The Bahá'í

The Bahá'í

The Religious Construction of a Global Identity

MICHAEL MCMULLEN

RUTGERS UNIVERSITY PRESS
New Brunswick, New Jersey, and London

Library of Congress Cataloging-in-Publication Data

McMullen, Michael, 1965–
    The Bahá'í : the religious construction of a global identity / Michael McMullen.
        p. cm.
    Includes bibliographical references and index.
    ISBN 0–8135–2835–6 (alk. paper) — ISBN 0–8135–2836–4 (pbk. : alk. paper)
        1. Bahai Faith—Georgia—Atlanta—Case studies. 2. Atlanta (Ga.)—
    Religion—Case studies. I. Title

    BP352.G4 M36 2000
    297.9'3—dc21   99-058719
                                                                                                      CIP

British Cataloging-in-Publication data for this book is available from the British Library

Manufactured in the United States of America

To my wife, Katie, and my daughter, Ivy

Contents

List of Tables

Preface

THIS BOOK began as a case study of the Atlanta Bahá'í community as an example of the social construction of a global religious identity. I wanted to explore how this religious movement makes the institutional and ideological connections between the local community and their vision of a global society. However, it would be more accurate to say that this is a multidimensional study based on qualitative sociological techniques of investigation as well as survey analysis and archival research. I have tried to combine these various methods of research into a single narrative about a particular religious community and their distinctive global identity.

My first encounter with the Bahá'í Faith was in a sociology class during the spring 1987 semester at the University of Kansas. Not only did it immediately pique my intellectual and sociological interests, but I also became personally drawn to it, and began to attend Bahá'í Firesides regularly. After several years, I myself "declared" and became a practicing Bahá'í. My involvement with the group I am studying raises valid questions about my objectivity.

However, I would assert that my status as an "insider" is a sword that cuts both ways. I already spoke the language of the group I was studying, and already had read several volumes of scripture that Bahá'ís find so important to their identity. I also have participated in the administrative structure that serves as the basis for local Bahá'í community life. I therefore had a firsthand understanding of how those institutions functioned.

But there were other, more practical advantages to being an "insider." As a Bahá'í, I could attend all Nineteen-Day Feasts (worship meetings) held throughout the metro Atlanta area—something non-Bahá'ís cannot do. My status as an insider granted me access to the diversity of various Nineteen-Day Feasts and the process of Bahá'í consultation, and especially the differences observed among local communities. I have not, however, betrayed any confidences I was made privy to through my attendance at Feasts. My status as an insider also facilitated my getting permission from the LSA of Atlanta to search through their archives, and to distribute a questionnaire. There is in the sociology of religion a precedent of quality research by "insider" researchers (see for example Ammerman 1987; Ebaugh 1993; Heilman 1976; Poloma 1989; Warner 1988).

While I cannot claim to be completely *objective* in studying the Bahá'ís—and I do not think any analysis is completely objective—I do believe that the study I present here is evenhanded. I have not tried to "prove the Bahá'ís right"; I have presented their beliefs and practices in their own words or through their own survey responses as much as possible. Any conclusions I have drawn or critiques I have made are informed by sociological theory; and I believe my sociological training as a researcher has given me the discipline to resist complete partisanship or advocacy. Most "research subjects" were aware that I was doing a research project on the Bahá'ís, and I was always willing to explain the details to those who asked. However, I did not announce my role as sociologist whenever I went to Bahá'í gatherings. Since it was not uncommon for people to take notes or record events, the presence of my notebook or tape recorder did not cause any undue concern. Overall, Bahá'ís in general recognize their own relative obscurity in U.S. society, and members of the metro Atlanta Bahá'í community were more than willing to be "studied" and "researched" by someone who was not automatically going to label them as a "cult" or "sect of Islam."

Finally, any concern about my objectivity may be further assuaged by the variety of methodologies I used. While potential bias was most likely introduced during participant observations, this possibility was offset by interviews and survey analysis. Each method was used to corroborate and cross-check the insights gained, the questions raised, or the conclusions drawn from the other methods throughout the research.

In this study I used four approaches: (1) participant observation; (2) archival research; (3) in-depth interviews; and (4) a survey questionnaire.

(1) My period of formal dissertation fieldwork lasted eighteen months, from November 1992 through April 1994, and included a Thanksgiving-week 1992 trip to the Bahá'í World Congress discussed in chapter 1. Participant observation events included as many Feasts, Holy Day celebrations, deepenings (including weekly attendance at the Sunday morning Study Class held at the Atlanta Bahá'í Center), town hall meetings (where several Local Spiritual Assembly jurisdictions would meet to consult about issues facing the Bahá'í community), Firesides, and public meetings as I could attend (all of which will be discussed in the text). Although my research was focused on the Local Spiritual Assembly of the city of Atlanta, I regularly attended events in neighboring suburban Bahá'í community jurisdictions. I also attended a variety of purely social events, such as "yard parties," picnics, and birthday celebrations. Sometimes I taped the

event (for example, a talk by a representative of the National Spiritual Assembly or Universal House of Justice), but most often I took field notes which I later used for detailed descriptive accounts.

(2) The Local Spiritual Assembly of Atlanta also gave me access to their archives, located at the Bahá'í Center near downtown Atlanta. I spent four to five hours each week, from January through May 1994, looking through file cabinets and boxes of notes, letters, pamphlets, and newspaper clippings. I had access to most of their records, except for Local Spiritual Assembly business of a personal or confidential nature. The Atlanta Bahá'í Archives Committee had just begun cataloguing all their records when I began my research; thus I did not have the benefit of a detailed written inventory to guide me. Needless to say, my research used only a fraction of the materials in storage. However, what I uncovered did provide the data for much of the history of race unity efforts of Atlanta Bahá'ís from the 1920s to the 1960s. A summary of this research can be found in chapter 8. My thanks to the Atlanta Bahá'í Archives committee for granting me access to these records.

(3) To flesh out and give voice to some of the statistical data, I conducted forty-three in-depth interviews with adult Bahá'ís. I chose not to study the perspective of Bahá'í youth, given my limitations as a sole researcher. Although I discussed with some Bahá'í parents the challenges of raising Bahá'í children in American culture, I did not feel I could in this context adequately address the viewpoint of younger Bahá'ís. I also did not interview anyone who had withdrawn membership from the Bahá'í Faith, again given research limitations. Interviews averaged 2.5 to 3 hours (although they ranged from 45 minutes to 6.5 hours), and were most often conducted in people's homes or offices, or in some cases, a coffee shop. Of the thirty-eight interviewees, 55 percent were women, 45 percent were men. The ethnic breakdown was as follows: 53 percent were white or European, 34 percent were African American, and 13 percent were of Persian background.

(4) Finally, I mailed out 487 surveys to a compiled list of metro Atlanta Bahá'ís, and received 241 back, for a total response rate of 49.5 percent (described as an "adequate" response rate in Babbie 1989, 242). The first mailing went out the second week of May 1994, and a follow-up questionnaire was sent to nonrespondents the first week of June 1994. I received surveys from individuals in seventeen different Local Spiritual Assembly jurisdictions (each comprising nine or more Bahá'ís), and from nine distinct "Bahá'í groups" (which number from two to eight believers). See Appendix A for a copy of the Atlanta Bahá'í questionnaire. I compiled my mailing list by contacting the secretaries of the metro Atlanta communities and getting permission to borrow their membership lists. Thus, I feel my final mailing list was as accurate a population record as I could have achieved for the metro Atlanta area.

To check for nonresponse bias, I compared those who answered immediately to those who responded only after the follow-up mailing was sent out. I assumed that those who failed to answer the questionnaire were more like those who delayed answering than those who responded right away (see Babbie 1989, 240; Fowler 1988, 48). I found absolutely no significant differences, on any variable (using two-tailed t-tests comparing means or proportions), between early and late respondents. I checked demographic measures (age, educational attainment, income, occupational status, marital status, race, partner's faith orientation [Bahá'í or not], sex, or previous religious background), and computed variables (such as level of teaching activity, measure of recognition of institutional authority, or level of organizational participation or devotion), but found no significant differences. Thus, I am confident that the degree of nonresponse bias is minimal.

Acknowledgments

MY THANKS go out to the many people who helped make this project a reality. Because this book began as a doctoral dissertation, I must first and foremost thank my dissertation committee, whose scholarly guidance and constant encouragement during my tenure at Emory University kept me sociologically grounded. Frank Lechner was a gifted dissertation director whose combination of attention to detail and ability to frame the bigger picture was invaluable in my conceiving and carrying out a project this large. Nancy Ammerman's direction in the actual *practice* of sociological research has instilled in me a lifelong ability to engage in participant observation, interviewing, and questionnaire construction; her skill in combining qualitative and quantitative research methods is one I hope to emulate. John Boli gave a *very* helpful critique of the first draft, as well as theoretical advice relating to globalization theory; and Steve Tipton framed some important initial questions and provided helpful critiques.

I am also indebted to Bahá'í researchers and scholars for their assistance in framing issues at the outset of the project. Special thanks go to Robert Stockman and Theresa Mullen at the Bahá'í National Center's Research Office for help in developing the questionnaire and getting access to comparative national Bahá'í data; Annette Prosterman at Our Lady of the Lake University in San Antonio for a helpful critique of survey questions; and Roger Dahl, chief archivist at the National Bahá'í Archives in Wilmette, Illinois for helping me find additional material on Atlanta and the American Bahá'í community during research trips in June 1994 and July 1998. A special thanks to Clark Denny for always lending an ear and his perspective throughout this process.

Money is always a vital resource in doing research of this kind. My sincere thanks go to the Society for the Scientific Study of Religion for their Research Award in 1994, and the Religious Research Association for their Constant H. Jacquet Research Award in 1994 while I was completing the dissertation. These two awards went a long way toward defraying the costs of copying and mailing out questionnaires and transcribing interview tapes. A special thanks to Maggie Stephens in the sociology department at Emory University for help in transcription. Additional credit goes to Terry Van Allen in the Office of Research Initiatives at the University of Houston-Clear Lake for help in securing Faculty Research and Support Fund #2-28211/1-11603 awarded on December 3, 1997, which enabled me to do follow-up fieldwork and interviews in Atlanta in 1998 to complete the epilogue to this book.

There are many in the Bahá'í community of metro Atlanta to whom I owe a most sincere thanks. Many were friends before they became "research subjects," and many became friends during the research process. They shared with me their hospitality, their stories, and their astonishment at what the Bahá'í Faith has done for their lives. I cannot mention them all here, so a general thank you to all those who filled out questionnaires, those whom I interviewed, and those with whom I had innumerable conversations about "being a Bahá'í." But special thanks are in order for the Local Spiritual Assembly of the Bahá'ís of Atlanta, Georgia, for their institutional support for this project. This support included a message on their letterhead sent out with the questionnaire encouraging Bahá'ís to fill out the survey; the LSA also granted me permission to search through their archives. I must also thank the Atlanta Bahá'í Archives Committee: Ann and John Haynes and Vera Taylor. I appreciate their time and energy in facilitating my access to the archive's files. A double tribute needs to be given to the Hayneses, for allowing me to sit at their dining room table once a week for three months looking through their personal records, for setting up several key interviews, and for granting me access to their historical photographs of the Atlanta Bahá'í community. I would also like to thank Patricia Steele and Carole Miller for their helpful information for the epilogue.

The editing process can be as frustrating as the writing process. I would like to thank several people who read through the manuscript during the rewriting process: David Myers at Rutgers University Press, an anonymous reviewer, and graduate student researchers Stephen Cherry, Angel Hagmaier-Duncan, Jay Linn, and Olive Oyango at the University of Houston-Clear Lake.

Finally, a special thanks goes to my wife, Katie, for putting up with my often nightly excursions to Bahá'í meetings, for stuffing envelopes with questionnaires and licking stamps, and for reading through much of the early drafts. She knew I would finish even when I couldn't see the forest for the trees.

The Bahá'í

Chapter 1   Introduction

*[The Bahá'í Faith] implies an organic change in the
structure of present-day society, a change such as the world
has not yet experienced. . . . It represents the consumma-
tion of human evolution—an evolution that has had its
earliest beginnings in the birth of family life, its subsequent
development in the achievement of tribal solidarity, leading
in turn to the constitution of the city-state, and expanding
later into the institution of independent and sovereign
nations. The principle of the Oneness of Mankind, as
proclaimed by Bahá'u'lláh, carries with it no more and no
less than a solemn assertion that attainment to this final
stage in this stupendous evolution is not only necessary but
inevitable, that its realization is fast approaching, and that
nothing short of a power that is born of God can succeed in
establishing it.*

Shoghi Effendi, great-grandson of Bahá'u'lláh,
World Order of Bahá'u'lláh

As THE WORLD ENTERS the third Christian millennium, social theorists, jour-
nalists, and political analysts are taking stock of the condition of humanity. While
some optimistically herald the fall of most communist regimes as the "end of
history" (Fukuyama 1992) and the triumph of democratic capitalism, others look
upon renewed global problems, such as ethnic conflict, economic development,
and environmental degradation, with considerable skepticism and anxiety. Representatives of the major religions are also addressing such global phenomena,
but they, too, do not speak with one voice. While the 1993 Parliament of the
World's Religions called for greater religious tolerance in dealing with the problems of humanity, the rise of fundamentalism in many parts of the world has
been raising doubt that religions can even agree to disagree. Across the religious
spectrum, however, there is a widespread sense that secularism might make religious worldviews increasingly irrelevant, and that religion might even be incompatible with global modernity.

In the face of perceived chaos and diverse responses to unsettling global changes, people from various religious groups nevertheless seek theologically grounded meaning and coherence. Amid shifting identities and institutions, movements around the world aim to construct a plausible cultural and organizational framework for the future. This book is about how one religious group—the Bahá'ís—attempt to meet global cultural challenges, and how the Bahá'í Faith confers upon its members a global religious identity in response to rapid social change.[1] The Bahá'í worldview embraces some aspects of modernity, but rejects others; it gives promise to humanity's future and explains its past; and it provides a foundation for a Bahá'í's moral and personal conduct. Unlike some who believe that the upcoming millennium signals the "end of the world" and requires a search for signs of the "end times" and the "Resurrection," Bahá'ís believe these events have already happened with the arrival of the prophet-founder of their faith—Persian-born religious leader Bahá'u'lláh (whose name means "the Glory of God" in Arabic). Bahá'ís believe that Bahá'u'lláh's teachings, to be discussed throughout this text, will bring about the unification of the world's people and global peace through "unity in diversity" (i.e., the Kingdom of God). See appendix B for a historical overview of the Bahá'í Faith.

A Bahá'í, then, is one who views the perceived tumult and uncertainty of our time with an assurance rooted in Bahá'í scripture: "That which the Lord hath ordained as the sovereign remedy and mightiest instrument for the healing of all the world is the union of all its peoples in one universal Cause, one common Faith. This can in no wise be achieved except through the power of a skilled, an all-powerful and inspired Physician" (Bahá'u'lláh 1976, 255). Bahá'ís believe this "universal Cause" to be the Bahá'í Faith, and the "inspired Physician" to be Bahá'u'lláh. This book analyzes the global ideology and the institutions of the Bahá'í Faith by highlighting the experience of the Bahá'í community of Atlanta, Georgia, and the world-embracing, universal identity of its members. The Bahá'ís are a sociologically interesting group because they consciously use ideological and organizational mechanisms to link the local and global levels of social, political, and cultural life. These links are constituted by the personal and collective practices, observances, and laws of the Bahá'í religion, and they form the core of this study. A sociological study of the Bahá'ís illustrates how one particular social movement manages the inherent tensions associated with globalization.[2]

The two discussions below, of two very different Bahá'í events, serve to illustrate what a global identity means for members.[3] The first event is the Bahá'í World Congress in New York City; the second is a typical Bahá'í "Fireside." A Fireside is the term Bahá'ís use for informal gatherings with friends, coworkers, and family members who want to learn about the Bahá'í Faith (discussed in detail in chapter 7). These two examples from my fieldwork—a large international conference in New York City and a small Fireside in metro Atlanta—demonstrate Bahá'ís' attempts to nurture a consciously global religious identity.

The World Congress as Global Bahá'í Dramaturgy[4]

During Thanksgiving week 1992 more than 27,000 Bahá'ís from 180 countries gathered in New York City to celebrate the Second Bahá'í World Congress.[5] It marked the one hundredth anniversary of the death of the prophet-founder of the Bahá'í Faith—Bahá'u'lláh—and was the largest gathering of Bahá'ís in the 153-year history of this 5 million member worldwide religion.

The World Congress attempted to crystallize for Bahá'ís the symbols and social relationships of the future global community and world civilization envisioned in Bahá'í scripture. One-half of the congress participants would attend the morning session, the other half a duplicate afternoon session. On entering the convention center, Bahá'ís would file past dozens of brightly colored, quilt-sized banners proclaiming verses from Bahá'í scripture and adorned with symbols from cultures across the globe. Once seated for the day's session, many believers would don headset receivers that provided translations of the proceedings in Spanish, French, Japanese, or Persian. On the front stage was a lectern surrounded by four large projection screens. When not showing video coverage of Bahá'í activity from around the world, the screens were illuminated by colored lights. The World Congress Choir would sing songs praising Bahá'u'lláh, at times prompting the audience to clap to the rhythm, or inspiring them to clasp each other's hands above their heads and sway to the music in the spirit of evangelical Christian revivals.

Many Bahá'ís indicated during interviews later that one of the most meaningful symbolic acts of the congress was a procession of Bahá'í representatives of the races and nations of the world to the center stage on the first day, setting the tone for the whole week. As stirring music played, each Bahá'í walked down the aisle arrayed in traditional native dress. The ceremony took more than half an hour to conclude, ending in a long standing ovation for this Bahá'í celebration of humanity that left many in the crowd in tears. In addition, prayers were read in a variety of languages at each session, and music was performed in Persian, Chinese, Hispanic, Pacific Island, African, Indian, and African American gospel styles, using native instruments. The event culminated in live satellite broadcasts from the Bahá'í World Center in Haifa, Israel, and from Bahá'í centers in Western Samoa, Argentina, Romania, India, Russia, Kenya, Panama, Malaysia, and Australia.

During the four days of meetings, Bahá'ís experienced "unity in diversity" as the sounds, sights, and symbols of the World Congress reminded them of their common allegiance to Bahá'u'lláh and the planet-wide institutions ordained in his writings. Many said that worshipping in the presence of more than 27,000 people from all walks of life who have adopted this "world-embracing" religious identity reinforced their hope for a united planet. In a message delivered to the congress from the Bahá'í World Center in Haifa, Israel, the Universal House of Justice (the elected authoritative body that governs the world's Bahá'ís) legitimated and fortified the Bahá'í vision of future global religious, ethnic, racial, and national harmony: "That so wide a diversity of the human race as you represent has assembled at this commemorative event is in itself history-making and is, indeed, an impressive demonstration of the potency and potential of [the Bahá'í Faith to lead to] the unification . . . of the nations and peoples of the earth" (quoted in *The American Bahá'í*, 31 December 1992, 2).

The affirmation of unity and fellowship was reinforced not only by official events, symbols, and messages as described above, but by informal socializing while waiting in line prior to Congress sessions, or during long bus trips to and from hotels. Such opportunities gave Bahá'ís a chance to renew old relationships or kindle new ones with "friends"[6] from around the world, exchange stories, recognize common Bahá'í concerns that span the developed and developing world, and learn about different cultures. A floral arrangement delivered to one session of the World Congress on behalf of the Iranian Bahá'í community also reminded participants that some of the friends were unable to join them in New York City because of continuing hardships facing Bahá'ís in the land of their religion's origin.[7]

The experience of the World Congress—the evident diversity of language, culture, and nationality, as well as the stories of Bahá'ís around the world facing opposition and discrimination—dramatized for participants the vision of global unity and peace outlined in Bahá'í scriptures. Bahá'ís feel that this global solidarity will come about through adherence to a common ideology and recognition of a common global authority institutionalized at the local, national, and international levels of social life (i.e., the Bahá'í "Administrative Order"—see chapter 3). For one forty-three-year-old Bahá'í from Atlanta, the congress strengthened his Bahá'í identity as one who celebrates "unity in diversity" and the "oneness of humanity": "I think it gave me a little real appreciation of the [Bahá'í Faith's] global perspective because I had never been to an international event before. I saw people from all over. . . . I think it's given me . . . a heightened awareness or appreciation for the changeable power in the Faith, the power to actually change the world. That maybe comes from seeing folks from all over the world."

The Bahá'í Faith actively fosters a new religious identity for its adherents (as followers of Bahá'u'lláh), one that is explicitly "world-embracing." Bahá'ís see themselves as "world citizens," actively engaged in "teaching work" to spread the news of the latest divinely guided "Manifestation of God,"[8] and inaugurating the Kingdom of God through the institutionalization of the Bahá'í "World Order" described in Bahá'í scripture.

The task of this book is to highlight the individual and collective practices that link local community life with a globalized ideology and network of institutions. The product of these mutually reinforcing sets of ideas and institutions is a distinct global religious identity for adherents of the Bahá'í Faith. The World Congress gives a vivid example of how Bahá'í participation in a global ritual reinforces their universal religious identity. But the practices of local community life function in this way as well, linking the local and global. The central research question to be addressed in this study is how participation in local community life shapes Bahá'ís' identity as "world citizens."[9]

Firesides as a Local Enactment of a Global Identity

The World Congress is an example of an event that reinforces Bahá'ís' identity as global citizens striving for "unity in diversity." But this self-conscious global identity is fostered at local meetings as well, as illustrated in the following description of one metro Atlanta "Fireside." A Fireside is an event held weekly or monthly in believers' homes that introduces non-Bahá'ís to the Bahá'í Faith. It may be an informal discussion, or a Bahá'í speaker may be invited to give a short talk followed by a question-and-answer session. Bahá'ís attend Firesides as a chance to socialize, and to bring along their non-Bahá'í friends, coworkers, and family members to join in discussions about the Bahá'í Faith. Some non-Bahá'ís attend Firesides without a Bahá'í "escort" after seeing an announcement placed in the newspaper by the local community, or after noticing flyers posted in coffee shops, stores, malls, universities, or community centers around the city.

At one "typical" Fireside I attended as part of my fieldwork, the speaker was a well-known and well-respected local Bahá'í who had served in several administrative positions at the local and national level of the Bahá'í organization. The speaker's talk was entitled "The Divine Plan Behind the Present Confusion," and was held in the home of a Persian Bahá'í and his Anglo-American wife. As is common in most Bahá'í homes, a picture of 'Abdu'l-Bahá, the son of the founder Bahá'u'lláh, was prominently displayed above the fireplace mantel. Samples of the world's religious scriptures, such as the Bible, the Qur'án, the Bhagavad-Gita, and Bahá'í texts, were on the bookshelves. The Persian man welcomed the fifteen to twenty guests (including seven non-Bahá'ís) seated in a semicircle in his living room, chanted an opening prayer in Arabic, and then introduced the speaker as someone who "has been serving humanity all her life."

The speaker said that since the end of the cold war, the world had been searching for principles upon which international cooperation and order might be based. She spoke briefly about the international paralysis in the Bosnian crisis, and the North American Free Trade Agreement (NAFTA) recently ratified by Congress. Both of these examples, she said, show a gradual movement toward internationalism, coupled with rising ethnic and racial tensions that produce behavior she characterized as "subhuman." The solution to these and other global crises, she explained to the mixed (Bahá'í and non-Bahá'í) audience, was the message of Bahá'u'lláh. She asserted, "The highest solution is world unity. If you took any of these problems, imagine a world in which there was something stronger than the U.N. that knew what its mission was . . . so that if any aggressor rose up against any other, an international force would do something about it." Coupled with this empowered global organization would be spiritual principles teaching the oneness of humanity, as taught by the Bahá'í Faith:

> We [Bahá'ís] believe in a oneness of the heart, a recognition that racial
> prejudice, national prejudice, religious prejudice must be swept away. . . .
> What is the source that will bring people around the world to an
> awareness of our oneness? . . . That is where the premiere of Bahá'u'lláh,
> the founder of the Bahá'í Faith, looms on the horizon, offering magnifi-
> cent hope to humanity. (Bahá'í talk, 27 November 1993)

As happens during most Firesides, the speaker went on to point out the connections between Christianity and the Bahá'í Faith. Bahá'u'lláh's coming, she claimed, fulfills the prophesies of all the religions of the world: for Christians especially, he is the return of Christ, the "Prince of Peace" foretold in the Old Testament book of Isaiah, upon whose shoulders will rest the government (i.e., the World Order of Bahá'u'lláh) that will unify the world. After a question-and-answer period, the Fireside ended with a prayer, and then people socialized over cookies and coffee while a videotape of Bahá'í activity from around the world played in the background (supporting the global themes of the talk). This particular Fireside, like most, was very civil and friendly, with most of the non-Bahá'í participants agreeing with general Bahá'í ideas of unity and world peace. However, occasionally at Firesides non-Bahá'ís challenge the claims of Bahá'ís, either expressing doubt that a unified world at peace is even possible (and thus accusing Bahá'ís of ignoring the dangers of "world government"), or disputing that Bahá'u'lláh could ever be the return of Christ.[10]

Progressive Revelation and Universal Ideology

I will begin this analysis of Bahá'í identity and investigation of their ideological and organizational mechanisms with an overview of Bahá'í beliefs, capturing their essential universal character.

In order to understand the universalizing goal of Bahá'í ideology and its promotion of global order and solidarity, one must understand the central ideological concept for Bahá'ís: "progressive revelation." Bahá'ís' vision of global unity includes the ideological claim that all of the world's major religions are only evolutionary stages in God's plan to educate and unify the whole planet—in effect, there is only *one* religion, but it is revealed by God in distinct historical periods. Bahá'ís claim that the *spiritual* truths of all religions are the same; religions *appear* to be in conflict due to their social laws, which differ because of the need throughout history for new moral and social codes by which larger segments of humanity may be unified.[11]

Thus, Bahá'ís believe that religious knowledge as recorded in the world's holy scriptures is revealed incrementally throughout history and educates humanity according to its collective ability.[12] Shoghi Effendi, the head of the Bahá'í Faith from 1921 to 1957, stated this in a social evolutionary context:

> The divine origin of all the [Manifestations] of God . . . is unreservedly
> and unshakably upheld by each and every follower of the Bahá'í
> religion. The fundamental unity of these messengers of God is clearly
> recognized, the continuity of their Revelations is affirmed, the God-
> given authority and correlative character of their Books is admitted, the
> singleness of their aims and purposes is proclaimed, the uniqueness of
> their influence emphasized, the ultimate reconciliation of their teach-
> ings and followers taught and anticipated. (Effendi 1980, 107–108)[13]

Confident that Bahá'í ideology and institutions can bring about global unity, Bahá'ís claim that Bahá'u'lláh shows how all the religions are logically and progressively linked. Bahá'u'lláh also condemns discrepancies in prophesy or conflict among religious ideologies as "priest-prompted superstitions."[14] Differences in the social laws of the various religions reflect the different requirements for social and moral solidarity of the age in which they were revealed.

Bahá'ís do admit, however, that there are differences in the content (but not the function) of the message brought by the "Manifestations of God."[15] For Bahá'ís, the function of religion is twofold: the spiritual education of individuals, and the social solidarity of humanity through various laws and institutions. Thus Bahá'ís consider that God's revelation to humanity has been evolutionary, teleological, functional, and progressive.[16] Bahá'ís believe that the solution to the problems of the modern age is global unity based on the recognition of one common faith that fulfills the prophesies of all the world's functionally equivalent, yet historically specific, religions. Bahá'ís do not think that theirs is the last stage of religious evolution for humanity, but they cite Bahá'u'lláh's statement that a full thousand years will pass before the next Manifestation will appear.[17]

One sociologically distinct feature of the Bahá'í Faith is its extreme rationalization of religious practice (further chapters will bear this out).[18] Sacraments are entirely absent from the Bahá'í Faith. In the place of sermons by clergy during worship services, religious ritual involves lay members taking turns reading from Bahá'í scripture (collectively known as "Bahá'í Writings," or just the "Writings" by Bahá'ís). Spontaneous prayer at religious meetings is rare; instead, praying usually involves the recitation of one of the literally hundreds of prayers revealed by the Báb,[19] Bahá'u'lláh, or 'Abdu'l-Bahá (collectively known among Bahá'ís as the "Central Figures"). Meditation is encouraged in Bahá'í scripture, not as a means of direct access to God, but to aid in the development of virtues.

Coupled with the Bahá'í global ideology is a network of organizations referred to as the Bahá'í "Administrative Order"—what Bahá'ís say will form the bedrock of the future world order and world government as the Kingdom of God. It consists of assemblies at the local, national, and international levels of Bahá'í administration. These assemblies are elected through a distinctive method of democratic participation couched in sacred symbols and considered a religious duty (to be discussed fully in chapter 3). Since 1937, when the first plans for expansion were developed, Bahá'ís have systematically dispersed throughout the world to establish functioning local Bahá'í communities (enabling them to be recognized as the second most geographically widespread world religion—see note 1).

In fact, the whole focus of "salvation" has shifted in the Bahá'í religion from its more traditional Christian connotation. Bahá'í ideology emphasizes the universal salvation of all civilization through the construction of a network of institutions called the Bahá'í Administrative Order bridging local communities and a global world headquarters. Bahá'ís claim the Administrative Order was revealed by God through Bahá'u'lláh, as a means of bringing about world unity and world peace. Individual salvation is achieved through the personal acquisition of "divine attributes" or "divine virtues," which ensures the progress of the soul in the "spiritual world." Concepts like "hell" and "Satan" are completely allegorized.[20] Religious salvation, then, is primarily a collective institution-building project requiring Bahá'ís to develop local and national community life and spread their "Cause."[21]

Social Science Views of Globalization and "World Order"[22]

Social scientists seek to provide a theoretical and conceptual framework to understand the efforts of social and religious movements to shape the identity and worldview of their adherents. An understanding of the global religious identity constructed by Bahá'í beliefs and institutions can best be framed by the concept of "globalization." Social scientific attempts to understand globalization have increased since the 1960s. One of the chief theorists of this sociological process has defined globalization as referring to "both the compression of the world and the intensification of consciousness of the world as a whole" (Robertson 1992, 8).[23] Globalization is the process by which the world has become a single place—where political, economic, and cultural spheres of life are becoming increasingly interdependent. However, globalization has not made the world a harmonious, integrated system. Historically, this process has been rife with conflict and reactionary movements, and is not reducible to monocausal forces like capitalist development (Robertson and Lechner 1985).[24]

Classical thinkers[25] in the social sciences were concerned with the issue of social order within the nation-state, and employed multiple theoretical frameworks to understand the basis for economic, political, and social cohesion. However, these classical thinkers make scant reference to the problem of social order on a larger, global scale. This problem has been left to more contemporary theorists, who have since the 1960s begun to address the issue of global order—asking if it is possible, and how it might be structured. These questions are similar to those asked by classical theorists about how social order is possible within bounded, national societies. One possible definition states that global order exists "if a number of significant actors across the globe engage in regular interaction and hold a cultural conception of 'globality' when they share a sense that they belong to and participate in one global cultural arena" (Lechner 1991, 263). Because this study focuses on the development of a Bahá'í's global identity, I use so-called "cultural globalization" theorists to help frame this study. These globalization theorists examine the cultural and ideological (especially religious) mechanisms that are emerging to understand global order.[26]

Globalization and Identity Formation

Issues of social identity are at the forefront in the cultural analysis of globalization processes. This study draws heavily from Robertson's work, since it explicitly deals with religion in response to, and as part of, globalization. Robertson provides theoretical clues concerning the challenges to individual and collective identity in the process of managing global tensions, without providing the theoretical mechanisms by which an aspiring global movement would manage those tensions. This study of a Bahá'í community attempts to fill in some of those theoretical gaps with empirical data about the ideological and organizational connections this movement makes between the local and the global.

Robertson's most pervasive theme involves issues of identity formation or reformation. This is the process by which, because of the "compression" of the world into such a small place, groups and individuals are forced to interact at new levels of intensity, and therefore to renegotiate their identity with respect to one another. This involves the alteration, retrenchment, or invention of new social identities and a transformation of symbolic boundaries.[27] The tightening of the world into a single interdependent system constrains societies and other groups to legitimate themselves in response to rapid global change and the instability and insecurity it engenders. Bahá'í theology claims that the solution to this identity insecurity is to redefine individuals as members of a universal humanity not divided by national, racial, or ethnic allegiances.

Issues of shifting identities are conceptualized by social scientists as tensions between local and global contexts. One social theorist has said that "transformations in self-identity and globalisation . . . are the two poles of the dialectic of the local and the global in conditions of high modernity" (Giddens 1991, 32).[28] Particularistic identities (national, ethnic, or religious) are reinforced[29] or transformed by globalizing processes that threaten the "plausibility" of a traditional worldview, culture, or sense of individual or collective self. At the same time, globalization processes "universalize" and aggregate identities as global tourism, travel, communication, and political and economic interactions bring people into regularized patterns of contact, leading some social movements to emphasize our common humanity and planetary homeland. Thus, social actors negotiate and reformulate their identity as part of the process of managing the tensions between the universal (global) and the particular (local).[30]

Many social and religious movements of the nineteenth and twentieth centuries are responses to and part of globalization. They are responding to the perceived sense that "my personal identity" and "my worldview of meaning" are no longer absolute and taken for granted. Social identity is contested and must take into account the growing diversity and plurality of ideas, institutions, and identities that penetrate into "my local community." Perhaps a unique feature of the late twentieth and early twenty-first century is that this infringement is happening globally. This study explores how a universal Bahá'í ideology is socially constructed in a local setting, creating in the process a distinctive Bahá'í global religious identity. To that extent, a Bahá'í identity is an example of the maxim "think globally, but act locally," which Robertson (1992) says is a phrase of "great sociological interest and of considerable relevance . . . because it involves the *strategic* attempt to link the local to the global" (1992, 177; emphasis added).

Globalization is therefore not without resistance, not only because the process threatens the economic, political, and social status quo, but because it calls into question our cultural, national, and religious identities.[31] Insurgency may take the form of opposition to the world as a single whole (which Robertson calls antimodernity), or opposition to the conception of the world as a series of equivalent, relativized ways of life (which he calls antipostmodernity). Some fundamentalist movements are examples of those "discontents"[32] who do not want their view of the world relativized or seen as equally legitimate with respect to others, and posit their own beliefs as the only "truth" (see Ammerman 1987;

Davidman 1990; Neitz 1987; Hunter 1983, 1987; Turner 1991). In an increasingly pluralistic world, it is not surprising that some groups feel the need to justify and preserve their own particular identity and way of life by vigorously distinguishing themselves from "others." But this becomes more difficult in modernity because the universalizing forces of globalization and commodity capitalism tend to identify the individual as part of a global humanity with a common destiny and purpose. This process is especially salient for religious communities that deal with questions of ultimate meaning or God's future for humanity.

Modern theorists grappling with issues of religion and globalization have generally dichotomized the *response* to globalization processes into (1) fundamentalism and (2) universalizing movements, with fundamentalism getting the majority of theoretical and empirical attention. This second, less studied response to globalization is similar to fundamentalism in that it is an implicit critique of modernity, yet it differs from traditional fundamentalisms in its ideology and the kind of identity it fosters in its adherents. Robertson says this of both movements:

> God has died at the societal level but is now all the more needed at the global-human level and constitutes an intellectual parallel to what is actually happening in the modern world. The fundamentalist movements concerned with the revitalization of their own particular societies—relative to other, culturally alien societies and the secular humanism of the modern state—are indeed attempting to bring back the tribal gods of society or community, while those movements which are more explicitly oriented to the global scene are attempting to vitalize and establish a universal God for a global humanity. (Robbins and Robertson 1987, 48)

The Bahá'í Faith falls into this less studied, universalizing category of religious responses to globalization.[33] The Bahá'í Faith claims a "universal God for a global humanity," as Robertson hints. This book, however, will investigate the relatively unexplored ways this religious movement employs ideological and organizational mechanisms to socially construct a universal global religious identity.

Summary and Book Outline

The Bahá'í Faith is a distinctive religious movement participating in globalization processes by creating a global religious identity for its adherents through both ideological and organizational means, systematically bridging the activities of a local Bahá'í community with a world center that provides ideological coherence and coordination. A study of such a movement reveals the ways in which local and global institutions are being actively created, connected, and

ordered through social and theological mechanisms. It also provides an empirical example of how the construction of a global identity is reinforced and "lived
out" in local community ritual.[34] This study of a Bahá'í community also contributes to social-scientific research on the Bahá'í movement, a relatively un-
studied *religious* aspect of globalization processes.[35]

The Bahá'í Faith inspires in adherents a globewide "collective consciousness" (Durkheim 1965) with a universal message and identity, and also links a
network of local communities to a global bureaucratic structure. This bridging
of the local and global establishes not only symbolic connections, but also lines
of authority and communication, making the movement sociologically worth
studying. Bahá'ís can be characterized as reflexive "situated universalists."[36] They
are universalists in that both their ideology and their ecclesiastical structures
orient their perspective toward the world-as-a-whole, promoting "unity in diversity," the "oneness of humanity," and the "oneness of religion." Bahá'ís are
conscious that what they are doing in Atlanta is similar to what Bahá'ís are doing throughout the world: erecting their version of the Kingdom of God. The
Bahá'í religion teaches Bahá'ís to "think globally, but act locally." Their global
worldview and concern is directed toward a situated, defined local community—
whose boundaries are decided by the religion's administrative officials. Bahá'ís
do not voluntarily choose with whom they worship: the geographical border of
a particular "Local Spiritual Assembly," like a Catholic parish, dictates the membership of one's local community. The daily practices of Bahá'ís to institutionalize their vision of world order begins in the local community. And finally, a
Bahá'í identity is reflexive, in that it is the product of a dialectical relationship
between the local and global levels of authority of the Bahá'í ecclesiastical government. Bahá'í evangelization efforts are "universalized" to all of humanity. But
the concern for the oneness of humanity leads them back to their local community as the crucible in which this universality is "particularized." In sum, a
"situated universalist" is taught to "think globally, but act locally."

I will use two strategies in analyzing the Atlanta Bahá'í community as an
example of a religious group's attempt to construct a global identity. The first
will be to quote at length throughout the text from Bahá'í scripture, referred to
by Bahá'ís as the "Bahá'í Writings" or just the "Writings." This is important for
two reasons. One is to expose the reader to what Bahá'ís consider holy scripture. Bahá'ís frequently remark among themselves and to non-Bahá'ís that unlike other religions whose scriptures were compiled after the death of their
founder or whose authorship is the subject of academic debate, the Bahá'í Faith
is based on writings Bahá'u'lláh dictated to an amanuensis or wrote himself, writings Bahá'ís consider to be the "word of God." For Bahá'ís, this imbues their
scripture with a unique authenticity. The other reason is that *reference* to Bahá'í
Writings constitutes a vital part of the *process* by which decision-making and

authority is distributed in the Bahá'í community, and how worship is conducted.[37] In a religion with no formal clergy who deliver sermons (discussed in chapters 3 to 5), collective worship consists entirely of "lay members" reading from Bahá'í Writings. It was also rare at the numerous meetings, study classes, or social gatherings I attended as part of my research that someone did not say, in effect, "Well, what do the Writings say about . . . ," or "What does Bahá'u'lláh (or other Bahá'í authority) say about that issue?" Bahá'ís argue a position, exert subtle moral pressure on one another, or make sense of current global issues, all by constant reference to their sacred texts. Thus, a sociological examination of a Bahá'í community would be incomplete without generous citation and analysis of Bahá'í scripture.

The second strategy I use throughout the book—but especially in chapters 3 to 8—is a general two-tiered approach to each chapter. The first part of these chapters provides readers with details of Bahá'í beliefs and theological doctrine germane to that chapter's topic. This should be particularly helpful to those readers unfamiliar with the Bahá'í Faith and its beliefs, practices, and values. The second part of these chapters provides the case-study material from my research in the Atlanta Bahá'í community. Sometimes I will stress my observational research, sometimes my interview results, and sometimes the empirical data from the questionnaire, as appropriate. As such, the empirical analysis explores the ways in which Bahá'ís in a local community do (or do not) enact or embody their global beliefs, doctrine, and worldview. In addition to participant observation, interviews, and archival material, I will discuss quantitative data from a survey questionnaire of the metropolitan Atlanta Bahá'í community—one of the first such empirical studies of a local Bahá'í group in the social science literature.

Specific topics addressed in this book include: the adherents of this globalized identity and why adherents became Bahá'ís (chapter 2); the organizational structure and authority relations in the Bahá'í "Administrative Order" (chapter 3 and 4); the socialization of a "Bahá'í perspective" among members through participation in Bahá'í rituals (chapter 5); the sociological boundaries between Bahá'ís and the wider culture, as well as among Bahá'ís themselves (chapter 6); Bahá'í evangelization efforts and the conflicts generated among Bahá'ís by their "teaching work" (chapter 7); and finally an examination of the importance of race unity efforts in the Atlanta context and its relationship to a global Bahá'í identity (chapter 8). Throughout the text, I have used the term "Atlanta Bahá'í community" sometimes to refer to the whole metropolitan Atlanta membership, and sometimes to refer to the city of Atlanta jurisdiction. This is the term Bahá'ís themselves use, and it should be clear from the context which group I am referring to. The term "Bahá'í community" is roughly analogous to the Christian term "congregation," referring to a local gathering of believers (although the Bahá'ís will also sometimes talk about the national or global Bahá'í community as well).

The Atlanta Bahá'í community is a test case in determining the ability of a religious movement to institutionalize global, universal values in a local, particular community, and the efficacy of the ideological and organizational mechanisms that make that possible. This study will analyze sociologically the nature of a Bahá'í's identity as a situated universalist: one who "thinks globally, but acts locally."

Chapter 2   Carriers and Converts

*To be a Bahá'í simply means to love all the world; to love
humanity and try to serve it; to work for universal peace
and universal brotherhood.*

'Abdu'l-Bahá, quoted in *Bahá'u'lláh
and the New Era*

To UNDERSTAND Bahá'ís as situated universalists, one must explore the organizational and ideological mechanisms that shape an adherent's global identity as
a "world citizen."[1] But first, it is helpful to know how people learn about the
Bahá'í Faith, and what draws them to it and keeps them committed to this relatively unknown religious movement.

Who Are the Bahá'ís?

PERSONAL CONTACT WITH OTHER BAHÁ'ÍS

In many respects, those who convert to the Bahá'í Faith are similar to those
who convert to other new religious movements (NRMs), with some exceptions
discussed below (see Bainbridge 1997; Stark and Bainbridge 1985; Dawson 1998).
The process of conversion to the Bahá'í Faith exhibits many of the theoretical
features discussed in the sociology of religion conversion literature (see Lofland
and Stark 1965; Lofland and Skonovd 1981; Richardson 1978; Snow and Phillips
1980). Research evidence indicates that social networks are the most crucial aspect in pulling individuals into nontraditional religious movements (Stark and
Bainbridge 1980).[2]

For potential Bahá'í converts, initial exposure and subsequent conscious
adoption and deepening of a Bahá'í identity and worldview involves being em-
bedded in a network of personal relationships with Bahá'ís, as well as adoption
of the role of "religious seeker" and an experience of tension with one's present
religious identity or affiliation.[3] However, an intellectual engagement with Bahá'í
global ideology and Bahá'í texts also contributed to drawing participants into

the Bahá'í fold. My research also indicates that for some, initial exposure to Bahá'í ideology corresponds with what Lofland and Skonovd call an "intellectual" conversion motif, sometimes also called an "activist" model of conversion:

> The "intellectual" mode of conversion commences with individual, private investigation of possible "new grounds of being," alternate theodicies, personal fulfillment, etc. by reading books, watching television, attending lectures, and other impersonal or "disembodied" ways in which it is increasingly possible *sans* social involvement to become acquainted with alternative ideologies and ways of life. In the course of such reconnaissance, some individuals convert themselves in isolation from any actual interaction with devotees of the respective religion. (1981, 376)

While some Bahá'ís indicated during fieldwork interviews that they basically "converted themselves" after attending a public lecture, or reading a Bahá'í pamphlet or book distributed at a Bahá'í information booth, most required more personal guidance to commit to this unfamiliar tradition. However, the "intellectual" motif highlights a recurrent theme (to be discussed more fully below) in the reasons given for why people convert to the Bahá'í Faith, and the mode in which Bahá'ís choose to evangelize their faith (see chapter 7): through written literature, public talks, and discussions of current social and global issues that are directly related to Bahá'í ideology. Given the Bahá'í affinity for the "intellectual" motif and their reliance on authoritative religious texts, it is not surprising that Atlanta Bahá'ís are characterized by a relatively high level of educational attainment.

How did Atlanta respondents first learn about the relatively unknown Bahá'í Faith? What was their first introduction, what captured their interest and prompted them to investigate further? As shown in table 2.1,[4] of those not growing up as Bahá'ís, overwhelmingly the most commonly mentioned introduction to the Bahá'í Faith was through friends who were themselves Bahá'ís—cited by almost 40 percent of respondents. Spouses or other family members were the agents of introduction for more than 24 percent of the respondents, and another 14 percent discovered the religion through more impersonal contact with Bahá'ís (a colleague at work, one's doctor, a teacher; one woman even learned about the Bahá'ís through her priest).

Other more institutionalized efforts were less likely to produce converts. The distribution of Bahá'í literature (pamphlets or flyers) at county fairs, college campuses, or city festivals was cited as an initial contact by only 2 percent, whereas outside media (newspaper accounts of persecution of Bahá'ís in Iran, for example) initially informed about 6 percent. Advertised public meetings were cited by only 9 percent of respondents as their introduction to the Bahá'ís and as the experi-

Table 2.1

Distribution of sources from which Atlanta Bahá'í converts first learned about the Bahá'í Faith

Friend	39.7 %
Informal contact	14.2
Other family members	12.8
Spouse	11.3
Bahá'í-sponsored public meeting	9.2
Outside media	5.7
Bahá'í shrine/House of worship	5.0
Bahá'í literature	2.1
TOTAL	100.0 %

According to a 1991 Bahá'í National Center survey, converts in the American Bahá'í community first learned about the Bahá'í Faith as follows: 31.2 percent from friends; 46.5 percent from family (including spouse, relative, parents); 3.4 percent from Firesides; 1.5 percent from public meetings.

ence that compelled them to investigate further.[5] These results indicate that 78 percent of those who did not grow up with at least one Bahá'í parent but who eventually became Bahá'ís heard about their religion through personal contact with Bahá'ís: either friends, family, coworkers, teachers, and so on. This finding also substantiates the importance of interpersonal networks in the conversion process.

These personal relationships with trusted friends and family help potential converts to overcome the initial "foreignness" of the Bahá'í religion. The host of Islamic references in Bahá'í scripture, the unpronounceable Persian names, and the introduction of ritual fasting and daily obligatory prayer all create boundaries that many potential converts find difficult to cross. At one point during my fieldwork, a recent declarant became embarrassed when she stumbled over a Persian word while reading aloud during a worship meeting. An elderly Persian woman gently reassured her that no matter how she pronounced it, "God *heard* you correctly." But as the empirical evidence described below will point out, current Bahá'ís' initial hesitation at investigating a "strange" or "Eastern" or "cultish" religion is usually overcome by their attraction to the Bahá'ís' global ideology and the lived example of its actual practice amid diverse local communities.

PREVIOUS RELIGIOUS BACKGROUND

Atlanta Bahá'ís began their "spiritual journeys" from many places; this is reflected in the diversity of converts' previous religious affiliation. In table 2.2, we see that nearly 30 percent of survey respondents were raised as Bahá'ís (this differs from the more than 36 percent who report that one or both parents are or were Bahá'ís, since some parents converted when the respondents were adults). More

Table 2.2
Distribution by previous religious background of metro Atlanta Bahá'í
community

AME	1.8%
Raised as a Bahá'í	29.7
Baptist	16.2
Buddhist	0.5
Church of God	0.5
Congregational	1.4
Dutch Reform	0.9
Episcopal	4.1
Greek Orthodox	0.5
Jewish	1.8
Lutheran	3.6
Mennonite	0.5
Methodist	10.8
Muslim	1.8
Nation of Islam	1.8
Nondenominational	6.3
Presbyterian	5.0
Roman Catholic	11.3
No religious background	1.8
TOTAL	100.0%

than half of Atlanta's Bahá'ís are from Protestant Christian background (with 16 percent of them previously Baptist, and 11 percent Methodist); nearly 12 percent were originally Roman Catholics; and less than 2 percent each are drawn from other non-Christian traditions, including those whose previous affiliation was "no religious preference."[6]

Although the questionnaire merely asked the respondent to "write in the space below your previous religious background (if you grew up in a Christian church, specify your denomination)," one-fifth of the respondents indicated that they had "switched" religious backgrounds before becoming Bahá'ís. Whereas most respondents indicated their faith-of-birth to be merely "Presbyterian" or "Lutheran," several gave a succession of religious organizations in their "spiritual journey." Exactly 13 percent who did not grow up in a Bahá'í home indicated that they switched between Christian denominations; another 6 percent switched eventually to a non-Christian faith; and 3 percent said they dropped out of religion entirely before converting to the Bahá'í Faith.

There is significant research amassed in the sociology of religion literature concerning "switching" religious affiliation—most of it concerning switching denominational membership within mainline liberal groups or between conservative evangelical and mainline denominations (see Kelley 1972; Hoge and Roozen 1979; Newport 1979; Bibby 1978; Bibby and Brinkerhoff 1973; Roof and McKinney 1987). Much of this research investigated the apparent growth of conservative, evangelical, or fundamentalist churches. However, it is well recognized from Gallup Polls that more than half of U.S. residents switch their denominational affiliation at some point in their lives (from Roberts 1995). What is most interesting for the purposes of this study is the documented emerging trend of switching into the ranks of the nonaffiliated (withdrawing membership from any Christian denominations or any other religious adherence—see Roof and McKinney 1987). These are the pool of potential converts most likely to be drawn to the unconventional ideological and organizational mechanisms of the Bahá'í Faith. Roof and McKinney indicate that "those who switch to no religious preference have significantly more education and higher occupational prestige than those who remain religiously affiliated [with Christian denominations]" (1987, 176). This accounts in part for the high level of educational attainment exhibited by Atlanta's Bahá'ís (discussed below). More than any other demographic variable, higher than average educational attainment is what distinguishes Atlanta Bahá'í converts from the wider population. This may also explain both the relative lack of growth of the Bahá'í religion in the United States (although not the relatively greater growth of the Bahá'í Faith in the developing world—see chapter 7) and the attraction an intellectualized religion with no clergy, one that emphasizes personal study and introspection, would have among the relatively higher-educated population.[7]

The limited data presented above—which arguably underestimates the amount of "switching" that went on in people's lives before they became Bahá'ís—in conjunction with interview results (discussed further below), indicate that many Bahá'ís were dissatisfied with organized religion, and defined themselves as active "seekers" looking for spiritual fulfillment. Many Bahá'ís expressed during interviews that they were initially impressed with the Bahá'í focus on the "independent investigation of truth" before committing themselves to a religious system, and the Bahá'í definition of "faith" as "conscious knowledge," eschewing blind imitation to the faith of one's parents.[8]

Much of Bahá'í ideology focuses on the role of human beings as "seekers" after truth. The Bahá'í Faith emphasizes that individuals are to search actively for truth in their lives—and thus stresses the importance of education.[9] This not only includes seeking the truth of the Bahá'í Faith, converting to the religion, and submitting to its laws and authority, but continuing in this role throughout life (the term in Bahá'í scripture for this is "seeker" or "wayfarer") through a process known as "deepening." Whether Bahá'í converts called themselves seekers prior to conversion or merely identified themselves that way retrospectively is difficult to determine. However, the focus on an individual's responsibility to seek truth does become an important aspect of a Bahá'í's socialized identity. Bahá'í scripture says that individual spiritual development is a lifelong, infinite process ('Abdu'l-Bahá 1993, 45).

Bahá'ís are therefore taught not to discriminate against the sources from which truth is sought. This reinforces the idea that spiritual knowledge is progressively revealed, and one should not expect to find truth only within Bahá'í writings or concepts. 'Abdu'l-Bahá states that for Bahá'ís:

> We must seek the fragrance of the rose from whatever bush it is blooming—whether oriental or western. Be seekers of light, no matter from which lantern it shines forth. Be not lovers of the lantern. At one time the light has shone from a lantern in the East, now in the West. If it comes from North, South, from whatever direction it proceeds, follow the light. ('Abdu'l-Bahá 1982, 248)

The seeker identity, however, depends upon the effort of the individual. Bahá'u'lláh tells his followers:

> O My servants! My holy, My divinely ordained Revelation may be likened unto an ocean in whose depths are concealed innumerable pearls of great price, of surpassing luster. It is the duty of every seeker to bestir himself and strive to attain the shores of this ocean, so that he may, in proportion to the eagerness of his search and the efforts he hath exerted, partake of such benefits as have been pre-ordained in God's irrevocable and hidden Tablets. (Bahá'u'lláh 1976, 326)

Bahá'u'lláh assures his disciples, however, that "He [God] hath extended assistance to every wayfarer, hath graciously responded to every petitioner and granted admittance to every seeker after truth" (Bahá'u'lláh 1988b, 255). A seeker should not, however, depend upon the learned of the world (whether a system of clergy, or theological specialists referred to in Bahá'í Writings as "ecclesiastics") to help him or her seek God. This is an individual, personal journey: "Blessed is the wayfarer who hath recognized the Desired One, and the seeker who hath heeded the Call of Him Who is the intended Aim of all mankind. . . . How vast the number of the learned who have turned aside from the way of God and how numerous the men devoid of learning who have apprehended the truth and hastened unto Him" (Bahá'u'lláh 1988b, 235–236).

The role of "seeker" is of sociological importance for two reasons. First, it reinforces the idea of an *individual* spiritual journey and development (in a globalized religious structure). Second, it bolsters the perspective of a universal humanity, wherein anyone can be defined as a "seeker" and become a Bahá'í, regardless of national, cultural, ethnic, or class distinctions. Bahá'ís are encouraged to read all the world's religious scripture, and to recognize the spiritual wisdom each contains. A Bahá'í identity, then, is a religious perspective that is inclusive, and one that celebrates diversity (truth comes in a variety of scriptures, languages, peoples, and religions from around the planet).

Attraction of Converts to the Bahá'í Faith

What initially attracts potential converts to the Bahá'í Faith? Again, the sociological literature is replete with examples of commitment mechanisms employed by organizations (see for example Miner 1988; Hirschman 1970; Kanter 1972). One of the most cited works in the area of organizational commitment as it relates to religious organizations is Kanter's (1972) study of utopian communities. She theorized that commitment to a religious group or organization occurs on three levels: (1) instrumental commitment (allegiance to the organizational structure or form); (2) affective commitment (fidelity to the members); and (3) moral commitment (adherence to the ideas or values espoused by the group).[10] Sociologically, the Bahá'í Faith uses all three of Kanter's commitment mechanisms, but with an intentional linking of local and global levels of social life. Organizational commitment links local Bahá'í communities to a World Center in Haifa, Israel; affective commitment is to the global family of humanity, beginning with the members of one's local community; and moral commitment is to values that are explicitly articulated in a global context in Bahá'í scripture. By far, however, the commitment mechanism most attractive to new believers is the moral commitments: those of one God, one humanity, and one religion that will usher in world peace and unity. Bahá'ís, when asked to summarize their religious beliefs, will frequently cite these "three onenesses" as an expression of a universal, global worldview.

Table 2.3 shows the various attractions and affinities initially felt by converts to the Bahá'í Faith. The second column represents the combined percentages of all those who indicated each response as being either the first, second, or third most important reason for their conversion to the Bahá'í Faith. Potential Bahá'ís are most attracted to the spiritual (81 percent) and social (49 percent) principles of their Faith. Spiritual principles include teachings on the ideology of progressive revelation, life after death, the nature of the soul, and the oneness of mankind. Social principles include concepts such as the elimination of all prejudice, the equality of men and women, universal education, and international disarmament and world government.[11]

Although there is one central text of Bahá'í scripture—the *Kitáb-i-Aqdas*, the "Most Holy Book" (often referred to as the "Bahá'í Bible"), all of the writings of the Báb, Bahá'u'lláh, 'Abdu'l-Bahá, and Shoghi Effendi and the UHJ—filling hundreds of volumes—are considered irrefutable scripture and are collectively referred to as "Bahá'í Writings." Bahá'í Writings cover a multitude of topics from philosophical and political commentary, mysticism, legal issues, administrative principles, Bahá'í history, to moral guidance. Given the wide array of scripture available, it is not surprising that 36 percent of Atlanta respondents report an "affinity for the Writings of Bahá'u'lláh" as being among the top three attractions to their faith. Another 35 percent cited the diversity of

Table 2.3
Distribution of metro Atlanta Bahá'ís' primary and top three reasons for
becoming a Bahá'í

Reason for Converting	*Top Reason*	*In Top Three*
Agreement with spiritual principles	41.3%	80.5%
Agreement with social principles	7.9	48.5
Affinity for Bahá'í Writings	6.7	36.4
Diversity within the Faith	5.0	35.3
Personal esteem for teacher	8.3	25.6
Raised as a Bahá'í	10.8	21.2
Love for the Central Figures of the Faith	6.3	19.3
Other	12.5	18.5
Absence of clergy in the Bahá'í Faith	0.8	11.6
Can find Bahá'ís anywhere in the world	0.4	2.5
TOTAL	100.0%	NA

In the 1991 Bahá'í National Center survey American Bahá'í community members indicated the following
as important reasons why they became Bahá'ís: agreement with spiritual principles, 67.7 percent;
agreement with social principles, 50.2 percent; affinity with Bahá'u'lláh's writings, 31.6 percent; love for
the Central Figures, 24.3 percent; personal esteem for those who taught them the Faith, 21.7 percent;
raised as a Bahá'í, 27.0 percent.

humanity represented in the Bahá'í Faith, evident at almost every meeting I attended as part of my fieldwork (see also chapter 8). More than one-fourth reported admiration or esteem for those who taught them their faith (again,
indicating the importance of personal contact and interpersonal networks in
bringing converts into the religion), and nearly one-fifth cited a love for one of
the "Central Figures" (the Báb, Bahá'u'lláh, and 'Abdu'l-Bahá). Of the almost
19 percent who wrote in "other" reasons, nearly half (47 percent) said it was
the claim to be the fulfillment of biblical Christian prophesy (see chapter 7)
that most attracted them to the Bahá'í Faith.[12]

Interview evidence confirmed the above survey results. Bahá'ís again and
again cited two factors as vital in their conversion: the diversity represented
among the Bahá'ís at every event and meeting (i.e., unity in diversity—a social
principle); and the feeling that ultimately, the Bahá'í Faith made rational, logical sense to people who were discontented and disaffected from religion in the
first place (i.e., progressive revelation—a spiritual principle).

UNITY IN DIVERSITY

The attractiveness of the racial, ethnic, religious, and class diversity among
Bahá'ís (an important aspect of a global Bahá'í identity) is perhaps captured best
by one Bahá'í's reflection on the time he was still a "seeker" attending a large
Bahá'í meeting at the Louhelen Bahá'í School in Michigan:

> I remember looking at this group and I had this sense of "this is where
> all the misfits go." Because there was such a wide range of people there.

It was like, you don't see that. There were old people, young people and different races and different economic classes and different parts of the country, the globe, and all that—and it looked so peculiar. I thought, "these people don't fit in anywhere else and now they've found a club to hang with." So that's kind of odd because usually the groups are so homogenous that you see—whatever it is, it was a bunch of long-haired people, or a bunch of black folks, a bunch of old folks, [but] you just don't see them all in one group. I remember that was really a shocking experience.

Another woman said that her first impression of the Bahá'ís was that "they were weirdoes, but weird in a good way"—reflecting a wide range of backgrounds.

Another convert said this about a film he saw recounting a Bahá'í youth conference, his first introduction to the Bahá'í Faith, in Birmingham, Alabama:

This man showed a movie of the Bahá'í Youth Conference—it must have been in the late '60s. On the movie, it showed all these young people with long hair, and some with short hair, blacks and whites, and American Indians and Hispanics and Orientals. And they were enjoying being with each other, and there were no conflicts between the various groups. It really looked like heaven.

An African American believer echoed this sentiment when she talked about her first encounter with the Bahá'ís in 1964:

We went out to Tucker, Georgia. I was excited the whole time. It turned out to be one couple, and another young lady that lived with them. . . . They were all white. And the greeting was so profoundly sincere. I essentially saw halos on their heads.

Over and over, Bahá'ís said it was the socially diverse, yet seemingly unified collection of people invariably present at Bahá'í gatherings that piqued their curiosity enough to lead them to investigate further. Especially for those who converted in the 1950s and 1960s in the Deep South, the diversity seen at nearly all meetings was unique among normally segregated religious organizations.

A RATIONAL AND PROGRESSIVE RELIGION

Interviews confirmed not only the "pull" of the diversity within the Bahá'í community, but the "push" of respondents' disillusionment with their religion of birth. The Bahá'í Faith satisfied many converts' desire for a more "logical and relevant" religion in touch with modern times, one that at the same time provided strong moral guidelines. Others said that their church or synagogue could not offer satisfactory answers to their questions. One woman expressed her disappointment with the church, and her subsequent ten years as an atheist:

My dad died when I was twelve, and the minister never came, or spoke
to me. . . . There was no pastoral [care] . . . and he'd been my parents'
minister forever. And then everybody said, "Oh well, it's God's will; we
have to accept it and it's good for you." And I'm like—I don't think so. I
wasn't buying it at all. And it took me a couple of years to disengage
myself and finally say I don't believe in any of that God stuff people talk
about—it didn't make any sense.

A psychologist said that he was already disillusioned with his Jewish upbringing
when he met his wife-to-be, a Bahá'í:

I was pretty much formally distanced from Judaism in a corporate
sense. . . . I slowly developed a disillusionment around Jewish
practice . . . as we know it in the synagogues and Jewish cultural life. . . .
It was without spirituality. . . . I was just feeling nothing there was
drawing me that was truly meaningful in a core sense, and I just floated
away. . . . Well, I wasn't satisfied with material life, because my soul was
aching.

One Persian man, a chemistry professor in Iran before he fled that country's
persecution, said he was torn between his Bahá'í father and his Muslim mother,
especially because the imams in the mosque would deride the Bahá'ís and spread
false accusations. But finally:

When I was seventeen, I realized that something was missing over there
[in Islam], and that was the reason I became interested in finding out
about the truth. I decided that there are so many accusations [about the
Bahá'ís], and I wanted to find out the truth. So, I went to a Fireside. To
be honest with you, [I went] to betray the Bahá'í Faith. And I got
trapped! (Laughter) I'm happy I did, or otherwise I don't know what
would be my fate.

Still others expressed their disillusionment with the hostilities fostered between religious groups, as well as the divisions among those who claim faithfulness to the same scripture and messenger. Several interviewees said that adopting
the Bahá'í Faith solved for them dilemmas about the seemingly peaceful messages of the world's religions and spirituality in general, which stood in stark
contrast to the perennial conflicts over which religious tradition was "true." This
exclusivity of religious groups bothered many (see chapter 6 about boundaries
between the Bahá'í and non-Bahá'í worlds). One woman said:

I would ask questions in the meetings [Campus Crusade for Christ] like
well, how is Christ going to reach somebody in Africa who has never
been exposed? Did that person go to heaven, what happens? And no one
ever had any kind of answer that satisfied me on a rational or spiritual or
emotional level. And I had read some things in high school, like the

Buddhist bible for one, and some other pieces, and I thought, you know, this is really uncanny, because the messages are all the same. And so that was for me a real unresolved issue until I ran into the Faith, because it's like, I always believed there was God, and Jesus was a real entity, a prophet, but I just couldn't handle the exclusivity of the traditional Christian religion at all.[13]

Another man expressed similar sentiments concerning divisions among the religions:

It is the exclusivity of religions that I think has been the impetus for most of us to look at the Bahá'í Faith. Some people appear not to be bothered by the exclusivity of Christianity, or Islam, or whatever, but I think that most of us who have accepted the Faith, we really have found that bizarre that only those in this [Christian group] are "saved."[14]

What Bahá'í ideology resolves for these people who are "pushed" away from "traditional" religion is what Berger (1969) called the "problem of plausibility" in a pluralistic, globalized world. Not only are various Christian denominations in competition with each other and with a secular worldview, but as a result of globalization processes Christian groups must now vie for ideological coherence with the other world religions. Berger said that "secularization has resulted in a wide-spread collapse of the plausibility of traditional religious definitions of re-ality" (1969, 127), which has forced religion's retreat to the private sphere of the family and the transformation of religious authority into a consumer com-modity proffered on an open market. Berger continues: "As a result of secular-ization religious groups are also compelled to compete with various *non*-religious rivals in the business of defining the world" (1969, 137). In this globalized situ-ation, the "world-building potency of religion is thus restricted to the construc-tion of sub-worlds, of fragmented universes of meaning, the plausibility structure of which may in some cases be no larger than the nuclear family" (1969, 134). Instead of a religious tradition providing certainty about one's identity and mean-ing in a confusing world, in modernity religious groups compete with each other for adherents' allegiance. The taken-for-grantedness of religion is lost in mo-dernity, calling into question the validity of religious authority, doctrine, mean-ing, and identity.

For many adherents, Bahá'í ideology solves the crisis in plausibility facing members of competing religious traditions that was so elegantly diagrammed by Berger. Instead of declaring one religion valid for all time and in exclusive pos-session of "Truth," and the others anathema or heresy, Bahá'í ideology claims all are valid within a given historical framework. This ideology provides adher-ents with a worldview that interprets humanity's religious history as a global, evolutionary, and teleological process of individual and collective advancement.

One woman described how this doctrine of progressive revelation (what might be considered *the* core spiritual principle in Bahá'í ideology) solved her personal dilemma:[15]

> I remember at one period I really seriously started studying some of the other religions. I came back and said, you know, they all claim to be right. They can't all be right. How do you sort this stuff out? [The man who taught her the Bahá'í Faith] turned to me and said, "Well, they were all right for their time." It was like light bulbs went off. God! Of course! . . . That really sort of set the stage, I think. My first encounter with the Faith was finding out about Bahá'u'lláh and then saying "Well all of the Manifestations have come from God." The concept of progressive revelation was what makes perfect sense. So that really attracted me.

One woman described how the Bahá'í spiritual principle of the unity of science and religion captivated her, thus resolving her personal struggle with religion:

> I am from a Baptist background. I didn't have a very good feeling toward Baptists. . . . Church never made sense to me . . . and it just seemed like the ministers were just there to get you to give money. . . . I guess what changed my life was in the eighth grade. I became fascinated with science . . . and one of the things that came up for me, was Darwin's theory of evolution. . . . That became very clear to me, so that technically became my religion per se.

When she was finally introduced to the Bahá'í Faith as an adult, she saw that Bahá'ís felt an evolutionary principle was operating in spiritual matters (progressive revelation) as well as in biology, and she then understood how science and religion "fit" together in harmony within a Bahá'í worldview. The unity of science and religion is another major principle of Bahá'í ideology.

These two themes, which recurred throughout the interviews and were corroborated by the questionnaire data, partially answered the question of who becomes a Bahá'í and why.[16] In general, Bahá'ís have been disillusioned with organized religion, or are searching for a "logical" or "rational" religious faith that makes sense and provides meaning in a globalized world. They are attracted by either the religious ideology (progressive revelation) or the corresponding community life (the unity in diversity in various local meetings) of the Bahá'í Faith. Both are crucial aspects of a Bahá'í identity, and both reflect the global worldview of the religion. Nor is it surprising that high education levels distinguish Atlanta Bahá'ís demographically from the wider metro Atlanta non-Bahá'í population (see note 24 on the demographic profile of the Atlanta area). Bahá'ís claim that theirs is a logical and progressive faith, explicitly global in its theol-

ogy and worldview, which downplays emotive elements, and therefore appeals
to professionals with relatively high levels of education.[17]

Not all Bahá'ís define themselves as "seekers" looking for meaningful answers to their religious questions; not all feel "pushed" from their religion of birth.
A few people said emphatically that they were *not* seeking a new religion and
were not dissatisfied with their church. A doctor, whose father was a Methodist
minister, said that a college friend was a Bahá'í and got her to go to a Fireside.
There she learned that, according to the Bahá'ís, Christ had returned. She eventually became convinced of these prophetic claims:

> Through the Bahá'í prayers, I knew that's who he [Bahá'u'lláh] was [the
> return of Christ]. I could not believe it [at first] because I had never
> thought that the return of Jesus would be like that. It had never
> occurred to me. . . . It took me a while to get my head adjusted. I went
> back home that night. I don't think I slept at all that night. I went
> tearing through the Bible comparing [Bahá'í claims] with the quotes in
> the Bible. I knew then who [Bahá'u'lláh] was. . . . Why in the world do
> these people [Bahá'ís] know this and I don't?

Another man expressed the emotional struggle of his becoming a Bahá'í and
reconciling it with Christian teachings about the return of Christ:

> It was difficult to some extent to switch loyalties. Because Christianity is
> centered on Christ, and he is your only door to heaven, so if you turn
> your back on Christ, you're doomed, you know? So it is a very serious
> consideration. . . . So the only way that I could make the switch was
> when I realized that I had the same feelings towards Bahá'u'lláh as I did
> towards Christ, and there was no conflict between them. That was it.
> When I realized Bahá'u'lláh had the same loyalty, and I wasn't diminish-
> ing my feeling towards Christ and my loyalty towards him. Bahá'u'lláh
> kind of stepped into Christ's spot, yeah, but without Christ moving.

This struggle was voiced by several interviewees who had converted to the
Bahá'í Faith. They pointed out that official Bahá'í doctrine states that in
accepting Bahá'u'lláh, one must accept the validity and equality of all the Manifestations of God. Bahá'u'lláh said to his followers: "Inasmuch as these [Manifes-
tations of God] are all sent down from the heaven of the Will of God . . . they
therefore are regarded as one soul and the same person. . . . In this respect,
if thou callest them all by one name, and dost ascribe to them the same attribute,
thou hast not erred from the truth" (Bahá'u'lláh 1989, 152). Bahá'í converts
from Christianity said that they had to learn that Jesus, according to Bahá'í theology, *was* "the way, and the truth, and the life" (John 14:6), but only during
Christ's dispensation.[18] Similarly, Muslim converts struggled to accept that the

Table 2.4
Activities that give respondents the most personal satisfaction as Bahá'ís

Activity	Top Reason	In Top Three
Prayer	41.6%	69.8%
Reading the Bahá'í Writings	11.8	52.4
Teaching the faith	20.6	46.6
Attending Feast	4.6	27.7
Talking with other Bahá'ís about the Faith	6.3	27.3
Taking action on social issues	3.8	20.1
Attending Firesides	3.4	17.1
Attending Deepenings	3.4	14.2
Following Bahá'í activities world-wide	0.8	8.6
Other	2.1	8.6
Serving in an administrative position	1.7	7.3
Attending District Convention	0.0	0.8
TOTAL	100.0%	NA

The 1991 Bahá'í National Center survey indicated that American Bahá'í community members found the following activities most satisfying to them as Bahá'ís: reading the Writings, 12.2 percent; daily prayer, 33.5 percent; teaching, 21.3 percent; talking with others about the Bahá'í Faith, 3.8 percent; attending Feast, 4.2 percent; taking action on social issues, 5.3 percent.

Báb and Bahá'u'lláh were the equals of Muhammad, despite their traditional understanding of Muhammad as the "Seal of the Prophets."[19]

Thus, while most converts were "seekers" who were dissatisfied with their previous religion, a small minority were "pulled" into the Bahá'í Faith by the prophetic claims in Bahá'í scripture, and not "pushed" by disaffection from their synagogue, church, or mosque.

COMMITMENT TO THE BAHÁ'Í FAITH

The aspects of the Bahá'í Faith that initially attracted converts include the global or universal principles of unity in diversity and progressive revelation. However, the characteristics that maintain commitment to a Bahá'í worldview and deepen a Bahá'í identity serve to reflexively reconnect the Bahá'í's global vision back to one's local community. Table 2.4 shows for each local activity or aspect of their faith the proportion of Bahá'í respondents who consider it the primary, or one of the top three, activities that give them the "greatest personal satisfaction."

The three features reported most often—daily prayer (70 percent), reading Bahá'í scripture (52 percent), and teaching the Bahá'í Faith (47 percent)—combine elements of personal devotion and active evangelizing. Other activities cited include attending the Nineteen-Day Feasts (the primary local worship activity in the Bahá'í calendar, discussed in chapter 5) and "talking with other Bahá'ís about the Faith" in more informal settings. Some of the "other" activities Bahá'ís wrote in were studying Bahá'í history or other religions, Bahá'í social activities,

Table 2.5
Distribution of respondents' household income

Less than $10,000	11.7%
$10,000–19,999	8.7
$20,000–34,999	18.7
$35,000–49,999	21.3
$50,000–74,999	21.7
$75,000–99,999	9.6
$100,000 or more	8.3
TOTAL	100.0%

Median income category for Atlanta Bahá'ís is $35,000–49,999. A 1991 Bahá'í National Center survey indicated that the mean income for American Bahá'ís is $38,800, slightly lower than the midpoint of the median income category for Atlanta Bahá'ís.

and attending Bahá'í summer schools and conferences. One of the most frequently mentioned "other" activities was participating in the Atlanta Bahá'í Arts Institute (a recently created organization that promotes teaching the Bahá'í Faith through the arts) and singing in the Bahá'í Gospel Choir. The least satisfying aspect of Bahá'í life, according to survey results, was engaging in administrative duties (to be discussed in chapter 3). Thus, as situated universalists, what attracts Bahá'í converts are universal ideological principles; what keeps Bahá'ís committed to their faith is engagement in Bahá'í activity in the local community.

Who Are Atlanta Bahá'ís?

This last section will address the issue of an "elective affinity" between the universalistic ideology of the Bahá'í Faith and its "carriers."[20] This more descriptive section presents the demographic characteristics of the Atlanta Bahá'í community, including socioeconomic measures and ascriptive variables.

Survey results indicate that Atlanta Bahá'ís are of average income but are well educated (see tables 2.5 and 2.6, as well as note 23 of this chapter). The median household income category is in the $35,000–49,000 range. Although income is fairly evenly distributed,[21] educational level is more skewed. As can be seen in table 2.6, more than 65 percent of Atlanta respondents have a college degree or higher educational level.

Similarly, Atlanta Bahá'í respondents are overwhelmingly (nearly 70 percent) white-collar or professional (see table 2.7). The occupational breakdown is: 18 percent are not in the labor force (including students, retirees, homemakers, and unemployed); nearly 13 percent are in blue-collar occupations (including skilled trades, factory and transportation work, and general labor); 35 percent are in white-collar jobs (which include sales, clerical, technical, and service professionals such as teaching and nursing); and 34 percent are professionals (engineers, doctors, lawyers, and professors).

Table 2.6
Distribution of Atlanta Bahá'ís' level of educational attainment

Some high school	1.7%
High school graduate	2.9
Some college or trade school	23.5
Vocational/Trade degree	6.3
College graduate	27.3
Some graduate study	10.1
Masters degree	17.6
Doctorate/Professional degree	10.5
TOTAL	100.0%

Data from my survey indicate that 65.5 percent of Atlanta Bahá'ís have attained a bachelor's degree or higher. According to a 1991 Bahá'í National Center survey, 54.0 percent of Bahá'ís nationwide have attained at least a bachelor's degree.

There is also moderate racial and ethnic diversity in the community. Survey results show about one-half (49.6 percent) of Atlanta Bahá'ís to be white or of mixed European background; one-fourth (24.2 percent) are African American; slightly more than 13 percent are of Persian ancestry (13.3 percent); and a nearly equal proportion (12.9 percent) indicate other racial classifications (Native American, Hispanic, Asian) or a mixture of racial/ethnic backgrounds (including a few people who responded "it doesn't matter" or indicated that they were just "human").[22] The female-to-male ratio is 3:2.

Although the metro Atlanta community as a whole displays relatively high ethnic diversity, not every local jurisdiction is equally diverse. No one local Bahá'í community is segregated, but there is a *tendency* for communities in different geographical locations in the metro area to duplicate the segregated housing market in Atlanta. For example, in the city of Atlanta Bahá'í community, known locally for its relatively high percentage of African American Bahá'ís, the proportion who identified themselves as "black" or "African American" was 45 percent. And in one northeastern metro Atlanta Bahá'í community, known for its Persian influence, 38 percent of those respondents identified themselves as such. Thus, while no ethnic group is segregated into any one Bahá'í locality, some communities exhibit a distinct ethnic "flavor," incorporating black or Persian culture into their rituals (which Bahá'ís consider beneficial, since the goal is unity in diversity, and not uniformity). Chapters 3 and 5 will discuss how Bahá'í institutional structures are flexible enough to incorporate local ethnic variation without losing their ideological coherence or global orientation.[23]

It could be argued that the level of racial and ethnic diversity in the Bahá'í community is a product of their global ideology, which stresses the "oneness of humanity" and "unity in diversity." While it is impossible to make a precise comparison between *one* Bahá'í community and Christian denominations nationally, it may be useful to contrast the percentage of African American adherents

Table 2.7
Distribution by occupation of metro Atlanta Bahá'í community

Homemaker	5.5%
Clerical	3.8
Technical	9.3
Managerial	17.8
Professional	16.5
Service professional	14.0
Sales	7.6
Other service work	7.6
Skilled trades	4.2
Factory Work	0.4
Transportation	0.4
Student	9.3
Retired	2.1
Unemployed	1.3
TOTAL	100.0%

Sixty-nine percent of Atlanta Bahá'ís have white-collar or professional jobs. A 1991 Bahá'í National Center survey indicated that nationwide the proportion is 75.4 percent.

among Atlanta Bahá'ís (more than 24 percent) with that of other religious denominations. From data compiled by Roof and McKinney (1987, 142), only the American Baptists (at 27 percent) and Seventh-Day Adventists (at 27 percent) have an equally high percentage of African American members—at least among the non-historically black denominations. African American representation among other groups include: Episcopalians—5 percent; Presbyterians—4 percent; United Methodists—3.8 percent; Lutherans—1.3 percent; Churches of Christ—8 percent; Roman Catholics—1.9 percent; and Southern Baptists—0.6 percent. Thus, one could argue that Bahá'ís in the Atlanta area (and nationally) have fostered a moderate degree of diversity, compared with other national mainline religious bodies. It is also commonly recognized within the sociology of religion, ever since H. Richard Niebuhr (1957) first formulated the argument, that American religious denominations are divided along class as well as racial lines (see also Ammerman 1990; Roof and McKinney 1987). However, Atlanta Bahá'ís have evaded this division to some degree, with members representing a fairly even distribution of family income—not too different, on average, from the general population in Atlanta (although, admittedly, the distribution of educational attainment and occupational status is very skewed for the Bahá'ís).

More than 65 percent of Atlanta Bahá'ís are presently married (65.4 percent); another 19.2 percent are single, and the divorced and widowed number 11.7 percent and 3.8 percent, respectively.[24] More than three-fourths of married respondents have a Bahá'í spouse (78 percent). In addition, more than one-third of all respondents report either one or both parents being Bahá'ís (36 percent).

The average Atlanta Bahá'í has been a member of his/her faith for 20.3 years (the data range from less than a year to 63 years). The average age is 42 (data from a 1991 Bahá'í National Center survey indicated that the average length of affiliation is 24.5 and the average age is 49). This is indicative of the relatively high percentage of "long-time" Bahá'ís, and the relative paucity of new members (to be addressed in chapter 7). On average, Atlanta Bahá'ís have lived in the metro area about 14.5 years, and have lived in their local community half as long (a little over 7 years).

Summary

On average, Atlanta Bahá'ís are well-educated, middle-class professionals, are moderately racially and ethnically diverse, and when married are most likely married to another Bahá'í, although most are not likely to have grown up with Bahá'í parents—more than two-thirds are converts (70.3 percent). It is also a fairly "old" community, with 25 percent of Atlanta respondents officially Bahá'ís less than ten years, but 25 percent more than twenty-eight years. The Bahá'í emphasis on personal reading of Bahá'í scripture, the universal social and religious themes, the lack of clergy, and the emphasis on individual spiritual development partly explain the attraction among those with higher levels of education. Most were dissatisfied with the authority and content of their religious roots, and considered themselves "seekers" actively looking for a worldview that answered their questions and had meaning in their lives. Unwilling to return to the religious worldview of their religion of birth, they were attracted to the global character of the Bahá'í Faith. The answers they found are grounded in a universal ideology of spiritual and social teachings—centering on progressive revelation and the oneness and unity of humanity, respectively. The global character of the Bahá'í Faith is initially the most attractive aspect for seekers, and solves the "problem of plausibility" many found in their previous religion. As situated universalists, Bahá'ís are attracted to their faith from diverse racial and religious backgrounds by universal, global themes. They remain committed to their faith because their universal ideology reflexively orients them back to their local situated community (as seen in table 2.4 by the satisfaction derived from local teaching activity, personal spiritual development, and local worship attendance).

This first glimpse at the Atlanta Bahá'í community has also shown that Bahá'ís are relatively successful in fostering "unity in diversity." Bahá'ís come from varied racial and religious backgrounds, and are evenly distributed throughout income categories (although skewed toward the high end of the educational and occupational scales). One could conclude that those with higher educational levels are predisposed to be attracted to the Bahá'í Faith's global message. Later chapters show that ascriptive and demographic characteristics of Atlanta Bahá'ís are not associated with participation in local community life. In the research literature on religious groups, this is an unusual finding, and indicates the possibility of distinctive mechanisms of commitment and participation operating in Bahá'í institutions (see Roberts 1995; Johnstone 1992). Having acquired some understanding of why "seekers" become Bahá'ís, we now direct our attention to the organizational, ideological, and ritual mechanisms that reinforce Bahá'ís' global religious identity as situated universalists (in chapters 3, 4, and 5, respectively).

Chapter 3

The Bahá'í
Administrative Order

The unity of the human race, as envisaged by Bahá'u'lláh,
implies the establishment of a world commonwealth in
which all nations, races, creeds and classes are closely and
permanently united.

Shoghi Effendi, *The World Order of Bahá'u'lláh*

THE BAHÁ'Í FAITH seeks to be a model for future world order, and to instill a "world-embracing" identity in its adherents. The preceding chapter discussed how Bahá'ís are drawn to their religion in part because of its universal ideology of unity in diversity and progressive revelation.[1] This chapter will begin to analyze the mechanisms by which Bahá'ís, as situated universalists, envision a reflexive connection between universal global society and situated local community, looking first at organizational structure. I will briefly discuss the expansion of the Bahá'í Faith on a global scale, its attempt to link scattered local communities to a global center, and its effort to foster local administrative participation that brings individuals into contact with institutionalized authority, reinforcing a global worldview. Bahá'ís refer to this combination of top-down authority and bottom-up democratic empowerment as their "Administrative Order," which reflexively links the local Bahá'í community with a global ecclesiastical structure.

The growth of the Bahá'í Faith into a truly *global* social movement continues today through the institutionalization of a network of structures at the local, national, and international levels of social life. This expansion to every corner of the globe has taken place through methodical, rational blueprints called "Teaching Plans," first developed by Shoghi Effendi (great-grandson of Bahá'u'lláh), and now coordinated by the Universal House of Justice (UHJ) in consultation with National Spiritual Assemblies (NSAs).[2] Systematic plans for growth have followed a pattern that seeks first to establish local communities through missionary activity, and then to utilize indigenous resources to expand—both horizontally in the local area, and vertically to link with the global headquarters.

34

This chapter will focus on the organizational mechanisms of this process; the two subsequent chapters will explore the ideological and ritual mechanisms, respectively. I will discuss first the doctrinal aspects of the Administrative Order, and then the empirical example of how Atlanta Bahá'ís participate in the Administrative Order.

Administrative Structure

Bahá'ís consider their ecclesiastical organization unique in the world, not only because it was designed, Bahá'ís claim, to be the model of world government, but also because Bahá'u'lláh was the first Manifestation of God to deliberately design the organization that would "routinize his charisma" (cf. Weber 1946, 297). Bahá'í sources say this about the Bahá'ís' "unique" organizational system:

> Not until the advent of the Bahá'í Dispensation did a Manifestation of
> God include administrative principles among His spiritual teachings.
> This is an entirely new dimension which Bahá'u'lláh has introduced; He
> has placed the spiritual and administrative principles on a par with each
> other. A violation of an administrative principle . . . is as grave a
> betrayal of the Cause of Bahá'u'lláh as breaking a spiritual law.
> (Taherzadeh 1992, 395)

The Bahá'í Administrative Order consists of two pillars, or functional branches. These two branches evolved, to use sociologist Max Weber's (1946, 1922) terminology, to routinize or bureaucratize the charismatic authority of the Central Figures of the early history of the Bahá'í Faith. This is significant for Bahá'ís, considering that Bahá'u'lláh has strictly forbidden the formation of clergy in the Bahá'í Faith (Bahá'u'lláh 1992, 195; Esslemont 1970, 139). As part of the ideology of progressive revelation, Bahá'ís believe humanity has developed beyond the need for a special class that monopolizes religious knowledge.[3] Bahá'ís claim that the lack of clergy protects their faith from corruption by the power that accrues to one individual. Theoretically, no one Bahá'í has any authority over any other. Instead, all religious authority rests with democratic councils, which operate at all levels of society. These two branches (or pillars) of the Administrative Order consist of (1) elected assemblies (the "Rulers") and (2) appointed boards (the "Learned") operating at the local, national, and international levels of society—see fig. 3.1.

THE RULERS

The first, and more important, of the two branches of Bahá'í organization is a series of democratically elected "spiritual assemblies" at the local, national, and international levels of social life (referred to as the "institution of the Rulers,"

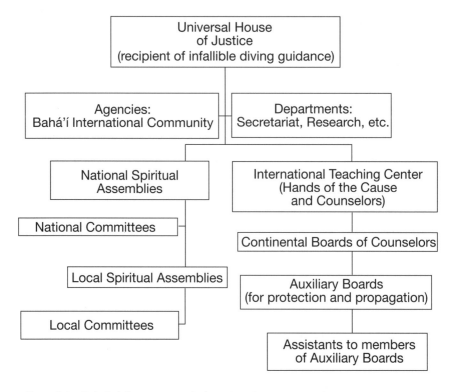

Figure 3.1 Bahá'í Administrative Order *(adapted from Smith and Momen 1989)*

since they are that branch of the Administrative Order that governs or has authority over the Bahá'í community). These assemblies constitute the core of the Bahá'í World Order, the object of all the (rationalized) teaching plans for growth, and the crux of Shoghi Effendi's work throughout his tenure as "Guardian of the Bahá'í Faith" from 1921 to 1957. Each year, wherever there are at least nine adult Bahá'ís (age twenty-one and older) within a recognized municipal boundary, an election is held to form a Local Spiritual Assembly (LSA) of nine members, which constitutes the foundational authority of local Bahá'í community life. Every community member votes for nine individuals, and the nine receiving the most votes become LSA members—this is true of Bahá'í elections at all three levels of the structure.[4] (If there is a tie for the ninth spot, administrative law dictates that the position goes to the individual who is a "minority" in the community—a form of electoral "affirmative action").[5] Local elections take place the first day of the twelve-day Festival of Ridván, held April 21 through May 2 each year.[6]

On the first weekend in October, Bahá'ís in the United States attend their District Convention, an administrative meeting where a National Delegate is elected—the first step in the formation of the National Spiritual Assembly (NSA), the next higher level in this branch of the Administrative Order. Districts are composed of somewhat arbitrary groupings of several LSA jurisdictions and Bahá'í Groups. There are 168 districts in the United States, three of which make up the metro Atlanta area. These elections—the April Ridván festival, and the October District Convention—are the two democratic rituals in which all Bahá'ís have a chance to participate; indeed, they are viewed as spiritual obligations for members.

The elected National Delegates then go to the National Convention (held in Wilmette, Illinois, site of the Bahá'í National Center) in May to elect the National Spiritual Assembly (NSA)—a nine-member body that oversees Bahá'í activity within a nation or region. For example, the United States has within it three NSAs: the National Spiritual Assembly of the United States (the forty-eight contiguous states), the NSA of Hawaii, and the NSA of Alaska. Often, the National Delegates will return to their districts and hold a meeting to report on the decisions made at the National Convention. The proceedings are also summarized in *The American Bahá'í*, the monthly publication of the NSA, and sent to every Bahá'í household in the United States. Unlike officials or representatives in many electoral systems, Bahá'í delegates or assembly members are not bound to "represent" the views of their "constituents"—rather, they are elected based on spiritual character to vote their own conscience.

The National Spiritual Assembly of the United States also has various departments and agencies. These include the National Archives, the Bahá'í Schools Committee,[7] the Persian-American Affairs Committee (to ease the transition of refugee Iranians to American culture), the National Teaching Committee, and the Office of External Affairs. The latter has lobbied the U.S. Congress to pass resolutions condemning the persecutions of Bahá'ís in Iran.[8]

Finally, once every five years, the members of all the NSAs in the world gather at the Bahá'í World Center in Haifa, Israel, to elect the nine-member Universal House of Justice (UHJ), the highest authority in the Bahá'í world. Unlike the LSAs and NSAs, the UHJ is restricted by Bahá'u'lláh's writings to males only (discussed in chapter 4). The first UHJ was elected in 1963, a few years after the death of Shoghi Effendi. None of the individuals who are elected to the assemblies have any authority—only the decisions arrived at through consultation by the institution are authoritative. Bahá'ís are not allowed to "run" for office, since in his writings Bahá'u'lláh strictly forbade campaigning. Instead, Bahá'ís are instructed to vote for any Bahá'í who is eligible based on their spiritual character.[9]

Bahá'u'lláh promised Bahá'ís that decisions made by the UHJ are divinely guided and infallible. Although the UHJ cannot change any law revealed by Bahá'u'lláh, it is empowered to legislate on all matters "which have not outwardly been revealed in the Book" (Bahá'u'lláh 1992, 3). Bahá'ís believe that through the collective decisions made by the institution (again, not in theory based on any charismatic authority or individual revelation) of the UHJ, the Bahá'í world, and eventually the global civilization to be generated from Bahá'í institutions and laws, is assured of divine guidance until the appearance of the next Manifestation of God.[10] Thus, Bahá'ís believe that infallible authority and guidance flow from the UHJ down through the NSAs to the LSAs and individual Bahá'ís.

Bahá'ís note that flexibility is built into their institutions. Although the UHJ is considered "the source of all good and freed from all error" (Taherzadeh 1992, 384), and can legislate on matters not covered in Bahá'u'lláh's writings, it can also modify its own laws as historical circumstances demand. It can therefore repeal or change its own legislation (but not those laws revealed by Bahá'u'lláh).[11] This administrative flexibility, Bahá'ís say, prevents the religious laws and organization of their faith from becoming obsolete, which in other religions often results in sectarian divisions.

THE LEARNED

The second pillar of the Administrative Order is known as the "Learned" branch, or the "protectors" and "propagators" of the Bahá'í Faith (see fig. 3.1). This function of protection and propagation was originally assigned to charismatic individuals known as "Hands of the Cause of God."[12] These individuals were appointed by Bahá'u'lláh, 'Abdu'l-Bahá, and Shoghi Effendi to offer guidance and encouragement in teaching efforts and to safeguard the development of Bahá'í communities.

Hands of the Cause of God are loyal and knowledgeable individuals who "propagate" their religion by active teaching and by assisting the NSAs in achieving national teaching goals. They "protect" their religion by defending the integrity of Bahá'í principles and institutions from external attacks as well as internal dissension. Hands of the Cause have the authority to expel Bahá'ís (this is now subject to the approval of the UHJ—see chapter 6) for unwillingness to acknowledge the legitimate chain of authority in the Administrative Order (Taherzadeh 1992).[13]

The function of protection and propagation, originally performed exclusively by Hands of the Cause, was transferred in 1968 by decision of the UHJ to the members of an institution called the Continental Board of Counselors (appointed by the UHJ for five-year terms), and below them the various Auxiliary Board members (appointed for one-year terms by the Continental Counselors, subject to UHJ approval).[14] Under the Auxiliary Board members are their Assistants, who are also appointed for one-year terms and work directly with Local Spiritual Assemblies. None of the Counselors or Auxiliary Board members and assistants have any individual authority over the Local or National Assembly or the UHJ; they also have no formal authority over any individual Bahá'í. As individuals who are knowledgeable about Bahá'í law and administrative principles (hence the expression "institution of the Learned"), their role is to offer assistance to newly formed assemblies just learning the principles of Bahá'í administration, to offer aid to teaching projects undertaken by LSAs, and to assist local or national communities in handling the expulsion of deviant members. In effect, they are Bahá'í "consultants" representing the UHJ in its work with the elected assemblies. In 1973, the whole appointed pillar of the Administrative Order (as opposed to the elected pillar of local and national assemblies) was put under the direction of the International Teaching Center in Haifa, which itself is under the authority of the UHJ.

In addition to these major components of the Administrative Order, the UHJ oversees a Research Department, an Archives division, a Center for the Study of Holy Texts, an Office of Social and Economic Development, and the Bahá'í International Community (BIC). The latter is the name of the nongovernmental organization (NGO) registered with the United Nations, first chartered in March 1948. BIC was granted consultative status with the U.N. Economic and Social Council in May 1970, and with UNICEF in 1976; in 1989 it developed a working relationship with the World Health Organization. BIC's goal is to promote "world peace by creating the conditions in which unity emerges as the natural state of human existence" (BIC document 92-0409—see website http://www.bic-un.bahai.org). The Bahá'í NGO also works to promote the advancement of women, just economic development, universal education, a sense of world citizenship, religious tolerance, the adoption of an international auxiliary language, and the protection of the environment.

This detailed discussion of the Bahá'í Administrative Order's background is important to this analysis for three reasons. First, Bahá'ís I interviewed often talked proudly about their Administrative Order as being the only ecclesiastical government designed by a Manifestation of God. Bahá'ís point out that Jesus merely said to Peter, "And I tell you, you are Peter, and on this rock I will build my church, and the powers of death shall not prevail against it" (Matthew 16:18). This sparse information on how Christ wanted his followers to govern themselves has, Bahá'ís claim, led to numerous misunderstandings and conflicts concerning the authority of Christian leaders. Second, Bahá'ís point out that the promises of Bahá'u'lláh guarantee that the collective decisions of the Universal House of Justice are "without error" and infallible.[15] Thus, Bahá'ís assert, the Administrative Order will not succumb to the corruption, decline, and divisions other ecclesiastical governments have experienced. Finally, Bahá'ís look to the global character of their institutions, which they say will provide a unifying force for all future social, political, and economic life on the planet. All of this combines to reinforce the global Bahá'í identity as "situated universalists": tied to a global network promoting universal principles, but acting as a force for change beginning at the local level.[16]

The Administrative Order and Global Expansion

Since Bahá'u'lláh declared His mission more than 130 years ago, the Bahá'í Faith has seen rapid development. According to the 1992 *Encyclopedia Britannica Book of the Year*, the Bahá'í Faith has established "significant communities" in more countries and territories than any other independent religion with the exception of Christianity. Its fastest growth has been in the developing world. The *World Christian Encyclopedia* (Barrett 1982) indicated that from 1970 to 1982, the Bahá'í Faith grew at an average rate of 3.63 percent, compared with 2.74 percent for Islam, 2.3 percent for Hinduism, 1.67 percent for Buddhism, 1.64 percent for Christianity, and 1.09 percent for Judaism. There are approximately 5.5 millions Bahá'ís worldwide, in 188 countries, organized into roughly 20,000 LSAs, with representatives from more than 2,100 ethnic groups. Their literature has been translated into 802 languages, and they have established 26 independent publishing trusts, 7 radio stations, 741 schools, and 873 literacy and socioeconomic development projects throughout the world (all statistics from *The Bahá'ís: A Profile of the Bahá'í Faith and Its Worldwide Community*, 1994).

The movement's most intensive growth globally came at the beginning of the 1950s, coinciding with the worldwide increase in transnational institutions (Waters 1995, Archer 1992).[17] For example, in 1953, there were 9 NSAs and 611 LSAs. By 1964, at the end of the Ten Year World Crusade (the first globally encompassing teaching plan inaugurated by Shoghi Effendi), there were 56 NSAs and 4,566 LSAs (from Smith 1987, 161). In 1954, the first year of the Ten Year Plan, 94 percent of the world's Bahá'ís lived in Iran, the land of its origin. By 1988, only 6 percent lived there (Smith and Momen 1989, 72). It is estimated that in 1963, at the end of the Ten Year Plan, there were approximately 400,000 Bahá'ís worldwide. That number increased to 3.5 million in 1985, and to 5 million six years later (a 43 percent increase from 1985 to 1991).[18]

Four ideological and organizational reasons can sociologically account for this expansion:

- Rationalized plans. The Bahá'í Faith has grown through a series of calculated teaching plans, first developed by Shoghi Effendi, and since 1963 developed by the UHJ. In each of these cases, and especially since the plans became "globalized" in the Ten Year World Crusade of 1953–1963, there have been numerical goals for new local and national assemblies, new believers, publishing trusts, and so on. This, in conjunction with expanded means of global travel and communications, has undoubtedly contributed to rapid expansion. Although the plans are in accordance with the blueprint for expansion set out in the *Tablets of the Divine Plan* ('Abdu'l-Bahá 1993), National Assemblies are having increasing input as to the more specific content of the generalized goals set by the UHJ (see chapter 7). At the time of my fieldwork, the Three Year Plan was considered by Bahá'ís as the latest stage in the rational construction of the Kingdom of God. The National Spiritual Assembly of the Bahá'ís of the United States took this plan from the UHJ and established explicit numerical goals for the U.S. Bahá'í community. These goals included: (1) dispatching at least three thousand travel teachers (those who travel beyond their own jurisdiction to teach their Faith); (2) settling at least five hundred homefront pioneers (missionaries) on Indian reservations, in the South, and in other areas of greatest need; and (3) establishing LSAs in every city with a population of 50,000 or more, resulting in no fewer than 150 new Local Spiritual Assemblies.

- The status and mission of the "Pioneer." When Bahá'ís volunteer to go "pioneering" (the term for Bahá'í missionaries), they travel to various parts of the world to evangelize and establish local assemblies. Their goal is for these assemblies to eventually become self-supporting groups of indigenous believers. Bahá'í pioneers attempt to recruit new adherents and assist in the development of fledgling LSAs. Thus, Bahá'í pioneers consider themselves part of a larger, divinely ordained project of global institution-building—institutions they believe constitute the Kingdom of God.[19] Once LSAs are formed, Bahá'ís will go to great lengths to make sure their institutions remain viable. When reports circulate that the number of believers has fallen below the required nine in some locality, stories appear in *The American Bahá'í* about Bahá'ís who sold their homes and quit their jobs to become "homefront pioneers," moving into that jurisdiction to save a "jeopardized assembly" that would otherwise have to disband. (Pioneering, and its role in the creation of a global Bahá'í identity, will be discussed further in chapter 7).

- Grass-roots construction of the Administrative Order. Shoghi Effendi set out to erect the Administrative Order from the ground up, using blueprints in the writings of Bahá'u'lláh and 'Abdu'l-Bahá. According to the scripturally defined rules, for an NSA to be elected a certain number of LSAs had to be established in the corresponding nation or region. And a certain number of NSAs had to be established before the UHJ could be formed.[20] The rapid growth seen in the decade preceding the first election of the UHJ in 1963 came from the

inspiration, generated by Shoghi Effendi, to elect that body on the
one hundredth anniversary of Bahá'u'lláh's public declaration of his
mission to the world. The yearly election of local and national
governing bodies, and the election every five years of the UHJ,
democratically renews Bahá'í institutions from the ground up; yet
authority flows downward from what Bahá'ís consider an infallible
source.

- Ideological principles. Finally, the very ideology of the Bahá'í Faith
  has also contributed to its attraction and growth. In Atlanta, for
  example (as discussed in chapter 2), social and spiritual principles
  (including unity in diversity and progressive revelation) were the
  prime source of attraction for most converts. Limited research among
  Bahá'í communities in the developing world confirms that the
  ideological elements of the Bahá'í Faith have affinity in a variety of
  cultural settings. The greatest concentration of Bahá'ís globally is in
  India (Smith and Momen 1989), where the Bahá'í emphasis on
  equality and unity in diversity has resulted in a relative breakdown in
  caste divisions among Bahá'ís (Warburg 1986; Garlington 1977). This
  has led to significant mass conversions in some areas of India, to the
  point that it has been reported that in some rural villages a majority of
  residents consider themselves Bahá'ís (Warburg 1986). Bahá'í ideology
  has come to the attention of the Indian government; a 1994 Indian
  Supreme Court opinion cited Bahá'í teachings on tolerance and unity
  in a decision concerning a dispute between Hindus and Muslims.[21]

The organizational structure and the method of expansion of the Administrative Order facilitates the development of a Bahá'í identity as situated universalists. Built from the ground up by universal participatory democracy, the
Administrative Order links Bahá'ís in a local jurisdiction to a global central authority believed to be infallible. As the highest Bahá'í authority, the UHJ reflexively acts back upon a Bahá'í's situated local community through the
development of regular, systematic teaching plans, which act as a blueprint and
guide for local activity. The teaching plans help coordinate an individual's and
a local community's vision as participants in universal salvation: building what
Bahá'ís believe to be the Kingdom of God. The next two sections look at how
the Atlanta Bahá'í community interacts with the Administrative Order as both
a theological and an administrative authority.

Atlanta Bahá'í Participation in the Administrative Order

LOCAL INSTITUTIONAL PARTICIPATION

The Bahá'í Administrative Order facilitates widespread community participation in local governance (see table 3.1). Nearly four out of five respondents to my survey had been elected to their Local Spiritual Assembly at some time. Nearly 70 percent had served as an officer of the LSA—either as chair, vice-chair, treasurer, or secretary.

More than 80 percent of respondents indicated that they had been on a local committee within their assembly jurisdiction. These committees included: a Feast and Holy Day committee to plan worship events; a deepening committee to plan for the continuing education of the community through study of the Bahá'í Writings (many communities with a significant number of children may also have a separate children's classes committee); a media or publicity committee to provide newspapers, radio, and TV with information about the Bahá'í Faith, or to announce meetings of interest to the general public; a social committee to plan fun events outside the Bahá'í calendar open to Bahá'ís and non-Bahá'ís; and a teaching committee to plan large public meetings or small Firesides.[22] This high rate of participation is also indicative of the small size of most local communities. Since a local jurisdiction needs at least nine believers in order to elect an LSA, communities with only twelve to fifteen members will

Table 3.1
Atlanta Bahá'ís' participation in governance and the Administrative Order

	No	Yes
Bahá'ís elected or appointed to an Order position		
Member of LSA	79.0%	
Officer of LSA	68.8	
Assistant to an Auxiliary Board Member	25.9	
Local Committee Member	81.6	
National Committee Member	17.9	
Other Position	58.9	
Bahá'ís participating in Administrative Order activities		
Voted in Ridván 1993 election	29.8	70.8%
Voted in 1993 District Convention	29.8	70.1
If no, ever attended District Convention?	37.8	63.2
Bahá'ís who find administrative activities satisfying		
Attending District Convention	0.8%	
Administrative duties	7.3	
Frequency of reading Shoghi Effendi's administrative writings		
Daily	3.2%	
Weekly	29.6	
Monthly or less	67.1	

elect the majority of the community to the LSA, and most members will be appointed to local committees. Communities with LSAs in metro Atlanta range in size from ninety in the city of Atlanta to just nine in suburban Decatur. Thus, for the average local Bahá'í community, high participation rates are virtually guaranteed by their small size.[23]

A typical LSA meeting begins when at least five of the nine assembly members arrive to establish a quorum, usually in one of the members' homes. The Atlanta LSA, however, meets at the Atlanta Bahá'í Center. Large assemblies, such as the city of Atlanta's, would often meet weekly. Other assemblies meet once every Bahá'í month (every nineteen days—see chapter 5), or perhaps once every Gregorian month. The meeting begins when one of the members reads a prayer by 'Abdu'l-Bahá specifically written for that occasion. The chairperson of the LSA then asks the secretary to read the correspondence. This can include letters from other metro Atlanta LSA jurisdictions inviting the whole metro Bahá'í population to a teaching or fundraising event; or a letter from the Bahá'ís of Albany, Georgia, asking for volunteers to come down to Albany and surrounding communities to help visit believers that are on Bahá'í membership rolls but are currently inactive. LSA correspondence frequently includes letters from the National Spiritual Assembly asking for information: updated local membership lists, the number of Firesides and new declarants in the community, or the number of socioeconomic projects undertaken by the LSA (such as literacy programs, neighborhood environment cleanup projects, and so on). NSA letters to the LSAs also remind Bahá'ís about national budget shortfalls, and the need for LSAs to remain committed to their monthly financial obligations to the NSA.[24] After the secretary reviews that month's correspondence, the chair asks the treasurer to review the community's financial health. The treasurer discusses monthly income, disbursements, payments to various Bahá'í funds (see chapter 5), and any correspondence sent from the NSA treasurer directly to the local treasurer.

The majority of the LSA meeting revolves around consultation on community issues. The chair of the LSA facilitates discussion that arises from the correspondence, or on any other agenda items. LSAs consult and make decisions on issues involving: advice to give a member of the local community about a personal problem she/he brought before the assembly; recommendations put before the LSA by a local community member (usually at a Nineteen-Day Feast) related to teaching or social events; fundraising opportunities to strengthen the local treasury; and local teaching projects (which can range from entering a Bahá'í float in a local parade to composing an advertisement for the local newspaper).

Bahá'ís place a great deal of importance on the process of consultation, the term Bahá'ís use for consensus decision making.[25] Shoghi Effendi said this about the need for consulting together to create and maintain unity in diversity:

The members [of an assembly] must take counsel together in such wise that no occasion for ill-feeling or discord may arise. This can be attained when every member expresseth with absolute freedom his own opinion and setteth forth his argument. Should any one oppose, he must on no account feel hurt for not until matters are fully discussed can the right way be revealed. The shining spark of truth cometh forth only after the clash of differing opinions. If after discussion, a decision be carried unanimously, well and good; but if, the Lord forbid, differences of opinion should arise, a majority of voices must prevail. (1974, 21–22)

Despite the above advice from Effendi, which Bahá'ís often quote, many interviewees admitted that consultation is sometimes not as open as it should be. One joke I heard several Bahá'ís repeat is that although Shoghi Effendi counsels "the spirit of frank and loving consultation" (1974, 63), "frank is left out in the car" when an LSA meeting begins. One long-time Bahá'í told me he felt that "we are supposed to be unified, and so there is a culture of not wanting to disagree, to challenge, or to voice dissent" when respected or senior local Bahá'ís present their views. "Bahá'ís are supposed to be nice, not confrontational," he went on, and this leads to "status quo thinking" when it comes to discussions of teaching plans, relationships within the Bahá'í community, or new ideas for outreach to the wider society.

Summarizing the substance of LSA meetings, based on what informants told me: LSA consultation revolves around the issues of: (1) teaching and evangelizing the wider Atlanta area about the Bahá'í Faith (to be discussed in detail in chapter 7); (2) communicating with other LSAs in the metro Atlanta area (to be discussed in chapter 4); and (3) internal matters, such as the scheduling of Bahá'í Feasts, Firesides, Holy Day celebrations, and children's classes. At the end of the LSA meeting, another special prayer written by 'Abdu'l-Bahá is read, and then refreshments are usually served.

A majority of Atlanta Bahá'ís (58 percent) have participated in the administration through "other" elected or appointed positions. Some of these might include: an officer of a college Bahá'í Club; a delegate to the National Convention (to elect the National Spiritual Assembly); a member of the Atlanta Bahá'í Task Force (an intercommunity planning committee); a librarian of a local community; or a member of a district, state, or regional Youth Committee or Teaching committee.

In addition to local administration, Bahá'ís in Atlanta may have some affiliation with an arm of the Bahá'í National Center. A much lower proportion of survey respondents (18 percent) had been or were currently on a national committee.[26] Atlanta Bahá'ís' participation on national committees may be lower than local committee participation for a couple of reasons, apart from the fact that these committees draw their membership from throughout the United

States. One is that the Administrative Order focuses individual activity on the local level, stressing that although the Bahá'í vision is "world-embracing," "thinking globally" should indeed be coupled with "acting locally" in one's Local Spiritual Assembly jurisdiction. As situated universalists, Bahá'ís' attitudes and ideology are very cosmopolitan and universal, but directives from the NSA ask that Bahá'í activity be focused on one's local situation: teaching and strengthening local institutions.

The second reason for much lower participation on national committees relates to the low turnover rate among national and international Bahá'í institutions in general. Local mechanisms of communication and participation allow people to rotate in and out of LSA and committee positions. The primary worship celebration of the Bahá'í community, the Nineteen-Day Feast (see chapter 5), facilitates community consultation and collaborative decision-making, and allows for individuals with new ideas and new talents to be noticed. This exposure can mean that Bahá'ís with unique ideas may get elected to the LSA at the next Ridván festival, or perhaps appointed to a local committee at the next vacancy. This type of exposure is not possible at the national level, where the same people tend to get elected to the NSA or appointed to national committees.[27]

A lower proportion of respondents have been Assistant to an Auxiliary Board member, as compared with election to the LSA. Only about one-fourth of Atlanta Bahá'ís have served or serve now on the institution of "the Learned." The lower echelons of this branch of the Administrative Order have received less attention within the Bahá'í community than do elected positions, and they have no decision-making authority as do LSAs.

The relationship between LSA members and Assistants to an Auxiliary Board member continues to evolve along with the whole Administrative Order, according to Assistants with whom I spoke. One young Persian man I interviewed said that the role of an Assistant is to be a "catalyst. We [Bahá'ís] have a process of growth, and we [Assistants] are like the spark plug." However, he pointed out that those in the Learned branch of the Administrative Order "should be very respectful of the authority of the LSA and their scope, and we are told [in the Writings] that the LSA will in a respective manner engage in a consultative relationship with the Assistants. It is up to them [the LSA] to adopt the suggestions or not." The two branches of the Administrative Order "need to work together like two teams of horses pulling a wagon." A woman I interviewed who had only recently been appointed to the one-year renewable Assistant post said this about her work in Atlanta: "The elected branch [LSA] has the authority, but the appointed branch has the responsibility to see that the decisions of the authoritative branch are carried out. The function of the Assistants are basically the functions of the Hands of the Cause: propagation and protection." Assistants for "propagation" do this, she said, by consulting with LSAs to develop formal teaching plans, and to encourage and offer advice and inspiration to individual Bahá'ís to engage in teaching work. She said that while the LSA develops a local teaching plan in accordance with the goals of the Three Year Plan, it is the responsibility of the Assistants to make sure that plan is carried out, ideally by promoting 100 percent community member involvement.

Another Assistant for "protection" said his role is to deal with issues of "the Covenant." He said his duties included working with the local assembly as "mediators and experts at conflict resolution." Individual Bahá'ís can come to him if they have conflicts in their life, and the LSA can consult with him if they have conflicts with a community member. In this way, Assistants have "pastoral" functions of counseling and encouraging members to apply Bahá'í principles in their lives. The Assistant role is the first line of intervention when concerns arise about disciplining members of the Bahá'í community for violation of Bahá'í law (those who lose their administrative rights or who become "Covenant Breakers"—see chapter 6). However, he said, "the Administrative Order is not meant to be the wrath of God. We must work with someone [who may transgress Bahá'í law], talk with them. The Assistant must be loving, must be a peacemaker, must not be judgmental. . . . Long before someone is deprived of their administrative rights, they will be given multiple chances to retract [their position] or change their behavior." Like LSA membership, appointment as an Assistant to the Auxiliary Board reinforces a Bahá'í's situated universalist identity. Assistants nurture new declarants and assist in teaching work in the designated local community, but receive guidance from successively more "global" perspectives: Auxiliary Board members, Continental Counselors, the International Teaching Center, and ultimately the UHJ.

BAHÁ'Í ELECTIONS

In addition to serving on local assemblies or committees, Bahá'ís can participate in the Administrative Order by voting in Bahá'í elections. One of the distinctive aspects of the Bahá'í system of government is democratic participation within a scripturally defined authority structure. How many Atlanta Bahá'ís vote? Table 3.1 suggests relatively robust participation rates. When metro Atlanta Bahá'ís were asked if they voted in the April 21, 1993, Ridván ceremony to elect their Local Spiritual Assembly, more than half indicated that they had showed up to vote, and another 20 percent said they had sent in absentee ballots. This represents a 70 percent participation rate in what Bahá'í scripture calls a "sacred duty" (Effendi 1974, 39).

Similar results were found for participation in the District Convention in October 1993 to elect a National Convention delegate. Nearly 53 percent of the respondents took part; another 17 percent sent in absentee ballots, resulting

in a 70 percent participation rate in the process that leads to the yearly formation of the national authority. Of those respondents who did not attend the 1993
District Convention, 62 percent indicated that they have attended a yearly convention at some point since becoming a Bahá'í.

Bahá'í elections should be conducted in an atmosphere of reverence and
solemnity. Before ballots are handed out, prayers are recited and passages from
the writings of Shoghi Effendi are read. Two common excerpts are:

> These local Spiritual Assemblies will have to be elected directly by the
> friends, and every declared believer of 21 years and above, far from
> standing aloof and assuming an indifferent or independent attitude,
> should regard it his sacred duty to take part conscientiously and
> diligently, in the election, the consolidation and the efficient working of
> his own local Assembly. (Effendi 1974, 39)

> Hence it is incumbent upon the chosen delegates to consider without
> the least trace of passion and prejudice, and irrespective of any material
> consideration, the names of only those who can best combine the
> necessary qualities of unquestioned loyalty, of selfless devotion, of a well-
> trained mind, of recognized ability and mature experience. (1974, 88)

These excerpts reinforce for voters the divine source of the Administrative Order, the sacred nature of the ritual, and one's role in the construction of a global order. Tellers are chosen to count the ballots; sometimes they need to refer
to the Writings to clarify a question in the balloting.[28] The person receiving
the most votes in a local election has the responsibility of calling the first LSA
meeting, at which time officers will be elected (or they elect officers right on
the spot if all nine members are in attendance).

At the District Convention I attended during my fieldwork, Bahá'ís had to
show their Bahá'í membership card to a representative of the LSA sponsoring
the convention during the morning registration period. Each individual's name
was checked on a master list provided by the NSA, to verify each attendee's
administrative rights. A dignified atmosphere is cultivated at these meetings
through prayers and scripture readings; the Convention also usually includes
musical performances from around the world (reflecting the ethnic composition
of the community), and a community-wide consultation on issues of importance.
Often the newly elected delegate to the National Convention is given recommendations or regional concerns to present to the NSA. Sometimes District
Convention will last all day (hence it is always held on a weekend, usually the
first in October), prompting complaints from participants that it is too long or
too boring.

The 1993 District Convention I attended was held at a local university.[29]

After checking in, attendees socialized over coffee and doughnuts before prayers were read to start the Convention. About forty-two people attended the meeting—not an especially good turnout, but it drew from throughout the diverse constituencies of the metro Bahá'í community (approximately equal numbers of white, African American, and Persian participants). The first order of business was to elect the Convention chair and secretary. The role of the chair is to facilitate the day's consultation and oversee the selection of the tellers and election of the delegate (several Bahá'ís told me that if the chair of the District Convention does a good job, he/she is often then elected to be the delegate to the National Convention—considered an honor in the Bahá'í Faith). The role of the Convention secretary is to take notes on the consultation and translate the resolutions and voting results onto preprinted forms to be sent to the Bahá'í National Center. These roles were performed by a white man and an African American woman, respectively.

The focal point of this District Convention's consultation was maintaining intercommunity communication among the various LSA jurisdictions in the district. As the chair of the Convention recognized participants who raised their hands to speak, several people pointed out that since "The Trumpet"—the recently defunct metro Atlanta Bahá'í newsletter—was no longer being published, it was difficult to know what other LSAs were doing, where Firesides or deepenings were being held in the area, or what major teaching events were being planned. After a half-hour of discussion without resolution, the chair of the Convention suggested that the host LSA follow up on the various suggestions presented in the Convention consultation, and prepare to present recommendations either at a future metro-wide town hall meeting attended by representatives from each of the district's LSAs, or at the next District Convention. In the face of a stalled discussion, this suggestion drew applause from the crowd (interviewees later told me there was no follow-through on how to revive intercommunity communication—no LSA wanted to take on the burden of establishing a metro-wide communication newsletter).

There was also consultation about the lack of planning and preparation for the current year's meeting. There were complaints about the lack of childcare, lack of music or other entertainment, lack of printed agenda, and insufficient time allotted for the meeting—many felt the three hours scheduled was too short to allow sufficient discussion of important issues such as metro-wide teaching events. (One Convention planning committee member of the host LSA later told me that the meeting was scheduled for three hours because there had been complaints about last year's meeting lasting too long). Someone pointed out that the NSA (which is responsible for choosing the LSA that will host the annual district meeting) had given the sponsoring LSA only two months' advance notice that they would be hosting this year's District Convention. After further consultation, it was decided to request that the NSA assign the duty of hosting District Convention at least ten months ahead of time to allow for adequate preparation. Someone else said that we should establish a standing metro Atlanta committee to plan year-round for each District Convention. Several people seconded that suggestion (which was never followed up), but under the provision that this newly formed committee would be under the "guidance and protection" of whichever LSA was asked to sponsor that particular year's Convention.[30]

The final issue that generated notable consultation was concern for Bahá'í youth; this discussion emerged from criticism of the lack of childcare at the Convention. Several participants wanted to know what other communities were doing to support the moral and spiritual development of Bahá'í children and youth. Most of the discussion centered around the Atlanta Bahá'í Youth Workshop (a performing arts group that teaches about the Bahá'í Faith through skits and songs—see chapter 7) and other ways youth might be "set on fire for the love of Bahá'u'lláh" via the arts. One mother said passionately that Bahá'í communities need to prevent Bahá'í children from abandoning their faith. "Our children," she said to the Bahá'í crowd, "are the next Universal House of Justice members." The final act of the Convention was to elect that year's delegate to attend the National Convention. The representative selected by the forty-two Bahá'ís in attendance and sixteen absentee ballots was a well-respected African American man from one of the southeastern LSA communities who had served as delegate on two previous occasions.

Although survey results indicate that Bahá'í institutions foster a great deal of participation in the Administrative Order, they also demonstrate that Bahá'ís don't enjoy it very much. When asked to rank the three most satisfying activities they are involved in, only about 7 percent of Bahá'í respondents listed serving in an administrative position, and only two people out of 241 (less than 1 percent) indicated that attending District Convention was among the top three. This makes the high voting rates in the election process all the more interesting. This participation can probably be attributed to a Bahá'í's view of the authority of his/her institutions, as well as the lack of distinction made between spiritual and administrative responsibilities. Participation in Bahá'í elections is socially constructed as a "sacred duty," and Bahá'ís are reminded that local elections culminate in the selection of the UHJ—believed by Bahá'ís to be a divinely inspired and infallible body.[31]

One final survey item relates to the issue of individual participation in the Administrative Order. Bahá'ís were asked how often they read the writings of "the Guardian," much of which focuses on administrative principles. As table 3.1 reveals, only 3 percent indicate they read Shoghi Effendi's writings daily as part of their personal devotions; and just under 30 percent read them weekly. This leaves more than two-thirds of the respondents who do not include study of administrative principles as a regular part of their personal "deepening." Thus, while 80 percent of Bahá'ís are now or have been on their LSA, and 70 percent participate in the election of the Local and National Assemblies, far fewer regularly study the more mundane and technical aspects of administering Bahá'í institutions.

Atlanta Bahá'í Characteristics and Administrative Participation

The Administrative Order encourages widespread local participation among Atlanta Bahá'ís. Democratic elections and consultative decision making empower believers at the local level; but Bahá'ís also believe that their participation is part of a global mission of institution building, preparing for the Kingdom of God. Voting in elections is socially constructed as a religious duty, whereby each believer is able to participate in the process of institutional renewal and community governance. This culminates in the election of their supreme, presumably infallible authority, the Universal House of Justice. Are the high rates of participation in the Administrative Order associated with demographic characteristics of the Bahá'ís themselves? I compared measures of association between membership on an LSA and appointment as Assistant to the Auxiliary Board, with participation in elections, reading administrative scripture, and demographic measures. I will discuss LSA membership and being an Assistant separately.

LSA MEMBERSHIP

Those who serve on an LSA are more likely to participate in local elections, but not more likely to read from Shoghi Effendi's writings on administrative principles. Thus, membership on an LSA may inculcate an awareness of the importance of voting in Bahá'í elections; or it may indicate that because one bothers to attend elections and vote, one is more active and consequently more likely to be elected by one's community. However, it does not necessarily mean one engages in personal devotion to educate oneself about the technicalities of administration (at least at the local level).

Gender is not associated with election to an LSA: results show that of survey respondents, 78.9 percent of the men and 79.1 percent of the women serve, either currently or in the past, on an LSA. Thus, Bahá'í women and men are equally likely to serve on the local governing authority. The Bahá'í ideology of promoting the equality of men and women seems institutionalized at the local level in Atlanta. However, other demographic characteristics are predictive of election to the assembly. Income, occupation, level of education, the number of years one has been a Bahá'í, and one's age all are statistically associated with LSA membership. In other words, the higher one's income, the more responsibility and autonomy one has on the job (as measured by white-collar, professional and managerial occupations), the more education one has, the longer one has been a Bahá'í, and the older one is, the more likely one will be elected to one's local assembly.[32] In addition, race is significantly related to LSA membership: 86 percent of white Bahá'ís have served or now serve on an LSA, while only 72 percent of both Persians and other nonwhite minorities have done so. However, this relationship disappears (i.e., becomes statistically insignificant) when we control for the local community in which one resides, since, as I discussed earlier, the composition of each LSA jurisdiction roughly mirrors the segregated housing patterns of the metro Atlanta area.

Whereas the number of years one has been a Bahá'í is significantly associated with assembly election, the number of years one has resided in one's local jurisdiction is not. This is probably because energetic, knowledgeable Bahá'ís who have just recently moved into an LSA jurisdiction are just as likely to be elected as are energetic, knowledgeable Bahá'ís who have lived there for several years. (This observation is borne out by interview results.[33]) Finally, marital status is also significantly associated with LSA membership: married Bahá'ís are twice as likely to be elected to an LSA as are single people.[34] In addition, being married to a Bahá'í is also significantly related to LSA participation: 91 percent of respondents with Bahá'í spouses are on an LSA, whereas only 73 percent married to a non-Bahá'í are. This is probably due to the fact that marriage to a non-Bahá'í often curtails the amount of time one can give to one's faith— one unofficial criterion considered in being elected to serve on the LSA.

ASSISTANT TO THE AUXILIARY BOARD

The results for Assistants to the Auxiliary Board are slightly different, possibly due to the very different role members appointed to this branch of the Administrative Order are asked to play. As with their LSA counterparts, being an Assistant is positively associated with voting in both District Convention and local Ridván elections. However, being appointed as an Assistant is also significantly related to the amount of personal study one undertakes of Shoghi Effendi's writings. This makes sense, given that the function of the "Learned" branch of the Administrative Order is to act as consultants with the Local Spiritual Assembly on administrative issues. Assistants are expected to have a more thorough knowledge of how the Administrative Order operates, and survey results show that they apparently make efforts to that effect.

Furthermore, as with their counterparts in the "Rulers" branch, higher incomes and longer tenures as Bahá'ís translate into greater likelihood of being appointed as an Assistant, as does being married, and if married, having a Bahá'í spouse. The length of residence in a local community is not relevant to being an Assistant, in part because their duties and sphere of influence extend beyond LSA jurisdictions. And as with LSA members, men and women are equally likely to be appointed to the "Learned" branch. In addition, race is significantly related to appointment as an Assistant; however, in this case both Persians and other nonwhite minority Bahá'ís are significantly *more* likely to hold this position than are whites.[35]

The differences with LSA membership appear when we consider the association between being an Assistant and age, education, and occupation. Survey results show no association between one's age level of education and being an Assistant. In other words, there is an equal likelihood of being appointed an Assistant at all ages, and at all educational levels. With occupation, the pattern also looks very different from LSA members. As I mentioned earlier, as you move from those not in the labor force to blue-collar to white-collar to professional workers, the proportion who have served on an LSA increases. This pattern does not obtain for Assistants to Auxiliary Board members. Instead, of those not in the labor force, 37 percent have been or are Assistants; for blue-collar workers, 24 percent fit this category; for white-collar workers, 11 percent; and for professionals, 38 percent. How can these differences be explained?

In part it has to do with what Bahá'ís consider to be the qualifications for being elected to the "Rulers" branch and being appointed to the "Learned" branch. Whereas both roles require "spiritual virtues," LSA membership and leadership in general requires greater managerial skills that come with more professional credentials, and higher levels of education and maturity. The LSA treasurer, depending on the size of the community, must also have some financial or accounting ability. LSA members are also more likely to interact with the "secular" or "non-Bahá'í" world as official representatives of the Bahá'í Faith, roles for which educational or professional credentials would be useful in facilitating interaction. Thus, secular standards influence what Bahá'í scripture indicates is a purely spiritual qualification.

On the other hand, Assistants to Auxiliary Board members perform a more "in-house" function (at least at the local level), acting as spiritual consultants on matters of Bahá'í administration—a role for which academic or professional credentials may be less crucial. Assistants to the Auxiliary Board, functioning as Bahá'í consultants, are often required to travel to various local communities to give advice and other assistance; thus these positions may require not so much managerial skill (although this would be useful) as the job flexibility to allow travel (as well as the financial resources to do so—and it was noted that income is positively associated with being an Assistant). Thus, we find that the highest proportion of appointees to the "Learned" branch are those not in the labor force (37 percent) and professionals (38 percent)—both of whom, for different reasons, have more time and flexibility to travel and consult with local communities.

Thus, the characteristics of Atlanta Bahá'ís help influence their election or appointment to local positions within the Bahá'í Administrative Order. One's income, occupation, marital status, and the number of years one has been an adherent all help predict the likelihood of serving in an administrative position. Educational level and age are significant for election to the LSA, but not for appointment as an Assistant to the Auxiliary Board. Gender does not influence one's level of participation in either branch. Race is significant, but only in favoring minority members of the Bahá'í community in appointment as Assistants. In all, the system of "rulers" and "the learned" generates a relatively high level of participation, with three-fourths of Atlanta Bahá'ís serving on the LSA, four-fifths serving on local committees, and one-fourth as administrative consultants to LSAs.

Summary

This chapter has analyzed the organizational mechanisms by which the Bahá'í Faith attempts to construct a coherent global authority, upheld by what Bahá'ís believe to be an infallible UHJ as a blueprint for global order. These organizational mechanisms link the local community and global hierarchy.[36] Jurisdictional "parishes" or assemblies at the local level facilitate widespread individual participation in organizational governance through democratic elections couched in religious symbolism. Two major election rituals at the local level annually renew the organization from the ground up, which culminates every five years in the election of the Universal House of Justice.

The attempts of the Bahá'í Faith to create a truly global structure in the hundred years since the death of its charismatic founder are attributable to the rational application of administrative principles through systematic plans: first under Shoghi Effendi, and then via elected assemblies and appointed boards. The combination of hierarchical centralization (to maintain ideological coherence and solidarity) with democratically empowered individual participation at the local level creates a distinct global movement. This combination also facilitates the institutional link between the global and local levels of Bahá'í life, shaping Bahá'ís' identity as situated universalists. In doing so, Bahá'ís attempt to "think globally, but act locally." This local action, at least among the Bahá'ís of Atlanta, revolves around issues of evangelizing their faith, institution-building, and family life—especially in socializing the next generation of Bahá'í children (an important concern among all religious groups in the United States in this period of pluralistic, market-oriented, individualistic religion—see Roof 1993).

The next two chapters will explore this theme further. In chapter 4 we will examine the role of ideological mechanisms that serve to promote "unity in diversity," and the degree to which Atlanta Bahá'ís adhere to their ideological authority. Then chapter 5 will investigate the personal and local ritual mechanisms by which Bahá'ís maintain connections between local activity and global ideology, and therefore strengthen their identities as situated universalists.

Chapter 4

Authority in the Administrative Order

A world federal system, ruling the whole earth and
exercising unchallengeable authority over its unimaginably
vast resources, blending and embodying the ideals of both
the East and the West, liberated from the curse of war and
its miseries . . . such is the goal towards which humanity,
impelled by the unifying forces of life, is moving.
  Shoghi Effendi, *The World Order of Bahá'u'lláh*

AUTHORITY HAS ALWAYS been an important concept in understanding any social organization. This is especially true of voluntary religious organizations,
which employ what sociologist Amitai Etzioni (1961) calls "normative compliance structures" to motivate commitment and legitimate authority. Shared values and normative authority, rather than coercion or remuneration, provide the
primary legitimacy for the use of power in religious organizations.

Researchers in the sociology of religion have found that even within religious organizations, all of which use normative compliance structures to some
degree, there is great variation in how authority is utilized and structured. *Polity*, or the structure of ecclesiastical governance, influences all the authority relationships within organizations, as well as how organizations such as churches
carry out their goals and mission (Takayama and Sachs 1976; Hammond, Salinas, and Stone 1978; Cantrell, Krile, and Donohue 1983; Hougland and Wood
1979). Even the ability of religious organizations to pursue controversial policies is dependent on the authority relationships characterizing their institutional
structures (Wood 1970, 1981).

Thus, it is important to look at the impact authority has on relationships
within the Bahá'í Administrative Order, which, as the preceding chapter has
shown, has a structure that differs markedly from the familiar episcopal, presbyterian, or congregational typologies of Christian denominations (see Moberg
1962; Cantrell, Krile, and Donohue 1983). One question to be addressed: does
the Bahá'í Administrative Order create for Atlanta adherents normative con-

sensus around core elements of a global ideology? This chapter will show that the institutional authority of the Bahá'í Administrative Order acts as another mechanism linking local believers to the global center from which this authority flows, and provides the ideological solidarity needed to maintain moral consensus within the faith. Bahá'í authority flows from the top down, yet it is enacted through participatory democracy in assemblies constructed from the ground up. This authority unites ideology and structure, attempting to establish "unity in diversity" in Bahá'í institutions. This chapter will explore the nature of authority in the Bahá'í Administrative Order, as well as its influence on Bahá'ís' identity as situated universalists.

The Bahá'í Concept of "The Covenant"

The concept of "the Covenant" is what provides ideological coherence and justification for the authority relationships within Bahá'í institutions. Bahá'í theology describes two types of Covenants made between God and humanity: the Greater and the Lesser. The Greater Covenant is the promise God made to never leave humanity without spiritual and moral guidance; Bahá'ís believe that God has sent humanity a succession of prophets or "Manifestations" to be the "educators of humanity." Bahá'ís believe that Bahá'u'lláh is the most recent Manifestation, but not the last one to be sent by God. Bahá'ís claim that the uniqueness of their faith lies in Bahá'u'lláh being the fulfillment of the promises made in all of the world's religious scripture.

The Lesser Covenant is the agreement made between the Manifestation of God and the followers concerning immediate succession—or the "routinization of charismatic authority" (cf. Weber 1922, 1946). Again, Bahá'ís consider this religious dispensation to be unique in that it is the first in which the Manifestation leaves a written document (*Kitáb-i-'Ahd* or "Book of the Covenant"— Bahá'u'lláh 1988b) that gives the followers clear instructions on successorship and the resulting polity structure for the religion. Bahá'ís also consider it significant that there are no clergy in their faith; they interpret this as signaling the maturation of humanity beyond the need for a special class of individuals who monopolize religious knowledge. Instead, for Bahá'ís authority resides in elected assemblies, although only the UHJ is believed to be divinely and infallibly guided.[1]

AUTHORITY IN THE UNIVERSAL HOUSE OF JUSTICE

Bahá'ís turn to the UHJ for guidance and inspiration because they believe it is the legitimate heir to Bahá'u'lláh's authority via the Covenant. The UHJ published its own *Constitution*, which claims authority by virtue of the Covenant established by Bahá'u'lláh:

It [the Covenant] continues to fulfill its life-giving purpose through the agency of the Universal House of Justice whose fundamental object, as one of the twin successors of Bahá'u'lláh and 'Abdu'l-Bahá, is to ensure the continuity of that divinely-appointed authority which flows from the Source of the Faith, to safeguard the unity of its followers, and to maintain the integrity and flexibility of its teachings. (Universal House of Justice [UHJ] 1972, 3–4)

The *Constitution* goes on to say that, "there being no successor to Shoghi Effendi as Guardian of the Cause of God, the Universal House of Justice is the Head of the Faith and its supreme institution, to which all must turn" (1972, 4), and that therefore the UHJ is responsible for ensuring the expansion of the Bahá'í Faith, protecting its integrity, and ultimately, Bahá'ís believe, becoming the foundation of the future world order and world government (although Bahá'ís are unwilling to say when the UHJ might take on this role of planetary governance).[2]

According to its own constitution, those elected to the UHJ, or any other Bahá'í institution, are "not responsible to those whom they represent, nor are they allowed to be governed by the feelings, the general opinion, and even the conviction of the mass of the faithful, or of those who directly elect them. They are to follow, in a prayerful attitude, the dictates and prompting of their conscience" (UHJ 1972, 6). Unlike secular, representative forms of governance, Bahá'ís elected to positions of authority are not bound to "represent" the desires of their constituents; instead they are to base their decisions in their understanding of Bahá'í scripture, and in consultation with other members of the institution.

The equality of men and women is a professed core principle of the Bahá'í Faith upheld by the UHJ. However, Bahá'u'lláh's writings restrict the membership of the UHJ (but not the local and national institutions) to men. This apparent contradiction is a frequent source of speculation among Bahá'ís, and is a source of disillusionment to many potential recruits and converts. When asked to explain, Bahá'ís quote 'Abdu'l-Bahá, who said that the reasons for this will become "manifest as clearly as the sun at high noon" (quoted in Taherzadeh 1992, 401) in the future. Most Bahá'ís I talked with, who recognize Bahá'u'lláh as the Manifestation of God for this Day, said they are willing to accept this. However, some admitted that this prohibition may appear to non-Bahá'ís as hypocritical, and calls into question the Bahá'í commitment to the real equality of women and men.

Several women (and a few men) said during interviews that they were bothered by this apparent contradiction, but saw so much good in what the Bahá'í Faith was doing that they were willing to accept 'Abdu'l-Bahá's cryptic explanation "on faith." Most pointed out that the Bahá'í Faith should be judged by its principles and its record of women's advancement at local and national levels (especially in the developing world), and not by this seemingly sexist restriction.[3] They explained that women and men serve as Counselors and Auxiliary Board members and Assistants in equal numbers in the appointed branch of the Administrative Order. Women also serve as Hands of the Cause of God (see chapter 3). Bahá'ís also highlight the passage of Bahá'í scripture that enjoins girls and boys to be taught the same curriculum in the world's schools, and women to receive training in all the professions and trades as do men.[4] Finally, Bahá'ís defend their faith's position on the equality of men and women by pointing to Bahá'u'lláh's law that states: "If it is not possible, therefore, for a family to educate all the children, preference is to be accorded to daughters since, through educated mothers, the benefits of knowledge can be most effectively and rapidly diffused throughout society" (1992, 200).

Also important for many Bahá'í women I interviewed was the symbolic example of Táhirih, one of the first Bábí women converts and heroine of the Bábí and Bahá'í faiths.[5] She was a leader, scholar, and poet, translating the *Qayyúmu'l-Asmá'* (Commentary of the Súrih of Joseph in the Qur'án) into Persian, one of the best-known early works of the Báb. Bahá'í legend (Effendi 1995) credits her act of appearing unveiled in 1848 at a gathering of Bábís in Badasht, Iran, as the symbolic severance of the Bábí Faith from Qur'ánic law, ushering in the new religious dispensation. Before Táhirih was martyred in 1852 for her Bábí allegiance, she was quoted as saying: "You can kill me as soon as you like, but you cannot stop the emancipation of women" (Effendi 1995, 75). Effendi calls her the "first woman suffrage martyr" (1995, 75).[6] Several Bahá'í women told me that the example of Táhirih was inspirational, and combined with the preference given in Bahá'í law to girls in education convinces them that the Bahá'í Faith per se is not sexist. But they also told me that the exclusion of women from the UHJ still causes many women concern and confusion. One middle-aged professional woman said: "I do believe that the Bahá'í Faith stands for the equality of men and women. The fact that the Universal House of Justice doesn't allow women does not negate that fact. . . . I just have to understand it *in light of* the principle of the equality of men and women."

However, this does not prevent speculation among Bahá'ís as to why women are not eligible for election to the UHJ. Throughout my fieldwork at deepenings and Firesides, I heard several rationalizations for this restriction. Many speculate that since the *Kitáb-i-Aqdas* indicates that future local, national, and international institutions could have more than nine elected members, those potential seats on the UHJ might be open to women. Others point out that the UHJ constitutes only the "legislative" sector of the future world government; the executive and judicial sectors, they speculate, might be open to women. Despite these explications, most Bahá'í appear willing to live with this apparent contradiction, believing 'Abdu'l-Bahá's assurance that the reasons for it will become clear in the future.[7]

AUTHORITY IN THE NATIONAL AND LOCAL ASSEMBLIES

Beyond the specific duties of the Universal House of Justice, the *Constitution* goes on to spell out the powers of the national and local assemblies, the obligations of assembly members,[8] and the electoral procedures of Bahá'í institutions. The UHJ claims authority to "review any decision or action of any Spiritual Assembly, National or Local, and to approve, modify or reverse such decision or action" (UHJ 1972, 14). The UHJ also outlines the rights of individual Bahá'ís and local or national bodies to appeal to the House of Justice decisions made at lower levels. Finally, it outlines the authority of the other branch of the Administrative Order under its wing—the "Learned," or appointed branch (see chapter 3 and fig. 3.1).

In 1929 the NSA of the United States became the first national body to create bylaws (National Spiritual Assembly of the Bahá'ís of the United States [hereafter NSA of the United States] 1975); these became the standard for all national assemblies throughout the world.[9] The bylaws outline the bounds of authority for both national and local assemblies, delineate the requirements for membership in the Bahá'í Faith,[10] describe voting procedures and officers, and circumscribe the authority of the LSA: "a Local Spiritual Assembly shall have full jurisdiction of all Bahá'í activities and affairs within the local community subject, however, to the exclusive and paramount authority of the National Spiritual Assembly as defined herein" (NSA of the United States 1975, 16).[11]

The NSA's *Declaration of Trust and By-Laws* also assigns specific duties to the Local Spiritual Assemblies. In addition to local teaching and administering marriages and divorces, these are specified as follows:

> The [Local] Assembly shall therefore above all recognize its sacred duty to maintain full and complete unity throughout the Bahá'í community, to relieve and comfort the sick and distressed, to assist the poor and destitute, to protect the orphans, the crippled and the aged, to educate the children of Bahá'ís according to the highest religious and intellectual standards, to compose differences and disagreements among members of the community, to promulgate the principles of divine civilization revealed by Bahá'u'lláh and to promote in every way possible the Bahá'í aim of the oneness of mankind. . . . It shall rigorously abstain from any action or influence, direct or indirect, that savors of intervention on the part of a Bahá'í body in matters of public and civil jurisdiction. (NSA of the United States 1975, 24–25)

This lengthy quotation is important because it emphasizes a key function future Bahá'í LSAs will supposedly carry out. Bahá'í scripture claims that as Local Assemblies mature and take on more of the above responsibilities, they will evolve into Local Houses of Justice, thereupon fulfilling many of the functions of local civil and municipal governments. Bahá'ís state that LSAs of the future will provide in every community for a Mashriqu'l-Adhkár (literally, "the Dawning-place of the mention of God")—otherwise known as a House of Worship. Bahá'ís envision the Mashriqu'l-Adhkárs eventually outnumbering mosques, synagogues, and churches as more and more people convert to their faith. Bahá'í scripture states that every Mashriqu'l-Adhkár is to be surrounded by various social insti-tutions: a hospital, an orphanage, a home for the aged, a travelers' hospice, and a university. Thus, Bahá'ís believe it will be the LSA's responsibility, as the Bahá'í Faith expands, to provide for the material and educational needs of all those within its jurisdiction, both Bahá'ís and non-Bahá'ís. While LSAs will take on greater political and economic functions in the future, say Bahá'ís, currently their sphere of activity is focused on nurturing the local Bahá'í community itself, as well as evangelizing the non-Bahá'í world.

Thus, Bahá'ís see the LSA as a liaison between the Bahá'í and non-Bahá'í world. Recent communication from the NSA has stressed that LSAs should con-ceptualize their ministry as being directed to all people in their jurisdiction, not just Bahá'ís (see *The American Bahá'í* 25, no. 2:4). During interviews Bahá'ís told me that LSA-sponsored religious education classes for children attract many non-Bahá'ís, with non-Bahá'í parents recognizing the value of the Bahá'í phi-losophy of religion and its focus on moral character development. In addition to this, many Bahá'í-sponsored race-unity or healing-racism workshops attract high numbers of non-Bahá'ís, reinforcing Bahá'ís' growing conviction that all community activities (with the exception of Nineteen-Day Feasts) are for the edification of all of humanity, and not restricted to members of the Bahá'í community.

From the above quote on the responsibilities of the LSA, we see that local institutions are enjoined not to interfere with "matters of public and civil juris-diction." Bahá'í scripture also instructs individuals within the Bahá'í Faith to follow all the laws of their government—even if at times such laws contradict specific laws of their faith.[12] In fact, Bahá'ís are not supposed to be involved with partisan politics in any way. Although encouraged to vote in civic elec-tions, they are counseled to register if possible as having "no party affiliation," to not vote along party lines, and to refrain from participating in campaigns or running for political office (cf. Hornby 1983).

The question then arises: given Bahá'í prohibitions against political involve-ment, what will be the future relationship between local and national Assem-blies and corresponding municipal, county, state, and national government? Bahá'ís envision their Administrative Order as being the basis for future social order, from the local up through the global level of society. Because they are forbidden to engage in politics, and because their scripture completely outlaws any form of military crusade, it is unclear for most Bahá'ís how Bahá'í laws and institutions will *become* the basis of social and global order. When I ask Bahá'ís what will be the relationship between the Atlanta LSA and the Atlanta City Council or Fulton County Commission, they confess they do not know, and are not sure how that relationship will evolve. Some point to passages by Shoghi Effendi, who said of a Bahá'í's relationship to social change via political involvement: "We must build up our Bahá'í system, and leave the faulty systems of the world to go their own way. We cannot change them; through becoming involved in them; on the contrary they will destroy us" (quoted in Hornby 1983, 450). However, Bahá'ís take it "on faith" that the UHJ will advise local and national institutions on these emerging relationships, which likely will evolve over hundreds of years.[13]

The Bahá'í concept of "the Covenant" is both mystical and administrative, but it functions to create what sociologist Emile Durkheim (1965, 1973) called a "collective consciousness," or a unifying set of moral and intellectual standards that promotes group solidarity. The authority of the Covenant, upheld by the UHJ, has protected the Bahá'í Faith from schism for more than 150 years, according to Bahá'ís. So important is this concept that Bahá'ís say prayers written by Bahá'u'lláh and 'Abdu'l-Bahá precisely to remain "firm in the Covenant."

The authority of the UHJ as protectors of the Covenant reflexively connects the local and global. As situated universalists, Bahá'ís are patient. Forbidden to impose their Administrative Order on the world militarily or through participation in secular politics, Bahá'ís patiently wait for direction and clarification on how their potentially revolutionary message and world order should interact with the secular world. For now, the highest authority in the Bahá'í Faith instructs Bahá'ís to live out their message of universal values locally, by hastening the maturation of their LSAs and teaching the non-Bahá'í world about Bahá'u'lláh.[14]

AUTHORITATIVE MESSAGES FROM THE UNIVERSAL HOUSE OF JUSTICE
Individual Bahá'ís have very little *direct* interaction with the UHJ. Only during the Bahá'í pilgrimage (see chapter 5) would the average Bahá'í have firsthand, personal contact with the UHJ. Typically any contact comes in the form of written documents. Throughout my fieldwork with Atlanta Bahá'ís, I had repeated opportunities to attend deepenings in believers' homes that focused on documents written by the UHJ. Sometimes messages or cablegrams from the Universal House of Justice are sent to the NSA, which then prints them in the monthly newspaper *The American Bahá'í*, or quotes them in the NSA's monthly letter to local communities, which is read at the Nineteen-Day Feast. Or Bahá'ís can write directly to the research department of the UHJ in Haifa for elucidation of an obscure passage of scripture. However, the most significant regular

communication from the UHJ comes in the form of yearly Ridván messages, which provide inspiration and guidance for individual Bahá'ís and the Bahá'í community collectively. The festival of Ridván is a twelve-day celebration (April 21 through May 2) commemorating Bahá'u'lláh's public declaration of his mission, and marking the beginning of the Bahá'í administrative year.

The fieldwork for this research was conducted from Ridván 1993 through Ridván 1994 (Bahá'í years 150 and 151, respectively). The previous year (1992, which the UHJ had declared a "Holy Year" commemorating the one hundredth anniversary of the death of Bahá'u'lláh) was also one of transition and new responsibilities for Bahá'ís. The complete English-language version of the *Kitáb-i-Aqdas* ("The Most Holy Book") was published for the first time that year, by the UHJ.[15] The primary scriptural text in the whole canon of Bahá'í scripture, the *Kitáb-i-Aqdas* is often referred to as the "Bahá'í Bible." The symbolic importance of this event cannot be overstated: it confirmed for English-speaking Bahá'ís a sense of independent identity with full access to the book Bahá'ís consider the blueprint for future world order.

The publication of the *Kitáb-i-Aqdas* reinforced Atlanta Bahá'ís' devotion and allegiance to their supreme authority. Several Bahá'ís said during interviews that the publication of the *Kitáb-i-Aqdas* was a "gift from God" and a "blessing to the Bahá'í world" and would hasten the maturation of the Bahá'í community by placing greater responsibilities upon them. Sociologically, the long-awaited English publication of their "blueprint for the future world order" served to strengthen Bahá'ís' sense of global identity.[16]

My fieldwork for this study, then, began just as Atlanta Bahá'ís were reading the full text of the *Kitáb-i-Aqdas* for the first time, and as the Bahá'í world was beginning the first year of the Three Year Plan outlined by the UHJ—setting the worldwide goals and direction of the Bahá'í community through Ridván 1996. The Ridván message of 1993 was of great importance to Atlanta Bahá'ís, because it set the stage for a new individual and collective effort of community maturation and expansion, not only for that year but for the duration of the Three Year Plan. The Ridván message brought Bahá'ís up to date on examples of the "clear indications that the profile of the community has been raised in the public eye," and announced the inauguration of the Three Year Plan. Although previous plans were at least five to ten years long, the Three Year Plan's "brevity is compelled by the swiftly changing tides of the times," and is "a measure of our determination to respond to the immense opportunities at this critical moment in the social evolution of the planet." The Three Year Plan (discussed further in chapter 7) revolves around "a triple theme: enhancing the vitality of the faith of individual believers, greatly developing the human resources of the Cause, and fostering the proper functioning of local and national Bahá'í institutions."[17]

Throughout the year, Bahá'ís—individually and in small groups, sometimes only two or three in a meeting—studied this guidance from the UHJ, going over the Ridván message sentence by sentence, paragraph by paragraph. At some of the deepenings, the discussion centered on the call from the UHJ to expand teaching not only to usher in "entry by troops" or mass conversion, but also to target "people of capacity." Bahá'ís discussed what "capacity" meant—was it people with money and professional credentials, or did it mean other things? Some suggested it might mean spiritual capacity, too. Others said that Bahá'í communities will need to mature if mass conversion begins, because it will mean the demographic profile of the community will change—especially if "entry by troops" means that many of society's problems (drugs or alcohol abuse, mental or emotional problems, etcetera) will become the Bahá'í community's problems as well (the implicit assumption made by Bahá'ís is that these problems are *not* part of the Bahá'í community at the present time). Still others made the connection between "developing the human resources of the Cause" and "attracting people of capacity." Bahá'ís said that if their community grows, their faith would need to attract people who can help solve society's problems and the problems within Bahá'í communities. Thus, Bahá'ís agreed that they need Bahá'í psychologists, Bahá'í businesspersons, and Bahá'í lawyers to help local communities mature and deal with their local problems, as well as humanity's global problems.

Bahá'ís frequently referred to the yearly Ridván message from the UHJ as a "letter from God"—not surprising given the Bahá'í view of the consensual decisions and directives of the UHJ as divinely inspired and infallible. The message gives Bahá'ís assurance that the chaos of the world has meaning and purpose, and that the UHJ will have authoritative solutions to this chaos. These documents serve to nurture a Bahá'í's situated universalist identity by creating a personal link between the individual and their faith's global center that redirects their focus back to the teaching work in the local community and individual spiritual development. Several people mentioned during interviews the frustration and confusion they feel their non-Bahá'í friends have about chaotic world events, and the hopelessness felt by many people in society. The UHJ reminded the Bahá'ís in their 1993 Ridván message that this global chaos is not a source of disillusionment or apathy, but an opportunity to teach people about their religion and its power to transform individual souls as well as society. To Atlanta Bahá'ís situated in local communities, the UHJ's message interprets the universal ailments afflicting the world, and prescribes a universal remedy in the Three Year Plan that Bahá'ís enact locally. Thus the UHJ warns Bahá'ís: "There should therefore be no hesitation or delay on the part of individuals or Spiritual Assemblies in attending to them [the goals of the Three Year Plan], lest the problems of mankind pile up unchecked, or the rise of internal crises slows us down."

Atlanta Bahá'ís and the Recognition of Authority

Given the clear organizational authority outlined in the UHJ Constitution, the sociological question is how readily Atlanta Bahá'ís recognize that authority. Included in my questionnaire were several items intended to assess Atlanta Bahá'ís' attitudes toward administrative authority. Responses can be used as a measure of agreement and assent to core Bahá'í principles, as well as the degree to which Atlanta Bahá'ís accept the concept of the Covenant.

The first set of items probes Atlanta Bahá'ís' level of agreement with the legitimacy of ecclesiastical authority within the Administrative Order ("Recognition of Legitimate Authority"). Table 4.1 shows that nearly 87 percent of respondents agree or strongly agree that "as a Bahá'í, I submit to the authority of the Administrative Order, even if I disagree with what it says." Nearly two-thirds disagree or strongly disagree with both of the following statements: "Bahá'ís should have a lot of latitude in following the decisions of the House of Justice," and "The NSA should not interfere in the decisions of the local community."

Overall, these results indicate a high degree of conformity with the ideology of divine authority in Bahá'í institutions. It should be pointed out, however, that the second question, concerning latitude in following the UHJ, displays moderate variance in individual responses, with more than one-third agreeing or unsure about the statement. This may reflect the fact that Bahá'í scripture does emphasize the importance of an individual's personal investigation of the truth—what I would consider a core spiritual principle among Bahá'ís. While the UHJ has absolute (and infallible) authority among Bahá'ís, and absolute obedience to that authority is demanded (this is the essence of living according to the Covenant of Bahá'u'lláh), Bahá'ís have considerable latitude in applying the principles championed by the UHJ. For example, there is no latitude in conforming to the UHJ's requirement of chastity outside marriage, but there is considerable latitude in how one might promote racial unity in one's local community. In addition to this, one-fourth of the respondents were "unsure" about the NSA's legitimate authority to "interfere" with the local community.[18]

The bottom two questions of table 4.1 substantively measure Atlanta Bahá'ís' attentiveness to the messages from the UHJ ("Attentiveness to Authoritative Directives"). Just as Atlanta respondents generally "submit" to the UHJ's authority, they also consider its messages "very important" to them personally as a source of information and direction about the Bahá'í Faith. While messages from the UHJ are overwhelmingly important to Bahá'ís, they are read less often than are the other Writings. As shown at the bottom of table 4.1, more than 80 percent of Bahá'í respondents indicated they personally read Universal House of Justice messages only monthly or less often.

Indicative of this respect for, and assent to, the substantial (and potentially

Table 4.1

Agreement with survey questions on attitudes toward authority and toward
authoritative messages from the Bahá'í Administrative Order

	Recognition of legitimate authority				
Question	1	2	3	4	5[a]
As a Bahá'í, I submit to the authority of the Administrative Order, even if I disagree with what it says.	54.0	32.9	10.1	1.3	1.7%
Bahá'ís should have a lot of latitude in following the decisions of the UHJ.	11.8	10.9	14.0	23.6	39.7
The NSA should not interfere in the decisions of the local community.	2.6	7.3	25.4	41.4	23.3

	Attentiveness to authoritative directives				
Question	1	2	3	4[b]	
How often do you read from the messages of the Universal House of Justice?	1.4	16.1	39.3	43.1	

Question	1	2	3	4	5[c]
How important to you are the Universal House of Justice messages in keeping informed about the Faith?	82.2	13.0	3.0	0.9	0.9

[a] 1 = strongly agree, 2 = agree, 3 = unsure, 4 = disagree, 5 = strongly disagree
[b] 1 = daily, 2 = weekly, 3 = monthly, 4 = less often
[c] 1 = very, 2 = somewhat, 3 = not very, 4 = not at all, 5 = never seen

repressive) authority of the Administrative Order are the comments Bahá'ís made
about it in interviews. Bahá'ís speak of this authority as a protection; as a blessing; as a source of guidance in a secularized, morally decrepit world. One African American man put it this way:

> I can't think of anything the UHJ has said that has caused me to want to
> rebel. . . . I have read every pronouncement it has written since I've
> been a Bahá'í. And I've found 100 percent of them illuminating and
> liberating.

A Persian man, reflecting on the fact that 'Abdu'l-Bahá acts as the "exemplar"
and the perfect model for Bahá'ís to emulate, said this:

> 'Abdu'l-Bahá says that any decision that comes from any institution he
> would obey. . . . Therefore, if 'Abdu'l-Bahá gives that weight, then, that
> is the only choice for us. You have to follow whatever comes from the
> institution, because it's guaranteed that if some decision is wrong, it will
> show up. And then improvement will happen.

Several Bahá'ís talked about the balance within their religion between obeying an infallible authority and exercising one's personal initiative and freedom. A young white woman said:

> A letter from the UHJ is more than guidance, it's more of a directive, I mean, it's . . . it has the authority of a divine institution and it's supposed to be followed. But since the addresses from the UHJ are directive and nondirective at the same time . . . I mean, they are explaining what's going on in the world, but putting it in a Bahá'í context so that you can understand it, and then giving you guidance as to what it is you can do. But, I mean, it's not like, you know, so specific that it doesn't leave room for your own creativity.

Another man from a Catholic background said, when asked how he viewed the authority of the Administrative Order:

> As absolute. The authority of the Bahá'í Faith is absolute, but the authority it chooses to exercise over my life and each aspect of my life, is minimal. But the authority of the Bahá'í Faith is absolute. The authority of the institutions, when they do choose to do something, is absolute. And I have no problem with that, none whatsoever.

His wife, also a Bahá'í, agreed, and added: "I guess in my head it all goes back to Bahá'u'lláh, and then comes down to us and the institutions. . . . Now once I figured out who Bahá'u'lláh was, then the authority wasn't an issue. Because if he is who he says he is, then everything else falls into place. So for me the question that I always come back to: is this guy really who he says he is?" (i.e., the return of Christ and latest Manifestation of God).

Not all Atlanta Bahá'ís, however, were willing to follow the authoritative laws as a matter of "faith," merely accepting them as divine protection. One man who had served on several LSAs said that he had to know the rational reason behind some of the restrictive laws before he would assent to them fully:

> I've always kind of rebelled against authority. But it depends on the credibility of the authority. . . . Christ has authority, that doesn't mean that I did everything that he says I should, and Bahá'u'lláh has the same authority, and I have no problem with 'Abdu'l-Bahá and Shoghi Effendi and the Universal House of Justice having that authority. And whatever they say is the law, I agree that's the law and that's the way it ought to be. I think that the Faith teaches that it doesn't matter whether you understand the law or not, you are still bound to abide by it. I haven't been able to buy into that. You know, I still have to understand, but I'm willing to break the law, I'm willing to be punished or whatever to find out.

As seen in table 4.1, however, the majority of Atlanta Bahá'ís agree that one should follow the laws or institutions even when one doesn't agree with them. This was true, some said, not only because Bahá'ís should set an example for the wider society, but because they are protected from the destructive forces of a secular society by doing so. One woman said this when talking about raising her children to obey Bahá'í laws:

> I tell you what they [her kids] have seen, and that's a constant living a life that is not Bahá'í and the difference of living a life that is Bahá'í. They've . . . see[n] the wisdom of the laws and to see the laws as protection, not as something designed to keep you from having a good time. Not something that sets out to make you miserable, but it protects you from things that could hurt you.

PREDICTORS OF RESPECT FOR THE ADMINISTRATIVE ORDER

What contributes to the respect Atlanta Bahá'ís indicate they have toward the laws and leadership of their faith? The most important possible predictor, one might assume from sociological research, for submission to the authority of the Bahá'í Administrative Order would be the respondent's previous religious background.[19] In the sociology of religion, both the polity (form of church government) and the liberal or conservative theological stance of one's denomination have proven to be significant in determining not only one's acceptance of ecclesiastical authority, but also one's measure of organizational participation (Takayama and Sachs 1976; Wood 1970).

This can be tested by recoding respondents' previous religious background into two different variables. The first is a liberal-to-conservative continuum of previous religious background, identifying groups as conservative, moderate, or liberal based on compiled theological profiles from Roof and McKinney (1987) and Backman (1983).[20] The second variable is based on the polity type of one's previous religious background—either hierarchically structured (including both episcopal and presbyterian polities) or decentralized (such as congregational polities—see Moberg 1962; Cantrell, Krile, and Donohue 1983).[21]

Analysis revealed that Bahá'í converts from theologically liberal religious backgrounds were just as likely to get high scores on the constructed authority measure as were converts from theologically conservative backgrounds. Even more interesting, Atlanta Bahá'í converts from hierarchical and decentralized religious backgrounds were equally likely to recognize the legitimate authority of their Administrative Order. This goes against the theoretically obvious assumption that those from hierarchically structured religious denominations would be more thoroughly socialized into viewing ecclesiastical authority as more legitimate. Survey results, however, indicate that this is not the case.[22] A Bahá'í convert's previous religious ideology and previous religious form of government do *not* predict the degree to which that individual perceives the Administrative Order as having legitimate authority. Bahá'ís come from a variety of religious backgrounds, but exposure to a universal ideology reflexively connects Bahá'í global institutions with situated local communities in a process that shapes diverse Bahá'ís into a unified identity as situated universalists.

It is also important to test whether there is any statistical association between my composite measure of authority recognition (the first three items from table 4.1) and various demographic measures. Statistical analysis revealed that the variables gender, race/ethnicity, age, education, income, occupational grouping, and whether or not one's parents were Bahá'í are not significantly related to the recognition of Administrative Order authority. However, some individual demographic characteristics were associated with recognition of authority. The longer one has been a Bahá'í, or if one is married—and especially if one is married to a Bahá'í spouse—the more likely one is to recognize the Administrative Order as possessing legitimate authority. This might be explained by the fact that the longer one has been a Bahá'í, the more socialized or "deepened" into the Bahá'í worldview one becomes, thus the more likely one is to adhere to the ideology of progressive revelation and the requirements of "firmness in the Covenant." Although being married makes one more likely to score high on the recognition of legitimate authority scale, when the religion of one's spouse is controlled for (either Bahá'í or non-Bahá'í), the original statistical association disappears. This suggests that it is being married to a Bahá'í that specifically contributes to the recognition of Bahá'í authority. Thus, a Bahá'í couple is more likely to fully integrate into their family life a sense of Bahá'í identity and recognition of the importance of Bahá'í institutions in reinforcing this identity. As situated universalists, Bahá'ís see the family as the core unit of society at the local level, and as the incubator of universal values of the oneness of humanity. Global unity cannot be achieved, Bahá'ís will say, unless you first begin with unity in your own household.[23]

Finally, membership on an LSA is also significantly related to scoring at the high end of the recognition of legitimate authority scale. This is not surprising, given that serving on a local assembly would bring one into contact with Administrative rules and procedures, as well as the socially constructed authority of Bahá'í institutions.[24]

LINK BETWEEN AUTHORITY AND BAHÁ'Í IDEOLOGY

There has always been a close relationship between recognition of ecclesiastical authority and credence given to the ideological principles espoused by that authority (see Wood 1970, 1981; D'Antonio et al. 1989). To explore this relationship within the Bahá'í Faith, one must test the statistical association between respect for authority and agreement or disagreement with various tenets

Table 4.2

Atlanta Bahá'ís' agreement and disagreement with statements expressing
Bahá'í principles

	1	2	3	4	5[a]
Bahá'í scripture is the authentic Word of God for this Day	80.2	14.3	5.1	0.4	0.0%
Bahá'í scriptures give me clear moral guidance in my daily life	73.8	22.4	3.8	0.0	0.0
I try to pattern all my daily activities around the laws and principles of the Faith	43.3	49.2	4.2	2.9	0.4
The Bahá'í Faith has had very little influence on my views of current social issues	4.3	4.7	4.3	30.6	56.2
It is important for me as a Bahá'í to make friends with people of other races/ethnicity	66.2	30.4	2.5	0.8	0.0
Bahá'ís have been in the forefront in promoting racial unity	27.4	42.3	19.7	7.3	3.4
The most important aspect of the Faith for me is spiritual growth based on the Writings	50.6	39.7	5.5	3.8	0.4
The most important thing for me to do as a Bahá'í is actively teach the Faith	38.6	43.2	10.6	5.9	1.7

[a] 1 =strongly agree, 2 = agree, 3 = unsure, 4 = disagree, 5 = strongly disagree

of Bahá'í ideology. Table 4.2 shows that Bahá'ís display a striking unanimity in their attitudes about their faith. More than 90 percent agree or strongly agree that "Bahá'í scripture is the authentic word of God for this day" (measuring recognition of progressive revelation). Similarly, more than 90 percent agree or strongly agree with the following statements: "Bahá'í scriptures give me clear moral guidance in my daily life" and "I try to pattern all my daily activities around the laws and principles of the Faith"; and nearly 90 percent disagree or strongly disagree that "The Bahá'í Faith has very little influence on my views of current social issues" (all three statements measure the salience of the Bahá'í Faith in an adherent's life). Nearly 97 percent agree or strongly agree that "It is important for me as a Bahá'í to make friends with people of other races and ethnic groups," and nearly 70 percent agree or strongly agree that "Bahá'ís have been in the forefront in this country in promoting racial unity" (both items measure acceptance of the concept of the oneness of humanity).[25]

Finally, two questions examined the importance of teaching the Faith, and the importance of individual transformation and spiritual growth—both foci, as discussed above, of recent UHJ communications. As can be seen in table 4.2, more than 90 percent and nearly 82 percent, respectively, either strongly agree or agree with spiritual growth and teaching items.

I tested for a statistical association between adherence to Bahá'í social and spiritual principles and their salience in one's life, and recognition of the legitimacy of the administrative authority in the Bahá'í Faith. With the exception of "patterning all my daily activities around the laws and principles of the Faith" and "Bahá'ís have been in the forefront in this country in promoting racial unity," all items in table 4.2 are significantly related to acknowledging the legitimate authority of the Administrative Order (at the p < .01 statistical level using Chi-square measures of association). Thus, the core principles of a Bahá'í's faith, as well as its salience in one's life, are significantly related to a Bahá'í's acceptance of the authority of the Administrative Order. This is also true of the importance of teaching one's faith and using Bahá'í scripture to improve one's character. In other words, socially ascribed personal characteristics have no association with agreement with core Bahá'í principles. Thus, blacks and whites and Persians, men and women, highly educated and less educated, and rich and poor Bahá'ís all were equally likely to acknowledge their acceptance of Bahá'í ideals. What *did* make a difference in whether an Atlanta Bahá'í agreed with the tenets of Bahá'í ideology was their recognition of the authority of the Administrative Order. Acceptance of Bahá'í institutional authority is therefore a key requirement in the construction of a Bahá'í's situated universalist identity.

The Challenges of Authority in the Atlanta Bahá'í Community

Bahá'ís readily recognize that their Administrative Order is in its infancy, and the exact relationships between its elected and appointed branches, as well as the relationships among local administrative units, are still unfolding. This maturation process often creates confusion and tension among Bahá'ís.

This confusion was dramatized at a meeting (which I attended as part of my fieldwork) with one of the Continental Counselors for the Americas, held in Atlanta in April 1994. Someone in the audience asked the Counselor: "What should be the best working relationship between the assemblies and the auxiliary board members, and between assemblies themselves?" He replied, "When you figure it out, please let us know!" The audience laughed, but the question pointed out one source of tension over authority evident in the Bahá'í community.

Part of the conflict arises because Bahá'ís themselves are unsure of where the legitimate authority of the assembly ends and the consultative relationship between assemblies and the "Learned branch" of the Administrative Order begins. One man who was an assistant to an Auxiliary Board member said he was glad when his one-year term ended and he was not reappointed. He told me that some Bahá'ís felt he was overstepping his authority, or "forcing" communities to do things they did not want to do, in his role as "consultant."

On the other end of the spectrum, some non-Bahá'ís I talked with indicated that the treatment accorded Counselors, Board Members, or even NSA or UHJ members who have visited Atlanta amounts to a clergy-laity relationship—this despite the prohibition against the creation of clergy in Bahá'u'lláh's writings. On one occasion, a former UHJ member spoke at an interfaith dialogue between Christians and Bahá'ís that I attended at a local Atlanta university. A Christian minister who attended the ecumenical gathering told me afterward that Bahá'ís should not boast about the absence of clergy in their faith, because the Bahá'ís "were hanging on his every word, and deferring to him during questions and answers," and treating him just like a "revered clergyman."

In theory, those who are appointed to the "Learned" branch (as opposed to being elected to the "Rulers" branch) attain that position because of their "expert" knowledge of Bahá'í scripture or administrative principles. Bahá'ís are encouraged to consult with them not only on administrative matters, but also with personal problems. Thus, esteemed Auxiliary Board members or their Assistants function at times in pastoral roles. However, it is also true that an assembly or an individual can reject any advice given them by a Counselor or Board Member or their Assistants, since decision-making authority resides only with the "Rulers."[26] Thus, deferential respect for the authority of Bahá'í institutions sometimes spills over onto individuals elected or appointed to those institutions.

This is a point many Bahá'ís I interviewed emphasized: in the Bahá'í Faith, there is a difference between individual and authoritative interpretation of Bahá'í laws. Only the Writings, Bahá'ís would say, and the decisions made through consultation by institutions, carry any weight. All assembly members, even UHJ members, when they are "outside the consultation chamber" (or outside an official assembly meeting with a quorum), are "just Bahá'ís" without any right to pass judgment on individuals or to make binding decisions about community issues.

One long-standing member of the Atlanta community summed up the Bahá'í Faith as a "do-it-yourself religion" that puts the onus on the individual for their own spiritual growth. However, another Atlanta LSA member emphasized that the Administrative Order was set up for a purpose—to get things done collectively. Bahá'ís shouldn't forget, he said, that their assemblies are invested with an authority all Bahá'ís, in keeping faithful to the Covenant of Bahá'u'lláh, must submit to and willingly support, even if they disagree.[27] He felt the assembly should mature and wield its authority because it is the leader of the whole community:

> I think the assembly needs to be more of a leader. . . . So I think the
> assembly has to mature first, and very rapidly after, or as it's maturing,

the community is gonna be coming right on its footsteps, or maybe even pushing it along, once it sees there is some momentum. They [his LSA] are good about it, you know, they don't dictate, they aren't authoritative. But I think it [the LSA] needs to be more pushy, more of a parent figure. Not dictatorial, but as far as a supervisor, a good leader, that type of concept.

Most often, the tensions concerning legitimate authority in Atlanta arise over intercommunity or inter-LSA relationships. Questions arise over the exact physical boundaries of an LSA (and thus over which community an individual lives in).[28] Tensions also arise when one LSA holds an event in the jurisdiction of another (possibly because of the availability of a public meeting space) without first obtaining permission.

Several times, metro Atlanta has seen the rise of an interassembly committee to coordinate citywide meetings or teaching events. The most recent attempt was in 1988, when the Atlanta Bahá'í Task Force was created to implement systematic communication and organization for Bahá'í events.[29] This was also in recognition of the fact that none of the seventeen Bahá'í LSAs in the metro Atlanta area individually had the resources to stage large teaching events, whereas pooling resources could allow for larger programs.

However, the Task Force encountered problems for two major reasons. The first had to do with confusion over jurisdiction and its proper authority within the Administrative Order. Bahá'ís expressed puzzlement and frustration as to what authority, if any, the Task Force had over any one particular LSA in metro Atlanta. The key issue was whether a "human-made" organization (the metro-wide Task Force) should have authority over any one "divinely ordained" institution (the Local Spiritual Assembly). Many LSAs also grew tired of the financial drain the Task Force became. The "Trumpet," the monthly newsletter of the Task Force, was sent free to every Bahá'í in metro Atlanta. Eventually the Task Force had to ask for donations, and when it could not secure enough funds, the "Trumpet" ceased publication (in late 1992).

The second problem concerned the way the Task Force was created. In 1988 the NSA appointed prominent or visible Bahá'ís from the Atlanta area to the Task Force and gave the group its mandate. This seemed for many Bahá'ís to be out of character in an administrative structure that stressed bottom-up, democratic participation. Bahá'ís also didn't feel that the mandate of the Task Force was communicated or understood. Was the Task Force created for communication among assemblies (essentially to publish the "Trumpet" newsletter), or was it intended to actually have the authority to plan metro-wide events? Eventually, around 1992, the Task Force crumbled, and few efforts were made to resurrect it during my period of fieldwork, mainly because Bahá'ís are unsure of what its function should be, separate from that of the LSAs. Despite this, almost all

Bahá'ís agree that there should be some kind of coordination among LSAs in
the metro Atlanta area.

Summary

However many questions Bahá'ís have about the efficacy of their institutions at
the present time, they are confident that the "divinely revealed" elected and
appointed branches of Bahá'u'lláh's Administrative Order will provide the pattern for future world order. Bahá'ís take a characteristically evolutionary view
of their present confusions, saying that the proper functioning of these institutions will "mature" over time (concomitant with the developing "spiritual maturity" of individual Bahá'ís in the community). This is a common theme that
emerges among Bahá'ís: they have faith that despite imperfections in the functioning of the Administrative Order, and despite apparent contradictions that
emerge between Bahá'í ideology and Bahá'í practice, the authoritative Universal House of Justice will provide the guidance and clarity needed to build the
Bahá'í vision of the Kingdom of God. Parallel to the idea of progressive revelation is progressive maturation: not only of individual Bahá'ís as they deepen their
spiritual life, but also of the Administrative Order under the guidance of the
UHJ. Bahá'ís themselves readily acknowledge these contradictions: the stated
importance of revealed scripture, yet a tendency toward a "cult of personality"
around those in high-status positions in the Administrative Order; an ideology
of equality of women and men, coupled with the exclusion of women from the
Universal House of Justice; an organizational structure that emphasizes social
change from the local level up through the global level (culminating in world
government), coupled with the faith's interdiction of individual participation
in political activity that might increase Bahá'í influence in society. Faith in the
UHJ stems from its socially constructed authority as an expression of Bahá'u'lláh's
role as most recent "Manifestation of God," fulfilling what Bahá'ís say are the
promises made by God's Covenant with humanity to bring about the Kingdom
of God.

Chapter 3 showed how the institutional structure of the Bahá'í Faith, characterized by a formal organization of democratically elected assemblies, reflexively links the local community with the world center. This chapter has shown
how authority acts as an ideological mechanism through which a coherent, unified worldview is constructed. The substantial authority resulting from the concept of "the Covenant" is communicated to adherents through widespread
participation in local governance, as well as through documents and letters from
a supposedly infallible source. This communication can be direct, as with the
yearly Ridván message addressed to the individual believer, or indirect, as when
the NSA acts as a mediating institution in a global dialogue. The authority of

the Administrative Order moves from the UHJ throughout Bahá'í institutions, acting as the "moral glue" that facilitates solidarity among Bahá'ís (cf. Durkheim 1965, 1973, 1984).

Authority appears to be a key variable operating in Bahá'í institutions. Whereas assent to core principles (such as progressive revelation or race unity) is significantly related to one's recognition of legitimate authority in the Bahá'í Administrative Order, it is not related at all to one's previous religious background, to most ascribed characteristics, or to demographic status. Evidence also indicates that acceptance of these core principles of Bahá'í ideology is widespread (see tables 4.1 and 4.2).

The organizational structure of the Bahá'í Faith, as well as the authority inhering to this structure, acts to inculcate a coherent global worldview among its diverse members. This combination of organizational and ideological mechanisms has constructed for the individual Bahá'í a distinctive global identity as a situated universalist—separate from other ascribed or achieved identities.

Personal Devotion and
Chapter 5 Organizational Participation

As to the Nineteen Day Feast, it rejoiceth mind and heart.
If this feast be held in the proper fashion, the friends will,
once in nineteen days, find themselves spiritually restored,
and endued with a power that is not of this world. . . . This
feast is held to foster comradeship and love, to call God to
mind and supplicate Him with contrite hearts, and to
encourage benevolent pursuits.

'Abdu'l-Bahá, *Selections from the Writings*
of 'Abdu'l-Bahá

THIS STUDY HAS demonstrated the importance of ideology in facilitating the "unity in diversity" that characterizes the Bahá'í Faith.[1] This ideology is upheld through the Administrative Order, which combines centralized ecclesiastical authority with empowering democratic participation. What are the practices and rituals that bring Bahá'ís into contact with the authority of the Administrative Order, and link the local and global to foster a Bahá'í's situated universalist identity?

It should be mentioned at the outset that Bahá'ís claim to have minimized the role of ritual in their faith. While practices such as routine worship or regular obligatory prayer and fasting sociologically constitute "ritualistic" behavior, Bahá'í scripture discourages overly formalized ceremonies or dogmatic rites. In theory, this theological flexibility serves to nurture the Bahá'í value of "unity in diversity," establishing global practices without becoming identified with one particular culture. Shoghi Effendi, for example, wrote:

> The Faith has certain simple rites prescribed by Bahá'u'lláh, such as the obligatory prayers, the marriage ceremony and the laws for the burial of the dead, but its teachings warn against developing them into a system of uniform and rigid rituals incorporating man-made forms and practices, such as exist in other religions where rituals usually consist of elaborate ceremonial practices performed by a member of the clergy. (Hornby 1983, 477–478)[2]

This said, however, rituals are the sociological backbone of a religious life, and I will use the concept of "ritual" here in its sociological sense, keeping in mind Bahá'ís' insistence that their faith keeps formal ritual to a minimum. The common practices and shared realities of religious life shape the worldview of its adherents. Geertz writes, "In a ritual, the world as lived and the world as imag-ined, fused under the agency of a single set of symbolic forms, turn out to be the same world" (1973, 112). This chapter will explore the ritual life of Atlanta Bahá'ís. It will show that both personal and collective rituals reinforce the uni-versal identity of individual Bahá'ís as situated universalists, and remind them of their faith's global vision. As Geertz said, the Bahá'í "image" of a global soci-ety is "lived" through the local collective life they share.

A Bahá'í's personal and collective life is divided up into daily devotional requirements, and also monthly and yearly festivals that conform to specific laws of Bahá'u'lláh and the dictates of the Bahá'í calendar. As Durkheim (1965, 1973) points out, ritual enacts the values and solidarity of a religious community. This is certainly true of Bahá'ís, as their rituals reinforce the authority and global worldview of the Administrative Order, and link them to the global center of their faith. While organizational structure and ideology provide the scaffolding and motivation to link *local community* with *global society*, ritual observance gives Bahá'í institutions the everyday, habitual practices that embody its global doc-trine (see Wuthnow 1987).

The Daily Devotional Life of Atlanta Bahá'ís

In the *Kitáb-i-Aqdas*, Bahá'u'lláh (1992) enjoined his adherents to follow a daily regimen of prayer and scripture reading, as well as periodic contributions to Bahá'í Funds, fasting during the month of 'Alá', and, if financially feasible, a pilgrim-age to the World Center in Haifa. I will cover each of these ritual practices sepa-rately; together they constitute some indication of a Bahá'í's devotion and commitment.

PRAYER

Bahá'ís have available to them hundreds of prayers written by the Báb, Bahá'u'lláh, and 'Abdu'l-Bahá; these prayers are used in private devotion and recited at Bahá'í gatherings.[3] One common denominator for nearly all Bahá'ís is possession of a prayer book (NSA of the United States 1985). The prayers found in Bahá'í prayer books are addressed to God, but Bahá'ís are free to pray directly to God, Bahá'u'lláh, or one of the other Manifestations of God. Prayers are usually arranged by topics, found in prayer books under headings such as "aid and assistance," "family members," "detachment," "spiritual qualities," "firmness in the Covenant," "protection," "steadfastness," or success in "teaching." This has the effect of further rationalizing devotional practice within the Bahá'í Faith.[4]

The majority of Bahá'í prayers are known as *munáját*, or "private communion," used for private devotion. There are thousands of such prayers, most of which usually appeared first in letters to individuals. Those available to English-speaking Bahá'ís are from the Báb, Bahá'u'lláh, and 'Abdu'l-Bahá; Shoghi Effendi also wrote prayers in Persian and Arabic, but as yet none have been translated into English (Walbridge 1996, 49). Some of the more popular prayers have been set to music and are sometimes sung at Bahá'í gatherings. Prayers are read at the beginning of every Bahá'í gathering, whether it is a worship gathering, a meeting to plan the next teaching campaign, or an administrative meeting. Some Bahá'ís stand when reciting prayers at a gathering; others chant them in English (with or without guitar accompaniment). Most, however, merely read the prayer. If elderly Persians are in attendance, they frequently volunteer or are asked to chant a prayer in Persian or Arabic (I rarely observed young Persians chanting in public). Those speaking other languages are also encouraged to recite prayers in that tongue. This has the effect of reinforcing Bahá'ís' global identity—in any local gathering, there is the potential for a diversity of the world's languages to be praying in unity.

Bahá'u'lláh forbade the congregational recitation of prayer, as is done by Muslims five times a day, with the exception of the Prayer for the Dead, usually recited at a funeral. Otherwise, prayers are said individually or recited by one individual while others listen. Bahá'u'lláh has, however, enjoined Bahá'ís to perform daily obligatory prayers, preceded by ablutions (washing of the hands and face).[5] To perform obligatory prayers, Bahá'ís must face the *qiblih* ("point of Adoration")—initially Bahá'u'lláh himself, but after his death, the location of his interred remains outside Haifa, Israel, near the Bahá'í World Center. During the Medium and Long Obligatory Prayers, certain genuflections must be performed (similar to Muslim prayers), involving bending down with one's hand resting on one's knees, raising one's hands "in supplication," and bowing one's forehead to the ground. Many Bahá'ís from Christian backgrounds told me that it took them a while to get used to this form of prayer; some even said they were Bahá'ís for years before they knew that ablutions were required (many said it wasn't until the full text of the *Kitáb-i-Aqdas* came out that this was clear to them).

Responses to the survey question "How often do you pray?" show that the vast majority of Atlanta's Bahá'ís engage in daily prayer. As can be seen in table 5.1, nearly half (48 percent) reported praying twice a day or more. Although the survey did not specifically ask about the Obligatory Prayers, one may assume that the 82 percent who report praying at least once a day fulfill this personal law of Bahá'u'lláh.

One Bahá'í author writes: "For Bahá'u'lláh, prayer and fasting are the fundamental religious observances" (Walbridge 1996, 30). This statement serves as a synopsis of the individualistic nature of the spiritual aspects of the Bahá'í Faith, in contrast to the collective ritual discussed below. While prayer (and fasting, also discussed below) are the essential religious observances, compliance with the laws of obligatory prayer and fasting are beyond the purview of LSA authority. Thus, central rituals of Bahá'í identity are private.[6] The obligatory prayers are binding upon believers between the ages of fifteen and seventy except those suffering from illness. Other exemptions in the *Kitáb-i-Aqdas* are given for travelers, menstruating women, and dangerous conditions.

Finally, there are some special prayers and invocations Bahá'ís often use during times of difficulty, ill health, or emergency. The "long healing prayer" (which lists more than 126 attributes and virtues of God) and the Tablet of Ahmad, as well as the daily obligatory prayers, "have been invested by Bahá'u'lláh with a special potency and significance" (NSA of the United States 1985, 209). One prayer frequently recited by Atlanta Bahá'ís is the "Remover of Difficulties" prayer, revealed by the Báb for difficulties in one's life. Sometimes Bahá'ís will repeat these or other prayers in multiples of nine or nineteen.[7]

FASTING

Part of a Bahá'í's devotional life is to follow the requirements in the *Kitáb-i-Aqdas* for the month of Fasting (the month of 'Alá', lasting March 2–20, the last month in the Bahá'í year), required of Bahá'ís between the ages of fifteen and seventy. Like Muslims during Ramadan, Bahá'ís fast from sunup to sundown, refraining from eating, drinking, and smoking (although unlike in Islam, believers are not required to abstain from sexual relations during the Fast). The *Kitáb-i-Aqdas* says, "the traveler, the ailing, those who are with child or giving suck, are not bound by the Fast; they have been exempted by God as a token of His grace" (Bahá'u'lláh 1992, 25). The purpose of fasting, according to Bahá'ís, is contained in one of the prayers written by Bahá'u'lláh for the Fast: "that through [the Fast] they may purify their souls and rid themselves of all attachment to any one but Thee" (Bahá'u'lláh 1987, 79).

The Fast is a time of extra prayer and reflection for Atlanta Bahá'ís—although many told me that it is difficult to engage in this type of spiritual discipline in a culture unaccustomed to its practice. Bahá'ís frequently gather to "break the fast" during the month of 'Alá', getting together at sunset for large meals in each others' homes or going out to breakfast before sunrise. But Bahá'ís also point out that the Fast is a good time to teach others about their faith— invariably a coworker's invitation to lunch will need to be declined, giving an opportunity to explain the Bahá'í Faith's laws and principles. Survey results indicate (see table 5.1) that more than half the respondents fully observed the 1994 Fast; another 20 percent partially observed it (many indicated that they

Table 5.1
Atlanta Bahá'ís' practice of personal devotional activities

	> twice daily	Daily	2–6 times/week	< weekly
How often do you pray?	47.7	34.3	11.7	6.3%
			Yes	No
Have you ever been on Pilgrimage to Haifa, Israel?			30.0	70.0
		Yes	No	Not acquainted with 3 Year Plan
Have you personally made individual goals for yourself based on the 3 Year Plan?		46.2	46.6	7.1
	Fully	Partly	No, excused	No
Did you observe the 1994 Fast?	51.5	19.9	16.6	12.0
	1	2	3	4	5[a]
I try to pattern all my daily activities around the laws and principles of the Faith.	43.3	49.2	4.2	2.9	0.4

[a] 1 =strongly agree, 2 = agree, 3 = unsure, 4 = disagree, 5 = strongly disagree

got sick during the Fast, or had to make a business trip and were therefore ex-empted travelers), nearly 17 percent were excused (again, because of age, ill-ness, pregnancy, etc.), and 12 percent reported not observing it at all.

READING THE WRITINGS

Bahá'u'lláh said to his followers: "Recite ye the verses of God every morning and evening. Whoso reciteth them not hath truly failed to fulfill his pledge to the Covenant of God and His Testament" (UHJ 1983, 1).[8] Bahá'ís are thus en-joined to read daily from Bahá'í scripture and meditate on what they read—a process known as "deepening".

Bahá'ís were asked on the questionnaire about the frequency of their own reading from various kinds of Bahá'í scripture or literature: the three Central Figures, Shoghi Effendi, the Universal House of Justice, and other Bahá'í au-thors. Bahá'ís are moderately active in reading their scripture; nearly 40 percent indicate daily reading of Bahá'u'lláh's writings, and 24 percent read 'Abdu'l-Bahá's writings daily.[9] When asked if adherents "regularly participate in deepenings"—small meetings where Bahá'ís gather to study and discuss Bahá'í scripture, sometimes referred to as "Bahá'í Bible study"—almost 45 percent indicate regular attendance at one of several advertised deepenings in the metro Atlanta area. Typical deepenings involve Bahá'ís sitting in a circle and taking turns reading from scripture. People give their interpretation or understanding of a particular passage, and sometimes lively discussions ensue. Further discussion of group deepenings as socialization into a situated universalist identity will be included below.

PILGRIMAGE

Bahá'u'lláh declared in the *Kitáb-i-Aqdas*, "It is an obligation to make pilgrimage to one of the two sacred Houses; but as to which, it is for the pilgrim to decide" (1992, 115), provided one is financially able to make the journey. The "two sacred Houses" refer to the House of the Báb in Shiraz, Iran, and the House of Bahá'u'lláh in Baghdad, Iraq. After the death of Bahá'u'lláh, 'Abdu'l-Bahá declared the Shrine of Bahá'u'lláh in 'Akká (outside Haifa, Israel) an additional pilgrimage site. Since the House of the Báb in Shiraz was destroyed by Iranian officials in 1979,[10] and the House of Bahá'u'lláh in Iraq was seized by authorities in 1922 and has been closed to Bahá'ís ever since, the World Center in Haifa is at present the only accessible pilgrimage destination for Bahá'ís around the world.[11] Bahá'ís can sign up for a three- or nine-day excursion (although the waiting list is now about three to five years). Bahá'ís must receive permission from the UHJ to come on pilgrimage—in part to make sure only Bahá'ís with their administrative rights are allowed to go, and in part to ensure accommodations for pilgrims in the limited quarters. While on pilgrimage, Bahá'ís visit the Shrines of Bahá'u'lláh and the Báb, the gravesites of 'Abdu'l-Bahá and his sister, and the various institutions of the Bahá'í Faith on Mount Carmel above the city of Haifa (such as the International Teaching Center, the Archives Building, and the Universal House of Justice). Every night, pilgrims meet with a UHJ member for dinner and discussion, or possibly with one of the three remaining Hands of the Cause. At present, approximately two thousand Bahá'í pilgrims visit Haifa each year (Walbridge 1996, 117). Exactly 30 percent of Atlanta Bahá'ís surveyed indicated that they have fulfilled this particular obligation of their faith.

No particular attire is required for Bahá'í pilgrimage (unlike the Muslim *hajj*), although some Bahá'í pilgrims wear their national/ethnic dress at formal occasions during their stay as a celebration of Bahá'í "unity in diversity." This particular ritual powerfully reinforces the global perspective of a Bahá'í's faith, as he/she meets Bahá'ís from literally all over the globe; it is not unlike the Muslim pilgrimage in this respect.[12] One African American woman who had just returned from her pilgrimage commented on how it influenced her and even her non-Bahá'í family:

I had the strongest confirmation of what this faith is about. There is no
question in my mind that it will lead the world. . . . I'm just amazed at
the power of God. To see Bahá'ís from all over the world working at the
World Center, and pilgrims from all over the world was just amazing. I
said prayers for my parents at the Shrine of Bahá'u'lláh, and my mother
declared [as a Bahá'í] when I got back. And my father hasn't had
anything to drink since I got back. . . . He's been sober since then. You
can just see the miracles.

FUND CONTRIBUTIONS

Bahá'ís are also, as in other religious organizations, encouraged to contribute
money to their faith. Table 5.2 shows the breakdown for contributions to the
various Bahá'í Funds.[13] Non-Bahá'ís are not allowed to give any money to Bahá'í
projects, nor are Bahá'ís who have lost their administrative or voting rights. It
is considered a spiritual bounty as well as a duty to give money to Bahá'í Funds.
Bahá'ís consider their projects—whether a health clinic in the developing world
or the House of Worship in Illinois—to be "gifts to the world" from the Bahá'í
Faith. Donating is thus a privilege reserved only for Bahá'ís. Table 5.2 shows
that nine out of ten Bahá'ís donate to the local Fund, although a majority of
Bahá'ís also contribute to the National and Arc Funds. Atlanta Bahá'ís favor
the local fund in their donations, by a ratio of two to one.

Survey questions examined two additional ways of measuring a Bahá'í's level
of devotion. The first asked whether the respondent had set individual teaching goals for him or herself based on guidance from the UHJ. The second asked
one's level of agreement with the statement, "I try to pattern all my daily activities around the laws and principles of the Faith." Nearly half of Atlanta
Bahá'ís set personal teaching goals for themselves, and more than 90 percent
agreed or strongly agreed with the above statement.

Statistical tests were performed to see if there were any significant associations between the measures of devotion listed in tables 5.1 and 5.2 (frequency
of prayer, contribution to local funds, observance of the Fast, etc.) and demographic variables.[14] As was found in the previous chapter, there was no association between piety/devotion and any demographic variable—gender, race,
income, occupation, marital status, or education. This was equally true for respondents with non-Bahá'í and Bahá'í spouses, for newly converted and longtime Bahá'ís, and for Bahá'ís from all previous religious backgrounds (comparing
both polity type and liberal-conservative theological stance—see chapter 4).
Apparently, commitment to conforming one's personal life to Bahá'í standards
is constant throughout the Bahá'í community, personal piety transcending
ascriptive background characteristics.[15]

This gives further evidence of the reflexive socialization taking place within

Table 5.2
Atlanta Bahá'ís' contributions to Bahá'í Funds

	% contributing in past year	% contributing to this fund most
International Fund	32.2	3.7
Arc Fund	58.4	7.8
Continental Fund	18.5	0.9
National Fund	70.4	29.5
Local Fund	91.8	58.1

Bahá'í institutions, shaping diverse individuals into a common devotional framework and linking the local with the global. Personal rituals reinforce the global identity of Bahá'ís by bringing them into (often daily) contact with authority that undergirds a universal ideology. Reading scripture or reciting prayers written by charismatic leaders personalizes one's relationship to that authority—which, as we saw in chapter 4, facilitates acceptance of and commitment to ideological claims. Giving material resources to local, national, or global funds helps Bahá'ís feel they are personally contributing to and sacrificing for a global institution-building project, as many indicated during interviews. And certainly fulfilling pilgrimage requirements brings believers face to face with their World Center in all its symbolic authority. Thus, personal devotional rituals are an essential element in creating a situated universalist identity that is globally oriented. In creating such an identity, ascriptive identities are "leveled" through personal religious practice, as Atlanta Bahá'ís are socialized into their situated universalist worldview.

The Bahá'í Calendar

A Bahá'ís daily life is governed by the personal laws given to the Bahá'í community by Bahá'u'lláh. But the organizational participation of the average Bahá'í is dictated by the rituals of the Bahá'í calendar. Bahá'í theology states that whenever a new Manifestation of God appears to humanity, they bring with them a new calendar to institutionalize a new pattern of worship, festivals, and holidays. In the future, Bahá'ís say, the Bahá'í calendar, first proposed by the Báb and sanctioned by Bahá'u'lláh, will become the accepted global standard for dividing the year.

Thus, for Bahá'ís time is sacred. This is true for the cyclical pattern of the year, with various festivals, Holy Days, and personal ritual observances. But time is also sacred throughout the entire scope of human history, and particularly in this period, Bahá'ís assert, because it is the hallowed culmination of God's plan for this planet. One Bahá'í author put it this way:

But to the Bahá'í it matters very much when he lives. History for the
Bahá'í is a teleological drama in which the maturation of the human
race is worked out through religious history. The prophets build on each
others' messages, slowly preparing humankind for a promised day in
which the kingdom of God can be erected by human hands according to
a divine plan with the stage of the world and historical time. A Bahá'í
seeks not only salvation for himself but an earthly paradise for those
who will come after him. He sees his place in historical time as a
particular stage in the building of a new world. He and all other people
are a caravan and their journey's end is no longer many years away.
(Walbridge 1996, 173)

The Bahá'í year is divided into nineteen months, each with nineteen days
(totaling 361), with the insertion of "Intercalary Days" (four in an ordinary year,
five in a leap year) between the eighteenth and nineteenth months to reconcile the calendar to the solar year. Each month (and each day of the month) is
named after an "attribute of God"—virtues Bahá'ís are supposed to acquire
throughout their lives (see appendix C for a table of the names and dates of
Bahá'í months and days of the week). During my period of fieldwork, I never
heard Bahá'ís use the Arabic name for the days of the week, or days of the month;
nor did they refer to Friday being the day of rest, as is the case in the Bahá'í
calendar. Bahá'ís did, however, use the Arabic name of the Bahá'í month, often
needing to specify whether they were talking about the Bahá'í month or the
Gregorian month.

THE NINETEEN-DAY FEAST

THE FEAST AS A SOCIAL INSTITUTION. On the first day of each Bahá'í month, Bahá'ís
gather for the Nineteen-Day Feast, which is the central worship experience in
the Bahá'í Faith, and which only Bahá'ís are allowed to attend. The Nineteen-
Day Feast consists of three loosely structured parts: (1) a devotional period, where
the writings and prayers of the Báb, Bahá'u'lláh, and/or 'Abdu'l-Bahá are read
(readings may also include passages from other Holy Scripture, such as the Bible
or Qur'án);[16] (2) an administrative period, where the chair of the LSA leads
communitywide consultation on important issues facing the community; and (3)
a social portion, involving fellowship and refreshments. Occasionally several LSA
jurisdictions will all meet together for what is known as a "Unity Feast," which
non-Bahá'ís are welcome to attend; in such cases the administrative period is
omitted.[17] The Universal House of Justice said this about the importance of the
Nineteen-Day Feast:

> The World Order of Bahá'u'lláh encompasses all units of human society;
> integrates the spiritual, administrative and social processes of life; and

canalizes human expression in its varied forms toward the construction
of a new [global] civilization. The Nineteen Day Feast embraces all
these aspects at the very base of society. Functioning in the village, the
town, the city, it is an institution of which all the people of Bahá are
members. It is intended to promote unity, ensure progress, and foster joy.
(dated 27 August 1989, quoted in *Bahá'í News*, November 1989, 1)

The administrative portion is in some ways sociologically the most important aspect of a Feast. Participants brainstorm new local teaching or service
projects. A treasurer's report updates members on the financial health of the community. Someone usually updates the community on future activities, deepenings,
or social events. Sometimes individuals give reports on teaching trips they have
recently taken, or relate a story they heard concerning successful teaching taking place in other parts of the world. Recommendations that require official approval are referred to the LSA for consideration. In a sense, each Feast represents
a mini–town meeting, where Bahá'ís can have input into community governance
and exchange information. It is the arena where "social capital" (Putnam 1995)
is created and methods of Bahá'í governance are honed.[18]

A letter from the UHJ dated 27 August 1989 also suggests the sociological
significance of the Feast:

Moreover, because of the opportunity which it provides for conveying
messages from the national and international levels of the administration and also for communicating the recommendations of the friends to
those levels, the Feast becomes a link that connects the local community in a dynamic relationship with the entire structure of the Administrative Order. But considered in its local sphere alone there is much to
thrill and amaze the heart. Here it links the individual to the collective
processes by which a society is built or restored. Here, for instance, the
Feast is an arena of democracy at the very root of society, where the
local Spiritual Assembly and the members of the community meet on
common ground, where individuals are free to offer their gifts of
thought, whether as new ideas or constructive criticism, to the building
processes of an advancing civilization. Thus it can be seen that aside
from its spiritual significance, this common institution of the people
combines an array of elemental social disciplines which educate its
participants in the essentials of responsible citizenship. (quoted in *Bahá'í
News*, November 1989, 1–2)

Most Feasts are accompanied by a letter from the Bahá'í National Center
informing local communities of decisions made by the NSA or of global activities of interest to the Bahá'í world.[19] Sometimes, letters sent from the UHJ to
all the NSAs are reproduced for local communities, with the NSA acting as an
intermediary in communication between the global and local levels. Several

times a year, the NSA of the United States distributes a videocassette called the "Bahá'í Newsreel," describing Bahá'í activity around the world as well as new developments at the World Center. These mechanisms of communication (the monthly Feast letter and "Bahá'í Newsreel"), linking the global with the local via the national institutions, help fortify local Bahá'ís' identity as situated universalists, and as members of a global movement. At each worship, Bahá'ís engage in democratic consultation about how they can act in their situated local community to promote the universal values of unity in diversity, the oneness of humanity, and their vision of the Kingdom of God. This includes teaching activity to spread their message and attract new converts; plans for race unity picnics; or literacy programs in partnership with local schools. However, this local discourse and planning takes shape in the context of guidance from the national and global institutions which embody Bahá'ís' universal worldview. The Nineteen-Day Feast is the essence of the socialization of a Bahá'í identity as a situated universalist, and is the regular, ritualized link Bahá'í institutions make between the local and global. And as can be seen from the above statement from the UHJ, these links are consciously fostered to strengthen the scope of a Bahá'í's identity. This intentional link between the local and global is summarized in a 1933 NSA statement about Feast as the core of community life: "Nineteen Day Feasts serve to renew and deepen our spirit of faith, increase our capacity for united action, remove misunderstandings and keep us fully informed of all important Bahá'í activities, local, national and international in scope" (quoted in *Bahá'í News*, November 1989, 5).

Feasts are usually held in members' homes, although the LSA of the city of Atlanta owns a Bahá'í Center in the city center. Although most communities attempt to rotate the responsibility of holding feasts to all community members, issues like non-Bahá'í spouses (who are not allowed to attend Feast) and the needs of small children often require small communities to designate two or three homes as permanent Feast sites. It is usually the "host" or "hostess" of the Feast who prepares the refreshments and chooses the readings from the Bahá'í Writings (since there are no clergy). This reinforces the "democratic" nature of Bahá'í collective ritual, as individual community members are given the chance to shape the devotional services.[20]

LSA jurisdictions the size of Atlanta (132 square miles) and larger face a challenge regarding where Feasts should be held. Some community members I talked with said that sometimes it is easier to attend Feast in neighboring suburban communities only a mile or two away than to drive to the downtown Atlanta Bahá'í Center. They complained that there was not enough parking at the Bahá'í Center, and that it was "in a dangerous part of town." Given the racial and class segregation of the metropolitan area, this could potentially segregate the Bahá'í community as well. This is even more likely in larger communities such as New York, Los Angeles, and Houston, where the LSA has approved "regional" Feasts within their jurisdiction, to cut down on travel time to worship. Because Bahá'í administrative institutions repeatedly point to the Feast as *the* social workshop in which to foster "unity in diversity," they counsel that the Feast location should not become barrier to the goal of unity. A letter written by the UHJ in 1967 to the NSA of the United States had this warning:

> We understand and appreciate the problems involved in the holding of Nineteen Day Feasts in the large cities such as New York and Los Angeles. . . . The tendency in metropolitan areas is toward segregation, and therefore the local Assembly should be alert to prevent a similar pattern developing in Bahá'í meetings by reason of the location of the Feast. The local Assembly should be watchful that neither the unity of the community nor control by the local Assembly is dissipated by this practice. (quoted in *Bahá'í News*, November 1989, 7)[21]

The Feast is given high priority in the Atlanta Bahá'í community for both its spiritual and its social significance. Every nineteen days, it offers the whole community an opportunity to participate in spiritual fellowship and democratic administration. The Bahá'í Feast originated in the writings of the Báb, enjoining believers to entertain guests once every nineteen days, even if only to serve them water, as a sign of unity and hospitality. Bahá'u'lláh confirms the institution of the Nineteen-Day Feast in the *Kitáb-i-Aqdas*, saying its purpose is to "bind hearts together with material means" (quoted in Walbridge 1996, 207). During the ministry of 'Abdu'l-Bahá (1892–1921), the Feast came to also incorporate devotional functions; not until the early 1930s, paralleling the rise of the Local Spiritual Assembly, was administrative consultation added (Walbridge 1996). Shoghi Effendi described the Nineteen-Day Feast as the "foundation of the New World Order" (quoted in Walbridge 1996, 209). Attendance at the Feast is encouraged but not obligatory. Nor can the LSA issue any sanctions against Bahá'ís who do not attend the Feast.

THE FEAST IN ATLANTA. Survey results show a high degree of Feast attendance among Atlanta Bahá'ís. As can be seen in table 5.3, although only eighteen percent indicate they attend all nineteen Feasts in a year, nearly half (48 percent) said they attend "often", or between twelve and eighteen Feasts in a year. Another 17 percent said they attend "sometimes", and an equal percentage indicated they "seldom" or "never" attended. Although this is difficult to compare with Christians who attend "weekly," results indicate that Bahá'ís display a relatively high degree of worship participation.[22]

Based on my eighteen months of fieldwork and drawing from the experience of several Feasts, I will first describe a composite "typical" Feast in Atlanta,

Table 5.3
Atlanta Bahá'ís' participation in organizational activities

	All 19	12–18/yr	6–11/yr	1–5/yr	None
How regularly do you attend Nineteen-Day Feast?	17.9	48.3	16.7	11.3	5.8%
	9–12/yr	6–8/yr	3–5/yr	1–2/yr	None
How often did you attend Holy Day celebrations this past year?	41.0	20.5	20.1	13.0	5.4
				Yes	No
Do you regularly participate in deepenings?				44.5	55.5
				Yes	No
Have you ever participated in any of the Bahá'í-sponsored MLK Holiday activities?				71.6	28.4

then illustrate how other communities in the metro area exemplify variations on a theme. Feast in the Atlanta community began at 7:30 p.m., but as with most events running on "Bahá'í time" (as Bahá'ís jokingly call it), Feast didn't actually get started until 8 p.m. People gathered in the small, upstairs meeting room at the Atlanta Bahá'í Center, greeting each other with hugs and "Alláh-u-Abhá," the usual Bahá'í greeting. There were approximately thirty-five people there, two-thirds African Americans, one-fourth whites, and the remainder a mix of Asian and Persian believers. The worshipers were evenly split among men and women. The chairs were in rows, facing the front of the room where a picture of 'Abdu'l-Bahá and flowers adorned a table. Also on the table was a small wooden box marked "Local Bahá'í Fund." Music from the Bahá'í Gospel Choir that sang at the World Congress was playing on the tape recorder. Although the room had a piano, I never saw anyone play it, during my entire period of fieldwork. While people were waiting for the devotions to begin, the hostess— a middle-aged white woman who had volunteered to organize this particular Feast—passed out the devotional readings. Since this was the Feast of Rahmat, or Mercy, all of the readings revolved around the theme of God's mercy. To some she handed out Bahá'í books with the passage marked, and to others she handed out computer printouts of Bahá'í scripture generated by the recently released software program "Refer," which contains all of Bahá'u'lláh's writings. She also asked those who could speak foreign languages to recite prayers in Spanish, Swahili, French, and Persian. The hostess for the evening welcomed everyone to the Feast, and asked for the opening prayer. Those who had been assigned readings read them one by one. Unlike Firesides or deepenings, where discussion of the scripture is encouraged, at Feast the passages were read without comment. Interspersed throughout the devotional readings, a Persian chant sung by noted Iranian Bahá'í singer Narges Nouhnejád Fání was played on the tape recorder, and a woman played the guitar and sang a song, a verse from Bahá'u'lláh's writings set to music. After the readings, the hostess led the worshipers in a Bahá'í song everyone knew by heart:

> Soon will all that dwell on earth
> Be enlisted under His [Bahá'u'lláh's] banner
> Ya, Bahá'ul Abhá

After the last assigned prayer, the hostess asked if anyone else had prayers they would like to offer. Several people used their own prayer books or borrowed the one provided by the hostess, and said prayers for the success of an upcoming teaching event in Atlanta, for the health of an ailing community member, and for world peace (no one prayed extemporaneously). Then the hostess said, "That concludes the devotional portion of Feast. I turn the meeting over to the chair of the Atlanta LSA," who would then lead consultation.

The LSA chair—a young African American woman who worked as an architect in Atlanta—first welcomed guests, asking each to stand up and introduce themselves. An elderly African American woman from Birmingham, Alabama, and a young man from Osaka, Japan received a round of applause. She then introduced two new members of the Atlanta Bahá'í community: a middle-aged white man who had moved from Maryland, and an African American woman who had recently "declared" her belief in Bahá'u'lláh as a result of an area Fireside. They also received a round of applause. The LSA chair then reminded the new members to speak with the LSA secretary during the social portion of Feast so that he could get pertinent information sent to the Bahá'í National Center so they would be properly accounted for in the membership records. Then the chair asked the secretary to read the LSA correspondence.

The LSA secretary, a middle-aged African American man, read through a stack of mail the assembly had received in the last nineteen days. The first letter, from the Universal House of Justice, related to the U.S. Bahá'í community the recent desecration of Bahá'í graves by authorities of the fundamentalist regime in Teheran, Iran, wherein a Bahá'í cemetery was bulldozed to make way for a parking lot. A letter from the National Spiritual Assembly's Office for External Affairs was next, encouraging Atlanta Bahá'ís to contact Sen. Paul Coverdell asking for his support of Senate Resolution 31 condemning recent persecutions of Bahá'ís by the Iranian government. This would be the sixth resolution put before Congress since 1982 in the wake of the 1979 Iranian revolution. There was also a letter of support and encouragement from the UHJ addressed to the youth in Atlanta. They had written the UHJ asking for its prayers for success in an upcoming teaching campaign. Next came a letter from the National Spiritual Assembly to all LSAs in the United States asking them to submit summaries of the local teaching plans that had been developed in response to the Three Year Plan. The last piece of correspondence was a letter from the Atlanta Bahá'í Arts Center sent to each metro LSA, asking for each community to send a representative to a planning meeting in two weeks to consult on how to use the arts to teach non-Bahá'ís about the Bahá'í Faith.

Then the LSA secretary read through various announcements, including a picnic at Chastain Park to welcome the newest converts to the Atlanta Bahá'í community. He reminded everyone who was thinking of attending the picnic to wear their Bahá'í T-shirts, so that it could be a teaching event to advertise the Bahá'í Faith as well as a social occasion. He then asked if anyone else had announcements, and several people reminded the community of upcoming Firesides and a work day to clean up the Atlanta Bahá'í Center. The secretary then turned the consultation over to the LSA chair, who asked for a treasurer's report. A white, middle-aged man with a ponytail pulled out a ledger and read the contributions and expenses of the community for the last Bahá'í month. He read a letter sent from the NSA to local treasurers describing the acute conditions of the National Bahá'í Fund, asking local communities to step up their level of donations to the National Center. He reminded the community that they could earmark checks directly to the national fund, or any other international fund, without having to contribute through the local fund. He pointed out the fund box on the front table, which contained an envelope with each Bahá'í family's name on it. People started pulling out checkbooks and wallets, and the fund box was passed around for community members to find their envelopes. The treasurer then turned the discussion back over to the LSA chair, who asked for committee reports.

First in line was the youth committee. A young African American boy reported that he had recently been able to tell his fourth-grade science teacher about the Bahá'í Faith, and received applause for doing his part in teaching efforts. He reported that the youth group BAM—Bahá'ís Against Madness—was planning some teaching events at the public schools, and were also hoping to have a fundraiser for the Arc Fund (for the building projects on Mount Carmel at the Bahá'í World Center). Next came a report from the Teaching Committee. A middle-aged Persian woman reported that the goals for the Atlanta community during the Three Year Plan were being mailed out to all community members, and that there were meetings every Saturday morning at the Bahá'í Center for those who wanted to meet and say prayers before fanning out to area malls to distribute Bahá'í literature. Finally, there was a report from the Feast and Holy Day committee. A middle-aged white woman reminded community members that no one had yet signed up to host next month's Feast, and asked for volunteers.

The administrative portion of the Feast ended when the LSA chair asked if anyone had any other issues to bring before the community, or recommendations to the LSA for consideration. An elderly African American woman said that she was going on pilgrimage the following week, and asked that anyone who wanted special prayers said for them at the Shrine of Bahá'u'lláh let her know. A middle-aged Persian woman pointed out that the next holy day celebration was the Martyrdom of the Báb, and suggested that the LSA consider putting an announcement in the *Atlanta Constitution* letting readers know more about who Bahá'ís are and what they believe. The LSA secretary noted the proposal and said it would go on their next meeting's agenda. Another young African American man suggested that the greater metro Atlanta Bahá'í community consider sponsoring a five-kilometer race to promote race unity, or an essay contest in the public schools on race unity. These ideas were also noted by the secretary. The LSA chair then asked if there were any teaching stories anyone wanted to share with the community. One Asian woman said that she had finally been able to talk to her mother about the Bahá'í Faith without getting into an argument with her. Another young white man said that racial tension at work between a black coworker and his white boss prompted him to share the Bahá'í message on the oneness of humanity with both of them. Another woman said that a salesclerk in the mall noticed her Bahá'í necklace recently, which led to a discussion about the Bahá'í perspective on progressive revelation.

The LSA chair called for a closing prayer, which was chanted in Arabic by an elderly Persian man. Everyone moved to the back of the room for refreshments and socializing. People hung around for another thirty to forty minutes before heading home. During the social portion, the LSA secretary set up a TV and VCR in one corner of the room and showed the latest "Bahá'í Newsreel." As people talked and ate, images from the Bahá'í World Center flashed on the screen, intercut with stories of Bahá'í communities in Nigeria and Bangladesh engaging in teaching activity.

THE FEAST AS A WORKSHOP IN PROMOTING "UNITY IN DIVERSITY". Not only is the Feast format (devotions, administration, socializing) flexible enough to incorporate the proclivities of the individual host/hostess; it is also able to incorporate the cultural expressions of the various communities themselves. The UHJ, in a 1989 letter giving guidance to Bahá'í communities on the Nineteen-Day Feast, encouraged the introduction of music and "uplifting talks" and the use of "quality consultation," and said this of the diversity possible in the Feast experience: "The effects of different culture in all these respects are welcome factors which can lend the Feast a salutary diversity, representative of the unique

characteristics of the various societies in which it is held, and therefore condu-
cive to the upliftment and enjoyment of its participants" (quoted in *Bahá'í News*,
November 1989, 1).

This diversity is evident in the various Feasts in metro Atlanta. While the
city of Atlanta Bahá'í community always held Feasts at the Bahá'í Center, no
suburban community was large enough to afford a center. Feast was therefore
rotated among community members' homes. Each community took on a distinct
flavor depending upon its individual strengths and the cultures represented. Some
Feasts were held in small homes with threadbare, rickety furniture, the host/host-
ess offering ice cream and soda for refreshments. Others in the same jurisdiction were held in expensive homes with plush furniture, the host/hostess serving
many varieties of teas, coffees, cheeses, crackers, and finger sandwiches. At some
Feasts, the host/hostess had participants choose their own devotional readings;
others had every prayer, reading, and song picked out. Most Feasts had no music present, but during my year of fieldwork music was becoming a more preva-
lent part of worship.[23]

In general, the rich attended Feast in the homes of the poor and vice versa;
and blacks, Persians, and whites visited each others' homes every nineteen days.
People of all colors and social strata invariably greeted each other with hugs and
mixed socially at the end of Feast.[24] The only outward display of segregation at
the Feast came from elderly Persians, many of whom could not speak English,
and thus tended to socialize together (although this was not true of their "as-
similated" children).

The "flavor" of the Feast changed with the community as well. As discussed
earlier, because of housing segregation in Atlanta, and because Bahá'ís are organized into parish-like geographic jurisdictions, there is a tendency for a local
community to have a significant "minority" population. For example, the rather
substantial Persian community in Atlanta has tended to concentrate in the north
and northwestern sections of the metro region. As families managed to get parents or relatives out of Iran (which was still difficult at times), new Persian im-
migrants tended to settle with or near their kin. Undoubtedly, the language
barrier for first-generation Persians also contributed to this "enclave mentality,"
as many freely admitted to me during interviews.

The result is that "local culture" tends to take on characteristics of its substantial "minority." In the city of Atlanta and the southern and southeastern
metro area where there is a large African American population, elements of the
"black church experience" (Lincoln and Mamiya 1990) surfaced during worship:
a tendency to incorporate gospel music into devotions (even singing nominally
"Christian songs" like "How Great Thou Art" or "Be Still My Soul," with Bahá'í
words substituted in key places), or raising one's hands in the air during prayer.
Frequently, "Amen," or "Yá Bahá'u'l-Abhá" (the Bahá'í equivalent) could be

heard during devotions, and individuals would "testify" during consultation to the miracles Bahá'u'lláh had worked in their lives that month. Worship tended to be much more expressive and emotive than in majority-white LSA jurisdictions.

Communities with a large Persian element predictably had more Arabic/Persian chanting, and an array of Persian desserts were served during the social portion of the Feast. If there were older Persians attending who could not speak English, a second-generation son or daughter would translate the NSA message, or translate the tenor of conversation during consultation. Frequently, the NSA's monthly letter to all community secretaries would include both an English and a Persian translation. Persian believers who suffered persecution before and after the Iranian revolution would sometimes tell stories about Iran and relate news from relatives who could not leave the country. For the non-Persians at the Feast, this raised awareness of their faith as a beleaguered movement in Iran which might have to face difficult times in this country too, as many explicitly told me during interviews. The Persian influence in the Atlanta area increases the solidarity of the Bahá'í community, as stories of the "martyrs for the Faith" are recounted. It also gave "American" Bahá'ís a glimpse of the internationality of their faith.[25]

Bahá'ís attempt to live out their diversity in their worship experience, reinforcing the idea in their own minds that there is no one right way to express their Bahá'í identity. However, several Bahá'ís during interviews described Feast as "boring." The devotions were sometimes dry and rushed, especially if there was no music (which is the thing Christian converts most frequently said they missed about church). Several Bahá'ís said that it was only when music or some other variation in the devotional format was added to the worship experience that Feast again became spiritually uplifting. In small suburban communities where the majority of active believers are on the LSA, some Bahá'ís said that the consultation during the administrative portion of Feast is almost "nonexistent," since most issues have already been discussed in the LSA meetings (leaving those few in the community not elected to the LSA feeling "left out"). Some Bahá'ís said that Feast did not take place often enough to allow community members to get to know each other and establish basic local unity. Some LSAs have therefore instituted weekly social meetings to supplement their regular nineteen-day worship cycle.

HOLY DAYS AND SPECIAL EVENT DAYS

The other principal collective rituals in the Bahá'í calendar are the ten Holy Days and six special event days that commemorate specific occasions in Bahá'í history or celebrate the global vision of the religion. Non-Bahá'ís are always welcome at any of the Holy Day or special event celebrations (Bahá'ís are encouraged to bring friends who are "seekers"). In the Bahá'í calendar, the numerous

Holy Day celebrations, with the exception of Naw-Rúz and Ayyám-i-Há, are related to the lives of the Báb, Bahá'u'lláh, and 'Abdu'l-Bahá. On nine of the holy days, work is to be suspended. The following are Holy Days observed by Bahá'ís (for a detailed description of each, see Walbridge 1996)—* indicates work is to be suspended:

- Feast of Naw-Rúz* (Bahá'í New Year), March 21
- Feast of Ridván* (Declaration of Bahá'u'lláh), April 21, April 29, May 2
- Declaration of the Báb,* May 23 (same as 'Abdu'l-Bahá's birthday)
- Ascension of Bahá'u'lláh,* May 29
- Martyrdom of the Báb,* July 9
- Birth of the Báb,* October 20
- Birth of Bahá'u'lláh,* November 12
- Day of the Covenant, November 26
- Ascension of 'Abdu'l-Bahá, November 28
- Ayyám-i-Há, or Intercalary Days, Feb. 26–March 1

And these are special event days given secondary importance:

- Race Unity Day, second Sunday of June
- International Day of Peace, third Tuesday of September
- Universal Children's Day, first Monday of October
- United Nations Day, fourth Tuesday of October
- United Nations Human Rights Day, second Sunday of December
- World Religion Day, third Sunday of January

Survey results show the pattern of participation in Holy Day celebrations is similar to that of the Nineteen-Day Feasts among Atlanta Bahá'ís. As can be seen in table 5.3, more than 40 percent of respondents indicate they attend Holy Day celebrations "most of the time" (nine to twelve per year), while 20 percent acknowledged attending "often" (six to eight per year) and 20 percent answered "sometimes" (three to five per year).

Holy Days tend to take on two distinct moods: one festive and celebratory, the other reverent and somber. For example, the festivals of Ayyám-i-Há (or Intercalary Days, right before the month of Fasting) and Naw-Rúz (the Bahá'í New Year) are bright, joyful occasions, with many Bahá'ís bringing "seekers" to introduce them to Bahá'í hospitality at its best. The Atlanta Bahá'í Center is decorated with balloons and banners, and festive music is played. Ayyám-i-Há is also a period of exchanging gifts and doing charitable work.

On the other hand, the Ascension of Bahá'u'lláh,[26] commemorating his death on May 29, 1892, has a more subdued atmosphere, evoking reverence and veneration among Bahá'ís for the founder of their faith. It is held at 3 a.m.—

the recorded time of Bahá'u'lláh's death—and the quiet stillness of downtown Atlanta surrounding the Bahá'í Center adds to the sense of the sacred.

Although work is to be suspended on the more important of the Holy Days (see above), most Bahá'ís are unable or unwilling to take the day off. Bahá'ís themselves talk about the importance of properly commemorating Holy Days by taking the day off from work or school to establish more clearly a sense of "Bahá'í identity." Many said this would also help legitimize their faith as an independent world religion.[27]

I will discuss in detail four of the Holy Day celebrations, and one special event day, to provide a sense of the diversity of these collective rituals.

BIRTH OF BAHÁ'U'LLÁH. The birth of Bahá'u'lláh is celebrated on November 12. During the period of fieldwork for this research, the Atlanta LSA held the Birth of Bahá'u'lláh celebration at a popular African American restaurant in Atlanta's West End. Approximately 260 people filled the large banquet hall; nearly one-third were seekers. A row of folding tables held a buffet-style meal complete with a large birthday cake saying "Birth of Bahá'u'lláh." Before the meal, prayers were read, and a film was shown entitled "The Secret of Our Century," about the life of Bahá'u'lláh in Haifa. One Bahá'í said that while this film was without much informational content, it was aiming for "the emotional impact, rather than information overload" for the seekers who attended.

After the meal, some Bahá'ís from the Atlanta community got up to say a few words about the Bahá'í Faith and its goals. One Persian man introduced a coworker whom he had taught and who had recently declared her faith in Bahá'u'lláh. The new declarant, an African American woman, gave an old-fashioned testimonial, saying how she felt "like a new person" after becoming a Bahá'í, that she felt "reborn," and that it had "changed her whole life." She introduced her teenage son, dressed in a "Malcolm X" leather jacket, who had signed his declaration card that night. Everyone clapped and the three of them hugged each other. The rest of the evening included musical entertainment: gospel/R&B styles with Bahá'í themes, a classical flute piece, and Bahá'í youth who rapped about racial unity. As the evening wore on, chairs were cleared off the floor and a DJ played songs while people danced. One white Bahá'í from the suburbs said he was happy to see such diversity at this Holy Day celebration—indicating the diverse mix of blacks, whites, and Persians. He said that even among the Bahá'ís, you would not have seen this much diversity even fifteen to twenty years ago. Another woman told me she was glad to see so many Persians from Cobb County attending this celebration here in the heart of Black Atlanta.

ASCENSION OF BAHÁ'U'LLÁH. Bahá'u'lláh died on May 29, 1892. The event is commemorated by Bahá'ís at 3 a.m., the recorded time of Bahá'u'lláh's death.

Needless to say, because of the time of night, it is one of the least attended of
the Bahá'í Holy Days, and Bahá'ís who do attend will try not to work on that
day (when work is to be suspended in any case).

The Atlanta Bahá'í community began to gather around midnight, and had
several hours of scripture reading and prayers before the reading of the Tablet
of Visitation for Bahá'u'lláh at 3 a.m. There was no official program, but people
were free to read from scripture, often very long passages about the last days of
Bahá'u'lláh, if they felt moved to do so. On this most solemn of Holy Day com-
memorations, Persian chanting was softly playing from the tape recorder as people
arrived, and lit candles were placed throughout the room. People took turns reading from Bahá'í Writings, and in between readings, participants were silent in
private meditation (or just trying to stay awake). This Holy Day has a high rate
of attendance among Persian believers, who said they were used to observing
this Holy Day back in Iran, when the entire Persian Bahá'í community would
attend. Precisely at 3 a.m., after several hours of readings and prayers, all Bahá'ís
stand and face toward Haifa and the Shrine of Bahá'u'lláh. The Tablet of Visitation is first chanted in Persian, and then read in English. After the reading,
Bahá'ís who are still awake enough will go out to breakfast at a nearby 24–hour
restaurant. Some Bahá'ís told me during interviews that they felt judged by other
Bahá'ís for not attending this particular observance, usually because they could
not get off work the next day or were unwilling to drive downtown at 3 a.m.
Some Bahá'ís, they said, treated them as if they were not as committed to their
faith, and were not willing to "sacrifice sleep for Bahá'u'lláh."

NAW-RÚZ. Naw-Rúz is the Bahá'í new year, presently celebrated on the fixed day
of March 21 (although Bahá'u'lláh defined it as the day on which the vernal
equinox occurs).[28] It parallels the new year in Iran, which is a national holiday.
'Abdu'l-Bahá indicated that Naw-Rúz has a spiritual significance in that it represents the new life of spring—akin to the new spiritual springtime brought to
humanity with Bahá'u'lláh's revelation (Walbridge 1996). Naw-Rúz is a special
holiday for Atlanta Bahá'ís not only because it marks the end of 'Alá', the month
of fasting (which for many hungry Bahá'ís is cause for celebration), but because
it connects the expatriate Iranian community to their home country's cultural
roots. During my period of fieldwork, I attended two different Naw-Rúz celebrations: one at the Atlanta Bahá'í Center, and one at a majority-Persian community in Cobb County (northwest suburban Atlanta). Each had a unique ethos.
Each started at sunset, when the Naw-Rúz tablet written by Bahá'u'lláh was read,
along with other prayers, before participants broke the fast. The commemoration at the Atlanta Center was potluck, and included a cake with "Happy
Naw-Rúz" printed in bright blue icing. Among the one hundred participants
were many out-of-town Bahá'ís, as well as non-Bahá'í guests, who are always

welcome at Bahá'í Holy Day celebrations. Children were entertained downstairs with games and a Bahá'í video, while adults socialized upstairs, sitting in folding chairs while balancing paper plates on their laps and swapping stories about their Fast experiences. Many speculated on what would await the Atlanta Bahá'í community during the Three Year Plan and upcoming new Bahá'í administrative year.

The second Naw-Rúz celebration, however, reflected the Persian majority. Traditional Persian dishes such as Sabzee Polo, which includes rice, vegetables, and fried white fish, covered the dining room table of the home hosting the Holy Day celebration. Persian music played in the background, and news from relatives in Iran punctuated the conversation. Many Bahá'ís confessed to me that they had attended this particular Naw-Rúz observance specifically because of all the Persian food available. Seekers attending this Bahá'í event rather than the celebration described earlier would have gotten a very different impression of the Bahá'í Faith. The atmosphere and tone of this latter event may account for the assumption among some non-Bahá'ís that the Bahá'í Faith is "that Persian religion."

AYYÁM-I-HA. This four- or five-day festival, between February 26 and March 1, is inserted before the last month of the Bahá'í calendar to complete the solar year of 365 or 366 days. The word Ayyám-i-Ha literally means "the days of H," where the letter "H" in Arabic has a numerological value of five (the symbol of the Báb). The Báb did not specify where these extra days should be placed, and so Bahá'u'lláh specified that they were not to be part of any month, but considered a special festival. Bahá'u'lláh said that during Ayyám-i-Ha, Bahá'ís should "provide good cheer for themselves, their kindred and, beyond them, the poor and needy, and with joy and exultation to hail and glorify their Lord, to sing His praise and magnify His name" (quoted in Walbridge 1996, 216). Bahá'ís see Ayyám-i-Ha as a time for exchanging gifts, socializing, doing service projects for the wider community, and preparing for the month of fasting.

Numerous Ayyám-i-Ha celebrations were held throughout the metro Atlanta area. In the city of Atlanta community, the Bahá'í Center was decorated in festive colored streamers, balloons were hung on which the phrase "God Loves You" was printed, and a cake with "Happy Ayyám-i-Ha" on it was provided for the eighty to a hundred Bahá'ís and their guests attending. The celebration began with the special scriptural passage written by Bahá'u'lláh for the occasion, followed by a meal. The festivities ended with a large gift exchange. Every Bahá'í who attended was asked to bring a simple gift, with the Atlanta LSA providing extra gifts for non-Bahá'í guests. Each gift was numbered, and then people drew numbers out of a hat and got the corresponding gift. Some gifts were practical (i.e., a picture frame or a book on African history), but some were "gag" gifts.

Everyone appeared to enjoy the food and fellowship, and the children played games and took turns hitting a piñata.

RACE UNITY DAY. The Race Unity Day celebration in June 1993 was held at a rustic community center just east of downtown Atlanta. It was decorated inside to look like an old barn with a loft, a large meeting space, and a kitchen facility. Approximately eighty people were there during the main talk, including a diverse ethnic and racial mix of Bahá'ís and their non-Bahá'í friends (around one-fifth Persians, and equal numbers of African Americans and whites). Several non-Bahá'ís also came as a result of newspaper advertisements. T-shirts proclaiming the message "Unity in Diversity" were on sale, and free Bahá'í literature and food were set out on tables in the back of the main meeting space.

The emcee for the event began by welcoming everyone to the celebration of the oneness of humanity, giving a special greeting to non-Bahá'í guests. After briefly explaining what the Bahá'í Faith was about (which Bahá'ís always do when they think they are addressing an audience with non-Bahá'ís who may know nothing about the religion), he read a little from the Bahá'í *Vision of Race Unity* statement, then quoted from Dr. Martin Luther King's 1968 "I've been to the mountain top" speech, and then said that those gathered in this room were also on the mountain top (Bahá'ís frequently allude to this metaphor at their large, ethnically and racially diverse gatherings). A Persian man then played a native song on a traditional Persian stringed instrument.

There were two speakers for the main program. The first was an Atlanta Bahá'í anesthesiologist, a white man, who spoke about the physiological aspects of race unity (what he called the "easy aspect" of recognizing the unity of humanity). He said that all the physical/anthropological evidence shows that humanity is one species: when he studied physiology, he only had to study one model, because there is only one humanity. He also pointed out that when doing organ transplants, the most important thing to match is one of the four blood types, and the least important thing is race.

Then an African American Bahá'í woman spoke. A doctoral student in psychology, who does diversity training workshops for corporations, she spoke directly and bluntly. She said that society cannot have diversity as "the parsley on the plate"—that is, as ornamentation added onto the existing situation. Nor should we, she said, see diversity as "the melting pot," creating uniformity. Rather, she said, diversity is a "tossed salad," embodying the idea of unity in diversity. She said that she believes that it is foolish for people to say "I don't see color." "What if you put a fair-skinned blond child next to a Nigerian child? You will see color," she said. We should not ignore color and racial differences, she said, but cherish and celebrate them.

She also talked about axiology—the study of different value systems among cultural groups. She said that the white/European value system is object oriented, and this causes them problems when encountering people of African origin, whose culture tends to be more person oriented. Europeans are "linear," and Africans are "relational" (no one seemed to question her ideas or their source).

She told the story of how the Ford Pinto automobile was made using linear thinking—too much concern for things and profit, not enough for people. She said that some white men got together and "counted and measured" and found out that it would cost Ford $11 million to recall the Pinto and fix a defect in the gas tank that caused it to explode on rear impact, but only $6 million to ignore the problem and pay for the litigation brought by the families of those who died. She said they also figured into their decision-making the customer profile of those who would buy the Ford Pinto—poor minorities who would not have enough resources to drag out the legal battles for years. She said this example is why diversity is needed in the corporate boardroom—so that other voices may be raised saying "It is immoral to put profit before human life." The solution to this and other problems, she said, was the Bahá'í message of unity in diversity and the realization of the oneness of humanity. She got a standing ovation from the whole crowd when she finished speaking. Several Bahá'ís remarked that they were glad to hear a Bahá'í speaker give a talk on race unity that "pulled no punches" and went beyond "clichés on race unity." Afterward, there was food and fellowship; entertainment was provided by Bahá'í youth, who sang songs with race unity themes.

Deepenings: Education for "Situated Universalists"

Deepenings are another collective ritual in the Bahá'í community; their purpose is to "deepen" an individual's love for and knowledge of the religion. Deepenings are often referred to as "Bahá'í Bible study," and those held on Sunday morning are often called "Bahá'í Sunday school." They are a primary component of Bahá'í socialization—what Bahá'ís call "immersion in the ocean of God's Word." Bahá'ís gather in groups as small as three or four to study the writings of Bahá'u'lláh, 'Abdu'l-Bahá, and Shoghi Effendi, and to a lesser extent those of the Báb (what little has so far been translated into English). Bahá'í Writings say this about the importance and necessity of deepening:

> Above all, the duty of deepening the spiritual life of your newly-enrolled
> co-workers is paramount, for the fate of the entire community depends
> upon the individual believers. . . . To deepen in the Cause means to read
> the writings of Bahá'u'lláh and the Master ['Abdu'l-Bahá] so thoroughly
> as to be able to give it to others in its pure form. . . . The more we read
> the writings the more truths we can find in them and the more we will
> see that our previous notions were erroneous. . . . A great harm is done

by starting to teach without being firmly grounded in the literature. . . .
The Teachings of Bahá'u'lláh are so great, and deal with so many aspects
of both the inner life of man and his communal life, that it takes years
to really plumb them to the depths. (Hornby 1983, 71, 566–568, 570)

Deepening not only facilitates a person's spiritual development, but also prepares them for evangelism (see chapter 7). Bahá'ís supplement their study of scripture with various authors' interpretations and commentary on Bahá'í scripture. Deepenings are sometimes facilitated by someone well versed in a particular topic, with the gathering organized as a short lecture or presentation followed by discussion. Most often, they consist of Bahá'ís sitting in a circle taking turns reading from the Writings, with individuals offering their own interpretation or application of a passage. If a Bahá'í tries to impose his/her interpretation as the correct "Bahá'í view," he/she is gently reminded by a fellow Bahá'í that individuals are free to interpret scripture for themselves—except for those things already given an "authoritative" interpretation by 'Abdu'l-Bahá, Shoghi Effendi, or the UHJ. Survey results indicate that nearly 45 percent of Atlanta Bahá'ís attend a regular (weekly or monthly) deepening.

The following section will describe a series of deepenings I attended as part of my eighteen months of fieldwork. Just before my fieldwork began, the Universal House of Justice published the full English translation of the *Kitáb-i-Aqdas*, the "Most Holy Book" of Bahá'u'lláh's writings. Bahá'í communities throughout the United States began earnest study of the book Bahá'ís felt would be the blueprint of a Bahá'í World Order. This was true in Atlanta as well, and from June 1993 through February 1994, anywhere from six to twenty-two people would gather for two hours every Sunday morning at the Atlanta Bahá'í Center to "deepen" on the *Aqdas*. On average, the deepening was divided equally between men and women, African Americans and whites, new believers and veteran Bahá'ís. There were usually one or two seekers attending as well. I will describe a composite, "typical" deepening session, including various topics from the *Aqdas* and related discussions about world events.

The deepening was led by a middle-aged African American man, a longtime Bahá'í who grew up in Atlanta. He would ask for prayers to start the session, and the mixed gathering of Bahá'ís and non-Bahá'ís sitting in folding chairs in a circle would take turns reading prayers from one of the Bahá'í prayer books. Some were general prayers for "detachment" or "praise and gratitude" of God; others were more specific, asking for God's blessing for a loved one or for help in teaching Bahá'u'lláh's message to a specific coworker. Bahá'ís would always read from their prayer books, while seekers, when they did offer prayers, would speak extemporaneously. Then the deepening leader would summarize where the discussion left off the previous week, and would pick someone to begin reading the text. The deepening would last two hours, with attendees taking turns reading a paragraph and pausing to allow others in the group to give their opinions about what the scripture meant to them, and how they could apply it to their everyday lives. The atmosphere was relaxed, and people were free to get up and get coffee and refreshments provided by the deepening leader. Downstairs we could hear Bahá'í children's classes discussing the basics of Bahá'í history and the Central Figures.

Atlanta Bahá'ís considered the English-language publication of the *Aqdas* an important milestone. They frequently mentioned the privilege they had of being both beneficiaries and defenders of "this Charter of the future world civilization," as Shoghi Effendi promised in his summary of the book (Bahá'u'lláh 1992, 13). One of the first discussions in this series of deepenings surrounded the passage "Think not that We [God] have revealed unto you a mere code of laws. Nay, rather We have unsealed the choice Wine with the fingers of might and power" (1992, 3). This led into a debate over the nature of law in the Bahá'í Faith. One Bahá'í participant said that failure to follow Bahá'í law would lead to the loss of one's administrative rights. Another Bahá'í countered that LSAs and Auxiliary Board members are also supposed to be patient with the shortcomings of new and old Bahá'ís. Someone else pointed out that Bahá'ís should not get into a divisive comparison as to who is the "better Bahá'í" by following all the laws to the letter, while losing the spirit of unity the laws are designed to foster.

A new Bahá'í asked why Bahá'u'lláh would refer to the laws he revealed as "wine," when the *Aqdas* also clearly forbids the drinking of alcohol. The deepening facilitator said that it is important to remember that spiritual concepts are of necessity communicated through language that uses physical symbols. This, he said, is why religious scripture has been historically misunderstood: people take the Bible or Qur'án literally, without looking for its metaphorical meaning (a trap that Bahá'ís, he seemed to be implying, would not fall into).[29] Wine, said the deepening facilitator, was a metaphor for the Word of God, because of its stimulating and transforming effect on one's soul, just as actual wine intoxicates the mind.

A Persian Bahá'í from the Atlanta community arrived to fix the second-story window in the kitchen right next to the meeting room. It had been broken out by rock-throwing vandals, a reminder to the Bahá'ís that their meeting place was in a deteriorating section of Atlanta's inner city. The deepening facilitator told the group that this was the third time the back window had been broken, and that recent thefts had prompted the LSA to decide to put bars on the widows. The group decided to take a break since fixing the window was making a lot of noise, and as people stretched their legs and got more coffee, a homeless man came up the stairs. While several people avoided him, the deepening facilitator approached and welcomed him. The homeless man said that since he saw the word "Faith" on the sign on the front of the building, he thought this must be a church where he could get some help. The facilitator said it was not a church, but the Bahá'í Center, and the man was welcome to stay for our discussion about religion from the Bahá'í perspective. The man declined, but was given some food before leaving.

When the deepening resumed, the issue of homelessness, poverty and begging were raised in response to the encounter with the homeless man. A "seeker" who had been brought to the deepening by one of the regular attendees asked what was the "Bahá'í position on how to address social problems like homelessness?" The deepening facilitator said we should look in the *Aqdas*. One person read the passage "It is incumbent upon each one of you to engage in some occupation—such as a craft, a trade or the like. We have exalted your engagement in such work to the rank of worship of the one true God " (1992, 30). Later in the text, someone read, "It is unlawful to beg, and it is forbidden to give to him who beggeth" (1992, 72). However, it "is the duty of those who are in charge of the organization of society [the Universal House of Justice] to give every individual the opportunity of acquiring the necessary talent in some kind of profession . . . for the sake of earning the means of his livelihood" (1992, 192).[30]

Finally, someone read the passage in the *Aqdas* which says that "The prohibition against giving charity to people who beg does not preclude individuals and Spiritual Assemblies from extending financial assistance to the poor and needy" (1992, 235). After reading all of these excerpts, one Bahá'í pointed out to the seeker that the *Aqdas* delineates both individual and social responsibilities, balancing them in a way no present political or economic system can. When the seeker asked for some details of this balance, the Bahá'í was unable to provide specifics, merely saying that the Administrative Order under the infallible guidance of the Universal House of Justice would balance these things in the future, in ways that capitalist and communist systems cannot.

This led to a discussion about whether or not Bahá'ís should give money to panhandlers on the street. Some said that in light of what had been read in the *Aqdas*, Bahá'ís should not give anything to beggars. Two other participants said that they would buy that person a meal, rather than just give them money. One African American woman who converted to the Bahá'í Faith from the Nation of Islam said that what Bahá'í scripture said reminded her of the "brotherhood and sisterhood" the Muslim community provided for each other, and Islam taught Muslims not to give others handouts, but to empower fellow Muslims. Since becoming a Bahá'í, she said, she sees the *Aqdas* saying the same thing to the Bahá'í community. The authority of the LSA has to create the same kind of community support—including housing assistance, job training, and child care, as well as day-to-day subsistence if needed, she said.

However, one strain of thinking that emerged most often from this and similar discussions I heard throughout my fieldwork was that the solution to social problems like homelessness was for Bahá'ís to teach their faith. One man pointed out that most of the laws in the *Kitáb-i-Aqdas* were for a future state of society, when the Bahá'í Administrative Order governed the world's affairs. There are, he said, just too few Bahá'ís anywhere in the world, and certainly in the United States, to have much effect on contemporary social problems. To have an impact on the values and governance of society, as intended in the *Aqdas*, Bahá'ís need to convert more people to their faith.

The deepening facilitator brought the group back to the study of the *Aqdas*. The discussion went on to the passage "Take heed not to stir up mischief in the land after it hath been set in order" (1992, 42). This led into a discussion about the law requiring Bahá'ís to be obedient to the government under which they live.[31] One woman said she interpreted that passage as saying that Bahá'ís should be critical of policy that is contrary to Bahá'í principles (as Bahá'ís were in Atlanta during Jim Crow segregation—see chapter 8); however, she said, that does not mean Bahá'ís should be critical of individual people in the government.

A recent African American declarant asked what Bahá'ís of South Africa should do, given the Bahá'í obligation to follow the laws of the country in which they reside, and to avoid involvement in partisan politics. One woman, who had recently talked with a pioneer from the United States who went to South Africa, said that the injunction about obeying the government is the single most debated issues for Bahá'ís in that part of the world. She said this pioneer said that Bahá'ís in South Africa do have interracial meetings, but do it very cautiously and never do anything that will knowingly put someone at risk. The recent declarant felt that would be very frustrating, to live as a Bahá'í under such a blatantly unjust system. The woman responded that her pioneering friend said that Bahá'ís in South Africa have had to learn patience, not wanting to "stir up trouble so that Bahá'ís become known to the government as 'troublemakers.'" Someone got the Webster's dictionary from the Bahá'í library at the far end of the room and looked up "patience." Of its definition in the dictionary as "forbearing, long-suffering, capable of enduring hardship," someone commented that those are all spiritual virtues Bahá'u'lláh displayed during his forty years in captivity.

Bahá'ís concluded the week's deepening after reading the passage "renew the furnishings of your homes after the passing of each nineteen years" (1992, 74), which most agreed was intended to teach them "detachment" from the physical world—another spiritual virtue praised by Bahá'ís (although one person pointed out that the *Aqdas* exempts antiques or jewelry). This prompted a discussion about what detachment as a spiritual virtue means in a materialistic culture such as the United States. At noon, the deepening facilitator asked for a closing prayer to be read. After cleaning up the food and moving the chairs from the deepening circle so they faced the front of the room, ready for that week's Feast, several participants went out to lunch at a nearby restaurant. This was done nearly every week (except during the Bahá'í Fast) by the interracial group, in part to socialize, but in part to engage in "indirect teaching" by providing a model of interracial fellowship in both West End (primarily African American) and Buckhead (primarily white) restaurants in Atlanta.

This account of a "typical" deepening on the *Kitáb-i-Aqdas* gives an example of how and what Bahá'ís do during this crucial ritual of practicing their faith. Most deepenings, but especially those on the *Aqdas*, bring the individual believer into greater contact with Bahá'í Writings, their source Bahá'u'lláh, and their defender the UHJ. This reinforces one's Bahá'í identity as a situated universalist, by offering one an opportunity to discuss the relevance of a text of (Bahá'í) universal values within one's local community.

This composite account is also instructive in that it highlights several themes of a Bahá'í's situated universalist identity. The focus, as in all Bahá'í discussions, is on what is considered divinely revealed text read by Bahá'ís all over the world. Bahá'ís attempt to relate this global scripture to the plight of the homeless right outside their front door, as well as to the situation of Bahá'ís in South Africa and attempts at social change and racial unity. Week in and week out during my fieldwork, the small group of Bahá'ís met to read from their scripture and deepen their knowledge and identity in their faith. Sometimes several pages would be completed; sometimes in two hours only one paragraph would be read, as Bahá'ís shared personal insights and their understanding of the text's application to geopolitical events. But it is a typically Bahá'í form of socialization: Bahá'í identity is shaped interactively by consulting with each other about a text that reflexively connects the local community with global institutions. It also shows that despite deepening their knowledge about their faith, Bahá'ís have trouble explaining to non-Bahá'í seekers, who are always welcome at deepenings, how exactly the Bahá'í World Order will come about, given the injunction to avoid involvement in divisive secular politics and secular social movements. The typically Bahá'í answer to this paradox is to "teach the Faith" (see chapter 7).

Organizational Participation among Atlanta Bahá'ís

One final important measure of Bahá'í activity in Atlanta relates to race unity efforts. Every year in January, Atlanta hosts the nation's largest Martin Luther King Jr. holiday celebration, and Bahá'ís since 1986 have been major participants in the commemoration of King's vision of a "Beloved Community"[32] (see chapter 8 for further details). Because of the importance of racial unity and the oneness of humanity in Bahá'í ideology, Atlanta Bahá'ís were asked whether or not they participated that year in any of the Bahá'í-sponsored King Day events.

Nearly 72 percent reported that they had, signifying a high degree of behavioral as well as ideological support for Bahá'í ideals of race unity.

It is now appropriate to provide an overview of Atlanta Bahá'í organizational participation (see again tables 5.3 and 3.1). Statistical analysis revealed two distinct types of organizational participation among Atlanta Bahá'ís.[33] The first, "Active Organizational Participation," is a composite variable summing measures of Feast and Holy Day attendance, the number of hours per week devoted to Bahá'í activities, participation in Bahá'í-sponsored Martin Luther King (MLK) events, and participation in regular deepenings. This variable was then tested for statistical association with demographic, authority, and personal devotion variables. As was found in earlier analysis using the personal devotion variable, organizational participation is unrelated to most demographic measures. Active Organizational Participation is, however, statistically associated with recognition of the authority of the Administrative Order. It is also associated with the measure of personal devotion discussed earlier in this chapter. This makes sense theoretically, since active participation would bring an individual Bahá'í into greater contact with the symbols and myths of authority of the Administrative Order (especially at Feast). It is also theoretically plausible that organizational participation and personal piety/devotion would be associated, together reflecting a wider pattern of religious commitment.

In addition, being married to a Bahá'í spouse made one significantly more likely to participate in Bahá'í organizational culture than being married to a non-Bahá'í. This may indicate that the family can act as a crucible of socialization and a foundation for Bahá'í identity. None of the other demographic variables, however, were significant in predicting this measure of organizational participation.

The second measure of organizational activity is "Participation in Administrative Ritual," which combines the following variables: membership on one's Local Spiritual Assembly and local committees, being an officer of one's LSA, and voting in local Ridván and District Convention elections (see table 3.1). Like the first measure, Participation in Administrative Ritual is significantly associated with recognition of legitimate authority, marriage to a Bahá'í spouse, and personal devotion. In addition, it is related to the number of years one has been a Bahá'í. In other words, those who have been in the Bahá'í Faith longer are more likely to score high on this measure of organizational participation. This probably reflects the fact that the maturity necessary for participation in leadership roles within one's local community takes longer to cultivate than other types of organizational participation. No other demographic variables were significantly associated with "Participation in Administrative Ritual."

Thus, one's race, gender, educational level, income, occupation, and age are unrelated to the likelihood of participating in Bahá'í collective ritual or of being

a practicing devout Bahá'í. The common theme that emerged from this analysis is that those Bahá'ís who take seriously the authority claims of the Bahá'í
Administrative Order (and hence those of Bahá'u'lláh) are more likely to participate fully in local community life. However, this relationship is dialectical,
since participation in personal and community practices would also strengthen
one's exposure to and affinity for authority symbols in the Bahá'í Faith (and
hence the universal ideology of that authority).

Summary

I began this chapter by discussing the importance of ritual in the life of a religious community. Ritual not only reflects the community's ideology, but it shapes
social relationships and religious action in accordance with that ideology. Ritual
becomes the "outward" sign of "inward" belief, and binds a religious community
in solidarity.

Ritual functions in this way for Bahá'ís as well. But it is distinct in two respects. First, not only does ritual establish local solidarity among a group of gathered believers; local Bahá'í ritual also reflexively brings them into regular contact
with higher levels of authority and globally encompassing symbols and institutions. The recognition of the authority in the Bahá'í Administrative Order is
important, for it is significantly related statistically to adherence to major tenets of Bahá'ís' global ideology, around which Bahá'ís are highly unified. Survey results discussed in this chapter show that one's recognition of authority is
statistically associated with measures of organizational participation and one's
level of personal devotion. Ritual and authority interact to unify Bahá'ís around
a coherent, global identity as situated universalists.

For example, the Nineteen-Day Feast always includes communication from
the national and/or global centers of the Bahá'í Faith, helping Bahá'ís to "think
globally." Regular messages of encouragement, advice, and hope come directly
from a universal source believed to be infallible. The "Bahá'í Newsreels" reinforce the global compass of the individual's faith, as one sees Bahá'ís from
Bangkok and Baltimore, Lagos and Los Angeles, engaging in similar teaching
efforts and administrative duties. It brings "unity in diversity" to life on a global
scale.

Feasts also encourage Bahá'ís to "[en]act locally" certain key features of their
ideology. The administrative portion of the Feast gives individuals a chance to
participate in communitywide consultation, itself a Bahá'í administrative ritual.
Every nineteen days, Bahá'ís discuss issues of relevance to their collective lives,
with direct access to participating Assembly members. This assures that community concerns will be heard by the local authority.

Feast, as ritual, also reinforces the unity of a community by accommodating its diversity. The structure of Feast is loose enough to allow the music, devotions, consultation, and food to reflect the community's diverse membership. And the presence of Persians in most communities means that Persian culture will, as Geertz said of ritual in general, "shape the spiritual consciousness of a people" (Geertz 1973, 113). Thus, ritual and authority reinforce each other to create situated universalists.

This is true not only of collective ritual, but of private ritual as well. Reading scripture and reciting prayers brings a Bahá'í into a personal relationship with Bahá'u'lláh's and 'Abdu'l-Bahá's perceived charismatic authority. This is even more true of pilgrimage, where Bahá'ís see some of their founder's personal effects, and meet UHJ members. In addition, nearly one-half of Atlanta Bahá'ís shape individual goals for themselves based on the Three Year Plan formulated by the global authority of their faith.

However, Bahá'ís fully admit that the Atlanta Bahá'í community in general does not necessarily fully practice the Bahá'í calendar. Work schedules, the dominant Christian culture, and just plain inattention served to dilute for some the ritual power of time intrinsic in the Bahá'í rhythm of the year. It also appears that Holy Day celebrations in particular are seen by many Bahá'ís less as solemn occasions of commemorating Bahá'í history, and more as teaching opportunities to which one should bring non-Bahá'í guests. The rote recitation of rationalized prayer among a highly educated religious community may also dilute the influence of these rituals.

The second way Bahá'í ritual functions differently from other religious groups is that all Atlanta Bahá'ís are equally likely to engage in devotional and collective rituals, regardless of demographic characteristics. This means that one's recognition of institutional authority is more important in explaining or predicting one's level of organizational participation than are demographic characteristics such as race, education, occupation, sex, and class. This is a unique finding, one that strengthens the argument that the Bahá'í Faith fosters a distinct situated universalist identity in its adherents. Local organizational participation reinforces a global Bahá'í identity by bringing one into contact with authority structures. One's religious identity overshadows ascribed characteristics to the extent that they are no longer associated with organizational participation or ideological fidelity.

This contradicts much of the sociology of religion literature that tries to explain commitment to religious organizations. Hoge and Carroll (1978) found that church commitment among Protestants is explained by "status group theory." This theory states that church participation is based more on social class and ethnicity than on theology, meaning that believers choose a church much like they choose any voluntary association: based on the status and recognition it would bring to them in the wider society.

Other researchers have found that one's type of religious commitment varies based on demographic characteristics. For example, Fukuyama (1961) found that dimensions of religiosity (such as attendance, acceptance of ideology, and level of devotion) vary by sex, age, education, and socioeconomic status. Good (1966), Lazerwitz (1961), and Roof and McKinney (1987) found that religious participation is strongly influenced by educational, income, and occupational factors. These patterns simply were not found among the Bahá'ís.

Although the Bahá'í Faith has a universal character and global structure, its ideology does set boundaries between the Bahá'í and non-Bahá'í worlds. The next chapter will explore those boundaries, as well as the institutional mechanisms that maintain them.

Chapter 6

Boundaries and Identity

*The Message of Bahá'u'lláh is not a particularistic appeal
to a group of people. It is a Universal Message, an
all-inclusive appeal.*

      Shoghi Effendi, quoted in *Pupil of the Eye*

*Ex-communication is a spiritual thing. . . . Only actual
enemies of the Cause are ex-communicated. On the other
hand, those who conspicuously disgrace the Faith or refuse
to abide by its laws can be deprived, as a punishment, of
their voting rights.*

      Shoghi Effendi, quoted in *Lights of Guidance*

ONE PROBLEM ANY religious group faces is that of boundaries—what are the ideological and behavioral landmarks that distinguish between "us" and "them"? This is a problem even for the Bahá'ís, whose professed goal is "unity in diversity" and the "oneness of humanity." Bahá'ís espouse the "unity of religion," and in so doing are often accused of syncretism (cf. Parrinder 1971; Kurtz 1995; Smith 1991). However, Bahá'ís conceive their religious ideas to be *more* relevant than others for today's world; they believe Bahá'u'lláh's World Order is the *only* salvation for a wayward humanity. Thus, they do erect boundaries and limit their universality, including institutional mechanisms to censure and even expel Bahá'ís who stray too far from what is "acceptably Bahá'í." However, we will see that Bahá'ís themselves are often unsure where these boundaries should lie.

Bahá'ís present a mixed picture of inclusion and exclusion. The way they treat the boundaries between the Bahá'í and non-Bahá'í world is indicative of the balancing act they perform as situated universalists. On the one hand, Durkheimian (1965, 1973) elements in Bahá'í ideology advocate a global collective consciousness, with the goal of fostering the oneness of humanity and the elimination of all prejudice through universal adoption of a common religious faith (see also Robertson 1992). This is inherent in the Bahá'í concept of "progressive revelation." On the other hand, the Bahá'í Faith's formal global institutions include mechanisms to sanction and even excommunicate rebellious members. We will see that the way Bahá'ís treat these boundaries reflects this attempted balancing act between the intimate local community and the global Administrative Order.

This chapter will investigate how "open" or "closed" individual Bahá'ís are with respect to the wider culture, and examine the ideological boundaries between the Bahá'í and non-Bahá'í world. These boundaries are especially evident when we consider how Bahá'ís envision the secular "old world order" as opposed to the Bahá'í "new world order," and how they view the sanctions placed upon individuals who pass beyond acceptable Bahá'í behavior.

Who Is Considered a Bahá'í?

As "situated universalists," Bahá'ís attempt to foster an identity that "thinks globally, but acts locally." They are asked by their scriptures to see all humanity as "the rays of one sun, as the waves of one ocean, and as the fruit of one tree" (NSA of the United States 1985, 102). However, this does not mean Bahá'ís should accept all perspectives, beliefs, and ideologies. Ask different Bahá'ís what it means to be a Bahá'í—and how they are distinguished from non-Bahá'ís— and the answers will vary, as is true in any religion. Some would quote 'Abdu'l-Bahá, who said, "To be a Bahá'í simply means to love all the world; to love humanity and try to serve it; to work for universal peace and universal brotherhood" (Esslemont 1970, 83). Some would hold up their Bahá'í membership card, noting the individual Bahá'í number that gives them voting rights in local elections. Others would note that they are followers of "the Manifestation of God for this day"—Bahá'u'lláh.

Despite variation in the definition of who is considered a member, the process by which one becomes a Bahá'í has become substantially more formalized and systematic since the days of 'Abdu'l-Bahá's pronouncement that a Bahá'í is any "lover of humanity." Since the inauguration of the Administrative Order, the boundary between who "is" and who "is not" has become much more rigid.

Most Bahá'ís would acknowledge a basic three-step process in crossing the threshold into the Bahá'í world, inaugurating a lifetime deepening process as situated universalists. Bahá'ís do not use terms like "becoming saved" to describe accepting the Bahá'í Faith (as in some Christian denominations),[1] but most Bahá'ís I interviewed acknowledge their "Bahá'í birthday" as the day on which they finally, often after years of investigation, "declared."[2]

The first stage in becoming a Bahá'í is belief in Bahá'u'lláh. This involves acceptance of the idea of progressive revelation and of Bahá'u'lláh as the latest Manifestation sent from God to humanity. Bahá'í theology states that in truly accepting Bahá'u'lláh, one must of necessity accept all the other Manifestations of God. Several Bahá'ís from Christian backgrounds told me that they accepted Bahá'u'lláh as the return of Christ, but had to overcome their reluctance to accept, for example, Buddha, Moses, Zoroaster, Christ, Muhammad, *and* Bahá'u'lláh as equal messengers from God.

The second stage is "declaration." Over the last seventy years this has become the most formalized aspect of Bahá'í membership. In declaring, one signs a card that states: "In signing this card, I declare my belief in Bahá'u'lláh, the Promised One of God. I also recognized the Báb, His Forerunner, and 'Abdu'l-Bahá, the Center of His Covenant. I request enrollment in the Bahá'í Community with the understanding that Bahá'u'lláh has established sacred principles, laws, and institutions which I must obey." Upon declaration, one is assigned a Bahá'í number signifying one's status as a full-fledged Bahá'í with the right to attend Nineteen-Day Feasts, vote in elections, and contribute to Bahá'í funds. This second, more formal step is administrative in nature.

Many converts who declared prior to the late 1950s told me that they first had to appear before the Local Spiritual Assembly to prove their readiness to become a Bahá'í. They were required to read several books of Bahá'í scripture, and correctly answer questions posed to them by the LSA. Several said this was a nerve-wracking experience, provoking anxiety over whether they were "worthy" to be a disciple of Bahá'u'lláh. Some even indicated they thought it was now too easy to become a Bahá'í (currently no LSA requires a convert to pass an "entrance exam"), and were uncomfortable with the mass enrollments of the 1960s, when hundreds would sign their declaration cards literally within moments after hearing the Bahá'í claim that Christ had returned as Bahá'u'lláh.

The third stage for a Bahá'í begins a lifelong journey, a personal transformation and socialization according to Bahá'í principles. This process also involves participating in the Administrative Order through voting, and, if called upon by one's fellow Bahá'ís, serving on the Local Spiritual Assembly. It also involves personal and collective deepening, or systematic study of Bahá'í Writings.[3] Thus, over time, the boundaries between the Bahá'í and non-Bahá'í world have solidified through the second, formal administrative step—part of the routinization process begun by Shoghi Effendi in the 1920s.

Distinctions between Bahá'ís and Non-Bahá'ís

Repeatedly throughout my fieldwork, in Nineteen-Day Feasts, in Firesides, in deepenings, and during interviews, I witnessed Bahá'ís discussing the distinction between the "old world order" and the "new" or "Bahá'í world order." This concept brings into relief that the worldview of Bahá'ís, while universal and global, also differentiates between what is of God and what is the result of "vain imaginings."

Atlanta Bahá'ís often discussed their understanding of the old and new world order, and how local teaching efforts and participation in the Administrative Order contribute to the construction of the Bahá'í new world order. In part, to be a Bahá'í means that one identifies with the divine mission envisioned for the Bahá'í Faith: to lay the foundation for a global civilization based on a common religious worldview and ecclesiastical authority. But to succeed in that enterprise, Bahá'ís must wait patiently for the disintegration of the old world order, while they themselves build the framework (the Bahá'í Administrative Order) for the new. The boundary between Bahá'ís and others lies in part in their ability to foster and inculcate new-world-order thinking. Often I heard Bahá'ís gently chastising each other for "old world order thinking" or "old world order habits." When asked to elaborate, Bahá'ís would answer that racism, sexism, partisan politics, and gossiping were all part of the old order of society.

Bahá'ís often referred to Shoghi Effendi's discussion of the disintegration of the old world order, which is "lamentably defective," and the organic growth of the new world order in Bahá'í institutions:

> We are indeed living in an age which . . . should be regarded as one
> which is witnessing a dual phenomenon. The first signalizes the death
> pangs of an order . . . that has stubbornly refused . . . to attune its
> processes to the precepts and ideals which that Heaven-sent [Bahá'í]
> Faith proffered it. The second proclaims the birth pangs of an Order,
> divine and redemptive, that will inevitably supplant the former, and
> within Whose administrative structure an embryonic civilization,
> incomparable and world-embracing, is imperceptibly maturing.
> (1980, 17)

It is this division of the world into "old" and "new" worldviews that shapes the relationships Bahá'ís will have with the non-Bahá'í world, and the boundaries Bahá'ís erect between themselves and those who live in the "old world order." Bahá'ís seek out and collaborate with other groups that embrace principles similar to those upon which the "new world order" will be based (to be discussed fully below). Examples include issues like racial unity (collaboration with the Martin Luther King Jr. Center for Nonviolent Social Change); universal education (helping to establish community literacy programs); and the use of consultation to solve disputes (neighborhood conflict resolution programs). This division of the world into old and new paradigms is also the rationale for Bahá'ís' refusal to support political parties or platforms: partisan politics is not only divisive, but part of the "old world order," which is beyond repair. Bahá'ís therefore focus their energies in two directions. The first is outward, in teaching efforts to spread the news about the Bahá'í revelation (see chapter 7). Bahá'ís consider partnership with groups that share similar goals part of the teaching process. The second is inward, fostering the growth and maturity of local and national assemblies for the expanding role Bahá'ís presume will be theirs in the future, as "secular" conditions deteriorate around the world. Bahá'ís feel that by building up their own local, national, and global institutions, and by making the world aware of their beliefs, they will be one (if not the only) viable model for social life as conditions in secular society steadily worsen.

Thus, Bahá'ís see simultaneous integrative and destructive forces—divine in origin—at work in the world, enabling the Bahá'í World Order to arise out of the collapse of the old. Bahá'ís turn to Shoghi Effendi's writings to put the world's travails in perspective. The calamities facing the world are part of the healing process, he said, and are necessary to cleanse humanity of its divisions and allow new ideals and institutions to take root. During deepenings, in Feast consultations, or while just socializing, Bahá'ís bring up current social issues. Events such as the conflict in the Balkans, rising crime rates, racial riots, or general immorality are seen as evidence of the collapse of the old world order, and a confirmation of Shoghi Effendi's wisdom.

Bahá'ís see no "quick-fix" solution to humanity's problems; rather, they see these problems worsening in the near future (thus the Bahá'í Faith often takes on an apocalyptic tone—see related Bahá'í scholarship in Stockman 1996, Smith 1982, MacEoin 1986). This creates for Bahá'ís a sense of urgency to reform their individual character, and institutionalize a new pattern of living via the Local Spiritual Assembly. Bahá'ís often speculate that some terrible catastrophe will plague humanity soon—nuclear war, environmental destruction, or global economic collapse. Others say modern society is already beyond hope. Part of the conscious division, then, between Bahá'ís and non-Bahá'ís is that Bahá'ís, through their scripture, have developed a distinctive perspective on these global problems. But they also have assurance and hope that the solution is already available in the Bahá'í Faith—and they therefore believe they are participants in the creation of the global institutions and universal values that are humanity's only salvation. Hence the importance of teaching as a way of making humanity aware of the Bahá'ís' ideological and organizational solution (see chapter 7).

Bahá'ís point out that humanity was not destined to go through this chaos. When Bahá'u'lláh was a prisoner in 'Akká, Palestine, he addressed letters (or "Tablets," in Bahá'í terminology) to various world leaders in politics and religion, asking them to investigate his claims. He told them he was the universal Manifestation sent by God to unite the world and end war—to establish what he called the "Most Great Peace." He praised their station of service to mankind, and urged them to reduce their armaments, protect the poor, and embrace his religion.[4]

Needless to say, none of these world leaders seriously heeded the claims of this imprisoned religious leader. Because the world's political and religious leaders did not convert to the Bahá'í Faith and urge their subjects or citizens or congregations to do the same, Bahá'u'lláh admonished the Bahá'ís themselves to "hold ye fast unto this, the Lesser Peace" (1976, 254)—a process of world unity that is more gradual and incremental. Bahá'ís claim that the political and religious rulers of the world had the authority, had they believed in Bahá'u'lláh's claims to be the inaugurator of the Kingdom of God, to declare their belief in Bahá'u'lláh and his plan for world order, and the masses of humanity would have followed. World peace would have been instantaneous, and humanity would not have been plunged into more than a century of wars, racial and ethnic conflicts, and political instability. However, Bahá'ís say that because the rulers of the world denounced Bahá'u'lláh, the world was destined to achieve peace through stages of strife and opposition. The Lesser Peace, Bahá'ís say, is one stage in this longer, evolutionary process brought into existence by Bahá'u'lláh.

The distinction between the Lesser Peace and the Most Great Peace confounds Bahá'ís, and was the topic of many deepening discussions during my period of fieldwork. The concept arises from a statement from 'Abdu'l-Bahá concerning stages in the unfolding unity of the human race. He said that the "unity of nations" will "in this century be securely established" ('Abdu'l-Bahá 1978, 32).[5] It is this vague reference to the "unity of nations," which will be established in this (twentieth) century, that creates for Bahá'ís a millennial speculation. Bahá'ís believe that the "Lesser Peace" will come about as a result of the spiritual influence of Bahá'u'lláh's revelation, but not necessarily through the explicit actions of the Bahá'ís. Non-Bahá'ís, especially world leaders, will usher in the Lesser Peace before the end of the century. However, Bahá'ís, knowing the "real" cause of the inevitable national unity, are to support those groups and causes that are unknowingly bringing it about.[6]

Bahá'ís, however, are vague about what this "unity of nations" or the Lesser Peace will actually entail. Some say that it will result in actual world peace. Others say that although peace treaties will have been signed by all of the world's nations by the end of the century, the lack of racial and religious unity will continue to make some warfare unavoidable. One introductory book on the Bahá'í Faith says this about the Lesser Peace:

> In the light of various statements in the Bahá'í Writings, it would
> probably be accurate to say that this second stage [after an initial stage
> of social breakdown] is seen as the permanent cessation of war rather
> than as a positive and complete global peace. The Lesser Peace is a term
> used to describe a political peace, which would be concluded by the
> nations of the world through international agreement. The fundamental
> feature of the Lesser Peace is the establishment of international security
> safeguards to prevent the recurrence of war among nations. (Hatcher
> and Martin 1985, 139)

Bahá'ís look upon the fall of communism in the former Soviet Union,[7] the peace treaties signed between Israel and Arab nations, the cease-fire between Catholics and Protestants in Ireland, and the democratization of South Africa as stages in the unfolding of the Lesser Peace.

Thus, Bahá'ís see themselves working in concert with other "new world order thinkers" to bring about the Lesser Peace. However, they see the Most Great Peace and the establishment of the long-awaited Kingdom of God as the result of exclusively Bahá'í efforts. Therefore, the boundaries between Bahá'ís and non-Bahá'ís shift: quite permeable when working for the Lesser Peace with like-minded groups, more solid and exclusive when considering long-term solutions to humanity's problems (which Bahá'ís consider to be nothing short of the universal adoption of the Bahá'í Faith and the establishment of a world commonwealth based on the Bahá'í Administrative Order—see Hofman 1982). The erection of the foundation of world order is, for Bahá'ís, a privilege in which only they can participate (especially evidenced by the fact that non-Bahá'ís are not allowed to contribute money to any Bahá'í project). It is the belief in Bahá'u'lláh's World Order as the exact cure for global disunity that prevents the otherwise inclusive Bahá'ís from allowing non-Bahá'ís to influence their particular system of global reconstruction.[8]

Sanctions in the Bahá'í Faith: Internal Boundaries

LOSS OF ADMINISTRATIVE RIGHTS

The most obvious boundaries between the Bahá'í and non-Bahá'í social worlds are the various laws Bahá'ís must follow as part of their Covenant with Bahá'u'lláh. Bahá'ís frequently divide their laws into those that are spiritual (personal) and those that are social (and therefore under the authority of the LSA). Personal laws include the daily obligatory prayers, fasting, and giving to the various Bahá'í funds. Compliance with these laws, Bahá'ís say, is between the individual and God. Those Bahá'ís who refuse to follow them are harming only themselves (since the laws are a source of spiritual protection), but not the Bahá'í Faith itself.

However, refusal to follow the social laws—laws of marriage and divorce, the prohibition of the consumption of alcohol or drugs, the prohibition of sex outside of marriage—harms not only the individual, but the image of the Bahá'í Faith as well. Bahá'ís believe that these laws are the foundation for future world order, and that violating them threatens the reputation of their faith and retards the development of the social order they are meant to secure. If an individual shows no willingness to correct unlawful behavior or actions, the LSA may petition the NSA to remove that individual's "administrative rights." This means that the sanctioned individual can no longer vote in Bahá'í elections, give to Bahá'í Funds, or participate in administrative processes or consultation (thus effectively ending one's attendance at the Nineteen-Day Feasts). This gives the NSA significant enforcement authority, a nearly ideal-typical example of Etzioni's (1961) "normative compliance mechanism."[9]

For example, under Bahá'í law, a couple wanting a divorce must separate for one full year (called the "year of patience") and attempt to reconcile. If this is unsuccessful, then the LSA may grant them a divorce. During fieldwork, I heard about one Bahá'í couple undergoing a year of patience, during which time the woman remarried. Since she had not waited until the divorce was granted by her LSA, her administrative rights were removed by the NSA.

To inform the whole American community of the removal of individuals' rights, and to advise local communities that those particular individuals cannot attend Nineteen-Day Feast anywhere in the United States, the NSA prints their names in *The American Bahá'í*, the organization's monthly newsletter. This places a social as well as a spiritual and administrative stigma upon the individuals concerned.[10]

Bahá'ís point out, however, that these sanctions are not quickly or carelessly applied. Bahá'í Writings emphasize that the Administrative Order must perform pastoral functions in slowly integrating new or wayward Bahá'ís into the community:

> [I]t would be most unwise, and unfair to those who apply for membership in the Community to require that they should at first accept all the laws of the Faith. Such a requirement would be impossible to carry out as there are many laws in the 'Aqdas' with which even the well-confirmed and long-standing believers are not yet familiar. As you rightly point out the process of becoming a Bahá'í is an evolutionary one, and requires considerable time, and sustained effort on the part of the new believer. (Hornby 1983, 344)

One man who was struggling with drug and alcohol addiction when he joined the Atlanta Bahá'í community told me he was grateful for the "support and love" he got from the LSA. He said: "They didn't come down real hard on me. They helped me find help and slowly exposed me to the laws." He went on to say that LSA members let him ask as many questions as he needed to, so that he would understand the importance of complying with Bahá'í law.

COVENANT-BREAKING

A far more serious boundary within the Bahá'í religion is the division between Bahá'ís and "Covenant-Breakers." Covenant-Breakers are those who are "immediately expel[led] from the faith" because they are "deemed to be deliberately attempting to subvert the unity of the community. The test [of faithfulness] is to determine the individual's attitude toward the central institutions established in the Covenant of Bahá'u'lláh" (Hatcher and Martin 1985, 190). Instead of merely breaking the laws of Bahá'u'lláh, a Covenant-Breaker refuses to acknowledge the Administrative Order's authority to uphold those laws, or challenges the legitimate succession of authority in the Bahá'í Faith. The latter problem is exemplified by the widespread Covenant-Breaking after the death of Bahá'u'lláh, 'Abdu'l-Bahá, and Shoghi Effendi (for a brief account, see appendix C. See also Stockman 1985; Taherzadeh 1992; Effendi 1995). One Bahá'í source said: "'Abdu'l-Bahá made it clear that he was not speaking here of differences of opinion or failures in personal behavior, but rather of deliberate efforts to create a schism by denying the authority established in the Bahá'í writings. He termed one who does this a 'covenant-breaker'" (Hatcher and Martin 1985, 190).

At present the authority to expel or excommunicate someone from the Bahá'í Faith rests with the UHJ and the Hands of the Cause of God. If an individual refuses to repent and acknowledge the legitimate authority of the Administrative Order, and thereby seeks to disunify the Bahá'í community, he/she is declared a Covenant-Breaker, is shunned by the entire global community, and is no longer considered a Bahá'í by the authorities of the faith.[11] No contact at all is permitted between Bahá'ís and Covenant-Breakers, nor should any Bahá'í read literature disseminated by Covenant-Breakers. The designation of Covenant-Breaking is the sociological mechanism by which the Bahá'í Faith seeks to avoid schism. Elements that might prove disunifying to the community are cast out, and the mass of loyal believers are completely forbidden any contact with the individual(s) attempting to subvert legitimate authority.

Taherzadeh (1992) says that the reason other religions of the world have split up into divisive sects is because of the lack of a written Covenant providing for the transfer of authority after the death of the founder, as well as the lack of powerful mechanisms to expel those who do not abide by that Covenant. Bahá'ís learn, then, that part of what presumably distinguishes them from other world religious communities is the existence of legal documents written personally by the Manifestation of God (Bahá'u'lláh) which have provided for such transfer, and have established penalties for those who break this Covenant. Bahá'ís often speak with pride of the purported absence of viable schism in their 150–year history, despite their faith's global reach and rapid growth.[12]

What Bahá'ís are referring to is the inability of any Covenant-Breaker thus far to establish a viable alternative organization. Although there have been schisms, none of the breakaway groups have grown substantially, and most have died off with the death of their leaders. This is probably due to their shunning at the hands of the mass of loyal Bahá'ís. Bahá'ís are encouraged to carry their Bahá'í membership card when traveling; especially if they travel overseas, they are also encouraged to take with them a letter of credentials from their National

Assembly, indicating their status as a Bahá'í in good standing with full administrative rights. In addition to guaranteeing the individual Bahá'í the right to participate in community activities, this helps protect Bahá'í institutions against
infiltration and disruption by Covenant-Breakers. At a Sunday morning deepening I attended at the Atlanta Bahá'í Center, a man who was in town from
Holland came to the Center to meet other Bahá'ís. He was greeted cordially,
and without being asked he produced a letter from his National Assembly giving proof of his good standing within the Bahá'í community. Another young
Bahá'í I interviewed said that when he began attending the University of Chicago recently, he was not permitted to attend Feast until he got his membership officially transferred from the local community in Atlanta to his new LSA
in Chicago. He said Bahá'ís in Chicago were particularly careful because there
are a few Covenant-Breakers in the Chicago area.

The sociological process of declaring someone a Covenant-Breaker, and subsequently shunning him or her, is given spiritual significance. Taherzadeh writes:

> Those who are expelled from the Faith as Covenant-breakers are left to
> their own devices. The believers will never oppose them in their
> activities and they are left free to continue their actions against the
> Cause of God. But the history of the Faith demonstrates that by their
> very opposition to the Centre of the Faith they sow the seeds of their
> own extinction, and after a while fade away ignominiously. Their
> position is like that of a branch once it is cut off from the tree. At first it
> is green and appears to have some life, but as it has no root, it will
> inevitably wither and die. (1992, 257)

One longtime Bahá'í I interviewed said that her good friend had been declared a Covenant-Breaker. She cut off contact with this person, and although
it had been a painful experience, she felt that her faith was more important.
Another Bahá'í told me he knew of a Bahá'í who had read some of the
anti-Bahá'í material written by Covenant-Breakers. Apparently, his friend's faith
was shaken, so vitriolic was the Covenant-Breaker's attitude toward the Bahá'ís.
During my fieldwork at the Second Bahá'í World Congress in New York City, I
was sitting with a group of Bahá'ís in a café. We were talking about the day's
events at the Congress, and one woman in our group was reading the *New York
Times*. Suddenly, she threw the paper to the table, distraught, and said that
Covenant-Breakers had placed an advertisement in the newspaper. When others went to pick up the paper to look at the ad, she said that they should not
even look at it, so polluted was its message. The announcement read:

THE BAHÁ'Í FAITH MUST HAVE A *LIVING* GUARDIAN. In her
Maxwell notes, Ruhiyyih Khanum, wife of the first Guardian, quotes

him as saying: "It is the Guardian's responsibility to prevent the International House of Justice from abrogating any of the laws of the Aqdas. . . . " Thus, the Bahá'í Faith *must* have a *living* Guardian. For more information on the continuing Guardianship, write: The Mother Bahá'í Council of the US in Roswell, New Mexico. (*New York Times*, 23 November 1992, B2)[13]

This ad was the subject of speculation for the remainder of the conference. Shoghi Effendi, "Guardian" of the Bahá'í Faith, died in 1957 without naming a successor (see appendix B). The UHJ, upon examining the issue in 1963 after its initial election, concluded that they did not possess the authority to name a second Guardian after Shoghi Effendi, leaving the UHJ as the sole authority in the Bahá'í world. Much of the Covenant-Breaking that has taken place in the last forty years involves those who disagree with the UHJ's conclusion and demand the appointment of a successor Guardian (or in the case of many, appoint themselves Guardian—see Taherzadeh 1992).

These anecdotes are consistent with what Piff and Warburg report about the prevalence of rumor in the Bahá'í community as it relates to boundary maintenance in the face of Covenant-Breaking. They said that "the unofficial oral discourse of the Bahá'í community elaborates and amplifies elements of the covenant doctrine, and provides a medium through which a community sense of the importance of this doctrine is reinforced" that contributes to "the control of community attitudes and protection of community boundaries" (1998, 66–67). Piff and Warburg describe the prevalence a "spiritual disease metaphor" in Bahá'í tales about Covenant-Breakers, stories also rife with anecdotes about the character defects, sexual deviance, cowardice, and preoccupation with evil surrounding these ostracized Bahá'ís.[14] For a Bahá'í, there can be no worse action than one for which the UHJ declares the sinner a Covenant-Breaker. Piff and Warburg conclude: "Such lore is aimed not at apostates or enemies, but at the faithful. It represents an attempt to post warnings at the boundaries of the community and to suggest the dangers of straying outside or crossing them" (1998, 77).

Regardless of the sociological efficacy of shunning Covenant-Breakers as a means of maintaining ideological unity within Bahá'í institutions, Bahá'ís *themselves* take seriously the potential spiritual hazards that supposedly result from interaction with excommunicated former believers. It is not known whether the presence of Covenant-Breakers in a community heightens the community's sense of internal unity; during my fieldwork, no Atlanta Bahá'í community faced this issue. However, the fear of falling outside the protection of the Covenant if declared a Covenant-Breaker would, presumably, promote ideological unity (see Coser 1956; Simmel 1955).

Atlanta Bahá'ís and Boundaries

Having explored the doctrinal issues of who is a Bahá'í, the distinctions Bahá'ís make between themselves and non-Bahá'ís, and the internal sanctions of the Bahá'í Faith, we turn to the issue of how boundaries are expressed in the Atlanta community. Survey respondents were first asked to think of their five closest friends, and to indicate how many of them were Bahá'ís. As shown in table 6.1, the modal category is three friends. Married respondents were also asked if their spouse was a Bahá'í; nearly 78 percent said yes. Bahá'ís are predominantly married to members of their own faith, but on average they have as many close friends inside as outside the Bahá'í Faith.[15]

Bahá'í scripture exhorts members to "consort with the followers of all religions in a spirit of friendliness and fellowship" (Bahá'u'lláh 1976, 95). One formal way to measure this is to ask Bahá'ís if they think it is "important for me as a Bahá'í to attend worship services of other religious faiths." From table 6.1, we see that nearly one-half of respondents disagree or strongly disagree, with the rest divided nearly equally between "agree" and "not sure." Another question asked how often respondents read the holy books of other religions (i.e., the Bible or Qur'án). Results indicate that although Bahá'ís are encouraged to read and learn about other religions (especially when preparing to teach others about the prophetic connections between all the world's faiths and their own), it is not very common.[16] Nearly 70 percent of Atlanta Bahá'ís reported reading either the Qur'án or Bible or other religious scripture less often than monthly.[17] These two variables (i.e., agreement with the importance of attending worship services of other religious faiths, and frequency of reading non-Bahá'í scripture) tell us something about the ways Bahá'ís understand the "oneness of religion," one of the central tenets of their faith. Survey results indicate that there is modest interest in learning about and interacting with non-Bahá'í religious groups, but that the longer one has been a Bahá'í, the less likely one is to read non-Bahá'í scripture or attend non-Bahá'í worship services.

Finally, Bahá'ís were asked whether or not they agreed with the statement, "Bahá'ís should cooperate with other religious and secular groups who have similar interests and goals as the Bahá'ís." As can be seen in table 6.1, there is almost no disagreement on this item; more than 95 percent of the respondents either agree or strongly agree. This probably reflects the fact that the Bahá'ís, who are still relatively unknown in the pluralistic religious marketplace of the United States, consciously seek coalitions with other groups to promote their ideals. During my fieldwork, I frequently heard Bahá'ís say, "That group is very Bahá'í-like," "They are almost Bahá'í," or "They are really Bahá'í, but they just do not know it." Forming coalitions with non-Bahá'í groups also serves as a good marketing strategy to help legitimize the Bahá'í Faith as a world religion on a

Table 6.1
Personal characteristics of Atlanta Bahá'ís

	None	One	Two	Three	Four	Five
Number of close friends who are Bahá'ís	12.1	14.2	15.0	25.8	14.6	18.3%

					Yes	No
If you are married, is your spouse a Bahá'í?					77.6	22.4

	1	2	3	4	5[a]
It is important to me as a Bahá'í to attend worship services of other religious faiths.	5.5	21.9	24.1	40.9	7.6
Bahá'ís should cooperate with other groups who have similar goals.	62.9	32.9	3.8	0.4	0.0

	Daily	Weekly	Monthly	Less often
How often to you read from the scripture of other religious faiths?	4.2	10.2	15.7	69.9

[a] 1 =strongly agree, 2 = agree, 3 = unsure, 4 = disagree, 5 = strongly disagree

par with the others, and not some "new age cult," as Bahá'ís feel they are often portrayed.

Tests of statistical association were used to see if a relationship exists between measures of social boundaries between the Bahá'í and non-Bahá'í world[18] and characteristics of Bahá'ís themselves. The strongest and most consistent finding was that the longer one had been a Bahá'í, the more likely one was to have erected barriers between the Bahá'í and non-Bahá'í worlds. In other words, one's intimate relationships (more likely to be married to a Bahá'í spouse, and more likely to have mostly Bahá'í close friends) tend to become more Bahá'í-centered the longer one has been a member of the religion. A similar relationship exists between length of membership and openness to other religions: respondents' worldviews became more exclusively Bahá'í-centered the longer they had been a declared believer (i.e., they were less likely to attend non-Bahá'í religious services and less likely to read non-Bahá'í scripture).[19]

This relationship between the strength of the boundaries dividing the Bahá'í and non-Bahá'í world and length of membership may be a result of the way the Bahá'í Faith is introduced to seekers. Initially, the universal character of the religion is heavily emphasized—the oneness of religions, the unity of the spiritual messages of all religions, the prophetic continuity linking Jesus, Bahá'u'lláh, and other religious figures. This is what attracts many people to the Bahá'í Faith in the first place (see chapter 2, table 2.3). However, members become more and more socialized over the years, not only into a Bahá'í worldview, but also into the *practice* of the Bahá'í Faith (as seen in chapter 5). As belief in the legitimacy of the authority claimed by Bahá'í institutions grows (recognition of authority is significantly related to length of membership), the symbolic boundaries between one's faith and other traditions become more solid. One possible conclusion is that the issue of the oneness of religion becomes less central to a Bahá'í's identity over time as one is deepened through personal and collective ritual. What might therefore become more important is a growing recognition of the global mission supposedly bestowed upon Bahá'ís by Bahá'u'lláh to construct the Kingdom of God. Bahá'í identity may shift its focus from "oneness of religion" to "unique mission," thereby strengthening the symbolic boundaries the longer one is an active Bahá'í. This study cannot confirm this speculation, but the issue deserves greater attention in the future.

There is also a strong association between marriage to a Bahá'í spouse and the exclusiveness of one's Bahá'í relationships. Marriage to a Bahá'í makes one much less likely to maintain friends outside of the Bahá'í Faith, or to agree that Bahá'ís should seek out contacts with non-Bahá'í groups. In other words, marriage to a Bahá'í creates a more insular home environment. Bahá'í activities are more likely to be held in the home, observance of Bahá'í Holy Days can be a family celebration, and private devotions (such as prayer, fasting, and scripture reading) are mutually supported by both partners. This relationship reinforces one's Bahá'í identity and solidifies the boundaries between Bahá'ís and the "outside" world.

This significant statistical association is not significant for the question about cooperating with other groups with similar goals. In other words, longtime Bahá'ís are just as likely to agree with seeking out relationships with like-minded groups as new converts. This is probably due to the fact that most Bahá'ís would agree that the Bahá'í Faith, which is still relatively unknown in U.S. society, gains legitimacy by forming partnerships on certain issues with established groups that have name recognition.

Although the length of membership in the Bahá'í Faith is significantly related to the symbolic and behavioral boundaries constructed between the Bahá'í and non-Bahá'í world, few other characteristics are. As has been true throughout this research, an individual's demographic characteristics are not related to these measures of boundaries with the non-Bahá'í world. Race, sex, occupation, income, and education were all found to have no relation to the likelihood of one's personal relationships being exclusively or predominantly within Bahá'í institutions.

NEGOTIATING BAHÁ'Í BOUNDARIES IN ATLANTA

It is instructive to mention one incident from my fieldwork that brings into focus the boundary tensions experienced by a religious group with universal values. Bahá'í hospitality extends to all individuals and groups who want to dialogue about religion and its purpose for humankind. This hospitality is also extended to those of other religions who are at times vocal about their own religious loyalties, even those who disagree with Bahá'í principles. It is not unusual for Jews, Christians, Muslims, or Hebrew Israelites[20] (who meet across the street from the Bahá'í Center) to join the meetings. However, this universal acceptance has limits. For a two- or three-month period during my fieldwork a man frequented the Atlanta Bahá'í Center not only to learn about the Bahá'ís, but to prove them wrong. He had started his own religious/nonprofit corporation, and saw himself as someone who would set the Bahá'ís straight. He often appeared at the Center in priestly garb, once even wearing an admiral's uniform, complete with a sword and plumed hat.

He would frequently take issue with Bahá'í teachings. This was generally not a problem for Bahá'ís who attended the deepening, whose own scripture encourages the independent investigation of the truth. He did become a problem when he began asserting that the Bahá'ís were interpreting their own teaching incorrectly, and that he would provide the "true" interpretation.

Eventually, his presence became disruptive not only to the Bahá'ís—who tend to be long-suffering toward those with nontraditional religious proclivities—but also to "seekers" who earnestly wanted to learn more about the Bahá'í Faith. This man began to abuse members of the deepening class—putting down their ideas, asserting his own as superior, and finally declaring himself to be a prophet. Bahá'ís later acknowledged that this person was not only rude, but probably psychologically troubled, and was not necessarily acting with malice.

Over a period of several weeks, longtime seekers stopped showing up, and during one tense meeting a long-standing member of the Atlanta community left in tears, saying later that while her Bahá'í Faith required her to love everyone, she did not have to put up with someone berating her faith to her face. As things came to a head, the disruption was made known to the Atlanta LSA, who finally decided to ask this person to never return to the Center. Some Bahá'ís told me later that this event was hard for them to deal with. The Bahá'í Faith is about the oneness of humanity, some said, and should be inclusive of all religions, races, nationalities, and perspectives. But others countered with the fact that Bahá'í scripture supports the removal of elements in the community that lead to disunity (such as the expulsion of Covenant-Breakers discussed above). This gentleman never did come back, and regular attendees of the Sunday morning deepening class entered a period of reflection on how they might better handle a similar situation in the future. Some said it was inevitable that as the Bahá'í Faith grew, and possibly became a threat to the religious status quo, others would consciously disrupt Bahá'í gatherings. Some chose to look upon the episode as a learning experience. A consensus was reached that when "internal" unity is threatened, then disruptive "external" elements should be excluded. This conclusion was legitimated by looking for guidance in Bahá'í scripture.

In a way, this incident illustrates the flexible nature of the Bahá'í/non-Bahá'í boundary. Bahá'ís are willing to accommodate "seekers," even those opposed to Bahá'í ideas. However, when the non-Bahá'í influence threatens internal unity, Bahá'ís are more than willing to shore up their boundaries, in order to maintain the integrity of their faith.

Summary

This chapter has shown that Bahá'í boundaries are real, but porous. There is openness to personal ideological diversity; however, it is when individuals begin to undermine the basis of legitimate authority in the Administrative Order that the most serious sanctions are imposed. Over time, membership has become formalized, following the general pattern of rationalization institutionalized since Shoghi Effendi's tenure. One example of this can be seen in Shoghi Effendi's insistence, toward the end of his ministry, that upon becoming declared believers Bahá'ís should withdraw their membership from their church or other previous religious organization.[21]

Several levels of boundary maintenance exist within the Bahá'í community. The distinction Bahá'ís make between the "old world order" and the "new world order" of Bahá'u'lláh becomes sharper the longer one has been a practicing member. As one becomes more socialized through Bahá'í rituals over time, the issue of the common themes found in all religions receives less attention, and the special mission Bahá'ís believe they have becomes more salient (at least this is one possible interpretation of the survey data). Over time, one's Bahá'í identity alters, solidifying the boundaries between the Bahá'í and non-Bahá'í world.

Bahá'ís also draw distinctions among themselves. Those Bahá'ís in good standing are differentiated from those who have lost their administrative rights. These distinctions are not permanent, however; with approval from the NSA, individuals can regain their administrative rights. The more serious divisions occur between the faithful and "Covenant-Breakers," who repudiate the legitimate authority of the Administrative Order. This distinction, theologically, is the closest Bahá'í parallel to the Christian distinction between the "saved" and the "damned." For a Bahá'í, it is worse to be declared a Covenant-Breaker than to never have become a Bahá'í.

The declaration of a Bahá'í as a Covenant-Breaker is the sociological mechanism intended to prevent schism. Bahá'ís allow great latitude in personal belief, as long as there is no flagrant violation of Bahá'í law. The Administrative Order takes no action if a Bahá'í refuses to give to Bahá'í Funds, refuses to pray, or refuses to attend the Nineteen-Day Feast. However, if distrust is fomented toward the authority of the Administrative Order, and this divisive behavior is not discontinued, then preserving the solidarity of the community necessitates expulsion of the offender. The Covenant-Breaker is shunned by the remaining Bahá'ís, making it difficult for him or her to gain a following.

In part, the flexibility of Bahá'ís' identity as situated universalists, and the boundaries they erect between themselves and non-Bahá'ís, are facilitated by Bahá'í theology. Theoretically, the principle of the oneness of religion prevents Bahá'ís from declaring all other religions "wrong"[22]; the vagueness of how and when the old world order will crumble, to be replaced by Bahá'u'lláh's new world order, promotes a long-term, patient perspective on social change; and partnerships with like-minded groups to help usher in the Lesser Peace keep Bahá'ís integrated into the wider society. Yet Bahá'ís do believe that their global ideology and Administrative Order is the only correct solution to humanity's problems. Thus, the relationship between Bahá'ís and non-Bahá'ís is paradoxically both inclusive and exclusive, creating tensions in the ways Bahá'ís present themselves to the wider public (see chapter 7).

Bahá'ís resolve apparent contradictions in their religion by relying on the guidance and authority of their Universal House of Justice (see chapter 4). Most individual Bahá'ís are unclear as to how and when the Most Great Peace will come about. Nor are they clear how Bahá'í ideals and institutions will revolutionize society when Bahá'ís are forbidden from engaging in political activity. All most Bahá'ís can do to resolve these ambiguities and seeming contradictions is to turn to what they believe is their source of infallible guidance on how the Bahá'í World Order will evolve.

Chapter 7

Teaching the Bahá'í Faith

*Let us arise to teach His Cause with righteousness,
conviction, understanding and vigor. Let this be the
paramount and urgent duty of every Bahá'í. Let us make it
the dominating passion of our life. Let us scatter to the
uttermost corners of the earth.*

Shoghi Effendi, *Bahá'í Administration*

As a global religious movement, the Bahá'í Faith aspires to remake world civilization according to the principles set out in its sacred texts. For this global aspiration to become a reality, the Bahá'ís must establish their faith as a model of world order and communicate its message to the world at large. Previous chapters on organization, authority, and ritual conveyed the substance of the Bahá'í Faith's self-directed institutional efforts; this chapter focuses on the way it reaches out to the world. Specifically, it shows how the universality of the religion is reflected in both the method and the substance of its teaching efforts.[1] Teaching does more than spread the message of global unity; it also reinforces the internal cohesion of the community, and fortifies a Bahá'í's global identity as a situated universalist. The practice of teaching also demonstrates the distinct Bahá'í approach to realizing their vision of the Kingdom of God. For Bahá'ís, such "world mastery" (cf. Weber 1922) cannot be a matter of rational control, forcefully imposed; rather, it takes the form of spiritual transformation through rational persuasion. Teaching is a demonstration in the public arena of a Bahá'í's situated universalist identity: a universal message (from a person Bahá'ís consider the "promised one" fulfilling the prophesies of all the world's religions) coordinated throughout the world by the Bahá'í World Center, but disseminated by Bahá'ís to their local communities.

The Importance of Teaching for Bahá'ís

Teaching is the primary focus of all Bahá'í institutional and personal labors. Bahá'ís realize that if their values and institutions are to have any impact on the development of a global civilization, they must communicate their message to the world. Bahá'ís engage in such communication according to rational, systematic plans for growth and development—"Teaching Plans." Shoghi Effendi crafted the first of these plans in 1937. Following Effendi's example, the UHJ has continued to promulgate plans that set goals for later stages in the spread of the Bahá'í Faith. These plans are a crucial part of the "spiritual conquest of the planet,"[2] and are based on 'Abdu'l-Bahá's (1993) *Tablets of the Divine Plan*, fourteen letters written in 1916 and 1917 to Bahá'ís in the United States and Canada. North American Bahá'ís believe that by adopting and executing teaching plans modeled after *Tablets of the Divine Plan*, they will assist in the growth of the Administrative Order and the global evolution of their faith (discussed in detail below). Teaching according to plan has become the hallmark of Bahá'ís' rationalized (Weber 1922, 1946) relations with the world.[3]

"Teaching the Faith" is socially constructed as a sacred duty for all Bahá'ís. Shoghi Effendi said in a letter: "We should therefore not sit idle; otherwise we would be failing in carrying out our sacred duty. Bahá'u'lláh has not given us His teachings to treasure them and hide them for our personal delight and pleasure. He gave them to us that we may pass them from mouth to mouth until all the world becomes familiar with them and enjoys their blessings and uplifting influence" (quoted in Hornby 1983, 586). Effendi counseled Bahá'ís to memorize passages from the Writings, since the words of the Manifestation, he said, have their greatest impact in their pure form, unencumbered by individual interpretation. Thus, often Bahá'ís will make efforts to memorize prayers and passages from scripture. Bahá'ís who have memorized large sections of the Writings, and can quote verbatim during Firesides or deepenings, have considerable status within the community.

Bahá'í Writings teach Bahá'ís that the study of their scripture will "attract" individuals to them who are interested in hearing the Bahá'í message. Effendi told believers that "success" in teaching depends not on one's social position, but on "to what degree we live the Bahá'í life, and how much we long to share this Message with others. When we have these characteristics, we are sure, if we search, to find receptive souls" (quoted in Hornby 1983, 586). Thus, Bahá'ís seek to transform their own character according to Bahá'í Writings not only for their own personal spiritual growth, but also to improve their ability to communicate their message to others.

While teaching is a consecrated duty enjoined upon all Bahá'ís, proselytizing is strictly forbidden—although Bahá'ís admit the line between merely teaching and proselytizing is often unclear.[4] Bahá'í scripture gives guidance to adherents as to how they should spread their message. For example, Bahá'u'lláh told his followers:

Consort with all men, O people of Bahá, in a spirit of friendliness and
fellowship. If ye be aware of a certain truth, if ye possess a jewel, of
which others are deprived, share it with them in a language of utmost
kindliness and good-will. If it be accepted, if it fulfill its purpose, your
object is attained. If any one should refuse it, leave him unto himself,
and beseech God to guide him. Beware lest ye deal unkindly with him.
(1976, 289)[5]

The prohibition against proselytizing requires the Bahá'í teacher to be in
tune with the receptivity of the individual being taught, as well as to achieve a
level of spirituality characterized by humility and respect. 'Abdu'l-Bahá also counseled Bahá'ís never to get into arguments about religion when teaching their
faith: "Do not argue with anyone, and be wary of disputation. Speak out the
truth. If your hearer accepteth it, the aim is achieved. If he be obdurate, you
should leave him to himself, and place your trust in God" (Universal House of
Justice 1977, 13). Even so, Bahá'ís themselves confess that they are at times unsure
where the line is between teaching and proselytizing. A nurse I interviewed said:

I work real hard to mention the Faith to people when people bring
religion up, but I always feel self-conscious. And then I realize on some
level, that seems to be an affront to God. . . . [I] shouldn't feel
self-conscious about that. I think that the point is to sort out in your
own head when you're proselytizing, and when you're actually doing it
with a pure heart.

His wife, a professor, added: "I don't know [where that line is]. Because you're
supposed to teach with no goal. You're supposed to teach out of the love of God,
not because you want them to become a Bahá'í. If I could figure that out."
    Another woman who has been a Bahá'í for twenty-five years said she is grate-
ful to the person who had the courage to first tell her about this religion, but
one needs to be careful of badgering people into hearing about Bahá'u'lláh:

I enjoy one-on-one teaching, enjoy firesides, and interacting with
people as friends. Whoever crosses my path will hear about the Faith,
but it's up to them to decide. 'Abdu'l-Bahá said that real teaching was to
live the life, live the life, live the life. That you can tell a person, but
then you leave them with it. If it gets into some debate or some challenge, you wear someone down, then you are not teaching, you're
proselytizing. If I feel a person stops asking questions [then it is
proselytizing].

THE THREE YEAR PLAN

The beginning of my fieldwork for this study coincided with the inception of
the Three Year Plan throughout the Bahá'í world. This was the eighth teaching

plan under which the Bahá'í Faith has grown and expanded (see note 3 to this chapter) since Shoghi Effendi's leadership. As mentioned earlier, the focus of the Plan for Bahá'ís individually and collectively was summarized in the UHJ's 1993 Ridván message: "The new Plan revolves around a triple-theme: enhancing the vitality of the faith of individual believers, greatly developing the human resources of the Cause, and fostering the proper functioning of local and national institutions" (quoted from a pamphlet entitled "The Three Year Plan" distributed by the Bahá'í National Teaching Committee, 1993). With guidance from the international level of the Administrative Order, the world's 188 NSAs formulate more specific goals for their jurisdictions; local assemblies in turn use these as blueprints to help plan local activity. Many individuals also create their own personal goals for the Three Year Plan (46 percent of Atlanta survey respondents indicated that they had done so), thus connecting personalized teaching efforts with direction provided by the Bahá'í Faith's highest authority. Thus, all levels of the Bahá'í ecclesiastical structure participate in what is believed to be divinely-inspired plans from the UHJ for the expansion of the Administrative Order and the dissemination of the Bahá'í message. This is a principal mechanism by which Bahá'í ideology and institutional processes link the local with the global, and it reinforces the individual's identity as a situated universalist.

The NSA of the United States said this in its April 1993 Ridván message concerning the goals for the U.S. Bahá'í community during the Three Year Plan:

> The Faith is emerging from obscurity and society, desperate for solutions to its intractable problems, is more willing to hear the truths proclaimed by [Bahá'u'lláh]. . . . Our own country is beset with problems to which it has failed to find solutions. Rampant materialism, the degeneration of morals, economic injustice, crime, and worst of all, inveterate racism, threaten the very fabric of American society. However, our capacity to influence the course of events, [and] to provide solutions . . . is gravely limited by the smallness of our numbers. . . . A large increase in the numbers of avowed adherents of the Faith is therefore imperative if we, Bahá'ís, are to fulfill our spiritual destiny. (*The American Bahá'í* 24, no. 7: 1)

The NSA went on to outline goals of the U.S. Bahá'í community for the next three years, which included greater study of Bahá'í scripture by individuals, more teaching activity, more racial unity events, expansion of Bahá'í educational classes for children, and a strengthening of the financial situation of the national community.[6] Two goals relate to explicitly global efforts at expansion: the NSA seeks closer ties to other national Bahá'í communities, and encourages individuals to practice "global citizenship" by traveling or living in another country expressly for Bahá'í evangelization. Progress toward those goals that can be measured quantitatively was tabulated in *The American Bahá'í* monthly to allow the whole community to follow its progress.

Support for these goals varies widely. Whereas about one-half of Atlanta Bahá'ís report setting individual goals for themselves based on the provisions of the Three Year Plan, only a fraction of the LSAs in the Atlanta area created local goals based on the UHJ or NSA messages (based on my informal discussions with community LSA secretaries). Some communities formulated no plan; others, like the Atlanta LSA, developed a very detailed plan. The goals of the Atlanta LSA are kept on a posterboard display in the main meeting room at the Bahá'í Center. In this way, the whole community can monitor progress toward each goal (a gold star was placed next to each numerical goal as it was achieved).[7]

ENTRY BY TROOPS

The NSA is encouraging mass growth at the insistence of the UHJ. They are calling for "entry by troops,"[8] in order that a larger number of Bahá'ís, and the concomitant increased human and financial resources, can begin to exert a greater influence on the non-Bahá'í world and address society's problems. In light of this, the NSA had, during my period of fieldwork, initiated several large teaching projects throughout the nation, such as "Vision in Action" and "HEAT Wave," to facilitate LSA initiative and expand local teaching campaigns (these will be discussed further below).

The Universal House of Justice sent a message to the Bahá'í world in October 1993, saying that the period when entry by troops would improve the fortunes of the Bahá'í Faith and help it emerge from obscurity had arrived. The phrase "entry by troops" comes from a statement made by Shoghi Effendi in 1953:

> The advent of the day which . . . will witness the entry by troops of
> peoples of divers nations and races into the Bahá'í world—a day
> which . . . will be the prelude to that long-awaited hour when a mass
> conversion on the part of these same nations and races . . . will suddenly
> revolutionize the fortunes of the Faith, derange the equilibrium of the
> world, and reinforce a thousandfold the numerical strength as well as
> the material power and the spiritual authority of the Faith of
> Bahá'u'lláh. (1965, 117)

The American Bahá'í published a statement by the UHJ offering guidance on specific activities Bahá'í communities might undertake to facilitate this entry by troops. In it the UHJ notes that their religion has not and will not grow uniformly throughout the planet; that the process of active hostility and even repression by the religion's opponents is accompanied by surges in the number of believers as the principles and aims of the Bahá'í Faith become known; and that the growth of the Bahá'í Faith is directly correlated with the "suffering and tribulation, associated with the process of social decline" experienced by the world (*The American Bahá'í 25*, no. 2:1a).

Bahá'ís say that various factors identified by the UHJ will aid in the process of entry by troops, with the goal of transforming individuals, community life, and eventually the whole planet: commitment to spiritual transformation, love and unity among the believers, love of Bahá'ís for the institutions of their faith, universal participation in their faith's institutions, maintaining a balance between expansion and consolidation, and developing the Bahá'í community as a "viable model and an alternative means of social organization" (*The American Bahá'í 25*, no. 2:1a). LSAs must develop and implement strategic and flexible teaching plans in order to achieve these goals. In addition, Bahá'ís must be able to relate their principles to contemporary social and humanitarian issues, and reach "people of capacity" (community leaders and those who influence public opinion) as part of reaching the masses.

The UHJ ends their statement on entry by troops by urging Bahá'ís to engage in "goal-directed behavior," reminding believers that Shoghi Effendi promised divine assistance for those who put forth individual effort to "teach the Cause." This serves to strengthen the formal and systematic character of Bahá'í evangelization mentioned above. The goals Bahá'ís focus on most are those most easily quantified and measurable.

Emphasis on entry by troops dovetails with a "shift in the public presentation of the message of the Faith." This was articulated by a letter dated April 1994 from the National Teaching Committee (NTC) about the need for Bahá'ís to emphasize the station of Bahá'u'lláh and to explicitly invite people to join the Bahá'í Faith when teaching. This will help "emblazon the name of Bahá'u'lláh across the globe" (*The American Bahá'í 25*, no. 5:2). The letter quotes Douglas Martin, who at that time was head of the Bahá'í World Center's Office of Public Information and a member of the UHJ. He said Bahá'ís need to move beyond merely teaching the principles of the faith (such as equality of women and men, progressive revelation, race unity, the harmony of science and religion) and instead talk about Bahá'u'lláh:

> Our task is to set in motion a broad array of initiatives that can establish Bahá'u'lláh's name as a familiar and authoritative voice in human affairs. The goal in the decades ahead is to reach the point where no responsible scholar will undertake work . . . without consulting Bahá'u'lláh's teachings and the models He has constructed. . . . Before anything else, we need to determine how are we to speak of *Bahá'u'lláh Himself*. (*The American Bahá'í 25*, no. 5:2; italics in original)

The letter goes on to say that Bahá'ís should not expect receptive souls to know, prior to declaring, all the laws and teachings, or to be acquainted with minutiae of history or administrative procedure. Rather, when seekers demonstrate that they believe in the truth of Bahá'u'lláh's manifestation, the Bahá'ís should invite them to join, expecting to rapidly "consolidate" the new believer through fellowship and deepenings.

This two-pronged message from the highest authority in the Bahá'í Faith (the need for mass conversion and a shift in teaching emphasis from principles of the faith to the person of Bahá'u'lláh) appeared in the Bahá'í Newsreels and in the pages of The American Bahá'í more and more frequently throughout my period of fieldwork.[9] Some Bahá'ís I talked with, however, expressed wariness in repeating the mistakes of the past by emphasizing mass growth. This was a favorite topic of consultation at Bahá'í meetings—how to prepare for and facilitate entry by troops, without repeating the failures of an earlier period of large-scale growth. Most Bahá'ís with whom I brought up the issue said that their institutions are presently ill equipped for that kind of change and expansion, and must prepare for the inevitable "old world order" problems—drugs, teen pregnancy, spousal abuse, and so on—that a substantial influx of new Bahá'ís would bring into the "new world order" (the assumption being, of course, that there are presently few "old world order" problems within the Bahá'í community).

A visiting NSA member met with a group of Atlanta Bahá'ís in mid-1993, and told them that they need not "fear" being overrun by masses of new believers. He pointed out that the dictionary definition of a "troop" was a relatively small number: eight to twelve people. He assured the group of Bahá'ís gathered that it did not necessarily entail the enrollment of hundreds, as had been reported in India in recent years, where sometimes whole villages would convert to the Bahá'í Faith. Rather, it implied growth on a much smaller scale. But it would, he said, require a change in the status quo if the Administrative Order is to act as an agent of change in a suffering world: "The Bahá'í Faith needs greater resources, more recruits, and therefore a new level of sacrifice and commitment to teaching." It requires Bahá'ís, he said, to move out of their "comfort zones" and envision their small, familiar Bahá'í communities becoming larger and taking on more responsibilities.

Despite the thrust by the national and international bodies to promote entry by troops, there was resistance among Atlanta Bahá'ís to this shift in perspective. Some Bahá'ís I talked with saw the intensified pleas by the Administrative Order for increased converts as merely part of a "numbers game," which made them uncomfortable. One woman, a member of metro Atlanta LSAs for two decades, said of the pressure from administrative bodies to engage in extensive teaching campaigns:

> It is just a numbers game—a product of the goals set by the NSA. Right.
> And I don't always think we know why we need them. I think it's the

fact of having them that's important. Having been involved in making paper assemblies, I'm never comfortable with it. I don't feel good about it. But, who knows what the mystical reason is for it?

Her reference to "paper assemblies" alludes to the process of waging a teaching campaign right before Ridván (April 21), when Bahá'í elections are held, to ensure the creation of a new Local Spiritual Assembly, thus fulfilling a national teaching goal. Teaching efforts are intensified in a municipal area that does not have an LSA, in the hopes that there will be nine Bahá'ís residing there by election time, allowing for the creation of a new LSA. Many Bahá'ís feel that since many of the newly converted assembly members are unacquainted with administrative principle or procedure, these LSAs are part of the Administrative Order in name only.

Another longtime member of the Atlanta community said this of the call for greater teaching activity: "I've heard this all before, you know? The NSA encourages teaching, and Bahá'ís rush around, but where are all the new Bahá'ís?" He went on to admit that he is not sure what would lead to large-scale growth, and is personally not motivated by what he called the latest "teaching fad." My observation from interviews is that those most likely to express reservations about the latest "teaching campaign" are Bahá'ís who have been members of their Faith longest, and that their skepticism has its roots in the perceived lack of success in the last twenty years. Newer converts tend to exhibit considerably more enthusiasm about implied teaching success and entry by troops.

Lack of Growth in the U.S. Bahá'í Community

While the *World Christian Encyclopedia* (Barrett 1982) identified the Bahá'í Faith as the fastest growing religious group in the world during the 1970s and early 1980s, the U.S. Bahá'í community has seen only marginal growth since the early 1970s.[10] Numerically, the Bahá'í community stands at about 120,000 believers, but one NSA member estimated that only about one-half can be thought of as even remotely active, in terms of Feast attendance, teaching efforts, or contribution to any Bahá'í Funds.[11] Atlanta Bahá'ís have described to me a period twenty-five to thirty years ago of dynamic growth, involving mass conversion, where sometimes hundreds of people would "declare" at one meeting. The problem, they told me, was that these widespread teaching campaigns, carried out mostly in the rural South, were conducted by transient travel teachers who made sacrifices to come to the South from across the country for a week, a month, or several months to teach about Bahá'u'lláh. But when the campaign was over they went home, leaving the few deepened, knowledgeable indigenous Bahá'ís in the South to undertake "consolidation"—helping raw, new believers create functioning LSAs. Bahá'ís told me that mass teaching ground to a halt after the early 1970s. The American Bahá'í community has not seen dramatic growth since that period. One longtime Atlanta Bahá'í couple describe that period, when they went to live in rural Georgia as part of the mass teaching efforts in the early 1970s. The husband said this about their experience:

> People were coming down [from the north] all the time for teaching projects. They would take their two-week vacation and come down and generate a lot of excitement and then go home. Consolidation didn't have that sort of glamour and excitement and energy to it. . . . Consolidation was just nuts and bolts, it was like watching grass growing. It is a very slow, tedious, and long path. And people didn't come here on their vacation for that!

His wife added: "We just got wore out, just could not get any help. People would come down and they would want to see and meet all these wonderful new Bahá'ís but they didn't want to stay and work. And actually they were more of a burden because it felt like we were running a tourist bureau there. People wouldn't take on the burden of deepening new believers." She went on to say that the Bahá'í National Center was out of touch with who the new Bahá'ís were. The National Center expected monthly treasurer's reports from the new LSAs, but in many cases the new Bahá'ís were illiterate rural farmers. She said it took a long time to get these new Bahá'ís to understand the faith they had joined, let alone get them to participate in any of the administrative processes. In the end, she admitted, "most of the mass-taught believers dropped out."

My fieldwork uncovered three major reasons Bahá'ís give for this stagnation in growth: (1) fears about who were then becoming Bahá'ís; (2) a lack of follow-up in nurturing the new recruits; and (3) unpreparedness and immaturity of Bahá'í institutions. Several Bahá'ís said that massive growth during this period changed the demographic makeup of the Bahá'í community and created internal stresses that took time to sort out. One Bahá'í leader remembers that period:

> Because when I became a Bahá'í in the seventies there were really two groups of people becoming Bahá'ís: poor rural southern blacks and hippie college groups. They came in more significant numbers at one time than this country had ever seen folks come into the Faith before. It really changed the character of the Faith at that point in time.
>
> Q: Will that kind of growth be seen again, do you think?
>
> A: My sense is that it's right around the corner. It's really hard to predict who those groups are going to be. But they're not going to be the groups that we would expect most likely. Not universally, and I don't know if even most folks felt that way, but there was a significant group

of Bahá'ís that really weren't so sure that that was the right thing to be doing. That's why mass teaching shut down after a couple of years.

The mostly middle-class, middle-aged white Bahá'í community in Atlanta thirty years ago were unprepared, he said, for the influx of African Americans and college youth influenced by the 1960s counterculture. He went on to say that it was not only the types of people who became Bahá'ís in the sixties and seventies, but the way they did it, that threatened the demographic status quo. Before the mass growth of this period, Bahá'ís usually declared their faith in Bahá'u'lláh after a rather lengthy period of study and Fireside attendance, having slowly become socialized into a Bahá'í worldview and identity. In fact, many longtime Bahá'ís indicated that before they could declare, they had been required to read several books about the Bahá'í Faith, and then appear before the LSA and demonstrate that they understood the step they were taking, knew who Bahá'u'lláh was, and knew the basics of Bahá'í law and history. In effect, they had to pass a Bahá'í entrance exam. However, mass growth during the late 1960s and early 1970s brought with it on-the-spot declarations, especially among rural, Southern blacks—people who, upon hearing from interracial teams of travel teachers the Bahá'í claim that Christ had returned, signed their declaration card immediately, without knowing much else.

Travel teachers would return boxes full of declaration cards to the National Bahá'í Center in Wilmette, literally overloading its capacity to respond. One Atlantan who worked at the National Center shortly after mass enrollments had subsided said that they were still trying to recover. At that time, he said, the membership records were literally kept on three-by-five index cards in a shoebox, and a three- to fourfold increase in membership incapacitated the National Center staff, most of whom were volunteers.[12] Consolidation—or the formation of functioning LSAs with deepened and knowledgeable Bahá'ís—was hampered by the lack of permanent, seasoned Bahá'ís in the South, as well as the inaccessibility of many of the rural, poor, mass-taught believers, some of whom didn't even have a full street address to which the NSA could send *The American Bahá'í*.

This is the history that informs many Atlanta Bahá'ís' perception of recent calls by the national leadership for entry by troops and mass growth. While supportive of these efforts in theory, some Bahá'ís told me they would rather grow slowly than repeat the mistakes of thirty years ago. Let us now look at two of the teaching campaigns begun by the NSA in which Atlanta Bahá'ís are cooperating.

National Spiritual Assembly Teaching Campaigns

In the June 24, 1993 issue of *The American Bahá'í*, the National Teaching Committee (NTC), with the approval of the NSA, announced a plan to accomplish the numerical goals of the Three Year Plan in nineteen Gregorian months, by November 1994 (*The American Bahá'í* 24, no. 9:1)—known as "Mission 19." From that point, numerical inventories were posted in *The American Bahá'í* to keep track of Bahá'í teaching progress in the United States. Checklists were published for individuals to cut out and enumerate their own efforts in meeting the goals of the Three Year Plan ("Have you made plans to become a traveling teacher this summer?" "Have you developed a personal plan for teaching?" "Have you reported your teaching activities to the National Teaching Committee office?" "Have you supported the Bahá'í Funds this month?"—*The American Bahá'í* 24, no. 11:3). They also published a form to be mailed to the Bahá'í National Center if a Bahá'í travel-taught—asking when and where one went, and what one did to teach the Bahá'í Faith (*The American Bahá'í* 24, no. 14:3).[13]

In order to achieve the numerical goals of the Three Year Plan via Mission 19, several new initiatives were launched by the NSA and NTC during my period of fieldwork.

HEAT ("HOLD EVERYTHING AND TEACH") WAVE

HEAT Wave was a campaign, inaugurated in the August 20, 1993 issue of *The American Bahá'í*, to encourage Bahá'ís to hold Firesides in their homes. As the NTC reminded Bahá'ís, Firesides were efforts "of the believers in that area to invite their friends, neighbors, and other associates to their homes and provide a warm and friendly atmosphere in which they can learn about the Bahá'í Faith. This, in essence, is fireside teaching" (*The American Bahá'í* 24, no. 12:3). HEAT Wave was to start in Chicago, and spread out to other parts of the country each Bahá'í month, culminating with the end of Mission 19 in November 1994 on the anniversary of the birth of Bahá'u'lláh. *The American Bahá'í* article quoted from a 1955 letter from Shoghi Effendi:

> It has been found over the entire world that the most effective method
> of teaching the Faith is the fireside meeting in the home. Every Bahá'í
> as a part of his spiritual birthright, must teach, and the one avenue
> where he can do this most effectively is by inviting friends into his home
> once in nineteen days, and gradually attracting them to the
> Cause. . . . This method is far more effective than advertising in
> newspapers, public lectures, etc. (*The American Bahá'í* 24, no. 12: 3)

The American Bahá'í would then keep track of Fireside progress, providing numerical totals in each month's issue. By the time the HEAT Wave campaign got to Georgia and North and South Carolina, beginning March 21, 1994, *The American Bahá'í* printed that the NTC registered 343 reported Firesides in the HEAT Wave campaign; and 2,352 reported attendees (of which 1,134 were Bahá'ís), which resulted in fifteen new declarations (out of 1,530 new believers enrolled since the beginning of the Three Year Plan in April 1993). The Mission 19 teaching campaign succeeded in achieving and surpassing the numerical goals of three thousand homefront travel teachers, five hundred homefront pioneers, and two thousand international pioneers (although the NSA was $9.5 million short of its goal of $25 million for that Bahá'í fiscal year). At the end of Mission 19, all the teaching activity had resulted in 2,349 new believers (*The American Bahá'í* 25, no. 8:3). During the HEAT Wave campaign, I counted a 20-percent increase in the average number of Firesides held in the metro Atlanta area (based on the number of upcoming Firesides advertised in the "Trumpet," the metro Atlanta newsletter). However, no one I spoke with in the Atlanta area knew if this elevated teaching level bore any fruit in terms of new converts.

FRUIT OF THE HOLY YEAR

This national campaign of teaching, also called the Bahá'í Youth Workshops Summer Teaching Project, was sponsored by the Atlanta LSA. *The American Bahá'í* promoted it through advertisements and feature stories. Bahá'í Youth Workshops (BYWs) are conducted mostly by young Bahá'ís who teach their faith through songs, dances, and dramatic performances. BYWs began in Los Angeles in the 1970s, and have since spread throughout the United States. The Fruit of the Holy Year project (an outgrowth of the declared Holy Year in 1992 commemorating the one hundredth anniversary of Bahá'u'lláh's ascension) was to last throughout the summer. BYWs would travel-teach across the country, converging on Atlanta the week of July 30 for a mass Fireside on August 7, 1993. According to *The American Bahá'í*, "This project has the potential of emblazoning the name of Bahá'u'lláh across the country like never before" (*The American Bahá'í* 24, no. 8:15).

The Fruit of the Holy Year Project was significant for the Atlanta Bahá'í community because of all the teaching activity generated in the area, as well as the media attention generated by the large-scale activities of the concluding week. More than three hundred Bahá'í youth from fourteen different BYWs converged on Atlanta during the first week of August 1993 and presented more than fifty public performances. This resulted in seventy-five new declarants in Atlanta, as well as an estimated fifty thousand area residents being exposed to the Bahá'í Faith through the teaching work (according to *The American Bahá'í* 24, no. 13:1). *The American Bahá'í* reported that the youth performed skits, songs, and dances that communicated Bahá'í themes of the oneness of humanity, the need to eliminate all prejudices, the equality of women and men, and abstinence from violence and drugs.

Workshop members performed at various locations throughout the city, including community centers, schools and recreational parks, and at sites suggested by the Martin Luther King Jr. Center for Nonviolent Social Change, Habitat

For Humanity, Hands on Atlanta (a community-oriented service organization), and the Southern Christian Leadership Conference (which expressed interest in working with the Bahá'ís in the future). Bahá'ís were also interviewed on several radio stations in Atlanta, giving them an opportunity to explain their faith and the message of the youth workshops. In the evenings, Firesides were held by the youth at Georgia Tech University.

The Fruit of the Holy Year Project culminated in a large public Fireside at Georgia Tech on Saturday, August 7. Nearly eight hundred people were there to watch the BYWs perform their vision of race unity. Prayers were chanted in Persian and Swahili, and sung in African American gospel styles. Youth performed a dramatic presentation of how the Manifestations of God, including Moses, Jesus, Muhammad, and Bahá'u'lláh, were all, according to Bahá'í theology, persecuted for shaking up the status quo. The connection between the Bahá'í Faith's principles of racial unity and the setting of Atlanta as the cradle of the modern civil rights movement was explicitly mentioned by several speakers. The large audience, which included nearly equal numbers of whites and blacks, frequently applauded Bahá'í ideals. It is difficult to say how many of the eight hundred people in the crowd were non-Bahá'ís, but I would estimate around one-fourth. At the end of the program, thanks were offered to all the adult sponsors of the fourteen BYWs that came to Atlanta, and a proclamation was read from Atlanta Mayor Maynard Jackson congratulating the Bahá'ís for their message of racial harmony and efforts to reduce youth violence. The event ended with all fourteen BYWs on stage rapping songs with Bahá'í themes.

When Pat Steele, NTC member from suburban Atlanta, was asked about the long-term impact of this kind of large-scale teaching event for the youth, she responded that in addition to new believers being added to Bahá'í rolls, "I also think this project raised the youth to a new level of identity as Bahá'ís. . . . It also dealt with raising up a generation that is free from prejudice. In fact, this is one of the strongest and most visible ways we have of making the Bahá'í teachings on race [unity] known outside the Faith" (*The American Bahá'í* 24, no. 13: 23). She indicated that this particular teaching project was responsible for fully one-tenth of the numerical goal established by the NSA for travel teachers for the entire United States.

While the Fruit of the Holy Year is an example of a well-organized and coordinated national teaching project, interviewees indicated later that the real frustration set in when trying to do follow-up work or consolidation. While most of the seventy-five newly declared believers were in the city of Atlanta itself, many were in small communities in the suburbs which had fewer resources to incorporate new people through regular deepenings, new believers' classes, or children's classes. The consolidation work moved slowly, and it was exacerbated by the problem of trying to figure out which community some of the new declarants lived in and how to contact that particular LSA secretary. Many of those who signed their declaration cards later became inactive and were never seen again, according to one person who worked to coordinate the follow-up efforts. Part of the problem, I was told, is that while many LSAs have "teaching committees," they do not have "new believers" or "consolidation" committees.

Throughout my period of fieldwork, the National Spiritual Assembly stressed the importance of attaining the goals of the Three Year Plan, especially measurable goals related to increasing the number of new believers and ushering in entry by troops. Using militaristic language characteristic of Bahá'í discussions of teaching the non-Bahá'í world, the chairman of the NSA was quoted as saying, "This is a spiritual war, and we're on a battlefield," and calling the Bahá'ís the "best equipped army ever to engage in battle" (quoted in *The American Bahá'í* 25, no. 2:6).

Tension among Atlanta Bahá'ís about Teaching Methods

Despite some Atlanta Bahá'ís' concern about pressure for entry by troops and mass enrollments as a "numbers game," the vast majority of Bahá'ís are serious about their duty of teaching the Bahá'í Faith. Throughout my fieldwork, I found that the greatest tension within the Atlanta Bahá'í community revolved around how exactly the teaching work should be carried out. This section will briefly outline some of the main debates concerning teaching among Atlanta Bahá'ís. It shows that while Bahá'ís are unified in recognizing the importance of local teaching activity as part of communicating a universal message and building global institutions, there is significant disagreement over the methods by which it is done.

TEACHING PRINCIPLES VS. THE STATION OF BAHÁ'U'LLÁH

Bahá'ís admitted to me that they are initially cautious when they teach their faith. They want to "feel out" the receptivity of the seeker, and introduce slowly the rather complex history, theology, and scripture. Bahá'í Firesides often comprise simplified discussions of the spiritual concepts from Bahá'í ideology (especially that of progressive revelation) or the social principles espoused in Bahá'í scripture.

Bahá'ís maintain that many of their historically controversial beliefs are now widely held in U.S. society, or are at least given widespread lip service. Principles such as the equality of women and men, universal education, the establishment of a global language, and racial unity were revolutionary even in America—especially in the Deep South—at the turn of the century, when the Bahá'í Faith was first being taught. Many Bahá'ís said during interviews that upon being introduced to the Bahá'í Faith and its social principles, many people's first

response is: "Yea, well, I believe that too! Why should I become a Bahá'í?" Reciting principles that have secular endorsement in the wider culture does not
set the Bahá'í Faith apart, nor does it communicate the importance Bahá'u'lláh
has for Bahá'ís.[14]

Bahá'í leaders feel teaching work must now focus on who Bahá'u'lláh is, as
was mentioned above.[15] Bahá'u'lláh, Bahá'ís claim, is the "promised one" (UHJ
1991) of all religions, the one who will bring world peace and unity. This approach should be the focus of teaching efforts: to "emblazon the name of
Bahá'u'lláh in the hearts." To this end, the Universal House of Justice (1991)
published a document entitled simply Bahá'u'lláh, to be used as a "teaching tool"
to help acquaint others not only with the Bahá'í worldview and perspective, but
with the source of this religion in the person of Bahá'u'lláh.

Some Bahá'ís have begun to reexamine their Bibles in an effort to understand the supposed references to Bahá'u'lláh and his dispensation.[16] Books by
Bahá'í author Michael Sours, who writes on Bahá'í-Christian dialogues, have
also become popular. For example, Sours writes, when using the Bible to show
how it heralds the Bahá'í Faith and Bahá'u'lláh:

> Courteously asking Christians to support their arguments with Scripture
> shows our respect for the Bible and helps keep the discussion centered
> on the Word of God. If the Christian can provide the verses to support
> the discussion, we and the Christian can examine them to see whether
> such verses are applicable. However, when we refer to the Bible it is
> important that we do so in an appropriate spirit and with sensitivity to
> our audience. We should avoid quoting verses in an over aggressive
> manner or needlessly reciting verse numbers in a way that appears
> pompous and arrogant. The objective is to show our acceptance of the
> Bible and to discuss issues in an atmosphere of mutual inquiry. (1990,
> 38–39)

When discussing the issue of Bahá'u'lláh as the "return of Christ," Sours counsels Bahá'ís to "present Christ in a way which reflects the particular language of
the Bible that is foremost in the minds of Christians. . . . We should avoid mentioning some details too early in our discussions, for example, references to the
Manifestations Zoroaster and Buddha" (1990, 155). As part of the Three Year
Plan, frequent deepenings were held in metro Atlanta to better understand how
a Bahá'í-Christian dialogue could be facilitated.

One man I interviewed said that while he worked at the Bahá'í National
Center in Wilmette in the late 1970s, the NSA hired a public relations consulting firm to see how the Bahá'í Faith came across to the public, and how teaching work might be made more effective. He said this of the firm's observations:

> They came back and they said (this was the end of the 70s) here's what's
> happening: There are two Bahá'í Faiths here. There's one that you

present to the outside world which is very nice, great social principles, global perspective on things, you're for peace, justice. . . . You're involved with the U.N., you're doing all these good things. . . . That is the Bahá'í Faith that you present to the world. Then if you sit down with a bunch of Bahá'ís and you penetrate things a little bit, then you start talking about Bahá'u'lláh. That's where the power is. But you don't share, you don't tell the outside world about [Bahá'u'lláh]. That's your problem.

My respondent went on to say that he felt that stories about how Bahá'u'lláh transformed people's lives should be used in teaching. Bahá'ís would sometimes use "conversion stories" (both among themselves and when teaching non-Bahá'ís) as a symbol and a way of talking about the transformative power of the Bahá'í message. In the context of Atlanta and the Deep South, these stories would include Ku Klux Klan members being won over to the Bahá'í Faith.

Many Bahá'ís also emphasize that an increasingly important part of teaching involves teaching each other as Bahá'ís. As their faith emerges from obscurity, Bahá'ís told me, they will come under increasing attack from those on the Left (alarmed at the Bahá'í notion of merging church and state in a world government, for example), as well as on the Right (fundamentalists who disagree with the station Bahá'ís reserve for Bahá'u'lláh—i.e., as the return of Christ). To prepare for these attacks, Bahá'ís must deepen more—become more knowledgeable about their faith and go beyond a simple, formulaic recitation of Bahá'í principles. They must also be able to relate the Bible, Qur'án, and other holy books to the claims made in Bahá'í scripture.

The challenge Bahá'ís face in focusing their teaching efforts more on the station of Bahá'u'lláh and less on a recitation of Bahá'í principles will be exacerbated by the lack of a professionally trained clergy. A significant number of Atlanta's Bahá'ís enrolled during the heyday of mass growth (late 1960s and early 1970s), when social conditions in the Deep South, and the United States generally, made the Bahá'í principles of race unity, world peace, and the equality of women and men attractive (as the data presented in chapter 2 suggest). As more social movement organizations espouse these ideas, a shift to the person of Bahá'u'lláh will require more Bahá'ís to have greater knowledge of the theological connections between their faith and others, and better command of the details of how Bahá'u'lláh supposedly fulfills the religious prophesy of other faith traditions. This knowledge has traditionally been the purview of professional clergy. Sociological research (cf. Roberts 1995) has shown that laity in most churches are generally ignorant of even basic church doctrine. Thus, as an institution governed entirely by laity, the Bahá'í Faith faces daunting challenges regarding its teaching efforts (especially given the difficulties many Bahá'ís face in moving beyond superficialities when explaining their tradition to seekers).

NEED FOR BAHÁ'Í CENTERS VS. INTIMACY OF BELIEVERS' HOMES

Several Bahá'ís expressed the opinion that teaching in the Deep South is hindered because Bahá'ís in general do not have "churches" to which people can be invited. Seekers are often uncomfortable coming to individual Bahá'ís' homes unless there is a preexisting personal relationship, even though individual homes can convey a hospitality and intimacy hard to match in institutional buildings. In the absence of permanent buildings with "Bahá'í Center" on the door, potential seekers might be discouraged from investigating further something that initially interests them. Although there is a Bahá'í Center in Atlanta, it is not always open, and getting there is a long trip for someone from an outlying area.

The lack of "churches" is especially problematic, many African American Bahá'ís indicated to me, in trying to teach Atlanta's black population. The church is an important institution among African Americans, and is symbolically significant in terms of status and autonomy for that community (Lincoln and Mamiya 1990). Some Bahá'ís said that the lack of "churches" in the Bahá'í Faith makes declaring difficult for blacks, who have to leave an institution that guarantees some status in their community for a relatively unknown religion that meets in adherents' homes.

The importance of centers in teaching was given some validity by one of the Continental Counselors, a former Atlantan, who gave a talk at a fundraiser for a Bahá'í Center in suburban Atlanta. She said that she recently consulted with the UHJ in her role as Counselor, and was asked by them what could be done to increase the number of believers in the American South and spur teaching activity. She told the crowd that she suddenly blurted out: "We need Bahá'í Centers in the South." She reiterated the problems of consolidation in the mass teaching campaigns in the rural South in the 1960s and 1970s, and said that the problem of losing all those people could have been ameliorated by establishing Bahá'í Centers that could anchor new converts in their chosen faith. Without an LSA to organize the Nineteen-Day Feast or deepening classes, and without a regular building to call their "spiritual home," many of these converts never established a Bahá'í identity, and ended up returning to the church. She said, "We tell them to come out of their churches, but we have no church for them to go to," even if it is only a double trailer with "Bahá'í Center" painted on the front.

The acquisition of a new Bahá'í Center for the metro-Atlanta community has been a source of conflict, however. The current Bahá'í Center in downtown Atlanta has inadequate space for large gatherings, and there is not enough parking. While all agreed that the downtown center should remain as a meeting place for the Atlanta LSA and for its historical importance (see chapter 8), there was no agreement on where a new center should be purchased or built. A center located in Atlanta itself would enjoy proximity to important Atlanta cultural institutions,[17] but real estate in the city is considerably more expensive. The less expensive suburbs tended to be less racially and ethnically diverse (again, mirroring the segregated housing patterns of the city). One African American Bahá'í told me that he thought efforts to locate a new center outside the city limits was a rare illustration of "racism within the Bahá'í community." He went on to say that the fundraising committee for the new center in the suburbs mentioned above included no African Americans. This raised doubts in his mind that it would truly be a "metropolitan" center, and was a sign that Bahá'ís needed to become more unified before purchasing any real estate.

CONFLICT OVER DIVERSITY OF TEACHING METHODS

Bahá'ís employ a variety of styles when telling others about their faith. There are four primary methods of teaching Bahá'ís engage in: (1) one-to-one teaching, or informally mentioning the Bahá'í Faith to friends, family, and coworkers; (2) "street" or "mass" teaching, whereby Bahá'ís canvass a neighborhood door-to-door or approach strangers in a shopping mall to deliver their message or pass out literature; (3) Firesides, as discussed in chapter 5; and (4) mass proclamation events, involving a lecture or performance format where the public at large is invited to attend, often through mass media advertising. The NSA has stated that no method is wrong, and there are as many methods of teaching as there are Bahá'ís. It encourages a plurality of methods, as long as the integrity of the Bahá'í Faith is never compromised, and as long as one does not proselytize. The principle of unity in diversity should be upheld even in the practice of teaching, according to Bahá'í officials.

However, one of the biggest tensions within the Bahá'í community is the categorization of teaching methods as "proper" or "improper." Energetic, visible teaching activity (especially door-to-door or "mass teaching") is seen by some Bahá'ís as too aggressive and not tactful; some prefer a more personal, low-key approach. This is related to the perceived higher status that dynamic Bahá'í teachers have over those who are less public in promoting their faith. One woman who preferred a more one-to-one style put it like this:

> But there is another division, another discrimination [among
> Bahá'ís]. . . . [Those Bahá'ís who go on mass teaching trips] and yes
> maybe taught, but then six months later all these people dropped
> out. . . . People were kind of looking down on those who didn't go on
> the teaching trip, feeling they were better Bahá'ís.

Another man, a Bahá'í for only a few years, echoed this sentiment:

> I think it is fine for people who want to [go on teaching trips, or mass
> teaching]. I disagree with putting pressure on people who don't want to,
> and I disagree with there being a caste system which says that the people

who do are somehow better Bahá'ís than the people who don't. And that's endemic to the Faith . . . but I resent the heck out of it and think it is wrong. Who's to say that doing that [participating in mass teaching] is a more effective way of being a Bahá'í or a better way to be a Bahá'í than people who are bringing up their children or people who are going about their business doing the best they can?

Many Bahá'ís showed reluctance to engage in "mass teaching"—in which Bahá'ís canvas a neighborhood or shopping center, passing out pamphlets or asking people "Have you ever heard about Bahá'u'lláh?"[18] Although some Bahá'ís think they might learn something from Jehovah's Witnesses and their evangelization methods, one woman disagreed:

> If I'm one on one or in a group, I don't mind talking about it if it comes up, but I can't imagine going out to a shopping mall. And I hate the idea of Bahá'ís going out to shopping malls accosting people, which is a very negative word, but that's what it feels like to me, because when people come to me with their religious tract, it feels like they are accosting me. So, some level of teaching is OK, but not proselytizing. To me it is proselytizing, I don't know what other word when you go out and pass out literature to strangers, that feels like proselytizing, and I'm not comfortable with that.

Another longtime Bahá'í expressed his reluctance about going out and teaching people with whom he has no prior relationship; he felt Bahá'ís should be teaching their neighbors, with whom they had a personal relationship, "not driving half-way across the state of Georgia to teach people I'll never see again."

However, most Atlanta Bahá'ís told me that they wait for the subject of religion to come up naturally, or learn to look for "teachable moments" in which to give non-Bahá'ís the message. Many Bahá'ís wear Bahá'í T-shirts or jewelry, or put Bahá'í calendars up at work, in the hope that others will ask them about it. One man, an officer in the Atlanta LSA, talked about "fishing" for teaching opportunities: "I guess it just has to come up naturally. I guess sometimes I'll fish. You know, I'll tell people I've got to go to an assembly meeting, or I'm not working late, I'm working on assembly business. Sometimes that will open a conversation." Other Atlanta Bahá'ís told me that they most enjoy supporting large-scale teaching events, where a dynamic Bahá'í speaker, or Bahá'í musicians such as Seals and Crofts or the late Dizzy Gillespie, are used in programs called "proclamation events." Survey data discussed in chapter 2 showed that people rarely get interested in the Bahá'í Faith and convert through such large, public events, even though these are the most expensive to plan and carry out. Instead, conversion is facilitated through friends, family members, or neighbors—in short, through personal contacts.

Perhaps the most interesting comment on large proclamation events was from a long-standing Bahá'í in the Atlanta area, a secretary of a suburban LSA. He had an interesting perspective on why Bahá'ís have expensive, time-consuming events that aim to communicate the Bahá'í Faith to "people of capacity"—movers and shakers, professionals in their respective fields—but rarely have a substantive "payoff" in terms of individual converts. He called it the "Houdini and the Elephant" system.

> But my answer is to put this [proclamation events] in a host of activities that I call the "Houdini and the Elephant" packet. [The Magician Harry] Houdini . . . would do a "free show" the first night [in a city] and would make an elephant disappear. And the next day on the front page of the local newspaper, it would say "Houdini makes an elephant disappear." Well, people would go "holy mackerel, that's incredible." And then people would come to the subsequent shows. Well . . . the elephant trick was a rotten trick for the people who were there, but it was wonderful PR. Now, I've seen the Bahá'ís do things that were worthless for the participants, but great PR. I don't think anybody is trying to be hypocritical, I don't think anybody is trying to make an elephant disappear, but I think that a lot of things are done because [of the publicity value].

For some Bahá'ís, a large proclamation event is money well spent (despite the lack of measurable converts), since it furthers a strategy of "emergence from obscurity." Bahá'ís realize that most Americans have never even heard of the Bahá'í Faith, or know it only as an "Eastern cult" or "that Persian religion." Thus, many Bahá'ís said that effort must be applied to garner some name recognition of their faith as a legitimate world religion, equal in status (if not adherents) to Islam, Christianity, or Buddhism, before teaching work can be effective in terms of converts produced.

Finally, whatever disputes Bahá'ís may have about the most "effective" and "tactful" teaching method, Atlanta Bahá'ís repeatedly indicated that the most important aspect of teaching was that of one's personal example—what Bahá'ís call "living the life," especially in terms of racial unity. Bahá'ís point out that lots of secular and religious groups talk about racial amity, but the Bahá'ís feel they are one of the few groups that live it out in nearly every Fireside, deepening, public meeting, and Feast.[19] One Atlanta LSA member summed it up best when he emphasized the importance of "teaching by example" (also called "indirect" teaching among Bahá'ís):

> It is not by what you say that this Faith is taught: it is by deeds, which speak louder than words. It is the sincerity of your personal relationships, and the love you manifest for humanity, is what teaches the Faith.

Whether or not a person becomes a Bahá'í, is not my reason for relating to them. Because if they don't become a Bahá'í when I think they should, then I've got a problem. All you can do is share the Faith with people. It's between them and God, is what it amounts to. You should just continue to love them.

This is a good encapsulation of a situated universalist perspective: teaching plans are promulgated from a global center that embodies universal values. But those values are best taught by personal example in one's situated community.

How Atlanta Bahá'ís Spread Their Faith

How active are Atlanta Bahá'ís in spreading their faith? Survey results indicate that only 12 percent of respondents report having done no teaching in the past year; most Bahá'ís are active teachers and employ a variety of methods in telling others about their faith. Table 7.1 gives the percentage of respondents who indicated that they engaged in each of the listed teaching activities in the past year, and the corresponding percentage who prefer that method over all others.

As the data show, the teaching activity Bahá'ís are most likely to engage in is one-to-one, personal teaching among friends, coworkers, or neighbors. More than 83 percent indicated that they had done this in the past year, and nearly one-half (47 percent) said this was the "teaching activity that I enjoy doing most." In addition, 40 percent of respondents indicated that they had hosted a Fireside in the past year or had brought a seeker to one, and another 31 percent had spoken at a Fireside on a Bahá'í topic of personal interest. More than one-fourth of the respondents had participated in "travel teaching"—where an individual or a group of Bahá'ís go outside their home community to give a Fireside, participate in a teaching event, or staff a booth at a county fair to tell people about Bahá'u'lláh. Another 15 percent engaged in "mass teaching." And 18 percent participated in "teaching institutes"—whereby several Bahá'ís get together to develop a strategy on how to teach a target population: possibly a minority community, people of "capacity" (i.e., professionals or leaders of thought and public opinion), or the elected officials in a community.[20]

Given that speaking with friends and coworkers personally is by far the most popular teaching activity, the next question is how often do Atlanta Bahá'ís talk with non-Bahá'ís about their Faith? Table 7.1 also shows the breakdown of responses to the question "About how often do you speak about the Faith with friends, coworkers, neighbors, or relatives who are not Bahá'ís?" More than one-third talk with others two or more times a week, and more than one-fifth do so weekly.

Despite the variation in favorite teaching methods, there is widespread agreement that teaching is an important aspect of being a Bahá'í, and a divinely

Table 7.1
Atlanta Bahá'ís' teaching activity

	Reported participation in teaching activities	
	% participating	% enjoying this activity most
Talking one-to-one	83.3	47.4
Hosting Firesides	41.0	10.0
Bringing seekers to Firesides	39.3	6.2
Speaking at Firesides	31.0	8.5
Other activities	27.2	13.3
Travel teaching	25.9	6.2
Teaching institutes	18.4	4.3
Mass teaching	14.6	4.3

	Reported results of teaching activities				
	1	2	3	4	5[a]
How often do you speak with non-Bahá'ís about the Faith?	37.7	22.6	15.9	10.9	13.0

	1	2	3	4	5[b]
The most important thing for me to do as a Bahá'í is to teach the Faith.	38.6	43.2	10.6	5.9	1.7

[a] 1 = twice a week, 2 = once a week, 3 = 2–3 times a month, 4 = once a month, 5 = less often
[b] 1 = strongly agree, 2 = agree, 3 = unsure, 4 = disagree, 5 = strongly disagree

commissioned responsibility, vital to a Bahá'í identity as a situated universalist. Bahá'ís encourage each other to overcome any personal fears or feelings of inadequacy, and to "audaciously" teach others about the Bahá'í Faith. The last item in table 7.1 shows the ideological agreement among Atlanta Bahá'ís concerning the importance of teaching. They were asked their level of agreement with the statement "The most important thing for me to do as a Bahá'í is to actively teach the Faith." More than 80 percent either strongly agreed or agreed with this statement.

The values of the top eight measures of teaching activity in table 7.1 were added together to create a composite measure of Atlanta Bahá'ís' teaching efforts. This new measure of teaching was then analyzed to determine whether a statistical association obtained between one's level of teaching activity and measures of demographic characteristics, organizational participation, adherence to authority, previous religious background, or personal devotion.[21] As we have seen in previous chapters, no demographic measure was significantly related to the likelihood of engaging in Bahá'í teaching activity (including gender, income, age, educational level, occupation, race, marital status, whether or not one's spouse is a Bahá'í, and the number of years one has been a Bahá'í). Nor is one's previous religious background significant in predicting the likelihood of engaging in teaching the faith. Most notably, those from conservative and liberal religious backgrounds are equally likely to be active teachers. This is significant, since one would expect that those who converted from conservative Christian denominations that tend to emphasize evangelism and "winning souls for Christ" would score higher on measures of teaching than those from more liberal backgrounds where evangelism is not so emphasized. This was not the case. Apparently, Bahá'ís from all backgrounds internalize equally the urgency for teaching that is instilled by Bahá'í authorities, and which constitutes a vital component of one's Bahá'í identity.

However, significant relations obtained between one's likelihood of teaching and the recognition of the legitimate authority of the Administrative Order, organizational participation, and personal devotion measures. Participation in the ritual life of the Bahá'í community (see chapters 3 and 5) exposes one to the authority of the Administrative Order (see chapter 4), whose central message is to "teach the Faith." Thus, the outgrowth of a Bahá'í's global identity as a situated universalist is the desire to teach. The inspiration of the Three Year Plan from the UHJ, coupled with the message that teaching is a religious duty, motivates the individual Bahá'í to teach his or her faith—creating a powerful sense of mission to bring the Bahá'í message to a chaotic world. Thus, organizational participation and personal devotion intensify the individual Bahá'í's recognition of the authority of the Administrative Order, impressing upon him/her the perceived critical need to engage in teaching.[22]

PIONEERING

One final aspect of teaching to be discussed concerns pioneering—the Bahá'í term for missionary activity. Shoghi Effendi designated those Bahá'ís who went to another country to teach the Bahá'í Faith as "pioneers" and those who moved to another city within their home country as "homefront pioneers."[23] A letter written on his behalf said:

> The Guardian has pointed out that the most important service anyone can render the Faith today is to teach the Cause of God. The degree of importance of areas of service is first, pioneering in a virgin area of the Crusade, second, pioneering in one of the consolidation areas abroad, and third, settling in one of the goal cities of the home front; and finally, teaching with redoubled effort wherever a Bahá'í may reside. . . . The perseverance of the pioneers in their posts, however great the sacrifices involved, is an act of devoted service, which as attested by our teachings, will have an assured reward in both worlds. (Hornby 1983, 439–440, 442)

The goal of the pioneer is more than simply teaching his or her faith so that a viable, functioning LSA is formed from members of the indigenous population. Pioneering, Bahá'ís said to me, is also a way to bear witness to the unity of humankind, in that a person from the United States would move to Brazil, or Nigeria, or Thailand, settle down, and manifest the characteristics of a "world citizen." Pioneers may receive an initial stipend from a local or national institution for the plane ticket to their new location, but they are then expected to find a job and become self-sufficient. (It is preferable, especially for foreign pioneers, to secure a job prior to entering the country.) Some Bahá'ís plan their education, or engage in a profession, with an eye toward using those skills as pioneers. One woman seeking a degree in public health said: "I'd like to get a job with Save the Children or some international relief agency. Health education, surveys, getting information about immunization, etc. That's the reason I went into public health, was to be able to go pioneering. That's always been my dream."

Survey results indicate a substantial level of pioneering activity among Atlanta respondents. Nearly 17 percent said they had been foreign pioneers during their membership in the Bahá'í Faith, while 35 percent indicated home front pioneering experience.[24] Pioneering, like missionary activity in any religion, is a sign of faithfulness and commitment. For Bahá'í pioneers, it requires a willingness to practice universal values in a situated local setting anywhere in the world, commitment to Bahá'í ideals of global citizenship, and a recognition that "the world is but one country, and mankind its citizens." One Atlanta Bahá'í summed up his experience pioneering in Liberia this way: "The world had grown. I had embraced the world. The world was my home. Wherever I was, it was home, wherever I laid my head, was home. If you go [pioneering] with respect, love and respect for people, you can go anywhere in the world and be accepted."

Summary

This chapter has shown that the average Bahá'í takes seriously the religious duty of teaching. Most Atlanta Bahá'ís have engaged in some amount of teaching in the past year; however, the "methods" by which teaching is done remain varied and debated. True to their ideology of "unity in diversity," most Bahá'í recognize the importance of all techniques when it comes to spreading their message.

Bahá'ís realize that in order for them to institutionalize the Administrative Order as the basis for a future global civilization and world order, they must not only inform others about the Bahá'í Faith, but attract others to become "declared believers." Bahá'ís utilize Teaching Plans developed by the UHJ to engage in rational, systematic recruitment of new converts. The Three Year Plan brings individual Atlanta Bahá'ís into a working relationship with all levels of the Bahá'í Administrative Order. This public way for Bahá'ís to live out their faith in the world reinforces the sociological mechanisms by which the local community and the global organization are reflexively connected.

Atlanta Bahá'ís of all demographic backgrounds are equally likely to engage in teaching work. Teaching is both the cause and consequence of a Bahá'í's identity. As their Bahá'í identity deepens, Bahá'ís will more likely engage in teaching work, since this is the primary emphasis of Bahá'í authoritative communication. But the more a Bahá'í engages in teaching, the more likely they will develop a sense of obedience to what are considered divinely ordained institutions, and value their role in building the Bahá'í version of the Kingdom of God.

Bahá'ís report noticing a shift in the focus of teaching messages from the authorities in their faith. The publication of *Bahá'u'lláh* by the UHJ (1991) called on Bahá'ís to spend more time teaching about the source and founder of their faith, and not just its social principles. For Bahá'ís, Bahá'u'lláh is the "universal Manifestation" who will usher in the Kingdom of God. This is the message Bahá'ís have been called upon to deliver more forcefully. Sociologically, this may have the effect of solidifying the boundaries between the Bahá'í and non-Bahá'í world, by highlighting the distinctiveness of the Bahá'í identity (see Kanter 1972 on boundary maintenance and commitment mechanisms in religious groups). Instead of saying to potential converts, "These are the principles we follow" (which may or may not be the same ones you adhere to), Bahá'ís are now advised to say, "This is the prophet we follow, and this is his message to the world." Sociological research suggests that highlighting that greater distinctiveness between Bahá'ís and non-Bahá'ís may lead to more recruits, since uniqueness helps "seekers" distinguish new ideologies in a pluralistic religious marketplace (see Bainbridge 1997; Stark and Bainbridge 1985).[25]

While most Bahá'ís recognize its importance, teaching is also the source of the greatest conflicts I observed during my fieldwork. There is confusion among Bahá'ís as to where to draw the line between "teaching" and "proselytizing." Some methods Bahá'ís employ to teach their faith (notably, "mass" teaching) are considered proselytizing by other Bahá'ís, creating the potential for divisions within the Atlanta community. There also exists the paradox that while the underlying goal of the national and local teaching plans is new converts, the goals themselves are for increases in the level of teaching activity (which may or may not bear fruit in new believers). Additionally, Bahá'ís themselves are often unfamiliar with many of the details of their theology, especially supposed Biblical connections to their faith; this makes it more difficult for them to move beyond the more superficial process of teaching Bahá'í principles.

Ironically, it may be the institutional emphasis on teaching that exacerbates the tensions that do exist within the Bahá'í community, and that has contributed indirectly to the relative lack of growth in membership. The role of "teacher" has a great deal of status in Bahá'í circles. Many of the heroes and heroines in Bahá'í history are those who selflessly taught their faith, often at great sacrifice; such teachers are lauded by Bahá'í leaders and given acclaim. While many Bahá'ís would deny it, and their scripture would not support it, there is also a status hierarchy for those teachers who get seekers to sign declaration cards. There was a sense among many Bahá'ís I talked with that those who engage in active, visible, and numerically measurable teaching activity (the more converts the better) are unfairly considered somehow "superior" Bahá'ís. *The American Bahá'í* frequently prints stories of "successful" teaching (defined in terms of new declarants), highlighting the importance of this activity. The couple I discussed earlier in this chapter described consolidation work as "tedious" work that did not have the same "glamour and excitement and energy." This perception only adds to the status distinctions Bahá'ís make among themselves, even though official doctrine gives equal importance to teaching and consolidating new believers. What is absent in Bahá'í culture is a corresponding role of "deepener" or "consolidator" to complement the role of "teacher."

This is reflected in the number of declared but now inactive Bahá'ís who came into the faith during its peak growth in the United States in the late 1960s and early 1970s. Being a teacher, traveling throughout the country or the world, brings acclaim, and helps one feel that one is actively helping the national and global institutions meet their numerical teaching goals and establish new Local Spiritual Assemblies. But then teachers go back home, and the difficult work of consolidating new believers and nurturing struggling LSAs is left to often small, overwhelmed communities, work that offers no distinction or status within the Bahá'í community. I spoke with two African American Bahá'ís, both converts from the early 1980s, who spent several weekends during my period of fieldwork seeking out "inactive" believers. With membership lists in hand, they went to rural communities south of Atlanta, knocking on doors and talking with nominal Bahá'ís. All of these "converts," who twenty years ago had signed a declaration card, had gone back to their churches. Some were glad to see Bahá'ís come to their door again, they said, and still enjoyed receiving *The American Bahá'í*; but an equal number were angry that Bahá'ís had come to their homes twenty years ago, generating excitement and hope, but had never returned.

This said, however, teaching remains a prime example of how Bahá'ís "think globally, but act locally" as situated universalists. Teaching Plans orient adherents to the goals of the Three Year Plan at the global level of their faith, but the adherent's arena of action is the local community. And while teaching activity has not recently had the numerical payoff they hope for, Bahá'ís still see their work as "planting seeds" that may bear fruit later, and at the very least as helping the Bahá'í Faith emerge from obscurity.

Chapter 8

"Thinking Globally, Acting Locally"

*I am Jewish, Christian, Muslim, Buddhist, Hindu,
Zoroastrian, Bahá'í and many other things as well. I am all
of these because I am a human being, for every human
being is an heir to the spiritual heritage which is ours.*

Suheil Bushrui, Bahá'í Chair for World Peace
at the University of Maryland

THIS STUDY HAS EXPLORED the sociological mechanisms by which local Bahá'í communities are connected to a global center, linking elements of local community and global Administrative Order. This reflexive connection between the local and global shapes what I have called a Bahá'í's situated universalist identity. I have also discussed the individual and collective rituals Bahá'ís engage in that bring them into contact with the authority of the Administrative Order, helping to unify the Bahá'í community around a global ideology. The preceding chapter looked at the kinds of teaching methods Bahá'ís employ to communicate their faith with others. Teaching is one way Bahá'ís "think globally, but act locally."

But there is another way Bahá'ís "think globally and act locally": in their promotion of racial unity with the goal of "unity in diversity." Bahá'ís strive for racial unity not only within their own community, but for society as a whole. The Bahá'í Faith and promoting racial unity often go hand in hand. What is distinctive about this social movement is the way Bahá'ís explicitly connect local race unity efforts and their global worldview. Bahá'ís declare that the elimination of all forms of prejudice is a fundamental requirement of achieving global unity and peace. The "oneness of humanity" is probably the most important social principle Bahá'ís champion. Atlanta Bahá'ís, practicing their faith in America's Deep South, find the greatest demonstration of the oneness of humanity in the promotion of racial unity and the elimination of racial prejudice. This focus emerged from fieldwork and interviews, but was also evident from

152

my research in the Atlanta Bahá'í archives. In Atlanta, this principle finds its greatest expression in the unity between the historically segregated black and white communities—although the influx of Persians into Atlanta area during the past fifteen to twenty years adds an extra ethnic and cultural dynamic.[1] Promoting racial unity is a local expression of thinking globally.

Bahá'í Focus on Race Unity

The history of Bahá'í struggles to live up to their ideology in the South penetrates the collective identity of Atlanta Bahá'ís. Bahá'ís draw from the symbolic and ideological resources found in Bahá'í history and scripture for examples of how to live their lives. These resources are woven into nearly every Atlanta area Fireside, deepening, teaching plan, and Feast consultation. This is especially true in particularizing the universal goal of the oneness of humanity. Followers of Bahá'u'lláh in Atlanta attempt to foster racial unity, hoping to act as a model for the non-Bahá'í world to emulate. One Continental Counselor, an African American woman who lived in Atlanta years ago, said to a gathering of Atlanta Bahá'ís: "The Bahá'í Faith does not have a perfect record on race relations. But, it is the oldest living workshop in the U.S. on racial unity." Bahá'ís draw from the example of 'Abdu'l-Bahá, and the guidance of Shoghi Effendi to learn how to advance racial unity locally.

THE EXAMPLE OF 'ABDU'L-BAHÁ AND LOUIS GREGORY
'Abdu'l-Bahá made a trip throughout Europe and North America in 1911–1912.[2] While in America, he traveled from New York to San Francisco, teaching his father's religion and preaching about the desperate need for Bahá'ís to practice racial unity among themselves.

While in Washington, D.C., 'Abdu'l-Bahá upset the city's racially segregated protocol by inviting a young black lawyer, Louis Gregory, to sit at his right hand in the seat of honor at a dinner reception. Louis Gregory—then a new Bahá'í—went on to become one of the most prominent travel teachers of the Bahá'í Faith in U.S. history. Gregory frequently passed through Atlanta as he traveled throughout the South spreading the message of racial unity. With the encouragement 'Abdu'l-Bahá offered during his 1912 trip, Louis Gregory married longtime friend Louisa Mathew, a British woman, and the two became the U.S. Bahá'í community's first interracial couple. Throughout his trip, 'Abdu'l-Bahá frequently spoke about the positive influence interracial couples would have on the elimination of racism in the United States. He said: "If it be possible, gather together these two races, black and white, into one assembly and put such love into their hearts that they shall not only unite but even intermarry. Be sure that the result of this will abolish differences and disputes between black and white. . . . This is a great service to the world of humanity" (quoted in Morrison 1982, 45–46).[3]

Bahá'ís in Atlanta, especially African Americans, look to Gregory as an important role model for behavior in the midst of a racist culture—a culture where separatism has become a compelling alternative to integration for some. Several African American Bahá'ís told me during interviews that stories of how Louis Gregory acted in various difficult situations instruct and inspire them in a way that Martin Luther King Jr. and Malcolm X do not.[4] One African American man who has been a Bahá'í for more than thirty years told me: "I never could be a follower of [Martin Luther King], but I can be a follower of Bahá'u'lláh."

Atlanta Bahá'ís also point out that while in the United States, 'Abdu'l-Bahá spoke about racial unity to the fourth annual meeting of the NAACP, undoubtedly because of Louis Gregory's influence within black intellectual circles (Morrison 1982). The importance of 'Abdu'l-Bahá as the "exemplar" of the Bahá'í Faith stems in part from his willingness to take a stand for racial unity, even upsetting Washington, D.C. society in the process. Bahá'ís thus turn to 'Abdu'l-Bahá as a role model. Many even said during interviews that they have had the courage to speak out against racist slurs or jokes because they feel 'Abdu'l-Bahá would have done so.

THE GUIDANCE OF SHOGHI EFFENDI

The second resource Bahá'ís draw from is the guidance Shoghi Effendi sent in a letter to the U.S. Bahá'í community in 1938, reminding them of the absolute necessity for Bahá'ís to embrace racial unity; the letter was published in 1963 in *The Advent of Divine Justice*. The criticism of the American Bahá'í community that Effendi expressed in this letter has left an indelible impression on U.S. Bahá'ís' identity, especially those living in the Deep South and Atlanta, and still challenges the Atlanta Bahá'í community sixty years later, if the continual reference to it during Bahá'í deepenings is any indication.

One section, entitled "The Most Challenging Issue," was frequently the topic of deepenings in Atlanta. In it, Shoghi Effendi wrote, "As to racial prejudice, the corrosion of which, for well nigh a century, has bitten into the fibre, and attacked the whole social structure of American society, it should be regarded as constituting the most vital and challenging issue confronting the Bahá'í community at the present stage of its evolution" (1963, 28). He sent this message during a period in U.S. Bahá'í history when Bahá'ís themselves, especially in the South, were making accommodations to Jim Crow segregation laws. Effendi censured the American community, measuring it against a different standard. After forewarning them that "a long and thorny road, beset with pitfalls, still remains untraveled, both by the white and negro exponents of the redeeming Faith of Bahá'u'lláh," and recalling the example set by 'Abdu'l-Bahá, Effendi said:

To discriminate against any race, on the ground of its being socially backward, politically immature, and numerically in a minority, is a flagrant violation of the spirit that animates the Faith of Bahá'u'lláh. The consciousness of any division or cleavage in its ranks is alien to its very purpose, principles, and ideals. . . . If any discrimination is at all to be tolerated, it should be a discrimination not against, but rather in favor of the minority, be it racial or otherwise. (Effendi 1963, 29)

Thus, the Bahá'í Faith advocates a form of "affirmative action" in promoting the diversity of its committees and assemblies. Bahá'í law requires that if a tie exists for the ninth spot in the election of an LSA, and if one candidate represents a minority in that society, then that minority candidate is elected to the position, in order to "further the interests of the community" (1963, 30).

In addition, Effendi explained that both whites and blacks have responsibilities in eradicating prejudice. He said:

Let the white make a supreme effort in their resolve to contribute their share to the solution of this problem, to abandon once for all their usually inherent and at times subconscious sense of superiority, to correct their tendency towards revealing a patronizing attitude towards the members of the other race. . . . Let the negroes, through a corresponding effort on their part, show by every means in their power the warmth of their response, their readiness to forget the past, and their ability to wipe out every trace of suspicion that may still linger in their hearts and minds. . . . Let neither think that anything short of genuine love, extreme patience, true humility, consummate tact, sound initiative, mature wisdom, and deliberate, persistent, and prayerful effort, can succeed in blotting out the stain which this patent evil has left on the fair name of their common country. (1963, 33–34)

The last sentence of the above quotation was the subject of several deepenings I attended as part of my fieldwork. While most of these gatherings were principally attended by African American Bahá'ís, they were always mixed-race meetings. Sometimes the whole hour would be spent just discussing what Shoghi Effendi meant by "forgetting the past," or what "extreme patience" or "consummate tact" meant from a Bahá'í perspective and in light of Bahá'í scripture. Sometimes tempers would flare and tears would be shed as whites and blacks would each struggle to understand the other's perspective. At the end of each deepening, however, everyone would exchange hugs and say "I love you."

The willingness to tackle the problem of racism is one of the most appealing characteristics of the Bahá'í community for many of its converts, and certainly is one of the most widely communicated aspects of the Bahá'í message. The confidence Bahá'ís as a group express in the eventual establishment of racial unity is noteworthy; non-Bahá'ís are more likely to be skeptical about the complete eradication of prejudice in a world filled with neo-Nazis, race riots, and ethnic cleansing. Non-Bahá'í seekers who attended Bahá'í events where the race unity message was discussed told me later that Bahá'í efforts are worthy of respect, but their goal is ultimately unrealizable. For many non-Bahá'ís, the assumed inevitability of racial unity is the hallmark of Bahá'í utopianism—a sort of naive vision of the world shorn of its hard political realities. However, the Bahá'í faith assures its adherents that the unity of humanity is already a "spiritual reality" prevailing since the advent of the Bahá'í dispensation, and will eventually become a "social reality" through the work of the Bahá'ís themselves.

RACE UNITY INITIATIVES BY THE NATIONAL SPIRITUAL ASSEMBLY
During my period of fieldwork, the National Spiritual Assembly of the United States initiated a series of programs and statements to highlight the Bahá'í community's commitment to race unity. The first was the 1991 publication of *The Vision of Race Unity: America's Most Challenging Issue*, a twelve-page pamphlet that outlines the "spiritual solution" to racism in this country and invites Americans to investigate the Bahá'í Faith as a "model" for bringing about social change. It has been used widely by Bahá'ís in teaching efforts, and has become one of the most popular handout pamphlets for promoting awareness of the Bahá'í Faith.

In this document, the NSA says that the problem of racism continues to grow in this country. Active steps must be taken, for "to ignore the problem [of racism] is to expose the country to physical, moral, and spiritual danger" (1991, 1). The pamphlet goes on to describe the Bahá'í perspective on unity: "The fundamental solution—the one that will reduce violence, regenerate and focus the intellectual and moral energy of minorities, and make them partners in the construction of a progressive society—rests ultimately on the common recognition of the oneness of humankind" (1991, 6). In addition, it states that "Our appeal is addressed primarily to the individual American because the transformation of a whole nation ultimately depends on the initiative and change of character of the individuals who compose it" (1991, 11).

The pamphlet goes on to discuss the importance of reforming the educational system and curricula in this country to reflect the biological, social, and spiritual oneness of humanity. It decries the "grim doctrine" of racial separation on the part of both blacks and whites, and offers the Bahá'í Faith as a model for the future: "We mention the experience of the Bahá'í community not from any feeling of pride and ultimate victory, because that which we have accomplished still falls short of that to which we aspire; nonetheless, the results to date are most encouraging, and it is as a means of encouragement that we call attention to them" (1991, 11).

This publication highlights an important aspect of a Bahá'í perspective on social change: their view that the problems of humanity are essentially spiritual, rather than economic or political, and so will require "spiritual solutions." However, when asked, most Bahá'ís cannot go much further in providing concrete examples of "the spiritual solution to social problems" than to recite that phrase, unsure of how a "spiritual solution" would be translated in actual social policy.[5] Bahá'ís claim that many of the "Bahá'í solutions" would be worked out in the future, in a consultative process with all parties involved, not by relying on formulaic doctrines or preset policies. This research has provided evidence that the Bahá'í Faith does reshape its diverse membership into a unified organization with a coherent global worldview and a distinct identity as situated universalists. This is in part a result of the initial acceptance of the legitimate authority of the Administrative Order, and acceptance of the claims of Bahá'u'lláh. Given that non-Bahá'ís do not have exposure to the authority of Bahá'í institutions, and cannot be resocialized by the religion's ideological and organizational mechanisms, it is unclear how the Bahá'í Faith could act as a widespread and effective model for the wider society, without the widespread conversion of the masses of the world's people to the Bahá'í Faith.

One final example of the National Spiritual Assembly's efforts to promote race unity was an open letter to the President of the United States (then George Bush) that appeared in the New York, Washington, D.C., and Los Angeles newspapers after the April 1992 Los Angeles riots following the initial Rodney King verdicts.[6] The NSA said: "the spiritual requirements [to solve the problem of racism] have been persistently neglected. America has not done enough to demonstrate her commitment to the equality and the unity of races, to the dignity of all human beings whatever their color, and to the moral imperative of extending love and respect to the entire human family."[7] It goes on to explain that the Bahá'í commitment to racial unity dates back to its founder Bahá'u'lláh, and urges united effort to address this problem. Bahá'í communities throughout the United States, including those in Atlanta, used the *Vision of Race Unity* publication, as well as the NSA letter to the president, to promote Firesides, deepenings, and public awareness of the Bahá'í perspective on America's "most challenging issue."[8]

History of Race Unity Efforts in Atlanta

The Bahá'í universal value of the oneness of humanity is being lived out in Atlanta principally through the promotion of racial unity.[9] These efforts to act locally on global thinking go back to the beginning of the twentieth century. Atlanta Bahá'ís take great pride in this history, which shapes the collective identity of the community. This section will give a brief account of early race unity efforts in Atlanta.

THE FIRST ATLANTA PIONEER

At the turn of the century, Atlanta was a city divided by race and class, deeply entrenched in the Jim Crow racial caste system institutionalized throughout the Deep South. Atlanta in 1895 was the site of the Cotton States and International Exposition, where Booker T. Washington, founder and president of Tuskegee Institute in Alabama, gave a speech that became known as the "Atlanta Compromise." His remarks, which have drawn much criticism from African Americans, gave de facto endorsement to segregation, saying "In all things that are purely social, we can be separate as the fingers, yet one as the hand in all things essential to mutual progress."[10]

Although the separate-but-equal "racial peace" prevailed on the surface,[11] events of the early 1900s revealed the depth of racial disunity. Atlanta experienced a race riot in 1906, and nine years later was the site of the rebirth of the Ku Klux Klan. Although Klan membership had declined in post-Civil War Reconstruction, it was resurrected in 1915 in suburban Stone Mountain by Colonel William Joseph Simmons (Tindall 1967).

This was the social context faced by the first known Bahá'í pioneer in Atlanta, Dr. James Charles Oakshette, who settled there in 1909 and taught the Bahá'í Faith for twenty-eight years before passing away in Atlanta on November 15, 1937. Oakshette was born December 25, 1858, in London, England. He grew up in London and was educated at Oxford, earning a doctorate in philosophy and theology; he was reported to have spoken Greek, Latin, Sanskrit, Hebrew, Gaelic, and German.[12] Apparently, his first vocation was a Congregational minister, and he led churches in London, Canada, and Chicago. He later studied medicine, and graduated from the University of Illinois Medical School in 1896. In addition to his medical duties, he also lectured in theosophy[13] and was a master of the Rosicrucian fraternal order.[14]

It is unknown when Oakshette first became a Bahá'í,[15] but he learned about the Bahá'í Faith while living in Chicago. It is also unclear what profession Oakshette practiced while in Atlanta—one would presume that it involved medicine. However, he actively taught the Bahá'í Faith, and is listed in early editions of *Bahá'í World* as the contact person for Atlanta's isolated believers.[16] Raymond Lindsey, an early Atlanta convert, said that Oakshette would hold weekly classes based on the introductory text *Bahá'u'lláh and The New Era* (Esslemont 1970) in his room at the Hotel Nassau, and that he would keep the local public library stocked with Bahá'í books—replacing them often when they vanished (Finke n.d., 4).

Records indicate that during the last ten years of his life, Oakshette entered a new profession to further the Bahá'í evangelization work in Atlanta, establishing the Liberal Catholic Church of St. Michael the Archangel (Finke n.d., 5). Its *Statement of Principles*, published in 1927, bear a resemblance to principles enunciated by Bahá'u'lláh.[17] Cleo Lindsey and her son and daughter-in-law, Raymond and Estelle Lindsey, all three of whom would eventually become loyal Bahá'ís in the Atlanta community, attended this church. They indicated that Oakshette would teach the Bahá'í Faith during the sermons, and would use Bahá'í prayers throughout the church services. Raymond Lindsey was so attracted to Oakshette's teachings that he approached Oakshette and said that he, too, wanted to be a Liberal Catholic priest. Oakshette reportedly told him "it was not the right thing to do; there was something better in store" for him, and gave him a copy of *Bahá'u'lláh and the New Era* (Finke n.d., 5).[18]

In 1927 when Oakshette organized his church, Shoghi Effendi had not yet decreed that Bahá'ís should withdraw membership from other religious organizations, let alone establish a church (see Hornby 1983, 160). This allowed Bahá'ís in the early years to be somewhat unorthodox in their teaching. When Oakshette learned of this requirement, he reportedly grew concerned. He consulted with the NSA, who allowed him to retain his association with the church. He died a few months later on November 15, 1937 (Finke n.d., 6).

There is evidence that Oakshette was actively engaged in early race unity work in Atlanta. Roy Williams, a frequent traveling companion of Louis Gregory (both African Americans) and a member of the Bahá'í National Center staff who made trips to Atlanta in the late 1910s and early 1920s, had this to say about Oakshette:

> During my first teaching trip I met Dr. Oakshette by arrangement with him in his office in the Hurt Building. This had to be done very secretly but he never showed any fear and we spent many happy hours discussing ways and means and contacts he knew among colored people. I have never met a more charming and lovable character—doing all that he possibly could almost alone under the harsh conditions then existing in Atlanta . . . he told me of his many persistent contacts with persons in all walks of life in Atlanta—whether black or white—Jew or Christian—Protestant or Catholic. No doubt these seeds have or will bear fruit as he was without doubt a true and selfless Bahá'í. (Finke n.d., 3)[19]

It was through Oakshette's efforts that the Atlanta Chamber of Commerce invited 'Abdu'l-Bahá to visit Atlanta during his trip to America. Finke's historical report quotes Louis Gregory as writing that "the year he [Oakshette] settled in Atlanta is unknown to me, but I am reasonably sure that he was resident there in 1912, since that year, the Atlanta Chamber of Commerce invited 'Abdu'l-Bahá to come to Atlanta. This was probably due to the influence and suggestion of Dr. Oakshette" (Finke n.d., 4).[20] Although 'Abdu'l-Bahá's trip did not take him into the Deep South, the fact that the Atlanta Chamber of Commerce invited him attests to the influence Oakshette had in certain spheres of Atlanta civic life.

NEW PIONEERS IN ATLANTA

The history of the Bahá'í community of Atlanta shifts to 1937, when two women, Olga Finke and Doris Ebbert, moved there. Interviews with local Bahá'ís who knew them indicated that Finke and Ebbert were both committed Bahá'ís. Finke was from New York City, and prior to coming to Atlanta had spent three years pioneering in Piney Woods, Mississippi, at a school for African American children. It was while at Piney Woods that she met Doris Ebbert, a fellow teacher from Ipava, Illinois, who became interested in the Bahá'í Faith, and later converted.

A month and a half before Oakshette died, the two women moved to Atlanta. A couple of days after arriving, Finke and Ebbert visited Oakshette, who was gravely ill. Finke reports:

> The picture of 'Abdu'l-Bahá was hanging on the wall at his bedside. He was very weak and hardly able to speak above a whisper and even this required great effort. Nevertheless Dr. Oakshette managed to convey to Miss Ebbert his conviction that Bahá'u'lláh is the Manifestation of God for this day. This statement made a great impression upon Miss Ebbert, coming as it seemed from a Catholic priest. So we find Dr. Oakshette loyal to his task of teaching the Bahá'í Faith to his dying day. (Finke n.d., 7)[21]

During the first few years in Atlanta, Finke and Ebbert tried to make a living operating a private school in which they taught Bahá'í principles.[22] However, it was never financially successful. After several years, they closed the school, and Ebbert eventually found work as a maid. Finke was employed by the city of Atlanta.[23] Throughout their tenure in Atlanta, the two women remained active in Bahá'í teaching efforts, and promoted Bahá'í ideals on various social issues in the public forum. Both frequently wrote letters to the editor that were published in Atlanta newspapers, even into the 1970s. Racial unity was often the theme. Ebbert, for example, once wrote a letter to the editor of the *Atlanta Constitution*. Referring to protests by state Democrats who denounced the invitation of African American leaders to an upcoming speech by Eleanor Roosevelt, Ebbert wrote, "it makes me wonder if there is any hope for a democracy in this state. These men must not have heard that Negro soldiers just finished fighting in a world war for democracy, liberty and justice."[24] Both Finke and Ebbert reportedly showed tenacity in teaching the Bahá'í Faith and promoting race unity, especially in the difficult context of 1940s Atlanta. Even an eviction notice, given them by their landlord after they had provided room and board for Louis Gregory during one of his visits in 1940, was not enough to deter them.[25]

THE FORMATION OF THE FIRST ATLANTA ASSEMBLY

Within two years of Finke and Ebbert's arrival in Atlanta, the community had grown to more than nine members, including the Lindsey family, who learned about the Bahá'í Faith through Oakshette's Liberal Catholic Church, and declared in 1938. Some of the Bahá'ís, including three African Americans, were only temporarily living in Atlanta in 1939. Efforts were made to form a local assembly that year, but records indicate that Horace Holley (a member of the NSA) notified the Atlanta community that it was not yet "strong enough" in terms of permanent, nontransient members.[26]

During this period, the small Bahá'í group in Atlanta held integrated Feasts and Holy Day celebrations, but Firesides were segregated by race (Finke n.d., 21). This was in accordance with the advice of Shoghi Effendi, who supported the National Assembly's policy of segregated teaching meetings when seekers were included, but racially integrated meetings when attendance was Bahá'í-only. This policy helped insulate Bahá'ís from the resentment and outrage of supporters of the Jim Crow system. In a letter from Charlotte Linfoot, secretary of the National Teaching Committee, dated August 4, 1937, Finke received the following counsel:

> Recent communications from the Guardian seem to imply that it would be wise for individuals to concentrate on teaching members of their own race rather than to follow the plan which many of the believers have followed in trying to bring the races together in study classes, etc. In other words, we feel that he [Shoghi Effendi] wishes the white people to teach the white people and the colored to teach their own race, and then when they have become believers, they will come together naturally, through the power of the Teachings. Unity is the result of the Faith, rather than the reverse, and it can be experienced in its fullness only among confirmed believers.[27]

It was through the efforts of Orcella Rexford, a full-time traveling lecturer on health foods in Atlanta in late 1939, that five individuals joined the Bahá'í Faith the following spring (Finke n.d., 22). Rexford would hold a series of classes on health foods, and during the last session she would give a talk on the Bahá'í Faith.[28] Terah Smith continued deepening classes for those interested after Rexford left town, and all those eventually joining the Bahá'í Faith were white— none of them ever having met any of the black believers (Finke n.d., 22). Thus, when elections took place on Ridván in 1940, the first Local Spiritual Assembly was not integrated.

EARLY CONFLICT IN THE ATLANTA COMMUNITY

With the new assembly finally elected, Atlanta Bahá'ís began planning various teaching activities. Raymond and Estelle Lindsey felt strongly that it was now time for mixed-race teaching meetings. They invited their black neighbors,[29] as well as the white and black members of the Bahá'í community, to a special dinner and deepening. Although things went well, after the meeting there was "vigorous protest" by some of the white Bahá'ís, and Terah Smith asked the Lindseys not to have any more mixed-race Firesides (Finke n.d., 23).

These events stirred a growing conflict in the nascent Atlanta community, one with the potential to divide the newly formed LSA over issues of teaching and race.[30] There also seems to have been little initial communication between black community members and the all-white LSA, since "the Local Assembly . . . was not cognizant of the fact that Mrs. Essie Robertson wished to be accepted into the group" (Finke n.d., 22). The following year (1941) Essie Robertson became the first native African American Georgian to accept the Bahá'í Faith, and was taught during the period of segregated Firesides. Robertson became a vital member of the Atlanta community—with Feasts, firesides, LSA meetings, and even regional teaching conferences held in her home (Finke n.d., 25). She was elected to the Atlanta LSA in April 1941—the first African American to hold that post in Atlanta—and the local assembly remained integrated for the rest of the decade.

To prevent schism in the struggling community, the National Spiritual Assembly decided to meet for the first time in the Deep South in November 1940, and to make racial unity their only agenda item. The NSA's public meetings and teaching conference in Atlanta healed many wounds and set an example in that community for ongoing race unity activities that continued throughout the decade, often receiving opposition from non-Bahá'í groups in the rest of the Jim Crow 1940s South. Shoghi Effendi subsequently sent a letter to the NSA commending them for their efforts in Atlanta:

> The Guardian is very pleased to learn of the success that has attended
> the sessions at Atlanta and the removal of the disagreement within the
> community of that city and the work achieved by the regional confer-
> ence and the public meeting open to both races. A special effort, he
> feels, should now be made to lay a foundation of unity between the
> white and colored Bahá'ís and lead the groups [in the region] into
> communities capable of forming Assemblies representative of both races.
> (quoted in Morrison 1982, 284)

THE 1940S

In the 1940s Atlanta was undergoing subtle changes. The decade saw the beginning of the twenty-three-year reign of Mayor William B. Hartsfield, known for his relatively progressive stance on racial issues and as the man who first described Atlanta as "the city too busy to hate" (see Allen 1971, 21). In 1944, the Southern Regional Council was formed to combat racial discrimination, and its headquarters was established in Atlanta. In 1947 a federal district court battle was won by Atlanta black public school teachers trying to equalize pay scales; and in the late 1940s Atlanta made efforts to integrate its police force (see King and Riley 1980, 124).

With its first major crisis over, the Atlanta community grew and expanded its activities throughout the 1940s. They grew from thirteen believers in 1940 to twenty-three in 1945, then membership leveled off for the rest of the decade.[31] The community legally incorporated in 1945. During its first decade the Atlanta LSA maintained an active teaching program of Firesides and public meetings. Some of the public meeting spaces in hotels like the Biltmore would allow mixed-race meetings; sometimes, however, the only available facilities would be in places like the Ansley or Henry Grady hotels, which were restricted to whites only because of the management's strict observance of Jim Crow laws. When only segregated facilities were available, then a second meeting with the same speaker would be held at a facility open to both races, most likely in one of the black churches or colleges, or the black YMCAs or YWCAs. This process helped to systematically strengthen ties between the Bahá'í community and Atlanta's African Americans—ties that built on the efforts of Roy Williams and Louis Gregory, who had spoke at these institutions in previous decades.[32]

The Atlanta community expanded its scope of activity throughout the decade. But two major events in the 1940s hastened the maturation of the community. The first was a visit by National Spiritual Assembly member Dorothy Baker, from September 29 to October 2, 1946. The result of this consultation was a nine-point policy governing aspects of evangelizing across the color line in the South. It emphasized that racially integrated meetings were "blessed" and should be encouraged, and stated that it was the LSA's responsibility to keep teaching activity truly "simultaneous" for white and black seekers. Firesides would be segregated by race to avoid dangerous situations fueled by racists, but with the ultimate goal of bringing the two races together once seekers had become practicing Bahá'ís.

The volatile nature of race relations in 1940s Southern culture can be clearly seen in the Atlanta community's second major turning point of the decade. Finding a safe location for Bahá'í-only, racially integrated meetings was often difficult, and served as the impetus for establishing a permanent Bahá'í Center. The Bahá'ís had gathered on April 28, 1947, for a Feast at Finke and Ebbert's house in southwest Atlanta. Right after the devotions, there was a loud knocking at the door, accompanied by the footsteps of many men. Ebbert answered the door, and one of many men who had gathered asked her, "Are there negroes and whites here? Bring the niggers outside!"[33] Ebbert refused, and Raymond Lindsey and David Ruhe moved forward to question the growing crowd. While this discussion was going on, the three blacks attending the Feast, along with some of the whites, went to the back of the house, called the police, and began saying prayers. In his official report to the NSA as chair of the Atlanta assembly, Ruhe wrote:

> One [of the men standing outside] stated that they did not want us to sell the house to negroes, to which Miss Ebbert told them she was the owner of the property and intended to keep on living in it, and that we would take the matter up with the police . . . as we were incorporated under the religious laws of the state.[34]

Ruhe goes on to say that the police finally came, dispersed the crowd, and escorted the black Bahá'ís to their homes, after telling all the Bahá'ís not to have any more integrated meetings in this part of the city. Although the men had placed a Ku Klux Klan sticker on Ebbert's door, the police said that the men were more likely part of the West End Cooperative Association, a white supremacist organization whose goal was to keep the West End of the city of Atlanta strictly segregated. This explained why Ebbert was asked if she intended to sell the house.

This event prompted the Atlanta LSA to find a building in a safe, nonresidential section of town where integrated feasts and other meetings could be held. Ironically, just two months prior to this incident, the Atlanta community had received a letter from Shoghi Effendi, which read in part:

> The friends must, at all times, bear in mind that they are, in a way, like soldiers under attack. The world is at present in an exceedingly dark condition spiritually; hatred and prejudice of every sort, are literally tearing it to pieces. We, on the other hand, are the custodians of the opposite forces, the forces of love, of unity, of peace and integration, and we must constantly be on our guard, whether as individuals or as an assembly or a community, lest through us these destructive, negative forces enter into our midst. . . . Love for each other, the deep sense that we are a new organism, the dawn-breakers of a New World Order, must constantly animate our Bahá'í lives, and we must pray to be protected from the contamination of society which is so diseased with prejudice.[35]

The community immediately began looking for rented space to use as a Bahá'í Center. Two months later, on June 29, 1947, the Atlanta Bahá'ís celebrated the grand opening of the city's first Bahá'í Center, a rented upstairs room in the Gazette Building in downtown Atlanta. Unfortunately, the rented room downtown was not the final solution. About a year and a half after the Bahá'ís began using the room, the whole building was shut down for renovations due to a change in the management of the property.[36]

The problem of being at the mercy of one's landlord was solved by Leroy Burns, an African American believer.[37] A postal employee, Burns already owned some property on Edgewood Avenue, one block off historic Auburn Avenue in the heart of the African American section of Atlanta, and he decided to build a Bahá'í Center for the Atlanta community at that location.[38] Burns and his son, Onslow, made the cement blocks for the building with their own hands, stacking them in the back yard until they were needed.[39] Raymond Lindsey, who worked as a building inspector for the city of Atlanta, used his professional skills to make sure the building passed city codes.[40] The community was able to move into their new home in late July 1949,[41] and it was dedicated the next year. All those I interviewed about this period in Atlanta Bahá'í history agreed that the location of the Atlanta Bahá'í Center was a source of conflict in the early stages. Some whites were uncomfortable with it being in a predominantly black part of town. But the genuine need for an interracial meeting space seems to have quickly won over most if not all community members, even those with initial reservations.

During my fieldwork, several Bahá'ís mentioned the need for a new Bahá'í Center, with space for larger crowds and adequate parking. However, there is talk among some Atlanta Bahá'ís that the Center should be registered as a historic site and preserved, and longtime members of the community told me with pride that the construction of the center was itself an interracial effort. As such, they said, it was a physical symbol of the Bahá'í principle of racial unity and the oneness of humanity.

Race Unity Efforts by Atlanta Bahá'ís

Atlanta's Bahá'ís take pride in their long history of race unity efforts, and how that history bears witness to their commitment to the oneness of humanity. These efforts continue today, and serve as an intensive focus of both deepenings and teaching. The Bahá'ís' willingness to confront racial prejudice was a factor in many individuals' declaration as Bahá'ís, especially African American believers. One relatively new African American believer said:

> My main problem at that age was racism [directed against himself]. And
> I tried to reconcile myself to it over the years, based on belief in Jesus
> and teachings of the other prophets, and I knew this [racism] was not of
> God, but it seemed it was getting stronger. Sometimes it looked like
> none of the prophets had ever showed up, in terms of the racism that
> was around!

He said that at a real low point in his life, he met his first Bahá'í, and was overjoyed that God had sent another revelation. He said, "The main teaching that attracted me was that Bahá'u'lláh taught that the whole earth is but one country, and mankind its citizens. God hasn't taught or created racism. It's men who instituted that." He went on to say that he initially saw Bahá'ís as "holy people," the first he had met who in his opinion confronted racial prejudice.

Another man, a community leader in suburban Atlanta, converted to the Bahá'í Faith from the Nation of Islam, and had to completely rethink his belief, as taught by Elijah Muhammad, that white men were "devils." He felt that the Bahá'í Faith was one of the few organizations in American society that systematically teaches racial unity as a core principle, and is structured in a way that facilitates interaction among different cultures and ethnicities (through its parish-like geographical boundaries and participatory Nineteen-Day Feast consultation). He recognized, however, that just because one believes in Bahá'u'lláh doesn't mean one's prejudices, learned throughout life, are automatically wiped away. This is true, he said, for blacks *and* whites:

> You know that there are racist attitudes that exist in some individuals in the Bahá'í community. The divine institutions of the Bahá'í Faith are capable of handling it. . . . Because there ain't no racism in the Bahá'í Faith, but there is racism in individual Bahá'ís. . . . Racism is a result of fear. . . . And I know the divine institutions, be they Auxiliary Boards, Counselors, National Assembly, or the Universal House of Justice, can handle it, no problem. . . . So, at one time, I would see these attitudes surface, and it would bother me, you know what I'm saying? . . . So my faith is more in the institutions than in the individuals.

Several African American believers expressed the above sentiment. Drawing from the spiritual resources in their scripture, Bahá'ís recognize that they must have patience with each other's at times imperfect attempts to put Bahá'í ideals into practice. Bahá'ís say that "progressive revelation" applies not only to the unfolding of God's plan over human history, but also to the slow evolution of the "Bahá'í perspective" within each adherent's life, as each Bahá'í learns through deepening to apply the Writings to personal and social circumstances. One African American woman who had been in the religion for twenty years said that "the Faith is perfect, but we [Bahá'ís] are not." She expressed confidence in the wisdom and guidance of the Administrative Order to overcome any individual shortcomings.

The next two sections examine two activities in the Atlanta community that illustrate the Bahá'í concern for eliminating racism: Pupil of the Eye and the Martin Luther King Jr. National Holiday Celebration.

PUPIL OF THE EYE

Every week throughout my period of fieldwork, the Pupil of the Eye Institute would meet, initially in individuals' homes, and then later at the Atlanta Bahá'í Center.[42] This gathering of Bahá'ís and non-Bahá'ís (of whom at least two converted) most often deepened on the *Vision of Race Unity* statement published by the NSA of the United States.

Most of the Pupil of the Eye meetings were dominated by African American men. Occasionally the group would be about half black and half white, but usually there were only two or three white Bahá'ís in attendance. Several of the new, active African American men in the metro Atlanta Bahá'í community had converted at this gathering, after attending as seekers for as long as eight months. Other than a white woman married to one of the African American men (she and her husband were both regulars), there were rarely women present at these meetings.

I will describe a composite, "typical" Pupil of the Eye meeting, held in the home of the interracial couple. Before the meeting, we gathered in their living room, venturing into the kitchen to help ourselves to the potluck dinner. The four or five children there went upstairs to play while the adults had their meeting. The formal meeting started with a one-man skit by the African American facilitator of the Pupil of the Eye, a monologue about the racism faced by black men growing up in the South, and about how young black boys do not understand the difficulties faced by their fathers and grandfathers only forty years ago. He ended the performance and received a huge round of applause. Then there was a slide show of pictures taken at the March on Washington in August 1993, commemorating the thirtieth anniversary of Dr. Martin Luther King's "I Have a Dream" speech. Several pictures showed general scenes of the Lincoln Memorial and the reflecting pool, but most were pictures of Bahá'ís who attended the event—most holding Bahá'í and race unity banners, with a quote from Bahá'u'lláh or a picture of black and white hands shaking.[43] In the background, the facilitator played one of the songs from the Bahá'í Gospel Choir tape.

To get discussion going for the evening, the African American facilitator, who had only been a Bahá'í for one year, read a story called "A Solo Song: For Doc" (McPherson 1972), about the life of a black waiter in a passenger car on the railroad, and the racism he faced. This took about thirty minutes. Discussion started slowly afterward, until one man said that he noticed that the only people talking were black, and that he would like to hear some white voices. One of the white middle-aged men attending said that he felt that it is good for whites to hear some of this stuff, and that he was appreciative of the blacks in the Bahá'í community who accepted him and taught him. He said he realized that as a white male, he was given all of the privileges in society. One young white man said he had heard Robert Henderson, secretary general of the NSA, say in a speech that given current trends, it will take more than four hundred years to eradicate salary discrimination, and that housing segregation will never end. He said he felt that integration has historically meant that blacks must blend in with the whites, and that as a Bahá'í he should move into a black neighborhood as an expression of his faith.

This launched the group into a discussion of what individuals can do to improve the racial climate in the United States. One black woman said she felt that the Bahá'í community should support individuals' attempts to teach non-Bahá'ís about race unity. She said that she was passing out the *Vision of Race Unity* statements at her place of work and the boss got very upset and said that they did not have those types of problems at her work site. She felt that if she had not stopped, she would have lost her job. She said that she felt vindicated later when the boss approached her, said that they needed to address racial issues, and asked if she could lead the effort.

An African American man said that Bahá'ís need to be able to go to their LSAs and ask for help in dealing with tough teaching situations, or in learning how best to employ their skills for teaching. By doing this, he said, Bahá'ís are helping their institutions mature, which is one of the goals of the Three Year Plan. He said that Bahá'ís need to become mature enough to deal with all of the problems of our society.

A white woman, wife of the facilitator, asked the African American Bahá'ís how they knew when to judge someone's behavior to be racist, and when they were just being "too sensitive." Two African American men explained that as Bahá'ís, blacks have had to learn to be very detached and patient during Feasts, and to not jump to the conclusion that there is purposeful racism in the community. One said that he had to realize that whites have been conditioned to act and say and believe the things that they do, and it takes a while to unlearn those habits. He said he felt he needed to be forgiving, and turn his energy to educating. A younger white man, who had been a Bahá'í for only a couple of months, said he felt that sometimes when others felt he was racist, he felt he was just being himself. He said that he has a tendency to interrupt people, and that when he does it to blacks, he doesn't feel that he is being racist, but just being himself. He said it hurts him to be called racist when he doesn't feel that's the issue.

The facilitator then said he thought it was appropriate to read to the group from Shoghi Effendi's *Advent of Divine Justice,* where he talks about the duties of both blacks and whites, which include "genuine love, extreme patience, true humility, consummate tact, sound initiative, mature wisdom, and deliberate, persistent, and prayerful effort" to achieve unity in diversity (Effendi 1963, 34).

Discussion of this quotation lasted until midnight. The facilitator made sure everyone got a chance to present their views or ask questions they did not feel they could ask in other settings (the goal of these deepenings, the facilitator said, was to create a "safe discussion" for both races to be "honest but loving"). After some dessert and more informal discussion, the group ended the meeting around 1:00 a.m. with a Bahá'í prayer for unity. While the discussion was sometimes tense, participants expressed their joy at being able to be open, honest, and yet unified.

MARTIN LUTHER KING JR. NATIONAL HOLIDAY CELEBRATION

Bahá'í involvement in Atlanta's Martin Luther King Jr. Center for Nonviolent Social Change has grown ever since the Bahá'ís marched as a group in their first parade in 1986 (the holiday has been officially celebrated since 1985). Over the years, Bahá'ís have gone from being one of many participant groups, to entering a large float, co-marshalling the televised parade, and serving on the Federal Holiday Commission that oversees the King national holiday.[44]

In 1993, the Bahá'ís had a much higher public profile and were especially prominent in the number of activities with which they were involved. The main event was the nationally televised March of Celebration on January 18; Robert C. Henderson, Secretary General of the National Spiritual Assembly, was co-grand marshal of the event. More than seven hundred Bahá'ís from all over the United States were reported to have participated in the march.[45]

Throughout King Week, Atlanta Bahá'ís intensified their teaching, fireside, and proclamation activities. For example, David Hofman, a former UHJ member, spoke at numerous locations around the city, including the Chamblee Chinese Community Center and the historically African American Interdenominational Theological Center (*The American Bahá'í* 24, no. 6:3).

The following year, King Week 1994 saw a similar level and intensity of Bahá'í activity. David Hofman, Robert Henderson, and Carole Miller (the latter two were the Bahá'í representatives on the King Federal Holiday Commission) were prominently featured in various marches, ecumenical services, and parades throughout the week. Bahá'ís once again sponsored the Martin Luther King Jr. World Prayer and Multicultural Day program at the King Center, and two hundred Bahá'ís—nearly half of the total marchers—marched in freezing rain on January 17 in the National March of Celebration (*The American Bahá'í* 25, no. 3:1). In addition, NSA member Patricia Locke read an American Indian invocation from Bahá'í Writings at the Nineteenth annual Labor/Management/Government Social Responsibility Awards breakfast, and the Atlanta Bahá'í Gospel Choir was featured in a "gospel/spiritual extravaganza" (*The American Bahá'í* 25, no. 3:11) at Spelman College sponsored by the Atlanta Bahá'í Arts Institute.

Finally, the Bahá'í perspective was prominent in a speech given by NSA Secretary General Robert Henderson at the King Center as part of the Martin Luther King Jr. World Prayer and Multicultural Day program. Henderson said:

> One of the lessons the civil rights movement taught us is that we can
> desegregate the lunch counter, and we can desegregate the bus station
> and the airport and the courtrooms, but until we desegregate the
> kitchen table and until we desegregate the living room sofa, until we
> desegregate those places where loving is done and where friends are
> made and where we express those things that really matter, we will not

have achieved the dream of bringing the human family together. (*The American Bahá'í* 25, no. 3:10)

Voices of Unity in Atlanta

Race unity activity is an important expression of Atlanta Bahá'ís' identity as situated universalists. From small interracial gatherings in Bahá'í homes (such as the weekly Pupil of the Eye meeting) to nationally televised events with significant Bahá'í involvement, concern for race unity is woven into Atlanta Bahá'í discourse and activity. Racial unity is the most tangible expression in Atlanta of how Bahá'ís "think globally, but act locally." It is for members of this religious movement the quintessential expression of a "situated universalist" identity. But racial unity is just one aspect of a global worldview Bahá'ís themselves refer to as "the Bahá'í perspective." When topics in the news were discussed at deepenings or Firesides, Bahá'ís frequently said, "Well, the Bahá'í perspective on that issue is. . . . " Many Bahá'ís would refer to "our perspective" as if every member of their faith would necessarily see an issue in the same way. This is definitely not the case, as the often spirited discussions during deepenings would attest.[46] However, numerous conversations and interviews with Bahá'ís revealed that an explicit "perspective" *does* emerge in the crucible of Bahá'í local institutions—one that is global and universal.

Some Bahá'ís come into their faith with a global perspective, which is why they initially found the religion attractive (see chapter 2). But most I talked with said that their universal worldview is enriched and deepened by reading the Bahá'í Writings and serving on Bahá'í institutions. One Bahá'í active on Atlanta's LSA said that he definitely sees the Bahá'í perspective as being different from the Christianity of his childhood:

> I think that's definite and always true. That we [Bahá'ís] are as concerned about Bahá'ís in China as we are in Europe, or anywhere—New Guinea—as we are about those that are similar to us [in the United States]. . . . I don't think Christians see Christians on the other side of the globe as part of their family. But I think Bahá'ís do.

He went on to talk about his "global family":

> I would like to say that I've become more global [as a Bahá'í]. . . . You become global in the sense that your family is scattered around the globe. That was one of the things that I remember when I first came into the Faith, realizing that no matter what city I was in anywhere, that if there is a Bahá'í community there, I've got family. And I think that contributes to a closeness in the Bahá'í community.

An African American woman spoke passionately of her concern as a Bahá'í for all of humanity:

> This society will not dictate to me how I will behave. . . . There are no leaders to stand for [everyone]. Nobody is standing for all humanity that can live a life that they love, that all humanity can have a future, all humanity can be related. No one is standing for that. But that is what we stand for. Bahá'u'lláh stood for that.

Most Bahá'ís I spoke with agreed that the large Persian influx into the metro Atlanta Bahá'í community has added to and enriched their global perspective. One married couple said this about the influence of Persian believers:

> A: To some degree at least, I think I attribute the emphasis on teaching, of constant teaching, a lot to the large number of Iranian believers. Because that is so foremost with them. Whatever you're doing, to be constantly teaching. Yea, I think it's changed the way we view ourselves.
>
> B: It also woke [Bahá'ís] up to some degree, and made whole bunches of provincial folk realize it is an international religion.
>
> A: That's just it. It's changed how we see ourselves as a community, that we are an international community.

They went on to say that the Persian community has taught Atlanta Bahá'ís a lot about their faith, and introduced new tensions. Having had access to Bahá'u'lláh's writings—especially the *Kitáb-i-Aqdas*—in Arabic long before the English translation became available, Persians were more educated on the nuances of the laws of Fasting and the prescribed way of doing certain prayers (for example, ablutions before daily obligatory prayers). Many Bahá'ís I spoke with said that Persians also were more conscious of the importance of celebrating the Bahá'í Holy Days and festivals, and thus helped to further incorporate the Bahá'í calendar into non-Persian Bahá'ís' identity.

Although Persians in general had a greater grasp of certain facets of their faith, most Bahá'ís agree that Persian believers in no way consider themselves "superior" or "exemplary" Bahá'ís.[47] One white man, who has served on numerous assemblies with Persian believers, said:

> They [Iranian Bahá'ís] are just so good about the fact that the way they do things as Iranian believers is not the way you have to do it. They are so welcoming of us [American converts] expressing our Bahá'í religion through our own culture or our own individual paths. It's like they love to see that happen. That to me is very unique. You know, what you'd expect is here's these people . . . their faith is so valuable to them, that they've lost their lives and left their homes [in Iran] and all their wealth, and started over here. You would think that people who are so attached to something like that would want it done their way. They don't.

It is not only those who grow up in America and convert to this religion who appreciate the Bahá'í Faith's worldview. Another Persian couple expressed these sentiments concerning the universality of their faith. The husband said:

> If you want to know what the Bahá'í Faith means, you better leave your
> country, and go to another country. Then you will really see the power
> of the Bahá'í Faith. Then you will see that people are wonderful, people
> are beautiful. We never felt like we are not home, because they [Bahá'ís]
> made us to feel at home. . . . The point I'm trying to make, that really if
> you get out of your country, and go to another country, you will see
> regardless of your race, regardless of your nationality, regardless of your
> background, immediately you are home. Immediately you have friends.
> Friends who are better than your relatives, in some cases.

His wife went on to discuss in detail the tensions that surfaced in the Atlanta Bahá'í community with the influx of Iranians after 1979. She confronted this issue when serving on the Persian-American Affairs Committee, a branch of the NSA. She attributes initial tensions between Americans and Persians to cultural unfamiliarity:

> We saw some difficulty because of culture, because Iranians had a
> different culture. Although we both [Americans and Iranians] believe in
> brotherhood and Bahá'u'lláh and Bahá'í ideas, we saw contrasts in
> culture. For example, the respect you show for your prayer book. For us,
> it is in the top place [indicates the top of the bookcase], not put on the
> carpet, or in the back pocket or something like that. We have more
> respect. That is the way we were brought up. But, there is nothing
> wrong: Bahá'í prayers can be everywhere.

One young Persian man, who along with most of his family converted in Iran from Shi'ite Islam, also talked about the universality of the Bahá'í perspective. When asked to compare the Bahá'í Faith in Iran and Atlanta, he said:

> Not really [any difference]. That is the beauty of the Bahá'í Faith.
> Everybody does it the same. As I said, I was in Africa before I came here.
> The Bahá'í Faith made people so unified, made the whole concept of
> religion so unique, you just go to Africa, you see Bahá'ís. The only thing
> you don't know about them is their name. When you find their name
> then you have the same religion, the same beliefs, they are striving for
> the same oneness of mankind, and unity of mankind, and reduction of
> all prejudices. Basically striving for the same thing, not like Christianity
> or Islam with all the sects fighting each other.

These quotations are instructive about the "Bahá'í perspective," because they illuminate the Bahá'í viewpoint on the intersection of religion and culture. What, for Bahá'ís, is the relationship between a universal ideology and pluralistic national/ethnic cultures? Bahá'ís frequently indicate that the future "world culture" and "global civilization"—which they believe will be based on Bahá'í principles and institutions—will be a fusion of the best in all existing cultures. One of the many "myths" that circulate among Atlanta Bahá'ís is that Persians are more "spiritual," while Americans are better "administrators" (see also Wyman 1985). Each can learn from the other, Bahá'ís point out. Aspects of traditional culture can be kept, Bahá'ís say, as long as it does not contradict the principles, laws, and spirit of their faith, which they feel transcend particularistic cultural expression. Unity in diversity is the ultimate goal. To this end, Atlanta Bahá'ís utilize the symbolic resources in their faith: the example of 'Abdu'l-Bahá, the guidance of Shoghi Effendi and the National Spiritual Assembly, and the Bahá'ís' own local history.

Summary

Given the prevalence of Bahá'ís' references to their global "perspective" during interviews and participant observation, statistical analysis was performed to explore whether or not there were measurable expressions of a global worldview. Three possible ways of measuring how Bahá'ís "think globally" while "acting locally" were constructed and tested: contribution to nonlocal Bahá'í Funds; staying informed about the national and/or international Bahá'í community; and the emphasis placed on participation in race unity activity.[48] The results of these analyses indicate that the common denominator in predicting the likelihood of an individual Bahá'í having a global perspective was the amount of teaching he or she did. Those Bahá'ís who scored higher on measures of teaching also tended to score higher on all three measures of a universal, global perspective.

This suggests that teaching, as an important way Bahá'ís act as reflexive situated universalists, helps confirm and sustain a "Bahá'í global perspective." I think this is due to the nature of teaching as an integral part of a Bahá'í identity. It is certainly the most important concern of the Bahá'í Administrative Order. This can be seen in the emphasis Bahá'ís place on the religion's teaching plans, where the focus is on educating humanity about the Bahá'í claim of universal salvation. Teaching in one's local community is a religious duty for a Bahá'í, and when done in the context of a universal ideology that values the oneness of humanity and world citizenship, it facilitates "thinking globally, but acting locally."

It is also true that the more important teaching is to the individual Bahá'í, the more likely one is to base one's teaching efforts on the directives and goals of the Three Year Plan. Because the teaching plans flow from the World Center through National Spiritual Assemblies, local teaching efforts by committed Bahá'ís are more likely to be linked to the national and global levels of the

Administrative Order. Active teaching also makes a Bahá'í conscious that he/she is fulfilling the directives of what is believed to be a divinely-inspired authority, and participating in the building of the Kingdom of God—both powerful motivators.

This, together with the analysis presented throughout this book, leads me to the following model of how living a Bahá'í life shapes and constructs a Bahá'í's identity as a situated universalist:

Organizational Participation → Exposure to Authority/Ideology →
Teaching Activity → Global Bahá'í Identity

Participation in local Bahá'í ritual (seen in various Bahá'í meetings, deepening, Firesides, Feasts, LSA meetings, etc.) exposes one to the authority claims of the Bahá'í Administrative Order, as well as the symbols and scripture that reinforce and enact that authority. Those socialized into the worldview of Bahá'í authoritative institutions hear one clear and constant message: teach the Bahá'í Faith for the salvation of the world. This constant grassroots activity helps in the construction of a global identity, since teaching (as discussed above) is directed toward one's local assembly jurisdiction, but within a global context. In this way, Bahá'í ideology and institutions shape an adherent's identity reflexively, encapsulating the sociologically significant phrase: "thinking globally, but acting locally."

Chapter 9   Conclusion

So powerful is the light of unity that it can illuminate the whole earth.

> Bahá'u'lláh, *Gleanings from the*
> *Writings of Bahá'u'lláh*

The Bahá'í Faith as Global Religion

I began this book justifying a study of the Bahá'í Faith using sociological theory derived from Roland Robertson. Robertson says that in the midst of modern forces of globalization, social and religious movements must manage the tensions between the global and local; between universal forces and particular cultures; between the "world at large" (literally) and specific places. Much of the academic work on religious movements has focused on various studies of "fundamentalisms." Fundamentalists (re)appropriate core elements of a religious tradition as the "fundamentals" or essence of their worldview, identity, and way of life. The identity fostered is "tribal" because it delineates a pure "us" versus an impure "them." A similar process occurs among secular tribal movements, where the core identity can be racial, national, or ideological. Tribal responses manage the tension between universal and particular (or between global and local) in one of two ways. The first is by isolating movement participants from the pluralism inherent in the modern world. Members of these movements often build their own set of institutions insulated from the power of the secular state. The other management strategy is to battle the secular state's power or policy on issues of recognition, resources, or rights. Either way, a tribal response seeks to circle the wagons and to remain isolated from, or fight against, the forces of globalization.

What has received little sociological attention, however, is what might be called a universal religious response. A viable universal religious response would have to manage global-local tensions in ways very different from a tribal response, by establishing explicit links between the global and the local and creating a distinct social identity. Studying the Bahá'í Faith gives us an empirical look at the mechanisms by which a religious movement might attempt to do this.

The goal of this research was to analyze the lived reality of the Atlanta Bahá'í community. I wanted to explore their practices and beliefs, and the process by which a Bahá'í's identity as a situated universalist is socially constructed. I found, however, that in order to understand Bahá'ís in Atlanta, I also had to understand the activity of Bahá'ís in Chicago at the national level, and in Haifa, Israel, at the international level. No local Bahá'í community exists in isolation. The Bahá'í Administrative Order is a distinctive ecclesiastical organization that links democratically elected local governance with globally centralized authority. This linkage I have called "reflexive," since there is frequent communication and consultation between the local, national, and global levels of Bahá'í administration: individual Bahá'ís email the Bahá'í World Center for clarification on a passage in Bahá'u'lláh's Writings; the Universal House of Justice establishes teaching plans for growth and direction that are utilized by national and local Bahá'í communities, as well as by individuals.

A Bahá'í's identity as a situated universalist is constructed by both ideological and organizational mechanisms. The ideology of the Bahá'í Faith is universal: it posits the oneness of humanity and the oneness of religion, claiming that Bahá'í institutions are the model for a future world order and that as such they will establish the Kingdom of God as foretold in all the world's religions. The faith envisions a world undivided by national, religious, ethnic, or racial prejudice. But this universal ideology must be lived out in the local community in which the individual Bahá'í finds her- or himself situated. It is not enough to "think globally" as a Bahá'í; one must "act locally" on that worldview by promoting Bahá'í ideals wherever one lives. This includes the development of local Bahá'í institutions that will be the framework of local community life in the future—local institutions that are reflexively linked to national and global institutions. In this way, a Bahá'í's identity is built upon not only cosmopolitan plausibility structures (see Roof 1976), but global plausibility structures.

The organizational mechanisms by which a Bahá'í identity is socialized have also been analyzed throughout this study. Personal devotion brings individual Bahá'ís into contact with the symbolic power of their faith: reading scriptures Bahá'ís believe were written by the Manifestation of God himself; prayer that has been formalized, again by the founder of the faith; pilgrimage to the global center of the Bahá'í Faith, from which Bahá'ís believe infallible divine guidance continues to flow a century after the death of Bahá'u'lláh. Community ritual also reinforces the reflexive connection Bahá'í institutions create between the local and the global. Local worship includes an administrative portion where local Bahá'ís receive communication, encouragement, and vision from the national and the global centers of their faith (in the form of letters from the NSA or UHJ, or videotapes of activity at the World Center in Haifa).[1] While other U.S. religious movements or religious denominations are also global in their outreach,[2] I argue that Bahá'ís are global in a different way, in that the ideology and ecclesiastical structure of the Administrative Order shapes a Bahá'í's identity as a situated universalist.

The authority inherent in the Bahá'í Faith, found first in the claims of Bahá'u'lláh and then in the Administrative Order he founded, turns out to be crucial to understanding how Bahá'í ideological and organizational mechanisms shape a Bahá'í's identity. As was seen throughout this study, the more an individual Bahá'í recognizes the authority of the Administrative Order, the more likely he/she is to participate in Bahá'í administrative and worship ritual, and the more devout he/she is likely to be in terms of prayer, fasting, or scripture reading. The kinds of statistical analysis performed in this study make it impossible to determine causation; therefore, it may be just as likely that the more an individual Bahá'í participates in Feasts, Holy Days, LSA meetings, and Bahá'í elections, the more likely she/he is to assent to the authority of the Administrative Order. However, recognition of authority, adherence to the ideological claims of the Bahá'í Faith, personal devotion, and organizational participation are all dialectically related, reinforcing sociologist Emile Durkheim's (1973) contention that participation in religious ritual reinforces the ideological components of a religious group and shapes its moral solidarity.

While adherence to authority is significantly related to numerous Bahá'í practices, only rarely are demographic characteristics associated with elements of Bahá'í identity. In other words, in the vast majority of cases, a Bahá'í's race, gender, age, occupation, educational level, income, and previous religious background are unrelated to the individual's likelihood of being elected to the LSA, of participating in Feast and Holy Day celebrations, of engaging in prayer or fasting, of teaching, or of adhering to ideological principles. As pointed out in chapter 5, this is a distinctive finding among religious groups. This strengthens my contention that Bahá'ís, as situated universalists, have moderate success in socially constructing a distinct religious identity, one that is universal and embraces "unity in diversity."

Recognition of the authority inherent in the Bahá'í Administrative Order is significant in another way, however. This research has discussed the paradoxes and contradictions in the ways Bahá'ís talk about their faith: Bahá'ís support of the equality of women and men as a core social principle, yet women cannot be elected to the UHJ; Bahá'í scripture contains the solutions to the world's vexing problems, yet most Bahá'ís are unable to articulate the policy implications of these solutions; Bahá'í ideology of "progressive revelation" resolves the apparent contradictions in the world's religious systems, yet most Bahá'ís are unfamiliar with the substantial theological discrepancies around which so many religious conflicts revolve; Bahá'í ideals and institutions will lay the foundation for future world order and the Kingdom of God, yet Bahá'ís are forbidden from engaging in political activism as an avenue of social change, and are unsure how Bahá'í prescriptions for the future will come to fruition.

How do Atlanta Bahá'ís resolve these contradictions and discrepancies? As in all religions, they do so through faith: faith in the ultimate infallible authority of the Universal House of Justice as the rightful heir of Bahá'u'lláh's authority. As the woman quoted in chapter 4 said: "If he [Bahá'u'lláh] is who he says he is, then everything else falls into place." For Atlanta Bahá'ís, if Bahá'u'lláh is the "Manifestation of God for this day," and if he conferred infallible decision making upon the Universal House of Justice, then one's faith in that authority can resolve any potential cognitive dissonance (Festinger 1957) that might result from the apparent contradictions and hypocrisy discussed above. Throughout my fieldwork, Bahá'ís would frequently say in effect when I brought up one of the paradoxes: "Well, I don't know the answer to that, but the Universal House of Justice will figure that out in the future," or "The Universal House of Justice will clarify that when the time is right." This kind of absolute faith in the authority of the UHJ and Bahá'u'lláh alleviates Bahá'ís' concern that they themselves do not have every answer, and is another hallmark of a Bahá'í's identity as a situated universalist.

Epilogue

In October 1998, I undertook a follow-up research trip to Atlanta to investigate changes in the Bahá'í community since my fieldwork had ended in 1995. Two events stood out in the minds of the Atlanta Bahá'ís: the acquisition of a new Bahá'í Center and a large media campaign to help the Bahá'í Faith emerge from obscurity.

BAHÁ'Í UNITY CENTER

In 1995, the Bahá'ís of South DeKalb County purchased a church in the southeast section of the metro area. Converted into the Bahá'í Unity Center (BUC), the building now serves as a worship and meeting space as well as a community center. The community of Bahá'ís in South DeKalb county had grown to the point where meeting in homes had become impractical, and they wanted to establish a social and economic development agency for the surrounding predominantly African American population. The purchase initially entailed a large debt and renovation costs, but an anonymous Bahá'í donor in the Atlanta area paid off the mortgage, giving the South DeKalb community more financial freedom to initiate neighborhood development projects. The BUC consists of two buildings: the main one a traditional-looking church building with a sanctuary seat-ing approximately 225 (with Christian symbols removed), a kitchen, and classroom space; and the second a fellowship hall with attached gymnasium.

The South DeKalb LSA established the Family Unity Institute (FUI) as a joint venture with the Mottahedeh Development Services[3] in late 1995. The FUI established a number of programs housed at the BUC, with the stated goal of promoting "the positive qualities, character and skills of successful family and community life as an antidote to social ills. . . . We believe that [the moral fabric of society] can only be restored by efforts that recognize and apply universal spiritual principles . . . found at the heart of all major religious systems."[4] In 1996, collaborating with the Georgia Human Relations Commission, the FUI sponsored "Educating the Mind and Heart," a literacy and parenting program serving public schools in the South DeKalb County area. The FUI also received a grant from the Georgia Children and Youth Coordinating Council to initiate "Camp LORE" (Love of Reading Early) as a youth summer enrichment program using tutors to enhance reading skills and teach self-esteem through the arts. This program also involved parents by hosting weekly parent nights. Volunteers I talked with said that the vast majority of the public school youth involved in these programs were non-Bahá'ís, and students improved their word recognition skills by 67 percent. Bahá'ís in the South DeKalb community feel that these programs have raised the public visibility of the Bahá'í Faith tremendously in the surrounding community: not only the building with "Bahá'í Unity Center" on the door, but the word-of-mouth endorsement of the FUI.

The BUC also serves as a community center, offering English as a Second Language courses, a multicultural mothering group for mothers and children called "One Garden," and the "Dawnbreakers" Toastmasters club. In addition to the community development projects supported by the BUC that serve both Bahá'ís and non-Bahá'ís, there are numerous Bahá'í-specific programs. There are Sunday morning devotional services, which routinely include four to seven non-Bahá'í guests; "Youth Night" for teenagers; weekly practices for the Atlanta Bahá'í Gospel Choir; and "Health and Healing" classes to discuss spiritual and physical health from a Bahá'í perspective. The BUC also houses a Bahá'í Speaker's Bureau[5]; the Atlanta Bahá'í Arts Institute, sponsoring musical, artistic, and literary efforts that promote the Bahá'í Faith; and the Atlanta Area Bahá'í Training Institute (AABTI). The AABTI offers weekly or weekend courses ranging in price from $5 per person to $40 per family on various Bahá'í topics, including: new believers courses; "Arming for Victory" (in Persian for Iranian believers); how to teach the Bahá'í Faith; "core curriculum" training written by the National Bahá'í Center staff for those who want to establish Bahá'í children's classes in their community; the importance of race unity; and the Bahá'í perspective on marriage and family relationships.

Most of those I spoke with about the new center said that the BUC has infused southeast suburban Atlanta Bahá'í communities with a new excitement and a higher level of activity. One woman I interviewed said that it has raised the level of intercommunity cooperation, and also raised her awareness of her Bahá'í identity. She said that large teaching events, or even Bahá'í weddings, previously had to be held in university auditoriums or community civic centers. Now these important occasions can be at a *Bahá'í* center. She said: "So all of a sudden Bahá'í activities start to take on more of a Bahá'í identity, because there is no [Christian] cross in the background, or seal of the government [on the podium]."

But this new level of Bahá'í activity and visibility was not achieved without tension in the Bahá'í community. Soon after the acquisition of the BUC by the South DeKalb LSA, a few Bahá'ís intensified their ongoing discussions about reuniting the three assembly jurisdictions in DeKalb County. One person I interviewed said he felt that the three communities (North, Central, and South DeKalb) were too small for any of them to be able to do much long-term planning, and were racially divided according to the segregated housing patterns of the county. The southern third of the county is primarily African American, while the northern two-thirds is primarily white. He thought that reuniting the three LSAs would promote racial unity in the area Bahá'í community, and would also be a powerful model to the non-Bahá'í world. He said, "from the perspective of American media coverage, here are three churches who decided to reunite to overcome [racism]. That's all the story you need. You would have people beating on your door [to join]."

The area Bahá'ís did some research, and found that while it was rare for assembly jurisdictions to unite, it was not unprecedented, and was not prohibited outright by Bahá'í guidelines. Usually, communities would unite because a community had lost members and their LSA would have to disband if the number of adult Bahá'ís fell below nine persons. The Bahá'í National Center said that while the DeKalb county situation was an unusual case, if the communities decided to go ahead, the NSA would consider it. The two main proponents of the merger also contacted their local Assistants to the Auxiliary Board to keep them informed.

A Town Hall meeting was convened to present the idea of a merger. There was vocal opposition. Given that the South DeKalb community now had a Bahá'í Center, some community members from the northern part of the county expressed reservations about the extra driving time to get to Feasts, Holy Day celebrations, or deepenings. Others expressed grave reservations at the idea of eliminating what for Bahá'ís were sacred institutions inaugurated by Bahá'u'lláh. Why eliminate two functioning, healthy LSAs? One of the Town Hall leaders with whom I spoke said "the idea was just too radical. That is something that you just don't do. If anything, you subdivide [to make new LSAs]. You never go backward."

After the Town Hall meeting, each of the three LSAs consulted and voted on the proposal. The predominantly African American LSA in South DeKalb voted in favor of the merger; the other two predominantly white LSAs voted against it. One of the initial proponents of the idea told me that if he had known how the vote would turn out, he would never have suggested it. "It was very divisive," he said. The perception on the part of some in the South DeKalb assembly was that the predominantly white communities did not want to join with the chiefly black community. Most in the North DeKalb community said that it was more the "sanctity of the LSA as a divine institution" that convinced them it would be a mistake, and they didn't want to assume any of the financial responsibility for maintenance at the BUC. One person said she felt that Bahá'u'lláh was sending the Bahá'ís in that area a message as a result of the failed merger. Bahá'u'lláh wanted the white Bahá'ís to teach more African Americans, and the black Bahá'ís to teach more whites, as a way to achieve greater racial unity. The attempt to manufacture a racially diverse community was merely a "Band-Aid solution," she said. Another Bahá'í saw the tensions in the three DeKalb County communities as an opportunity to use the institutions of the Bahá'í Faith and the guidance in the Writings to foster greater intercommunity collaboration and dialogue.

Tensions have died down and community cohesiveness has improved, sources told me; volunteers for the various social and economic development projects have included North and Central DeKalb community members, and the three communities have continued to meet at the BUC for joint Feasts and Holy Day celebrations.

RACE UNITY MEDIA CAMPAIGN

Atlanta was chosen by the NSA to be the test site for a new nationwide media campaign. "The Vision of Race Unity" was a half-hour video produced by the NSA that communicated the Bahá'í perspective on race unity and the oneness of humanity. The NSA covered the costs of production and paid for air time on cable access channels and a local interfaith channel in Atlanta. From June through September 1997, the program aired twice a day for two weeks, and then twice a week throughout the remainder of the campaign. During my follow-up research trip to Atlanta in October 1998, I was told that on average, eight people called the local Bahá'í number given at the bottom of the screen every time the program aired, for a total of three hundred calls. Two-thirds of the callers only wanted literature sent to their homes; the other one hundred people wanted to be contacted personally for more information about the Bahá'í Faith. The majority of respondents were African American females, and to the surprise of the Greater Atlanta Task Force, which coordinated the effort, none of the calls were negative. Some of those who called pursued their interest further by attending specially arranged Firesides or "seekers classes" at the BUC. In all, three people signed declaration cards as a direct result of the media campaign (a "disappointing" outcome, according to one organizer).

However, those involved in the process told me that they considered it money and time well spent, for several reasons. First, it helped unify the metro Atlanta Bahá'ís, since all the communities had to work together to coordinate advertising for the cable program, and the Firesides for interested seekers. One man said that it was the best example he has seen of local and national Bahá'ís institutions working together in his twenty-five years as a Bahá'í. The NSA appointed the Greater Atlanta Task Force after considerable dialogue with local communities and several Town Hall meetings (instead of making appointments without soliciting input from the local community, which some Bahá'ís had complained about in the past).

Second, it "energized" the Bahá'í teaching activity in Atlanta. One leader in the effort said that it "made the Bahá'ís feel like we were legitimate. We were on TV, and that made us more visible and known. It really increased our teaching work." She said that for a period of three to four weeks, the campaign doubled the number of regular Firesides and deepenings. Third, the Bahá'ís learned more about promoting their religion in an already pluralistic religious market. "I think it was a good experience in a lot of ways. It was the first time we got our feet wet [using TV]," said one man. Another woman very active in coordinating the program said that this video was tested by the NSA with focus groups, and Bahá'ís learned a lot about marketing: talking about Bahá'í World Order and world government tended to scare people off; referring to "the Bahá'í community" made Bahá'ís sound like a cult; and using pictures of 'Abdu'l-Bahá had no resonance with non-Bahá'ís.

Not everyone in the metro community felt the energy of the media campaign, however. Some told me that unless you were directly involved in the planning or coordinating follow-up Firesides and literature distribution, it could easily have passed you by. One woman did say, however, that it did feel good to be able to say to friends and coworkers who expressed some interest in the Bahá'í Faith, "if you want more information in a low-key, nonconfrontational setting, check out the Bahá'í TV program."

CONTINUED COMMUNITY INVOLVEMENT

Those I talked with in 1998 reported that Atlanta Bahá'ís continue to make connections to the wider non-Bahá'í world, both as a method of teaching and to further their own social concerns. While Bahá'í involvement with the Martin Luther King Jr. Center for Nonviolent Social Change has diminished, mostly because of a change in leadership at the King Center that has resulted in the cancellation of many of the events Bahá'ís used to be involved in during the

January celebration, Bahá'ís have expanded their active participation in other venues. Bahá'ís were involved in the Olympic Interfaith Advisory Council during the 1996 Atlanta Olympics, and they have worked with the Georgia Human Relations Council, the DeKalb County Board of Education, and the Carter Presidential Center's Committee on Religion for the Atlanta Project. Bahá'ís continue to support those non-Bahá'í efforts that promote "unity in diversity."

Appendix A

Atlanta Bahá'í
Questionnaire

To answer the questions in most cases simply put an "X" or check in the blank in front of the answer you want to give. In some instances you can give more than one answer. For a few questions you will be asked to write your answer in the space or blank provided. Please complete both sides of each page.

On Becoming a Bahá'í

1. How long have you been a Bahá'í? _____ years.

2. In the space below, write the source from which you <u>first</u> learned about the Bahá'í Faith? (for example: your parents, a friend, a public meeting, a fireside, grew up in a Bahá'í home, etc.):

3. As you think back to when you enrolled, what things most convinced you to become a Bahá'í? <u>Rank</u> the top three reasons by putting a "1" in the blank next to your top reason, a "2" by the next most important reason, and a "3" by the third most important reason:
    ____Personal esteem for the person(s) who introduced me to the Bahá'í Faith.
    ____Agreement with Bahá'í spiritual principles
    ____The diversity within the Bahá'í Faith
    ____Felt an affinity for the Writings of Bahá'u'lláh
    ____Agreement with Bahá'í social principles
    ____I was raised as a Bahá'í
    ____Felt a love for one or more of the Central Figures of the Faith
    ____The fact that the Faith has no clergy
    ____The fact that I can go anywhere in the world and find Bahá'ís
    ____Other (specify): ____ __ .... __ _____.

IF YOU WERE NOT RAISED AS A BAHA'I, please write in the space below your previous religious background (if you grew up in a Christian church, specify your denomination):

On Being a Bahá'í

1. Please indicate below which Bahá'í positions you now hold or have held in the past.

	Now hold	Held in past but not now	Never held
Member of Local Spiritual Assembly	____	____	____
Officer of Local Spiritual Assembly	____	____	____
Assistant to Auxiliary Board	____	____	____
Member of local committee	____	____	____
Member of National committee	____	____	____
Other elected or appointed position (specify:_____)	____	____	____

2. Think for a moment of your 5 closest friends. How many of them are members of the Bahá'í Faith?

    ____None   ____One   ____Two   ____Three   ____Four   ____Five

3. On average, about how many hours per week do you devote to Bahá'í activities, including study, administrative work, prayer, teaching, and attending Bahá'í meetings?

    _____hours per week on average

4. Which of the following 3 activities give you the greatest personal satisfaction? Rank the top three most satisfying activities that you as a Bahá'í are involved in, putting a "1" in the blank next to the activity that gives you the most personal satisfaction, a "2" by the next most satisfying activity, and a "3" by the third most satisfying activity.

____Daily prayer
____Talking with other Bahá'ís about the Faith
____Attending Nineteen Day Feasts
____Attending local Bahá'í firesides or public meetings
____Reading the Bahá'í Writings
____Attending District Conventions
____Taking action on social issues
____Teaching the Bahá'í Faith
____Attending deepening classes
____Serving in an administrative position
____Keeping informed of Bahá'í activities around the world
____Other (specify): _____.

5. How often do you pray?

____Two times a day or more
____Once a day
____2 to 6 times a week
____Once a week
____Less often

6. How often do you personally read from each of the following kinds of Bahá'í literature?

Writings of	Daily	Weekly	Monthly	Less Often
Bahá'u'lláh				
The Báb				
'Abdu'l-Bahá				
Shoghi Effendi				
The Universal House of Justice				
Other Bahá'í authors				
Other Holy Books (Bible, Qur'án, etc.)				

7. Did you observe the Fast this year (in March, 1994)?

____Yes, fully   ____Yes, partly   ____No, for an excused reason   ____No

8. Have you personally made individual goals for yourself based on the Three Year Plan from the Universal House of Justice?

____Yes   ____No   ____I am not acquainted with the Three Year Plan

9. How regularly do you attend Nineteen Day Feasts?

____Always (all 19 Feasts in a year)
____Often (between 12-18 Feasts in a year)
____Sometimes (between 6-11 Feasts in a year)
____Seldom (between 1-5 Feasts in a year)
____Never (did not attend Feast in this last year, May 1993-May 1994)

10. Please check "Yes" or "No" on the following questions.

                                                                        Yes   No

Have you ever been homefront pioneering in the US?   _____   _____
Have you ever gone pioneering in another country?   _____   _____
Did you attend the Bahá'í World Congress
   in New York City in November, 1992?   _____   _____
Do you regularly participate in deepenings?   _____   _____
Have you ever been on pilgrimage to Haifa, Israel?   _____   _____
Have you ever <u>personally</u> participated in any of the Bahá'í-
   sponsored events celebrating the Martin Luther King,
   Jr. National Holiday here in Atlanta in January?   _____   _____

11. Did you attend District Convention last year (October, 1993) to elect a National Delegate?

    ____Yes   ____No   ____No, but I sent in an absentee ballot

    If no, have you <u>ever</u> attended a District Convention meeting?

        ____Yes   ____No

12. How often do you attend Holy Day celebrations throughout the Bahá'í year, in either your community or another?
    ____Most of the time (between 9-12 Holy Day celebrations in a year)
    ____Often (between 6-8 Holy Day celebrations in a year)
    ____Sometimes (between 3-5 Holy Day celebrations in a year)
    ____Seldom (between 1-2 Holy Day celebrations in a year)
    ____Never (did not attend any Holy Day celebrations this last year, May 1993-May 1994)

13. Did you vote in the latest Ridván election on April 21, 1994?

    ____Yes, in person   ____Yes, by absentee ballot   ____No

14. About how often do you speak about the Faith with friends, coworkers, neighbors, or relatives <u>who are not Bahá'ís</u>?
    ____At least two or more times a week
    ____About once a week
    ____About two or three times a month
    ____About once a month
    ____Less frequently

15. What teaching activities have you been involved with this past year? (Check all that apply)
    (1)____Hosting Firesides
    (2)____Speaking at Firesides
    (3)____Bringing seekers to others' Firesides
    (4)____Mass Teaching (for example: door-to-door or street teaching)
    (5)____Participation in teaching institutes
    (6)____Speaking with friends and coworkers one-to-one
    (7)____Travel teaching
    (8)____Participating in other teaching activities (specify): _____.
    (9)____Not involved in any teaching activities this last year (May 1993-May 1994)

    Write the number of the one teaching activity that you enjoy doing <u>most</u>: _____.

16. To which of the following Funds have contributions been made by you or your family either directly or by earmarking them through your local or national treasurer in 1993 or 1994? (check all that apply)
    (1)____The Bahá'í International Fund
    (2)____The Arc Fund
    (3)____The Continental Bahá'í Fund
    (4)____The National Bahá'í Fund
    (5)____The Local Bahá'í Fund

    Write the number of the Fund to which you or your family contributed the most: _____.

Organizational Participation Other Than Bahá'í

1. In the space below, list the names of all the non-Bahá'í organizations of which you are a member (for example: professional organizations such as the AMA, civic organization such as Rotary, organizations dealing with social or health issues such as Habitat for Humanity or the Red Cross, cultural organizations, alumni organizations, etc.). Please include local, state, national, and international organizations:

2. In the space below, list the names of the non-Bahá'í organizations to which you made a financial contribution in 1993 or 1994:

3. If you now do volunteer work of any kind, in the space below list the names of all the organizations for which you do volunteer work:

Keeping Informed About the Faith

Below are some possible ways which you might use to keep informed about the Bahá'í Faith. Check the blank under the heading which best describes your feelings about how important each source of information is for you personally.

	Very important	Somewhat important	Not very important	Not at all important	Does not apply; never seen
The American Bahá'í	____	____	____	____	____
House of Justice Messages	____	____	____	____	____
Feast Letters	____	____	____	____	____
Local newsletters	____	____	____	____	____
Bahá'í Newsreels	____	____	____	____	____
Individual conversation	____	____	____	____	____
Visiting speakers	____	____	____	____	____
Local computer bulletin board	____	____	____	____	____
National computer bulletin board	____	____	____	____	____
Other Bahá'í magazines or journals	____	____	____	____	____

Your Attitudes As a Bahá'í

Please answer the following questions by checking the blank which corresponds to whether you strongly agree, agree, are unsure, disagree, or strongly disagree with each of the statements.

	Strongly Agree	Agree	Unsure	Disagree	Strongly Disagree
Bahá'ís should cooperate with other religious and secular groups who have similar interests and goals as the Bahá'ís.	___	___	___	___	___
The Bahá'í Sacred Writings give me clear moral guidance in my daily life.	___	___	___	___	___
Bahá'ís should have a lot of latitude in following the decisions of the House of Justice.	___	___	___	___	___
I try to pattern all of my daily activities around the laws and principles of the Faith.	___	___	___	___	___
As a Bahá'í, I submit to the authority of the Administrative Order, even if I disagree with what it says.	___	___	___	___	___
The Bahá'í Faith has had very little influence on my views of current social issues.	___	___	___	___	___
Bahá'ís have been in the forefront in this country in promoting racial unity.	___	___	___	___	___
The most important thing for me to do as a Bahá'í is actively teach the Faith.	___	___	___	___	___
It is important for me as a Bahá'í to attend worship services of other religious faiths.	___	___	___	___	___
Bahá'í scripture is the authentic Word of God for this Day.	___	___	___	___	___
The National Spiritual Assembly should not interfere in the decisions of the local community.	___	___	___	___	___
The most important aspect of the Faith for me is spiritual growth based on the Writings.	___	___	___	___	___
It is important for me as a Bahá'í to make friends with people of other races and ethnic groups.	___	___	___	___	___
What happens at the national or international level is more interesting to me than what goes on in my local Bahá'í community.	___	___	___	___	___

Personal Background

1. What is your age? _____years

2. Sex: ____Male ____Female

3. Are you:
   ____Single, never married
   ____Married
   ____Divorced or separated
   ____Widow(er)

   If you are presently married, is your spouse a Bahá'í?

   ____Yes ____No

4. Are or were your parents Bahá'ís?

   ____Yes, both ____Yes, mother only ____Yes, father only ____No

5. What was the last year of school you completed?
   ____Some high school, but did not graduate
   ____High school graduate
   ____Some college or trade school
   ____Trade school or vocational degree
   ____College degree
   ____Some graduate study
   ____Master's degree
   ____Doctorate or professional degree (PhD, MD, Law degree, etc.)

6. Write in the space below your ethnic or racial background:

7. Write in the space below your occupation or job title:

8. In which Local Spiritual Assembly or group jurisdiction do you now live? (for example--Atlanta, Marietta, North Gwinnett, Southwest Cobb, South Dekalb, isolated believer, etc.) Write in your community's name: _____.

   How long have you lived in your present local Bahá'í community? _____ years

   How long have you lived in the metro-Atlanta area altogether? _____ years

9. What was the approximate total income of your household in 1993 before taxes?
   ____less than $10,000
   ____$10,000 to $19,999
   ____$20,000 to $34,999
   ____$35,000 to $49,999
   ____$50,000 to $74,999
   ____$75,000 to $99,999
   ____$100,000 or over

THANK YOU VERY MUCH FOR PARTICIPATING IN THIS SURVEY!

Appendix B   Historical Overview

The Bahá'í Faith was preceded historically by the Bábí religion, which began in 1844 when a Persian merchant named Siyyid 'Alí-Muhammad revealed himself to be the Qá'im ("He Who Ariseth"—the Promised one in Shi'ite Islam), or Twelfth, Hidden Imam (Hatcher and Martin 1985). He took the title of the Báb ("the Gate" in Arabic) and began to reveal new religious teachings. The thrust of his message was to herald the coming of "One Whom God Will Make Manifest," a prophet of greater importance who would lead humankind into a new era of peace. Thus, many Bahá'ís compare the Báb to John the Baptist, who heralded the coming of Christ. The Báb attracted a substantial following among Shi'ite Muslims, arousing the suspicions and distrust of Islamic authorities, especially the Islamic clergy. To crush this religious movement, the government of Persia executed the Báb in 1850 (Esslemont 1970), almost destroying the new religious movement. The Báb had not revealed when the "One Whom God Will Make Manifest" would come, but had indicated the time would be soon.

The narrative then shifts to Mírzá Husayn-'Alí, a Persian whose family was part of the governing class of the country. Upon hearing of the religion of the Báb, he converted and began teaching its message. His growing leadership role within the Bábí movement revitalized and invigorated the new religion. His social position protected him at first from the persecutions of the Persian authorities, but as fervor increased, he too was imprisoned (Hatcher and Martin 1985). Bahá'ís believe that while Mírzá Husayn-'Alí was in prison in Tehran in 1852–1853, God revealed to him that he was the "One Whom God Will Make Manifest" prophesied by the Báb, and that his teachings would usher in the long-awaited Kingdom of God. Persian authorities exiled Mírzá Husayn-'Alí, his family, and his fellow Bábís to Baghdad. Once in Baghdad, he took the title Bahá'u'lláh

("The Glory of God" in Arabic), and announced that he was the one promised by the Báb, whereupon the vast majority of Bábís pledged allegiance to Bahá'u'lláh and proclaimed his authority as their religious leader.

In 1863, the Bahá'ís (the new name given to the followers of Bahá'u'lláh) were banished from Baghdad and sent first to Constantinople (now Istanbul) and then to Adrianople (now Edirne) in Turkey. Finally, in 1868, the group was exiled permanently to 'Akká, Palestine, the prison-city of the Ottoman empire ('Akká [Acca] is near present-day Haifa, Israel, the location of the Bahá'í World Center). Here, as in the other cities of his exile, Bahá'u'lláh carried on his ministry; he wrote nearly one hundred volumes that today form a large part of Bahá'í scripture, and met with pilgrims who traveled to 'Akká to see the man whose message was spreading throughout Persia and the Middle East.

When Bahá'd'lláh died in 1892, he left behind a growing movement, and a will and testament that named his eldest son, 'Abdu'l-Bahá ("Servant of the Glory" in Arabic), his successor and the authoritative interpreter of Bahá'í writings. After the Young Turk revolution in 1908 (Hatcher and Martin 1985), all political and religious prisoners of the Ottoman Empire were released. 'Abdu'l-Bahá too was free to begin establishing his father's Covenant: the institutionalization of the Bahá'í Administrative order as set out in Bahá'u'lláh's writings.

In implementing Bahá'í teachings, 'Abdu'l-Bahá helped define two major institutions: the Guardianship and the Universal House of Justice (UHJ). The Guardianship imparted sole authority of the religion to 'Abdu'l-Bahá's eldest grandson (Bahá'u'lláh's great-grandson), Shoghi Effendi Rabbani, who would continue the consolidation of the religion's Administrative Order. Upon 'Abdu'l-Bahá's death in 1921, Shoghi Effendi as Guardian became the leader of the Bahá'í Faith, and served in that capacity until his death in 1957. From 1957 until the first election of the UHJ in 1963, the "Hands of the Cause of God," a temporary administrative institution (inaugurated by Bahá'u'lláh) of charismatic, faithful Bahá'ís governed the Bahá'í Faith. Since 1963 the UHJ has been the recognized global authority of the world's approximately five million Bahá'ís.

Toward the end of his life, Bahá'u'lláh appointed four persons as "Hands of the Cause of God," and charged them with promoting the interests of the Bahá'í Faith. 'Abdu'l-Bahá later conferred this rank on a few individuals after their deaths. However, it was Shoghi Effendi who most effectively used these individuals in building Bahá'í institutions. In 'Abdu'l-Bahá's *Will and Testament*, Shoghi Effendi (as Guardian) was given the authority to appoint Hands of the Cause, and to appoint the succeeding Guardian of the Bahá'í Faith. The successor to the Guardian was to be the "first-born" of his lineal descendants; if his first born lacked the spiritual qualifications, then Shoghi Effendi was to appoint one of the male descendants of Bahá'u'lláh (Taherzadeh 1992).

During his tenure as Guardian, Shoghi Effendi appointed thirty-two Hands of the Cause (Taherzadeh 1992) to be his personal deputies in the establishment of the Administrative Order. However, Effendi and his wife never had any children, and all of Bahá'u'lláh's descendants had been excommunicated because of their opposition to the Bahá'í Faith and "violation of the Covenant." Since there was no provision in 'Abdu'l-Bahá's *Will and Testament* for these circumstances, there have been no further Guardians in the Bahá'í Faith since Shoghi Effendi's death in 1957. However, Bahá'ís say that the "institution of Guardianship" continues through the guidance given to the Bahá'í world in Shoghi Effendi's voluminous writings and personal correspondence. Since 'Abdu'l-Bahá conferred authority to appoint Hands of the Cause on the Guardian alone, upon the death of the three remaining Hands of the Cause still alive at this writing, this institution of the Administrative Order will also lapse; at that point the authority to excommunicate therefore falls solely to the UHJ.

It is important to note that at several times during a transition in charismatic authority in the Bahá'í Faith, a schism was attempted by what Bahá'ís call "Covenant-Breakers" (discussed in chapter 6). When Bahá'u'lláh declared his mission in 1863, his younger half-brother, Mírzá Yahyá, refused to acknowledge Bahá'u'lláh's claim to be the prophet promised by the Báb. Yahyá eventually declared himself to be the Báb's successor. When Bahá'u'lláh was banished to 'Akká, Palestine, Yahyá and his small group of followers were exiled to the island of Cyprus. Upon Yahyá's death in 1912, his group died out. Similarly, when 'Abdu'l-Bahá died in 1921, his half-brother, Mírzá Muhammad-'Alí, claimed to be 'Abdu'l-Bahá's successor. These claims were repudiated by the vast majority of Bahá'ís, given 'Abdu'l-Bahá's written will. Muhammad-'Alí's followers became disorganized, and most abandoned him even before his death in 1937. Finally, when Shoghi Effendi died in 1957, an American named Mason Remey, appointed a Hand of the Cause of God by Effendi, declared himself to be the second Guardian of the Bahá'í Faith. Despite the fact that he was neither Shoghi Effendi's son nor a descendent of Bahá'u'lláh, some American believers, distraught at the loss of the Guardian, followed Remey. All were declared "Covenant-Breakers" by the other Hands of the Cause, and were expelled from the Bahá'í Faith. When Remey died, several of his lieutenants vied for the position of "third" Guardian, dividing his followers into numerous sects, none of which have grown. So, while there have been several schisms in Bahá'í history (contrary to the claim of some Bahá'ís that there have been no divisions in the Bahá'í Faith's 150–year history), none has succeeded in garnering substantial support, with most groups eventually dying out altogether (see Taherzadeh 1992; Stockman 1985).

For a more detailed account of Bahá'í history, see Effendi 1932, 1995; Esslemont 1970; Hatcher and Martin 1985; Smith 1987; Stockman 1985, 1995; Taherzadeh 1974, 1992.

Appendix C   The Bahá'í Calendar

The Bahá'í religious calendar, called the *Badí'* (wondrous) calendar, was formulated by the Báb and refined by Bahá'u'lláh. It is based on the Zoroastrian calendar, which places the new year, or *Naw-Rúz*, on the vernal equinox—the first day of spring, usually March 21 (Walbridge 1996, 181). Like the Persian calendar, the *Badí'* calendar begins the week on Saturday. Friday is the Bahá'í day of rest. Years are grouped into two different types of cycles: the *váhid* ("unity"), which is nineteen years; and the *kull-i-shay'* ("all things"), which is 361 years (Walbridge 1996, 186).

The following are the names of the months and days of the Bahá'í year:

Month of year	Arabic	English	First day of month
1st	Bahá	Splendor	March 21
2nd	Jalál	Glory	April 9
3rd	Jamál	Beauty	April 28
4th	'Azamat	Grandeur	May 17
5th	Núr	Light	June 5
6th	Rahmat	Mercy	June 24
7th	Kalimát	Words	July 13
8th	Kamál	Perfection	August 1
9th	Asmá	Names	August 20
10th	'Izzat	Might	September 8
11th	Mashíyyat	Will	Seotember 27
12th	'Ilm	Knowledge	October 16

Month of year	Arabic	English	First day of month
13th	Qudrat	Power	November 4
14th	Qawl	Speech	November 23
15th	Masá'il	Questions	December 12
16th	Sharaf	Honor	December 31
17th	Sultán	Sovereignty	January 19
18th	Mulk	Dominion	February 7
Intercalary Days February 26 to March 1, inclusive			
19th	'Alá,	Loftiness	March 2

In addition, each day has not only its corresponding day of the month, but a name for the day of the week—another similarity to the Zoroastrian calendar. The names of the days of the week are:

Day of the Week	Arabic	English
Saturday	Jalál	Glory
Sunday	Jamál	Beauty
Monday	Kamál	Perfection
Tuesday	Fidál	Grace
Wednesday	'Idál	Justice
Thursday	Istijlál	Majesty
Friday	Istiqlál	Independence

Notes

Chapter 1 **Introduction**

1. The 1992 *Britannica Book of the Year* declared that the Bahá'í Faith had established significant communities in 205 countries, second only to Christianity in its geographic distribution. The *World Christian Encyclopedia* (Barrett 1982) estimated that the world-wide Bahá'í community had grown by 3.63 percent since 1970—the fastest growing of the independent world religions. For a brief outline of the history of the Bahá'í Faith, see Appendix B.
2. Globalization is the name given to the process of rapid social change that affects all increasingly interdependent global relationships and worldviews—to be discussed further below.
3. This study is a result of eighteen months of intense fieldwork among the Bahá'ís of metropolitan Atlanta, Georgia. This fieldwork included participant observations, in-depth interviews, archival research, and distribution of a questionnaire to nearly five hundred members of the metropolitan Atlanta Bahá'í community.
4. Sociologist Robert Wuthnow (1987) points out the importance of religious gatherings for enacting a group's essential values and worldviews. This is what he calls the "dramaturgical" aspects of religious faith. Wuthnow says: "Ideology, for example, is pictured as a set of symbols that articulates how social relations should be arranged. . . . [Culture] communicates information about morally binding obligations and is in turn influenced by the structure of these obligations. . . . The term 'dramaturgic' is used to describe this approach because of its emphasis on the capacity of rituals, ideologies, and other symbolic acts to *dramatize* the nature of social relations" (1987, 13–14). A comparable Christian ritual might be the periodic meeting of the World Council of Churches.
5. The First Bahá'í World Congress was held in 1963, after the election of the first Universal House of Justice (the highest governing body of the world's Bahá'ís), and marked the centenary of the public declaration of Bahá'u'lláh's worldwide mission (Esslemont 1970).
6. Bahá'ís refer to each other collectively as "friends" or "the friends." This term is also applied to those who are not Bahá'ís, but are supportive of Bahá'í ideals ("friends of the Faith").
7. The Bahá'ís have suffered persecution throughout their 150–year history. This oppression

has intensified since the Iranian Islamic Revolution in 1979, including the confiscation of Bahá'í assets, homes, and businesses, and the execution of several hundred Bahá'ís (see Nash 1982; Dowty 1989).

8. "Manifestation of God" is the name Bahá'ís give to those individuals possessed of what Max Weber (1922, 1946) called "charismatic authority" who inaugurate a new cycle of divine religion. For Bahá'ís, these individuals are all sent by the one God, and include (but are not limited to) Abraham, Krishna, Buddha, Zoroaster, Moses, Jesus, Muhammad, the Báb, and most recently, Bahá'u'lláh.

9. See also Warburg (1992), who also discusses Bahá'í identity in terms of "world citizens." The process by which one's identity is shaped by everyday social practices is called by Berger and Luckmann (1966) "the social construction of reality."

10. Accounts of how these conflicts between Bahá'ís and non-Bahá'ís are managed will be covered in chapter 7 on how Bahá'ís "teach the Faith."

11. The degree to which Bahá'ís do or do not address the real conflicts between the world religion's theologies will be addressed below. It is interesting to note that sociologist Max Weber has a view opposite that of the Bahá'ís, saying that the world's religions are "historical individualities," and not in any way part of a progressive, evolutionary whole. Weber says: "In no respect can one simply integrate various world religions into a chain of types, each of them signifying a new 'stage.' All the great religions are historical individualities of a highly complex nature; taken all together, they exhaust only a few of the possible combinations that could conceivably be formed from the very numerous individual factors to be considered in such historical combinations" (1946, 292).

12. Bahá'u'lláh told his followers: "Know of a certainty that in every Dispensation the light of Divine Revelation hath been vouchsafed unto men in direct proportion to their spiritual capacity" (1976, 87). In another context: "'The Revelation of which I am the bearer,' Bahá'u'lláh explicitly declares, 'is adapted to humanity's spiritual receptiveness and capacity'" (in Effendi 1938, 60).

13. In another context, Effendi wrote that the Bahá'í Faith's teachings "revolve around the fundamental principle that religious truth is not absolute but relative, that Divine Revelation is progressive, not final. Unequivocally and without the least reservation it proclaims all established religions to be divine in origin, identical in their aims, complementary in their functions, continuous in their purpose, indispensable in their value to mankind. . . . To contend that any particular religion is final . . . would indeed be nothing less than sheer blasphemy" (1938, 58). It is in this way that Bahá'ís contend that religious truth is relative. The teachings of a Manifestation of God are true in any particular dispensation, but are subject to revision when a new Manifestation is sent by God. Religion, for Bahá'ís, is relative in that no religious system is ever the final and complete message from God.

14. The average Bahá'í has difficulty in adjudicating and accounting for the differences in theology among the world's religions. Although they claim that the spiritual teachings of all the religions are "one" and without contradiction, Bahá'ís handle real differences in theologies by simply explaining that human error is the source of any discrepancy between the various views on the nature of God, free will, etcetera. This will be discussed at length in chapter 7. There is, however, a growing body of Bahá'í scholarship that seeks to reconcile seemingly incompatible theologies among the world's religions. See, e.g., Fazel 1997; Fazel and Fananapazir 1997; Momen 1988; Cole 1993; Lambden 1997; and Fananapazir 1997.

15. Bahá'u'lláh told his followers: "The measure of the revelation of the Prophets of God in this world, however, must differ. Each and every one of them hath been the Bearer of a distinct Message, and hath been commissioned to reveal Himself through specific acts" (1976, 79).

16. See references to progressive revelation in "Bahá'í Studies" literature: e.g., Laszlo 1989;

Barnes 1992; McLean 1992; Van Es 1995; Bartholomew 1989; Buck 1991; White 1989; Stoddart 1988; Chew 1991; Heller and Mahmoudi 1992; Fazel 1994; Schweitz 1994; Lalonde 1994; Pokorny 1996.

17. See Bahá'u'lláh: "Whoso layeth claim to a Revelation direct from God, ere the expiration of a full thousand years, such a man is assuredly a lying impostor. . . . Whosoever interpreteth this verse otherwise than its obvious meaning is deprived of the Spirit of God and of His mercy which encompasseth all created things" (1976, 346).

18. The term "rationalization" used here comes from sociologist Max Weber, and is not meant to imply a "rationality" in the Bahá'í Faith at odds with the "irrationality" of other religious traditions. Weber felt that ideology in general, and religious ideology in particular, in modernity was more and more influenced by the methods of scientific inquiry, as opposed to supernatural "magic" (see Weber 1922). One way of understanding the rationalism of the Bahá'í Faith or any religious system comes from Roth and Schluchter, who proposed three uses for Weber's term "rationalism" or "rationalization": "First rationalism refers to the capacity to control the world through calculation. Here rationalism is a consequence of empirical knowledge and know-how. . . . In its second meaning rationalism refers to the systemization of meaning patterns. . . . Third and last, rationalism also refers to the achievement of a methodical way of life. Here rationalism is the consequence of the institutionalization of configurations of meaning and interests" (1979, 14–15). As this study will show, the Bahá'í Faith has rationalized worship, prayer, administration, and evangelization.

19. The Báb is a Persian religious figure who claims to have foretold the arrival of Bahá'u'lláh. Bahá'ís consider the Báb to have proclaimed an independent religious revelation that paved the way for the Bahá'í Faith. See Appendix B, Esslemont 1970, and Hatcher and Martin 1985.

20. For Bahá'ís, hell is not an actual place of damnation, but a description of the condition of a soul who is distant from God. Satan is not an evil being, but a symbol of human ignorance and depravity.

21. In this sense, Bahá'í religious activity would parallel Weber's (1996) view of Protestant "inner-worldly asceticism." Fazel writes: "Another feature of soteriological language in the Bahá'í texts is that collective salvation is its main emphasis. . . . The question of salvation is reframed as a communal one. . . . One way to understand the Bahá'í view is that Bahá'u'lláh has no exclusive claim to individual salvation, but that the social salvation of humankind does exclusively depend on the adoption of the principles of the Bahá'í Faith" (1997, 264).

22. For those readers not interested in the sociological theory used to frame the discussion in this book, skip to the next section, "Summary and Book Outline."

23. Waters has defined it as "a social process in which the constraints of geography on social and cultural arrangements recede and in which people become increasingly aware that they are receding" (1995, 3).

24. Globalization as a historical process is usually discussed in economic terms, resulting in the integration of the world's economy (as measured by a larger volume of international trade, a reduction in global tariffs, growing foreign direct capital investments, and the rise of regional trade agreements such as NAFTA and the EU). See for example a series of articles on globalization in *The Economist*, October 18–December 6, 1977.

25. Turn-of-the-century classical social scientists include Max Weber (1946), Emile Durkheim (1984), and Georg Simmel (1971).

26. Also see Roof 1991; Giddens 1991; Robertson 1992; Robertson and Garrett 1991; Beyer 1994. Other models of globalization include economic or "World-Systems" theories (Wallerstein 1974, 1979, 1984), and "World-polity" theories (Meyer 1980; Bergesen 1980; Meyer, Boli, Thomas and Ramirez 1997). A related patchwork of disciplines, loosely known as "Cultural Studies," also looks at emerging global culture

through ethnic and colonial identity, media studies, art, and literature (see King 1991; Featherstone 1991).

27. Beyer reiterates the importance of studying the effect on personal and corporate identity of social changes brought about by globalization: "the global system corrodes inherited or constructed cultural and personal identities; yet also encourages the creation and revitalization of particular identities as a way of gaining control over systemic power. . . . It is in the context of this last feature that religion plays one of its significant roles in the development, elaboration, and problematization of the global system" (1994, 3).

28. Giddens also says "the more tradition loses its hold, and the more daily life is reconstituted in terms of the dialectical interplay of the local and the global, the more individuals are forced to negotiate lifestyle choices among a diversity of options" (1991, 5).

29. This is also referred to as engendering a "tribal view of the world" (Marty and Appleby 1992, 14). Most of the fundamentalist movements of the past century would fall into this category, whereby faithfulness to a traditional religious identity reinforces social boundaries (see Ammerman 1987; Davidman 1990; Lechner 1990).

30. Examples of this can be seen in such diverse movements as the development of the European Union (Greathouse 1998; Bhabha 1998; Sancton 1998; Latham 1998), fundamentalism (Marty and Appleby 1991; Marsden 1980), and global environmentalism (Beyer 1994).

31. An article by Samuel Huntington (1993) describes the debates surrounding the continued viability of the sovereign nation-state. He writes that "nation states increasingly define their identity and their interests in civilizational terms" (1993, 191), which he defines as Western (Christian), Confucian, Japanese, Islamic, Hindu, Slavic-Orthodox, Latin American, and African. According to Huntington, although nation-states will remain the most important actors in world affairs, conflicts in the future will be over civilizational fault lines that divide these major religious/cultural traditions (i.e., fault lines of personal and collective identity).

32. The term "discontents" comes from Lechner (1985), who defined the discontents of modernity as constituting "fundamentalist" movements, "ethnic or national" movements, "expressive-therapeutic" movements, or "Marxist" movements (1985, 165–170).

33. Beyer writes: "In sum, there are two formal directions for religion under conditions of globalization, one that approaches the global system from the perspective of a particular, subglobal culture, and one that focuses on global culture as such" (1994, 10). The Bahá'í Faith falls into Beyer's latter category. Beyer's work also examines the globalization-inspired, universally oriented movements of Liberation Theology in Latin America and religious environmentalism.

34. Robertson and Lechner point out that "there is of course no shortage of academically produced alternative images of future world order. There is, on the other hand, a paucity of academic discussion of rival images of world order among the movements of our time" (1985, 112). A sociological analysis of a local Bahá'í community contributes to the latter discussion.

35. There is, however, a growing social science literature that investigates the Bahá'í Faith. See van den Hoonard 1996; Warburg 1986, 1991, 1993; Berger 1954; Smith 1978, 1982, 1987; Archer 1977; Garlington 1977; Wyman 1985; Hassall 1991; and MacEoin 1986.

36. This identity is contrasted with R. Stephen Warner's (1988) study of evangelical Christians, whom he describes as "elective parochials." These Christians voluntarily elected to join a religious congregation whose activity remained oriented toward the local association of believers.

37. The importance of Bahá'í scripture in understanding a Bahá'í identity is supported

from research by Ebaugh, Richman, and Chafetz (1984), who show that Bahá'ís are more likely than other sectarian groups to seek answers and advice in times of crisis from interpretations of their sacred scripture.

Chapter 2   *Carriers and Converts*

1. 'Abdu'l-Bahá, son of founder Bahá'u'lláh, admonished Bahá'ís in the United States to "strive, in your capacity as a citizen of the world, to assist in the eventual application of the principle of federalism underlying the government of your own country to the relationships now existing between the peoples and nations of the world" (Esslemont 1970, 275).

2. Lofland and Stark (1965) posit a seven-stage progressive model of conversion to a new worldview, whereby a potential convert passes through the following stages: tension with one's environment, adopting a religious (as opposed to a political or psychological-therapeutic) problem-solving perspective, defining oneself as a seeker, reaching a turning point in life, developing affective bonds with the new group, withdrawing contact with non-group members (especially family), and finally cementing close relations with the new group's members. As the following discussion will also show, some elements of the Lofland-Stark conversion model are important for understanding Bahá'í converts: tensions felt with one's social context, and religious seekership (although I agree with Snow and Phillips's [1980] criticism of the necessity of a "turning point" and severing extracult attachments in the conversion process).

3. This was also found by Archer (1977) and Wyman (1985).

4. Surveys came from individuals representing seventeen Local Spiritual Assemblies (or LSAs, which are parish-like jurisdictions having at least 9 members), and nine Bahá'í "Groups" (jurisdictions with 2–8 members), resulting in a representative geographical cross section of the metro Atlanta community. Nearly 26 percent of the respondents are from Fulton County (18 percent from the LSA of the city of Atlanta), 31 percent from DeKalb County, 12 percent from Gwinnett County, and 24 percent from Cobb County. The remaining 8 percent come from more rural counties south of Atlanta (Coweta, Rockdale, Fayette, Spalding, and Clayton counties).

5. In addition, the Bahá'í House of Worship in Wilmette, Illinois outside Chicago (site of the Bahá'í National Center), or the Shrines at the Bahá'í World Center in Haifa, Israel, introduced another 5 percent to the Bahá'í Faith. There are at present several Bahá'í Houses of Worship in the World: in Wilmette; Sydney, Australia; Frankfurt, Germany; New Delhi, India; Kampala, Uganda; Apia, Western Samoa; and Panama City, Panama. The Shrines at the World Center (which are a pilgrimage destination for Bahá'ís around the world) include the burial sites of the Báb, Bahá'u'lláh, 'Abdu'l-Bahá, and Bahíyyih Khánum ('Abdu'l-Bahá's sister). Shoghi Effendi was buried in London, England, where he died—since, according to Bahá'í law, one must be buried no more than a one-hour travel distance from the city where one dies.

6. Based on comparisons with Glenmary Research data (Bradley et al. 1992), the previous religious affiliations of converted Atlanta Bahá'ís mirror the proportion of the Christian population of the metro Atlanta area, with the exceptions of Lutherans and Catholics, which were more heavily represented among the Bahá'í converts.

7. Dawson quotes research into why NRMs tend to attract well-educated members: "'To be properly understood, the teachings [of most NRMs] demand literate intelligence, a willingness to study, and lack of fear in the face of unfamiliar concepts and language'" (1998, 87–88).

8. For example, Bahá'í scripture states: "Where is the man of insight who will behold the Words of God with his own eyes and rid himself of the opinions and notions of

the peoples of the earth?" (Bahá'u'lláh 1988b, 188). In addition: "The essence of all that We have revealed for thee is Justice, is for man to free himself from idle fancy and imitation, discern with the eye of oneness His glorious handiwork, and look into all things with a searching eye" (Bahá'u'lláh 1988b, 157). 'Abdu'l-Bahá reinforces this: "Furthermore, know ye that God has created in man the power of reason, whereby man is enabled to investigate reality. God has not intended man to imitate blindly his fathers and ancestors" ('Abdu'l-Bahá 1982, 291).

9. For example, 'Abdu'l-Bahá said: "Were there no educator, all souls would remain savage, and were it not for the teacher, the children would be ignorant creatures. It is for this reason that, in this new cycle, education and training are recorded in the book of God as obligatory" (1978, 126–127).

10. The Bahá'ís, however, differ from the communities studied by Kanter in that processes of "mortification" and "transcendence," in the ways she defined them, are not employed by the Bahá'í Faith. See chapters 6 and 7 for further discussion.

11. Bahá'í theology divides religious teachings into spiritual and social elements: the former never change; the latter change with every new Manifestation according to the exigencies of the age. 'Abdu'l-Bahá said: "The first aspect of the revealed religion of God is that which concerns the ethical development and spiritual progress of mankind. . . . These ordinances are changeless, essential, eternal. The second function of the divine religion deals with material conditions . . . and social regulation. These are subject to change and transformation in accordance with the time, place and conditions" ('Abdu'l-Bahá 1982, 97–8).

12. Further analysis revealed no association between one's educational background or occupation and one's primary reason for converting. There was, however, a slight correlation between gender and an individual's most important reason for becoming a Bahá'í: women were more likely than men to cite personal esteem for the person who taught them their faith (11 percent vs. 3 percent), and men were slightly more likely than women to cite spiritual principles as their primary reason for converting (45 percent vs. 39 percent). In addition, Persians were more likely than other ethnic groups to indicate as their primary reason either being raised as a Bahá'í or having a love for one of the central figures of the Bahá'í Faith. This is not surprising, since in the interviews several Bahá'ís expressed the feeling that whereas Americans come into the religion because of the social and spiritual principles, Persians have a greater understanding of the station ("charismatic" status) of the Báb and Bahá'u'lláh due to their upbringing in Islamic culture (see also Wyman 1985). Finally, nonwhite, non-Persian respondents were significantly more likely than either whites or Persians to indicate their faith's diversity as the most important factor in their conversion.

13. When asked what she meant by the statement that the religions' "messages are all the same," she could only reply that all religions teach one to love one's neighbor. When confronted with seemingly real paradoxes and contradictions between theological positions from the world's faith traditions, Bahá'ís frequently are unable to reconcile them within the generalized "unity of religion" paradigm of their faith.

14. This individual also expressed the "hypocrisy of the clergy" as an additional reason for his disassociation from his Episcopal upbringing. He said the consensual decision making within the Bahá'í community, and the absence of status distinctions between clergy and laity, further "pulled" him into the Faith. The nearly 12 percent of survey respondents who indicated the lack of clergy in the Bahá'í Faith as one of their top three reasons for "declaring" are probably articulating similar "push" and "pull" sentiments.

15. Bahá'ís readily say that this doctrine also implies that in the future the Bahá'í Faith will become outworn and will be superseded by another progressive revelation from God.

16. The "pull" or the attractiveness of social and spiritual principles in a rational, pro-

gressive religion, and the "push" of being disillusioned with one's religion of birth and subsequent personal religious search and adoption of a "seeker" identity.

17. This may be peculiar to the United States or the industrialized world. Research by Garlington (1977) and Warburg (1986) suggest that Bahá'í ideology also appeals to lower-class individuals in the developing world (probably for its empowerment at the local level—see chapter 5).

18. Bahá'í theology claims that the spiritual aspects of religion do not change with the appearance of successive Manifestations of God (the essence of the unity of religion). However, the social laws intrinsic to every religion are superseded when God sends a new Manifestation (the essence of progressive revelation).

19. Bahá'í theology states that all previous Manifestations of God existed in the larger Cycle of Prophecy, teaching about a yet-to-come Kingdom of God on earth. With the Bahá'í dispensation, religious history enters the Cycle of Fulfillment, since Bahá'ís claim that Bahá'u'lláh fulfills all religious prophesy by bringing the laws and institutions to establish the Kingdom of God. Thus, Muhammad was the last Manifestation of the Prophetic Cycle and therefore its "Seal," but not the final Manifestation to be sent to humanity (cf. Hornby 1983).

20. The term "elective affinity" comes from sociologist Max Weber, who said there exists a "correlation" or "fit" between ideas or worldviews and the segments in society who adopt or "carry" those ideas forward as a social movement. "Ideas, selected and reinterpreted from the original doctrine, do gain an affinity with the interests of certain members of special strata; if they do not gain such an affinity, they are abandoned" (Weber 1946, 63).

21. Although income is evenly distributed throughout the community (with approximately one-fifth making less than $20,000, one-fifth making $20,000–35,000, one-fifth making $35,000–50,000, one-fifth making $50,000–75,000, and one-fifth making more than $75,000), there is a statistical association between race/ethnicity and both income and occupation (but not education). For example, of those making between $35,000 and $49,999, 57 percent are white, 16 percent are black, 14 percent are Persian, and 12 percent are of mixed ethnicity. There is also an association between race and occupation. Of those with blue-collar jobs, 33 percent are white, 43 percent are black, 7 percent are Persian, and 17 percent are multiethnic. Of professionals, 49 percent are white, 19 percent are black, 17 percent are Persian, and 15 percent are of mixed ethnicity.

22. Data from a 1991 Bahá'í National Center survey indicate the following ethnic composition in the American Bahá'í community: 58.6 percent are white; 20.4 percent are either African American, Hispanic, Asian, Native American, or other; and 21.0 percent are Persian.

23. As a reference point, it is helpful to compare the demographic profile of the metro Atlanta Bahá'í community with selected measures in the Atlanta general population. Using 1990 census data from Fulton, DeKalb, Gwinnett and Cobb counties (which constitute part of the Atlanta SMSA), I found that black residents make up 31 percent of the population, and whites 66 percent; average median income is $43,623; nearly 32 percent have completed a bachelor's degree or higher educational level; and there is a female-to-male sex ratio of 53:47. This means that compared to the wider population, the metro Atlanta Bahá'í community is "less white" (i.e., more racially diverse); is comparably wealthy (with $43,623 being slightly higher than the midpoint of the median income category for Bahá'ís); is much more highly educated (with 65 percent having at least a bachelor's degree); and has a slightly higher proportion of females.

24. Bahá'í divorce law is distinct among the world's religious systems. Although divorce is allowed under Bahá'í law, it is "strongly condemned" and granted by the Local Spiritual Assembly only after a "Year of Patience," during which the couple lives apart

and seeks reconciliation. Bahá'ís pride themselves on their high moral standards (especially with respect to chastity and abstinence from alcohol or drugs), but frequently mention that the divorce rate among their own community is too high (although it is lower than the general population, who report an 18.7 percent incidence of divorce—Stark 1989, 390). Provisions for a Bahá'í to marry a non-Bahá'í are given explicitly in Bahá'í scripture. Data from a 1991 National Bahá'í Center survey indicate the following about the American Bahá'í community: 64.7 percent are married; 14.8 percent are divorced; 13.7 percent are single; and 4.9 percent are widowed.

Chapter 3   The Bahá'í Administrative Order

1. My contention is that any organization that seeks to expand globally would have to utilize mechanisms of symbolic and ideological solidarity and a legal-rational bureaucratic structure (see Durkheim 1973, 1984 and Weber 1946, 1978). This is what Roland Robertson calls a connection between "Global Gemeinschaft 2" and "Global Gesellschaft 2." He defines the former as follows: "This image of the world situation maintains that *only in terms of a fully globewide community per se can there be global order*" (1992, 78). One possible image of the world "insists that there must be a globewide Durkheimian 'conscience collective'" that emphasizes "*mankind* as the pivotal ingredient of the world as a whole. Thus the dangers of globalization are to be overcome by commitment to the communal unity of the human species" (1992, 79). Of the latter, Global Gesellschaft 2, Robertson writes: "This conception of world order claims that it can only be attained *on the basis of formal, planned world organization*" (1992, 79). As one socioreligious movement responding to globalization, the Bahá'í Faith conforms to elements of both Global Gemeinschaft 2 and Global Gesellschaft 2 as theorized by Robertson.

2. Shoghi Effendi, using the framework of institutions laid out in Bahá'u'lláh's *Kitáb-i-Aqdas* and 'Abdu'l-Bahá's *Will and Testament*, and the program of expansion devised by 'Abdu'l-Bahá (1993) in the *Tablets of the Divine Plan*, instructed Bahá'ís to begin setting up the institutions of the Administrative Order through a series of formalized plans. Beginning with the first Seven Year Plan in 1937, he directed Bahá'ís to travel to specific parts of the world as "pioneers" to teach the Bahá'í Faith and to establish local Bahá'í communities across the globe. Since then, Bahá'í administrative and teaching activity has operated under two Seven Year Plans (1937–1944, 1946–1953); a Ten Year World Crusade (1953–1963), which was the first global teaching plan in the Bahá'í world; a Nine Year Plan (1964–73); a Five Year Plan (1974–1979); a Seven Year Plan (1979–1986); a Six Year Plan (1986–1992); a Three Year Plan (1993–1996); and presently a Four Year Plan (1996–2000). The Three Year Plan, in effect during my period of fieldwork, and related documents will be discussed in detail in chapter 7.

3. Thus, the impetus for internalizing religious knowledge falls to the individual believer. In Bahá'í ideology, the individual is given a circumscribed freedom to interpret scripture without interference from anyone else. However, as I will discuss below, the highest level of the Administrative Order has a monopoly on definitive interpretive authority when it comes to adherence to social laws.

4. The number nine appears regularly in Bahá'í symbols, and is explained in Bahá'í writings: "Nine is the highest digit, hence symbolizes comprehensiveness, culmination; also, the reason it is used . . . is because 9 has the exact numerical value of 'Bahá' (in the numerology connected with the Arabic alphabet) and Bahá is the name of the Revealer of our Faith, Bahá'u'lláh" (Hornby 1983, 416)

5. If fewer than nine, but more than two, Bahá'ís reside in a locality, they are known as a "Bahá'í Group." As such, however, they do not collectively have the same authority as a "spiritual assembly."

6. Ridván (meaning "paradise" in Arabic) commemorates what Bahá'ís believe to be the public declaration of Bahá'u'lláh as a Manifestation of God, which took place in 1863 in a garden outside Baghdad, Iraq, during his exile.

7. There are four permanently staffed Bahá'í schools that sponsor conferences and retreats for both Bahá'ís and non-Bahá'ís: Bosch Bahá'í School in Santa Cruz, California; Louhelen Bahá'í School in Davison, Michigan; Green Acre Bahá'í School in Eliot, Maine; and the Louis Gregory Bahá'í Institute in Hemingway, South Carolina.

8. Discussion of these resolutions can be found in issues of *Bahá'í News*, a news magazine published by the NSA of the United States: April and June 1982; May 1983; February, May, July, August, and September 1984; January, February, April, and October 1985.

9. Shoghi Effendi instructs Bahá'ís in all elections to vote only for those "who can best combine the necessary qualities of unquestioned loyalty, of selfless devotion, of a well-trained mind, of recognized ability and mature experience" (1974, 88).

10. Bahá'ís frequently say among themselves that since, from their perspective, the UHJ is infallible, it will be able to recognize the appearance of the next Manifestation of God, avoiding the confusion of past dispensations.

11. 'Abdu'l-Bahá said, "Those matters of major importance which constitute the foundation of the Law of God are explicitly recorded in the Text, but subsidiary laws are left to the House of Justice. The wisdom of this is that the times never remain the same, for change is a necessary quality and an essential attribute of this world, and of time and place. Therefore the House of Justice will take action accordingly" (quoted in Bahá'u'lláh 1992, 4–5).

12. For more information about Hands of the Cause of God, see Taherzadeh 1992; Stockman 1985; Hands of the Cause of God 1992.

13. While Bahá'ís can legitimately claim that there exists no formal clergy that wields authority within their organizational chart, figures such as Hands of the Cause often are given clergy-like status by individual Bahá'ís. Many Bahá'ís I interviewed told me that part of the necessary maturation of Bahá'í institutions will involve quelling the tendency to look to these individuals, as well as NSA and UHJ members, for the "right answers." Although Bahá'í theology says that collective decisions of the UHJ are unquestionable, individual members—while deserving respect—do not have any inherent status, nor can they make any authoritative claims. There are currently only three Hands of the Cause living: Amatu'l-Bahá Rúhíyyih Khánum (wife of Shoghi Effendi), 'Alí-Muhammad Varqá, and 'Alí-Akbar Furútan. Since Shoghi Effendi had no successor, and the UHJ does not have the constitutional authority to appoint further Hands of the Cause, this institution will end upon the deaths of the current Hands.

14. Shoghi Effendi first instructed the Hands in 1954 to appoint a set of Auxiliary Boards as their own assistants, under their direction, for propagation, and another set in 1957 for protection. In 1968 these Auxiliary Boards were put under the authority of the Continental Board of Counselors (Smith 1987, 127).

15. Taherzadeh writes: "Never before has a Manifestation of God given authority to a council elected by universal suffrage to enact laws and administer the affairs of His religion in the assurance that it will be guided by God in its decisions. . . . The only way that the individual can become convinced of the authority and infallibility of the Universal House of Justice is to recognize Bahá'u'lláh as God's Messenger for this age" (1992, 394, 398). Bahá'ís frequently pointed out in deepenings I attended that the Roman Catholic Church did not confer "papal infallibility" until the 1869–1870 First Vatican ecumenical council—after Bahá'u'lláh had publicly declared his mission in 1863 (a fact of no small significance, according to Bahá'ís). Bahá'ís regularly suggest that many of the ideas and inventions of our modern world did not come

about until after the beginning of the Bahá'í era, and see these discoveries as a direct consequence of the spiritual and intellectual energies Bahá'u'lláh's revelation released into the world.

16. For additional perspective on the Bahá'í Administrative Order and world governance, see Abizadeh 1989; Lerche 1994.

17. Further research utilizing the "institutionalist" or "world-polity" theoretical perspective in organizational sociology could analyze the similarities between Bahá'í growth and the development of the United Nations and affiliated global institutions (see Powell and DiMaggio 1991; Meyer 1980; Meyer et al. 1997). However, this question is beyond the scope of this book.

18. For further data on the rate of growth of the Bahá'í Faith globally, see Smith 1987; Smith and Momen 1989. It is only in the last forty to fifty years that the Bahá'ís have become a truly "global" movement—expanding beyond a bipolar concentration in the "Islamic heartland" (primarily Iran, but also Iraq) and "the West" (primarily the United States and Canada).

19. In fact, the title of "Knight of Bahá'u'lláh" was conferred by Shoghi Effendi upon Bahá'ís who were the first to enter a new territory in which no Bahá'ís or local assemblies existed. This was a mark of considerable status for that individual within the Bahá'í community.

20. Some conflicts over authority arose in the 1920s when some Bahá'ís argued that the UHJ had to be established immediately after 'Abdu'l-Bahá's death. When Shoghi Effendi announced that Bahá'í scripture decreed that its election could only come through the initial development of local and national institutions, some Bahá'ís questioned the authority of Shoghi Effendi himself, leading to their expulsion from the Bahá'í ranks (see Effendi 1995, Taherzadeh 1992).

21. See the on-line Bahá'í journal *One Country*, vol. 7, no. 1, June 1995 (www.onecountry. org/oc71/oc7115as.html).

22. Some LSAs in the metro Atlanta area have other specialized committees, such as Atlanta's Race Unity committee. Members plan the myriad events surrounding the Martin Luther King Jr. national holiday celebration, in which Bahá'ís have been heavily involved. Atlanta also has an Archives and Building committee, which preserves Bahá'í historical records and maintains the Atlanta Bahá'í Center's physical plant.

23. Data from a 1991 Bahá'í National Center survey found that one-fourth of American Bahá'ís live in communities of 16–40 believers, and another one-fourth live in towns with 2–8 believers.

24. The National Spiritual Assembly had asked each LSA in the United States to commit voluntarily to a monthly pledge of financial support to the NSA. Those LSAs who fulfilled their obligation over the course of the nineteen months of a Bahá'í calendar year were then recognized in the NSA's monthly newspaper, *The American Bahá'í*.

25. For a Bahá'í perspective on consultation, see Rosenfeld and Winger-Bearskin 1990.

26. These include the National Teaching Committee; one of the National Center's Bahá'í Schools Committees; the Office of External Affairs in Washington, D.C.; the Persian-American Affairs committee; the Youth Committee; and the Race Unity Committee.

27. The power of incumbency in National Spiritual Assembly elections conforms to theories of incumbency in secular electoral politics, but is exacerbated by the rules of Bahá'í elections. Political science research shows that incumbents are more likely to win elections over their challengers because they are better known; they can provide more services to their constituents; they get more media exposure in the performance of their elected duties; they can send out free ("franked") mail; and they have already been evaluated by the voting public in a "leadership" role on familiar job

performance criteria (see Jacobson 1992; Fenno 1978; Cain, Ferejohn, and Fiorina 1986; Popkin 1991; Butler, Penniman, and Ranney 1981; Dawson 1987; Wilson and DiIulio 1995). Jacobson writes: "Typically, more than 90 percent of the candidates are incumbents, and more than 90 percent of them win" (1992, 26). Cole reports that "since 1961, no member of the National Spiritual Assembly of the United States who has stood for reelection has been unseated" (1998, 240). This represents a turnover rate of less than 10 percent. However, in a Bahá'í system that scripturally does not allow campaigning for elections, and in which any Bahá'í with voting rights is eligible for election to the NSA, the rate of incumbency is no different from that found in the studies cited above. Thus, Cole's assertion of intentional "manipulation" (1998, 241) of national Bahá'í elections is not essential in explaining the lack of leadership turnover.

28. At one Bahá'í election I attended during my fieldwork, there was a tie for the ninth position, and neither person was a member of a minority group (Bahá'í law dictates that the person with minority status is chosen). The chief teller (a Persian man) and the chair of the outgoing LSA (a white woman) did not know whether to call a new vote for all nine LSA positions, or merely for the ninth spot. Since no one else attending the election ceremony knew the answer, they consulted the writings of Shoghi Effendi for the definitive answer.

29. In order to accommodate higher attendance, large events in the metro Atlanta area were often held in a meeting room at one of the local universities, because space could be reserved free of charge by the university's Bahá'í Club.

30. As will be discussed further in chapter 4, Bahá'ís in large urban areas face the following conflict: the Administrative Order is considered by Bahá'ís to be divinely ordained, and therefore sacrosanct. NSA goals for meeting quotas of new believers and assemblies compel LSA jurisdictions to be drawn at the lowest common denominator: municipal city or subdivided county boundaries. This results in a lot of small LSA jurisdictions, each with few Bahá'ís, in large urban areas. On their own, few LSAs have the human and financial resources to engage in large evangelization efforts. Such efforts require coordinated action among the area LSAs. Atlanta's efforts to elect a metro Atlanta Bahá'í Task Force raised practical as well as theological concerns: does a human-made coordinating Task Force have authority over a divinely ordained LSA? At minimum, most Bahá'ís said, the Task Force should be under the "guidance and protection" of a sponsoring LSA.

31. Bahá'í writings say this about obeying administrative standards: "Not until the advent of the Bahá'í Dispensation did a Manifestation of God include administrative principles among His spiritual teachings. This is an entirely new dimension which Bahá'u'lláh has introduced; He has placed the spiritual and administrative principles on a par with each other. A violation of an administrative principle, such as electioneering, is as grave a betrayal of the Cause of Bahá'u'lláh as breaking a spiritual law" (Taherzadeh 1992, 395).

32. For example, results show that of Atlanta respondents, 58 percent of those not presently in the labor force are on or have been on the LSA; 78 percent of blue-collar workers respond affirmatively; 80 percent of white-collar workers are or have been; while almost 90 percent of professionals have served or are serving in an elected position.

33. Some people told me that when they made it known that they were looking to move within the metro area, members of several assemblies lightheartedly coaxed them to move into their community to bring new members to their assembly.

34. Survey results show that of those who are single, 44 percent have been or are on an LSA; of those divorced or widowed, 78 percent have been elected; and of those who are now married, nearly 90 percent have served or now serve on the local institution. Interviews with Atlanta area LSA members, as well as my own observations,

indicate that in many cases where both partners of a couple are Bahá'ís, both tend to be elected to the assembly (although this cannot be statistically confirmed by the current data).

35. Unlike the statistical association between race/ethnicity and LSA membership, which became insignificant when local community was controlled for, the likelihood of being a nonwhite Assistant remains robust even when controlling for one's local community residence.

36. This is not unique among the Bahá'ís—many of the social and religious movements of our time are responding to globalization by trying to link the local and global. However, I would argue that Bahá'ís attempt to do this in a *distinctive* way, one that combines ideology and organizational structure to create a global religious identity that I have called a "situated universalist." One fruitful area of future research would be to compare the way Bahá'ís link the local and global to how this is attempted in other religious systems, such as the Roman Catholics, the Latter-Day Saints, pan-Islamic movements, and the religiously oriented environmental movement, among others. However, this is beyond the scope of this book.

Chapter 4 *Authority in the Administrative Order*

1. Although other religious groups claim divine successorship, as evidenced by "apostolic succession" in the Roman Catholic or Orthodox Christian traditions (cf. Marty 1959; Latourette 1953), or the Imamate in Shi'ite Islam (cf. Loeffler 1988; Mottahedeh 1985; Rippin 1990), Bahá'ís would respond that their organizational arrangement is unique in that the Covenant of Bahá'u'lláh has prevented organizational schism. Despite attempts by members of Bahá'u'lláh's family to form sectarian groups, and the fact that Bahá'í leaders were under house arrest in Palestine for the first 40 years of the movement's 150–year history, Bahá'ís claim that no viable (growing) competing organization has arisen also claiming to be "Bahá'í" (see chapter 6 for further discussion).

2. The UHJ *Constitution* enumerates some of the following responsibilities: "to preserve the Sacred Texts and classify the Writings; to defend and protect the Cause of God and emancipate it from the fetters of repression and persecution; to advance the interests of the Faith of God; to proclaim, propagate and teach its Message; to expand and consolidate the institutions of its Administrative Order; to usher in the World Order of Bahá'u'lláh; to promote the attainment of those spiritual qualities which should characterize Bahá'í life individually and collectively; to enact laws and ordinances not expressly recorded in the Sacred Texts; to abrogate, according to the changes and requirements of the time, its own enactments; to safeguard the personal rights, freedom and initiative of individuals, to give attention to the preservation of human honor, to the development of countries and the stability of states; to promulgate and apply the laws and principles of the Faith; to administer the affairs of the Bahá'í community throughout the world; to adjudicate disputes falling within its purview; to give judgment in cases of violation of the laws of the Faith and to pronounce sanctions for such violations; to be the exponent and guardian of that Divine Justice which can alone ensure the security of, and establish the reign of law and order in, the world" (Universal House of Justice 1972, 5–6).

3. For more information on the growing Bahá'í scholarship on feminist and gender issues, see: Mahmoudi 1989, 1995; Mahmoudi and Dabell 1992; Maneck 1989; Hatcher 1990; Gilstrap 1990; Drewek 1992; Woodman 1995; Miller 1998; Ma'ani 1997; Khan and Khan 1998; Caton 1987; Schoonmaker 1984; Schweitz 1995; Ray 1995. See also compilations from the Bahá'í Writings: National Spiritual Assembly of the Bahá'ís of Canada 1983, 1986.

4. 'Abdu'l-Bahá said that world peace will not be achieved until women receive equal

educational opportunities, and move into all levels of the professions that men now often solely occupy ('Abdu'l-Bahá 1982, 174–175).

5. Táhirih was the only woman among the Báb's "Letters of the Living"—an honorific title conferred upon the Báb's first eighteen disciples (Effendi 1995).

6. For more Bahá'í perspective on Táhirih, see Effendi 1932, 1995; Maneck 1989; Edge 1964; Root 1981. Maneck said Táhirih "is remembered by Bahá'ís not as the ideal wife, mother, and daughter but as the courageous, eloquent, and assertive religious innovator whose actions severed the early Bábís from Islam completely" (1989, 39).

7. The potential for "cognitive dissonance" (Festinger 1957) resulting from the perceived tension between Bahá'í ideology and organizational reality with respect to the status of women on the UHJ may explain the slightly negative tone taken by some Bahá'í women I interviewed when discussing issues of Bahá'í administration.

8. It says in part: "Among the most outstanding and sacred duties incumbent upon [Assembly members] are: to win by every means in their power the confidence and affection of those whom it is their privilege to serve; to investigate and acquaint themselves with the considered views, the prevailing sentiments and the personal convictions of those whose welfare it is their solemn obligation to promote; to purge their deliberations and the general conduct of their affairs of self-contained aloofness, the suspicion of secrecy, the stifling atmosphere of dictatorial assertiveness and of every word and deed that may savour of partiality, self-centeredness and prejudice" (Universal House of Justice 1972, 10).

9. The first local incorporation came from the New York City LSA in 1931, when they drafted bylaws that became the global standard for all local Bahá'í constitutions (Smith 1987). The ability of the local and national Bahá'í institutions in the United States to become global standards probably arises from the relative freedom of religion there, as compared to Iran, the other country with a significant concentration of Bahá'ís at the time. It may also result from the cultural profusion of voluntary associations in the United States, and the political context that allows for their legal incorporation (cf. Toqueville 1863; Wuthnow 1988; Curtis, Grabb, and Baer 1992).

10. Membership can formally begin at fifteen years old—the "age of maturity" as described in Bahá'í scripture. Membership is also dependent upon one's belief in the Central Figures of the Faith and adherence to the laws upheld by the UHJ. Eligibility for election to Bahá'í office begins at age twenty-one.

11. While much of this chapter focuses on the local-global authority relationship in the Bahá'í Faith, it should be noted that the NSA does wield significant authority as a mediating institution of the Administrative Order. Local Assemblies orient their teaching efforts around the rationalized plans devised by the NSA and the National Teaching Committee. Whereas the UHJ provided general goals in broad strokes for the Three Year Plan (1993–1996), it is the NSA that turns these into numerical goals and rational teaching campaigns appropriate to its jurisdiction. It is also the NSA that has the authority to sanction individuals for flagrant violation of Bahá'í law (see chapter 6).

12. For example, Bahá'í burial law decrees that individuals are not to be embalmed. However, in the United States, if being embalmed is required by state law, then Bahá'ís are instructed that they are exempt from this Bahá'í law.

13. These issues, while beyond the scope of this research, would most fruitfully be addressed through a world-polity perspective that seeks to uncover the relationship between the authority of the nation-state, and social movements contained within or transcending the nation-state. In contrast to such movements as the New Christian Right, which directs collective action toward state power and policy, the Bahá'ís seem thus far content to build their own global-ordering institutions, rather than influencing state policy (see Thomas et al. 1987). The only exception to this has been NSA efforts to get the U.S. Congress to condemn Iranian persecution of Bahá'ís in Iran (see Nash 1982).

14. Cole (1998) notes the inherent tension in a religious movement whose message is revolutionary but whose members are forbidden to engage in institutionalized methods of political activism (i.e., running for office, campaigning for candidates, etc.).

15. Until that time, Bahá'ís in the United States had available only the *Synopsis and Codification of the Laws and Ordinances of the Kitáb-i-Aqdas*, published in 1973 based on a partial translation from Shoghi Effendi.

16. Many of the laws in the *Kitáb-i-Aqdas* are to be only gradually applied to the whole Bahá'í community at the discretion of the UHJ (which, Bahá'ís say, follows the logic of "progressive revelation" discussed in chapter 1).

17. Quotes from the 1993 Ridván message from the UHJ come from a pamphlet distributed by the NSA entitled "The Three Year Plan."

18. The UHJ (1989) wrote a document addressing the Bahá'ís of the United States entitled *Individual Rights and Freedoms in the World Order of Bahá'u'lláh*. The UHJ (1989) wrote that the "excesses" of Western civilization have led to an exaggerated concern with individual liberty to the detriment of collective responsibility and authority. The UHJ pointed out that within the Bahá'í framework, there is a balance between recognized individual rights of expression, speech, press, etcetera, and the need for collective authority to maintain global civilization. Therefore, it asks Bahá'ís to look at freedom of speech within the Administrative Order as a constructive example. Individuals are free to express their views (respectfully, of course) at all community or assembly consultations, and even to explore issues so completely that ideas come into conflict. Once an LSA makes a decision, the individual is obligated to uphold that decision, even if he or she disagrees. Individual free speech comes before the vote is taken; afterward, solidarity is the primary value. Bahá'ís assert that if an individual were allowed to criticize an institution, or to try to lobby a vote one way or another, it would undermine the unity that should be the hallmark of Bahá'í decision making and action.

19. Statistical analysis was conducted on the first three questions in Table 4.1. Factor analysis showed all three questions clustered together as one factor, with Cronbach's alpha = .53. The scores from all three questions were added together to create a composite variable called "Recognition of Legitimate Authority."

20. Of the 70 percent of Atlanta Bahá'ís who are converts, 32.2 percent come from theologically "conservative" religious backgrounds (Baptist, nondenominational affiliations, the Church of God, Islam, various Black Protestant denominations, and Greek Orthodox); 24.0 percent come from "moderate" religious backgrounds (Methodist, Lutheran, Roman Catholic, Dutch Reformed, Mennonite); and 14.6 percent come from "liberal" religious backgrounds (Presbyterian, Episcopal, Jewish, Congregational, Buddhist, and those with "no religious affiliation").

21. Of the 70 percent of Atlanta Bahá'ís who are converts, 32.7 percent come from "decentralized" or congregational polities (Baptist, Jewish, Islam, Congregational, Mennonite, Black Baptist, nondenominational affiliations, and those with "no religious affiliation"); 38.1 percent come from "hierarchical" or episcopal or presbyterian polities (Greek Orthodox, African Methodist Episcopal, Methodist, Lutheran, Roman Catholic, Presbyterian, Episcopal, Reformed churches, and Black Methodist).

22. One must admit that "selection bias" may be operating in this sample of Bahá'ís: those who choose to become Bahá'ís may be predisposed to look upon the Bahá'í Administrative Order with reverence and obedience, and do not come to that viewpoint as a result of participating in Bahá'í institutions.

23. 'Abdu'l-Bahá wrote: "Compare the nations of the world to the members of a family. A family is a nation in miniature. Simply enlarge the circle of the household and you have the nation. Enlarge the circle of nations and you have all humanity" (National Spiritual Assembly of the Bahá'ís of Canada 1983, 29).

24. In order to rule out other predisposing factors in predicting one's recognition of au-

thority, I also tested to see if the source from which each respondent first learned about the Bahá'í Faith, as well as the primary reason that "most convinced you to become a Bahá'í," was significantly related to recognition of legitimate authority. I found that *how* one learned of the Bahá'í Faith made one no more likely to accept the authority claims of Bahá'í institutions (although of those who scored "high" on recognition of authority, 37 percent were raised as Bahá'ís). However, *why* one became a Bahá'í was statistically significant. Indicating one's "love for one or more of the Central Figures of the Faith" made one twice as likely to score high on the recognition of the legitimate authority of Bahá'í institutions as did any other reason. This may be because attraction to the founders and initial charismatic leaders (defined as the Báb, Bahá'u'lláh, and 'Abdu'l-Bahá) would translate into acceptance of the authority claimed by institutions designed or constructed by them. Interestingly enough, those who indicated their agreement with spiritual or social principles, who had an affinity for Bahá'u'lláh's Writings, who were raised as a Bahá'í, or who had personal esteem for those who introduced them to their faith, were all *equally likely* to score high on the measure of recognition of legitimate authority. But by far, attraction to the founder of the Bahá'í Faith, and concomitantly to his claims to be the return of Christ and "promised one" of all the world's religions, make one twice as likely to respect the authority of the Bahá'í Administrative Order. This indicates that a vestige of "charismatic authority" persists in this rationalized religion (cf. Weber 1922, 1946).

25. It is important to note that *none* of the demographic measures discussed in this study are significantly related to agreement or disagreement with *any* of the statements in table 4.2. In other words, there is no statistical association between Bahá'ís' demographic characteristics and adherence to key tenets of their faith. It is also important to restate that selection bias may be operating here: it is not known whether the 70 percent of the Atlanta Bahá'í community who converted to their faith were already in agreement with core ideological tenets of the Bahá'í Faith, and thus converted because this religious group espoused them; or if they came to uphold these ideas after conversion.

26. Cole (1998), based on research involving anecdotal personal communications and email forums, describes the institution of the Learned as performing surveillance on rank-and-file Bahá'í adherents to report unorthodox attitudes and behavior. I did not find this attitude among Bahá'ís I interviewed.

27. He also pointed out, however, that a Bahá'í has the right to appeal any decision made by the Local Spiritual Assembly to the National Spiritual Assembly, and if dissatisfied with its ruling, can take the issue to the Universal House of Justice, at which point the final pronouncement would be binding.

28. In fact, during my fieldwork, the secretary of the Atlanta LSA was forced to resign because it was discovered that he actually lived in an adjoining, suburban LSA jurisdiction.

29. The information on the Atlanta Bahá'í Task Force came from newsletters and personal interviews with community members.

Chapter 5 *Personal Devotion and Organizational Participation*

1. Some of the information in this chapter has already appeared in an edited volume containing ethnographies of religious communities in the United States. See Becker and Eiesland 1997.

2. Shoghi Effendi continues, saying that dogma describes "that body of rigid doctrines that have accumulated in a religion after the passing of its Founder; such man-made dogmas are entirely absent from the Bahá'í Faith, nor can it ever acquire them" (Hornby 1983, 477). For further information on this debate within the Bahá'í

community as to whether or not their faith is ritualistic, see a book review by Buck (1996).

3. I have never heard a Bahá'í pray spontaneously during a Bahá'í gathering, even though extemporaneous prayer is not forbidden in Bahá'í scripture. In every case, a prayer was read from one of the "Central Figures" of the Bahá'í Faith.

4. Bahá'ís are encouraged to memorize the written prayers, instead of using their own words. This might have the effect of making prayer formulaic, since Shoghi Effendi counseled Bahá'ís: "Regarding your question as to the changing of pronouns in Bahá'í prayers: The Guardian does not approve of such changes, either in the specific prayers or in any others. They should be read as printed without changing a single word" (Hornby 1983, 459).

5. Bahá'ís can choose between the Short Obligatory Prayer (to be said between noon and sunset); the Medium Obligatory Prayer (to be said in the morning, at noon, and in the evening); or the Long Obligatory Prayer (to be said once in 24 hours).

6. Walbridge continues that "the obligatory prayers and fasting are the most important ritual obligations of Bahá'ís and the Bahá'í writings warn strongly against neglecting them or minimizing their importance. . . . Obligatory prayer is a personal spiritual obligation and as such is not enforceable by Bahá'í administrative institutions" (1996, 46).

7. In Arabic numerology, *Bahá* ("glory") has a numerical value of nine, and *váhid* ("unity") has a numerical value of nineteen.

8. Bahá'ís in Atlanta told me that "reciting" scripture can mean anything from reading silently to reading out loud, chanting, or reciting from memory.

9. Survey results showed that 11 percent of Bahá'ís read daily from the writings of the Báb, 3 percent from Shoghi Effendi, 1 percent from the Universal House of Justice, and 5 percent from other Bahá'í authors.

10. As part of the continued persecution of Bahá'ís in Iran—see Nash 1982.

11. Pilgrimage to Shiraz and Baghdad are considered obligatory rituals that will be practiced only in the future, Bahá'ís say, once access to those locations is permitted.

12. One Bahá'í author wrote: "Many Bahá'ís recall pilgrimage as a pivotal experience in their spiritual lives. The diversity of the pilgrimage groups powerfully reinforces the pilgrim's sense of belonging to a world community and deep friendships are formed. Shoghi Effendi said that 'the flow of pilgrims' constitutes 'the lifeblood' of the Bahá'í World Center" (Walbridge 1996, 118).

13. International funds are moneys used by the UHJ for social and economic development projects around the world, such as schools and health clinics. Continental funds are those used by the Continental Counselors and the appointed branch of the Administrative Order. The Arc fund consists of moneys used to facilitate the construction projects at the World Center on Mount Carmel in Haifa. The UHJ has been making strong appeals to the Bahá'í world for increased contributions to the Arc fund, so that the buildings housing the various institutions of the World Center will be completed by the end of the twentieth century.

14. Factor analysis revealed that measures of personal devotion separate into two factors: one measuring the frequency of scripture reading (computed by summing the scores from items in table 5.2) and the other capturing a more general measure of devotion. The latter measure included the following variables: the frequency of prayer, observance of the Fast, contributions to the local Fund, taking Pilgrimage, the number of hours per week one devotes to Bahá'í activities (the average was 9.2 hours), level of agreement with the question "I try to pattern all of my daily activities around the laws and principles of the Faith," and finally, one's answer to the question "Have you personally made individual goals for yourself based on the Three Year Plan from the Universal House of Justice?" (either "yes," "no," or "not acquainted with the Plan"—see Table 5.1). Although the above variables separated into two factors, to-

gether they created a higher score in reliability analysis (Cronbach's alpha = .852) than either factor did separately. It could be argued that scripture reading is theoretically related to a general measure of piety or devotion. Thus, all the above variables were summed to form a general measure of piety/devotion. Chi-square tests of association between this measure of devotion and various demographic measures were then calculated.

15. High levels of devotion were, however, statistically associated with the recognition of legitimate authority in the Administrative Order. In other words, the more authority one recognized in the Administrative Order, the more likely one was to display high levels of personal devotion.

16. Bahá'í writings counsel that "the Feast is opened with devotional readings, that is to say, prayers and meditations, from the Writings of Bahá'u'lláh, the Báb and ['Abdu'l-Bahá]. Following this passages may be read from other Tablets, from the Holy Scriptures of previous Dispensations, and from the writings of the Guardian" (Hornby 1983, 245). However, "although in principle there is certainly no reason why excerpts from other Sacred Scriptures should not be read in the spiritual part of our Feasts, that as this is particularly an occasion when Bahá'ís get together to deepen their own spiritual life, it is, generally speaking, advisable for them to read from their own holy Writings in the spiritual part of the Feast" (Hornby 1983, 246). Only rarely during my fieldwork did I hear non-Bahá'í scripture read at Feasts.

17. "The rule that only Bahá'ís may take part in Nineteen Day Feasts is not a new one. . . . However, when a non-Bahá'í does appear at a Feast he should not be asked to leave; rather the Assembly should omit the consultative part of the Feast, and the non-Bahá'í should be made welcome. Of course, if the non-Bahá'í is well known to the Bahá'ís and no hurt feelings would be caused, he might be asked to retire during the consultative part. . . . During the period of consultation the Bahá'ís should be able to enjoy perfect freedom to express their views on the work of the Cause, unembarrassed by the feeling that all they are saying is being heard by someone who has not accepted Bahá'u'lláh and who might, thereby, gain a very distorted picture of the Faith. It would also be very embarrassing for any sensitive non-Bahá'í to find himself plunged into the midst of a discussion of the detailed affairs of a Bahá'í community of which he is not a part" (Hornby 1983, 241).

18. "Social capital," according to Putnam, "refers to features of social organization such as networks, norms, and social trust that facilitate coordination and cooperation for mutual benefit" wherein "networks of civic engagement foster sturdy norms of generalized reciprocity and encourage the emergence of social trust" that "probably broaden the participants' sense of self, developing the 'I' into the 'we'" (1995, 67). In Putnam's language, for Bahá'ís the "we" is universal and global, but the "cooperation for mutual benefit" focuses on one's situated local community: this is the essence of being a situated universalist.

19. Examples of such letters include these topics: the shortfall in the national Bahá'í funds (7 February 1993); the importance of the Fast for Bahá'í youth (2 March 1993); the publication in English of the *Kitáb-i-Aqdas* (8 March 1993); the election of the Universal House of Justice (30 April 1993); the importance of attaining the goals of the Three Year Plan (1 August 1993 and 17 May 1994); the importance of modeling racial unity in the Bahá'í community (9 August 1993); warning against the activities of Covenant-breakers (25 August 1993); the importance of "entry by troops" (2 March 1994); attitudes Bahá'ís should foster for successful teaching (5 June 1994); and the campaign to defend persecuted Bahá'ís in Iran (4 November 1994). Letters cited may be found in the National Bahá'í Archives, Wilmette, Illinois.

20. 'Abdu'l-Bahá stated: "The owner of the house must personally serve the beloved ones. He must seek after the comfort of all and with the utmost humility he must show forth kindness to every one. If the Feast is arranged in this manner and in the way

mentioned, that supper is the 'Lord's Supper', for the result is the same result and the effect is the same effect" (Hornby 1983, 243). Bahá'ís sometimes would comment, during Feasts, that 'Abdu'l-Bahá indicated that every 19 days, Bahá'ís should have a spiritual experience the equivalent of the Christian Lord's Supper, and that 'Abdu'l-Bahá would be present "in heart and soul" (Hornby 1983, 240).

21. In 1987 the UHJ elaborated: "The sub-division of the city should be seen merely as an administrative necessity meant to serve the good of the whole community.... Given the racial and social stratification of large cities, the Spiritual Assembly would also have to exert the utmost care not to allow the Bahá'í community of _____ to become, in effect, racially or socially fragmented, even though one race or stratum of society may be dominant in a sub-unit of the city. [The LSA should] uphold at all times ... the primary principle and goal of our Faith, namely, the unity of the human race" (quoted in *Bahá'í News*, November 1989, 7).

22. Recent research by Hadaway, Marler, and Chaves (1993) suggests that weekly church attendance rates are only about half of the commonly accepted rate of 40 percent. They found that 19.6 percent of Protestants attend church during an average week, while 28 percent of Catholics actually do so. This corresponds to the nearly 18 percent of Bahá'ís who report attending all nineteen Feasts, the 48 percent who report twelve to eighteen Feasts per year, and the 41 percent who attend "most" Holy Day celebrations (see below). However, direct comparisons are impossible.

23. This was especially true after a collection of Bahá'í songs sung by the "Bahá'í Gospel Singers" came out on CD. The group became well known in the Bahá'í world after its performances at the Second Bahá'í World Congress (see chapter 1).

24. Although survey data cannot address the issue of interracial friendship, my observation is that interracial unity is not limited to official meetings or structured worship. I attended many Bahá'í social gatherings where people of all ethnic backgrounds would socialize. This was especially evident among Bahá'í youth, some of whose parents told me that their kids had always had interracial playmates, and that these relationships continued into young adulthood.

25. Sociologically, the very act of using stories about martyrs and religious oppression reinforces the internal solidarity of a group (see Coser 1956, Simmel 1955).

26. This Holy Day is called the "Ascension" of Bahá'u'lláh, expressing the Bahá'í belief in the "ascent" of Bahá'u'lláh's soul to the spiritual world.

27. Unfortunately, I did not ask a question on the survey about taking off from work or school on Holy Days. However, my impression from discussions with Atlanta Bahá'ís is that a significant number work on those Holy Days when work is to be suspended, either because it was not allowed by their workplace, or because vacation days were saved for family trips and not used for Holy Day observance.

28. The Naw-Rúz festival is to be held separate from the Feast of Bahá (the first month of the year in the Bahá'í calendar); however, most communities combine the two celebrations.

29. See MacEoin 1986 and Cole 1998 for another perspective on Bahá'í fundamentalism or orthodoxy.

30. This obligation to work for a living does not include those who stay home to take care of children, because the *Aqdas* states that "homemaking is a highly honourable and responsible work of fundamental importance to society" (Bahá'u'lláh 1992, 193).

31. Shoghi Effendi counseled Bahá'ís: "The cardinal principle which we must follow ... is obedience to the Government prevailing in any land in which we reside. We cannot, because, say, we do not personally like a totalitarian form of government, refuse to obey it when it becomes the ruling power. Nor can we join underground Movements which are a minority agitating against the prevailing government. ... We cannot start judging how a particular government came into power, and therefore whether we should obey it or not. This would immediately plunge us into politics. We must

obey in all cases except where a spiritual principle is involved, such as denying our Faith. For these spiritual principles we must be willing to die. . . . If [Bahá'ís] become involved in the issues the Governments of the world are struggling over, they will be lost. But if they build up the Bahá'í pattern they can offer it as a remedy when all else has failed" (quoted in Hornby 1983, 446).

32. Several years ago, some Bahá'ís questioned the wisdom of becoming too closely allied with an institution that takes definite, partisan political stances, something forbidden in Bahá'í scripture. However, the NSA allayed these fears by clarifying for Bahá'ís around the country that Bahá'í support was for the King Center's continuing mission of promoting a racism-free society, and not for any political issues.

33. To create measures of organizational participation, factor analysis was performed on a variety of organizational variables, and two distinct factors emerged: one measuring "active organizational participation" (Cronbach's alpha = .703), and the other measuring "participation in administrative rituals" (Cronbach's alpha = .823). The Chi-square statistic was used to measure statistical association.

Chapter 6 *Boundaries and Identity*

1. See Fazel 1997; Fazel and Fananapazir 1997.

2. Some non-Bahá'ís I spoke with at Firesides said that while they feel various levels of pressure to "declare," they generally always feel welcome at Firesides or deepenings, even if they have participated for several years without declaring.

3. The secretary of the Atlanta LSA was giving a deepening on Bahá'í spirituality, and said there were three stages to becoming a Bahá'í: (1) developing your personal discipline of reading scripture and fasting; (2) participating in community life through Feasts and the Administrative Order; and (3) gaining a perspective on how the Bahá'í Faith will establish future world order (fieldwork notes, 10 October 1993). He explicitly defined the process as becoming more universal and global over time. In effect, he was describing a Bahá'í identity as a situated universalist: acting locally while fostering global-level thinking.

4. Bahá'u'lláh wrote to: Napoleon III, Pope Pius IX, Czar Alexander II, Queen Victoria of Britain, William I of Prussia, Francis Joseph of the Austro-Hungarian monarchy, Sultan Abdu'l-Aziz, Nasiri'd-Din Shah of Persia, and the leaders of the Republics of the Americas (Effendi 1980).

5. 'Abdu'l-Bahá said that unity of the planet will be accomplished in seven stages, which he called the "seven candles of unity": unity in the political realm, unity of thought in world undertakings, unity in freedom, unity in religion, unity of nations, unity of races, and unity of language (1978, 32). According to Bahá'í theology, what Bahá'u'lláh called the "Most Great Peace" or the Kingdom of God will result when all seven stages are completed—most likely, Bahá'ís say, at different historical times and through various travails. The unity of nations, which 'Abdu'l-Bahá predicts will occur by the end of the twentieth century, constitutes the "Lesser Peace," but is only one-seventh of the promised unity of humanity in Bahá'í scripture.

6. For more on a Bahá'í perspective on the teleological unfolding of world peace, see Hayes et al. 1986, Lee 1989.

7. Shoghi Effendi called communism, along with nationalism and racism, the "three false gods" that are at the heart of the corruption of the "old world order" (1980, 113).

8. Bahá'ís say that no compromises can be made with the interests of non-Bahá'ís who may water down or corrupt the supposed "purity" of Bahá'í laws and principles.

9. Adib Taherzadeh, member of the UHJ and Bahá'í author, said this about those who break the social laws of the Faith: "There is another category of believers who become deprived of their administrative rights by the sanction, at the present time, of

the National Spiritual Assemblies. This happens when the individual flagrantly breaks certain laws of Bahá'u'lláh which are related to social or administrative activities and by so doing brings disgrace upon the Faith. Although not Bahá'ís in good standing, these people are nevertheless part of the community and may, under certain conditions, regain their administrative rights" (Taherzadeh 1992, 260).

10. One topic not explored in this study was the attitudes and perspectives of those who had lost and regained their administrative rights, or who were still under administrative discipline. How would these stigmatized Bahá'ís understand their global, universal identity? Future research should make efforts to study this subset of Bahá'ís (see Goffman 1986). The same can be said of "Covenant-Breaking," discussed below.

11. Bahá'ís point out that because this is such a serious issue, the UHJ goes to great lengths to persuade the individual to mend his or her ways, before expelling him or her from the Bahá'í Faith. Sociologically, this is similar to the excommunication and *Meidung*, or social avoidance or shunning, practiced by the Amish (see Hostetler 1993; Kraybill 1989; Kraybill and Olshan 1994).

12. However, Bahá'ís often gloss over this topic, and report that there has *never* been a schism within their faith, claiming that it has maintained its unity over its entire 150–year history. This is not accurate, as the early records of attacks against Bahá'u'lláh, 'Abdu'l-Bahá, and Shoghi Effendi clearly indicate (see Taherzadeh 1992; Stockman 1985), although none of the splinter groups have grown.

13. News of another Covenant-Breaking group was reported in *Harper's* a few years later. The February 1995 issue printed a series of press releases from the "Bahá'ís Under the Provision of the Covenant" in Missoula, Montana. This group claims that Biblical prophesy predicted the World Trade Center bombing, as well as a future nuclear attack on New York City.

14. Taherzadeh says that 'Abdu'l-Bahá likens Covenant-Breaking to a contagious disease: "He ['Abdu'l-Bahá] used to explain that physical health is not contagious. The health of one individual has no effect on another individual. But an infectious disease spreads rapidly and can affect a multitude. 'Abdu'l-Bahá often explained that the protection of the believers from the deadly disease of Covenant-breaking was imperative, and could be achieved only by cutting off association with them" (1992, 254).

15. Research indicates that religious endogamy (marrying within one's religious group) is decreasing in the United States (McGuire 1997). Bahá'ís, however, are more likely to be married to someone within their faith than are members of all Protestant, Catholic, and Jewish groups in the United States (although high Bahá'í endogamy rates are more similar to those of conservative Protestant groups than of more mainline, liberal groups—McCutcheon 1988; Glen 1984). It is impossible to determine from my data if Bahá'ís tend to choose Bahá'í marriage partners, or if one spouse converts in anticipation of, or after, marriage.

16. It should be kept in mind that Bahá'ís are much more likely to read their own scripture: for example, nearly 40 percent of the respondents reported daily study of Bahá'u'lláh's writings, and another 30 percent said they read them at least weekly.

17. Those most likely to read non-Bahá'í scripture were disproportionately converts from conservative Christian religious backgrounds—those that tend to stress the primacy of the Bible in revealing religious knowledge, rather than human experience or reason.

18. Which include, as the above discussion suggests, the likelihood of having friends within the Bahá'í Faith, whether or not one is married to a Bahá'í, one's relationship to other religious faiths, and one's willingness to cooperate with other groups with similar goals. For the following discussion, statistical association was measured using Chi-square tests.

19. This relationship is even stronger among those who grew up as Bahá'ís, as one might expect. Those raised as Bahá'ís from birth would be more likely to have their Bahá'í identity shaped by Bahá'í parents during formative years, and to attend Bahá'í

children's classes and youth conferences. This parallels the greater commitment found among Roman Catholics who grew up going to parochial schools (D'Antonio et al. 1989).

20. "The African Hebrew Israelites of Jerusalem" is a predominantly African American sectarian group led by Ben Ammi, who led an "exodus" of followers back to their assumed historical homeland of Israel in 1969.

21. Shoghi Effendi said this about the need for converts to withdraw membership in churches: "We, as Bahá'ís, can never be known as hypocrites or as people insincere in their protestations and because of this we cannot subscribe to both the Faith of Bahá'u'lláh *and* ordinary church dogma. The churches are waiting for the coming of Jesus Christ; we believe He has come again in the Glory of the Father. The churches teach doctrines . . . which we as Bahá'ís do not accept; such as the bodily Resurrection, confession, or, in some creeds, the denial of the Immaculate Conception. . . . We should, therefore, withdraw from our churches but continue to associate, if we wish to, with the church members and ministers" (quoted in Hornby 1983, 159).

22. One event in which I participated as part of fieldwork highlighted this paradox. During an interfaith dialogue conference, Bahá'ís were presenting their perspective on the oneness of religion, and their belief in Bahá'u'lláh as the latest Manifestation of God. Finally, a professor of Christian theology pleasantly but firmly exclaimed: "I want Bahá'ís to tell me they think they are right and I am wrong!" No Bahá'í took up the challenge, but they did reiterate their view on the oneness of religion. When I spoke to him later, he said he could tell Bahá'ís were passionate about their faith, but he wanted them to convince him of the truth of their beliefs. They seemed to him, however, to not want to "step on any toes" by making exclusivist claims. This almost made Bahá'ís sound insincere, he concluded.

Chapter 7   *Teaching the Bahá'í Faith*

1. Bahá'ís refer to all evangelization efforts as "teaching work," "teaching the Cause," or just "teaching."

2. Bahá'ís often ironically use militaristic language to speak about their mission in the world—to bring about their version of a peaceable Kingdom of God. Bahá'í discourse frequently compares dedicated teachers to soldiers, as in one advertisement for a youth conference: "Army of Light Book Camp: National Youth Conference for Preparing the Soldiers" (*The American Bahá'í* 25, no. 14: 3). This can also be seen in the discussion of "entry by troops" below. When asked if that poses a contradiction, Bahá'ís point out that while Bahá'í law allows for collective security at the global level, Bahá'u'lláh forbade *jihad* (or "holy war"), and called on national leaders to reduce their stockpiles of weapons.

3. For Bahá'í scholarship on the history of the teaching plans, see Dahl 1993; Hassall 1995. As discussed in chapter 3, since 1937 Bahá'ís have operated under three Seven Year Plans (1937–1944, 1946–1953, 1979–1986); a Ten Year Plan (1953–1963); a Nine Year Plan (1964–1973); a Five Year Plan (1974–1979); a Six Year Plan (1986–1992), a Three Year Plan (1993–1996), and a Four Year Plan (1996–2000).

4. While Bahá'ís frequently told me that they are to "teach" but not to "proselytize," that latter term cannot be found in the writings of Bahá'í Central Figures or Shoghi Effendi, and its meaning therefore remains vague for Atlanta Bahá'ís. The UHJ, in a statement published to commemorate the one hundredth anniversary of Bahá'u'lláh's death, said "Bahá'u'lláh's writings forbid the aggressive proselytism through which many religious messages have been widely promulgated. . . . The aggressive proselytism that had characterized efforts in ages past to promote the cause of religion is declared to be unworthy of the Day of God" (Universal House of Justice 1991, 2, 18). One introductory Bahá'í source (Hatcher and Martin 1985) also says proselytizing is

forbidden, but references the quote below from Bahá'u'lláh, saying Bahá'ís "face a challenge to find ways of sharing their beliefs that do not infringe on the privacy of others or offend the customs of the society in which they reside" (Hatcher and Martin 1985, 174).

5. 'Abdu'l-Bahá also gave Bahá'ís guidance on the attitudes that would advance successful teaching: "The teacher should not consider himself as learned and others ignorant. Such a thought breeds pride, and pride is unconducive to influence" (Universal House of Justice 1977, 11).

6. The NSA outlined the following goals for the U.S. Bahá'í community as part of the Three Year Plan: intensify study of the Sacred Writings as a means of fostering spiritual strength and transformation; expand vastly the human resources of the Faith; raise at least 3,000 traveling teachers; settle at least 500 homefront pioneers on Indian reservations, in the South and in other areas of greatest need; establish local Spiritual Assemblies in every city with a population of 50,000, resulting in no fewer than 150 new Spiritual Assemblies; strive to become leaders in the movement for race unity and to make Bahá'í communities models of unity that inspire emulation and lead to growth; teach Bahá'í and other children and youth to become the first generation of Americans free of all prejudices and truly united; expand programs of education for Bahá'í children, youth, and adults and for the strengthening of Bahá'í family life; promote the advancement of women and publish a statement on women; foster the maturation of local and national institutions with particular emphasis on the development of spiritual assemblies, the refinement of the art of consultation, the refinement of the Feast, and the operation of the Funds; strengthen the financial position of the national community; extend the range of the NSA's collaboration projects with the Bahá'í communities of Alaska, Australia, Brazil, Canada, China, Eastern Europe, Greenland, Mexico, the countries of the former Soviet Union, and the United Kingdom; send at least 1,368 pioneers and traveling teachers abroad (quoted in *The American Bahá'í* 24, no. 7: 2).

7. The city of Atlanta's LSA goals included: develop community deepenings, initiate group teaching projects, expand children's classes, plan prayer chains, give certificates to people who reach goals, include music in the Feast, help establish an LSA in south Fulton county, become models in the race unity movement (from "Atlanta Bahá'í Bulletin" newsletter, 3 November 1993).

8. This is a phrase commonly used in Bahá'í circles to denote large numbers of converts, again using militaristic language.

9. Bahá'ís might read in *The American Bahá'í* encouraging news of entry by troops campaigns in San Francisco (vol. 24, no. 3: 1), where thirty new enrollments have been recorded; or fifty new declarations in St. Petersburg, Florida (vol. 24, no. 18: 2) and dozens of new Southeast Asian Bahá'ís in Merced, California (vol. 24, no. 7: 31). Or, one could read about global efforts and successes of entry by troops: 300 new believers in India the first week of the teaching campaign (vol. 25, no. 6: 13), or 200 new enrollments in Peru after thirty LSAs collaborated with the Bahá'í radio station in that country (vol. 25, no. 3: 15). This reinforces a Bahá'í's situated universalist identity. Seeing stories about mass conversions from across the globe provides inspiration, Bahá'ís told me, to redouble their own teaching efforts in their local community.

10. Rationalizations for the lack of growth given to me by Atlanta Bahá'ís range from a lack of teaching efforts by individual Bahá'ís, to the fact that people just do not like to talk about religion in the United States, to the fact that materialism in American culture distracts people from religious issues.

11. The NSA member's comments came at a fundraiser in Atlanta on November 6, 1993 to raise money for a new Bahá'í Center in the northwest section of the metropolitan area.

12. Confirmed by discussion with a Bahá'í representative at the Bahá'í National Center.

13. To avoid repeating what were considered mistakes committed in previous mass-growth campaigns, the NSA unveiled a model for expansion and consolidation during Mission 19. Teaching should "engage in a number of steps that guide individuals along a path from learning about Bahá'u'lláh to arising independently to serve His Cause." These steps include (1) finding and teaching receptive souls, (2) declaration and enrollment, (3) strengthening bonds of fellowship, (4) systematic deepening, and (5) continued learning and service. National Bahá'í leaders criticized Bahá'ís for only completing steps (1) and (2), without the harder and less visible work of consolidating new declarants (which garnered less status within the Bahá'í community itself). Focus on teaching should permeate all aspects of a local Bahá'í community's life, including: spiritual meetings, teaching activities, Feasts and LSA meetings, individual and family life, youth activities, children's classes, deepenings, schools and institutes, social activities, and social and economic development projects. Only Feasts and LSA meetings, NSA members stressed, were limited to declared Bahá'ís; all other activities in the Bahá'í community *should* involve non-Bahá'í friends. This, according to one NSA member, is a paradigm shift in conceptualizing the Bahá'í community: all of humanity is a part of the Bahá'í community, but only a fraction are declared members with voting rights at this time. An NSA member said, "Get your mind into a teaching mode—then everybody you see you see as a potential Bahá'í" (*The American Bahá'í* 25, no. 2: 4).

14. There is a growing literature in the sociology of religion that examines the ideological distinctiveness of a religious group and its corresponding ability to recruit and maintain new members. Those religious movements whose ideas and practices have minimal tension with the wider socioreligious environment have difficulty recruiting members because they offer nothing "new" to a convert; while those existing in extremely high tension with their environment also have difficulty, because they provide no continuity with the existing social system. See Stark and Bainbridge 1985; Bainbridge 1997; Kelley 1972; Finke and Stark 1992; Perrin and Mauss 1991; Iannaccone 1992, 1994.

15. Shoghi Effendi wrote this of the station or rank Bahá'u'lláh holds in Bahá'í theology: "To Israel He was neither more nor less than the incarnation of the 'Everlasting Father,' the 'Lord of Hosts' come down 'with ten thousands of saints'; to Christendom Christ returned 'in the glory of the Father,' to Shí'ah Islam the return of the Imám Husayn; to Sunní Islám the descent of the 'Spirit of God' (Jesus Christ); to the Zoroastrians the promised Sháh-Bahram; to the Hindus the reincarnation of Krishna; to the Buddhists the fifth Buddha" (1995, 94).

16. For example, Bahá'ís claim that Isaiah 9:6–7—"and the government will be upon his shoulder, and his name will be called 'Wonderful Counselor, Mighty God, Everlasting Father, Prince of Peace.' Of the increase of his government and of peace there will be no end"—refers to Bahá'u'lláh and His World Order; and Isaiah 35:2—"The glory of Lebanon shall be given to it, the majesty of Carmel and Sharon. They shall see the Glory of the Lord, the majesty of our God"—refers to the Bahá'í World Center on Mount Carmel in Haifa, and the "Glory of the Lord" is Bahá'u'lláh (see Sours 1990).

17. Bahá'ís frequently mention the Jimmy Carter Presidential Center, the Martin Luther King Jr. Center for Nonviolent Social Change, and CNN Center.

18. One student I talked with, discussing his disapproval of mass teaching, pointed out to me that when Shoghi Effendi was asked about this method of teaching, he said in a letter written on his behalf: "He feels that to distribute Bahá'í pamphlets from door to door . . . is undignified and might create a bad impression of the Faith" (quoted in Universal House of Justice 1977, 37–38). This passage was never a topic of group discussion as far as I know. Most Bahá'ís, when asked, felt that some people can use this method tactfully and effectively, while others are just uncomfortable with it.

19. During my year of fieldwork, I rarely attended an event that did not have a diverse mix of people from various racial, ethnic, and national backgrounds.

20. Another 27 percent of survey respondents indicated "other" teaching activities not listed in the survey. By far, the most popular "other" teaching activity (one-third of respondents) involved youth activities: teaching Bahá'í youth classes, helping out with youth conferences, and sponsoring the Bahá'í Youth Workshop. Another 23 percent answering "other" indicated race unity activities as an important part of their personal teaching efforts, whether it be through participation in Race Unity Day in June, Race Unity conferences, or through involvement in Martin Luther King Jr. holiday activities in January (72 percent of Atlanta respondents indicated that they have participated in this form of "indirect teaching"). Finally, the third most often "other" category mentioned was participating in the Bahá'í Gospel Choir or the Atlanta Bahá'í Arts Institute—groups that use song and drama to promote the religion.

21. All eight teaching variables at the top of Table 7.1 loaded on one factor in factor analysis, with Cronbach's alpha = .750. Chi-square analysis was then used to determine statistical association, discussed below. In addition, all eight teaching variables are positively correlated with each other at significant levels—even such teaching activities as talking one-to-one with others and mass teaching. This would indicate that, for most Bahá'ís, none of the teaching methods widely used are necessarily mutually exclusive, even though Bahá'í discourse may label some methods as more or less appropriate.

22. In fact, when asked which aspect of the Bahá'í Faith gives one the greatest personal satisfaction, more than 20 percent of the respondents listed "Teaching the Bahá'í Faith" as the most satisfying aspect of being a Bahá'í, and nearly one-half (46.6 percent) listed teaching as one of the top three activities that give them the most personal satisfaction. The emphasis given to teaching efforts is a critical component of a Bahá'í's identity as a situated universalist, and reinforces the connections individual Bahá'ís have between their activity in a local community and the Bahá'í mission on a universal scale.

23. Those who first pioneered to a country or territory were given the laudatory title "Knights of Bahá'u'lláh" by Shoghi Effendi, thus acquiring considerable status within the Bahá'í community. Shoghi Effendi coined the term during the Ten Year Plan or World Crusade (1953–1963).

24. Statistical analysis indicates that one is more likely to be either a foreign or a homefront pioneer if one's parents were Bahá'ís, the longer one has been a Bahá'í, the greater authority one assigns to the Administrative Order, the greater devotion one displays for one's faith, and the more actively one engages in teaching.

25. Bainbridge writes: "A novel religious movement that lacks cultural continuity demands that recruits learn an entirely new set of beliefs and practices which at the very least requires a substantial amount of education and indoctrination. In contrast, a movement that has continuity can present itself as the fulfillment of the faith the recruit already possesses, and it demands far less labor to learn" (1997, 412). Sociologically, the Bahá'í Faith's self-presentation contains both elements: on the one hand it is novel, in that a whole new ritual, organizational, and language system must be slowly inculcated. This puts it in moderate tension with the religious culture of the United States, and social movements in exceptionally high tension with the wider society "will be unable to build bonds with potential recruits because [they are] stigmatized" by society (1997, 412). On the other hand, the Bahá'í Faith presents itself as having some continuity with U.S. secular and Christian ideas, since Bahá'ís teach socially progressive values (such as racial unity and the equality of women and men), and also teach that the Bahá'í Faith is the culmination of Christ's promised return. However, a religious movement in "exceptionally low tension [with society] will be unable to provide the motivation necessary for successful conversion" (1997, 412).

It remains to be seen if the greater emphasis on the station of Bahá'u'lláh moves the public presentation of the Bahá'í Faith into higher, but not excessively high tension, resulting in more successful recruiting efforts.

Chapter 8   *"Thinking Globally, Acting Locally"*

1. Bahá'ís I have talked with say that the oneness of humanity finds expression in other ways outside the southern United States: for example, by promoting unity among the white, American Indian, and Hispanic communities in the Southwest; and among the Pacific Islanders, Southeast Asians, and whites in Hawaii.
2. 'Abdu'l-Bahá's trip through Europe and North America was possible because of the 1908 Young Turk Revolution, whereby all political and religious prisoners of the Ottoman Empire were set free (Hatcher and Martin 1985).
3. At the time 'Abdu'l-Bahá was saying this, miscegenation was illegal in most of the U.S. South. It was not until 1967 that the U.S. Supreme Court declared antimiscegenation laws unconstitutional. My impression from fieldwork is that the Atlanta Bahá'í community has a relatively high proportion of interracial couples. However, I have no statistical data to confirm this, in comparison with the wider society. The Atlanta Bahá'í community does not keep those kinds of records, and when I asked about the rate of interracial Bahá'í marriage, individuals gave a widely varying range of possibilities, making even an estimate difficult.
4. Louis Gregory went on to become a member of the NSA of the United States and a pioneer to Haiti, and was appointed as a Hand of the Cause of God before his death in 1951, remaining married to Louisa Mathew for thirty-nine years. One of the four permanent Bahá'í Schools in the United States, the Louis Gregory Institute in South Carolina, also bears his name.
5. Bahá'í scripture states: "The contribution of the Faith to this subject is essentially indirect, as it consists in the application of spiritual principles to our present-day economic system" (Hornby 1983, 551). While greater details appear in Bahá'í literature (see Thomas 1984; Robiati 1991; Dahl 1984, 1991; Fish 1997), few Bahá'ís seem knowledgeable about them.
6. In a letter to the LSA of Los Angeles, the NSA said that the L.A. riots were an example of how "The old world order is collapsing before our eyes," and encouraged the Bahá'ís of L.A. to fulfill their "sacred obligation" to "dispense the healing medicine" of Bahá'u'lláh to their city. Letter dated 30 April 1992, National Bahá'í Archives, Wilmette, Illinois.
7. Letter entitled "A Call to Eliminate Racism" sent to all Local Spiritual Assemblies in the United States from the National Spiritual Assembly; dated 10 June 1992. General Correspondence, 1992. National Bahá'í Archives, Wilmette, Illinois.
8. The NSA consciously promotes race unity efforts, and this was one of the principle goals of the Three Year Plan. In September 1993, the NSA printed a message to the American Bahá'í community counseling vigilant action in the promotion of race unity. In it, the NSA said, "For a Bahá'í, racial prejudice is a negation of faith. Freedom from prejudice is the supreme injunction of Bahá'u'lláh and the 'hallmark of a true Bahá'í character'. . . . As the Bahá'í Writings clearly state, the fundamental solution to racial conflict rests ultimately in recognition of Bahá'u'lláh, obedience to His commandments and acceptance of the principle of the oneness of humankind" (*The American Bahá'í* 24, no. 14: 1). But the NSA goes on to note that various "secular" methods by which local Bahá'í communities have tried to promote race unity have themselves been divisive at times. They cite a number of Institutes for the Healing of Racism around the country that have led to "disunity, contention and even paralysis of Bahá'í community life" because they have "relied on theories and methods that are not entirely consistent with Bahá'í teachings and principles." The NSA

was especially critical of twelve-step programs (upon which the Institute for the Healing of Racism is based), which use confession of "sins" and admission of guilt as part
of the therapeutic process.

9. This section contains information that appeared in McMullen 1995.

10. Quoted in Cooper and Terrill 1991, 543.

11. The 1910 City Code of Atlanta indicates that bars should be licensed to sell alcohol
to either blacks or whites but not both; barber shops must display signs indicating
whether they serve blacks only, whites only, or both; and restaurants cannot "sell to
the two races within the same room or at different tables within the same room, or
at different portions of the same table within the same room or serve the two races
anywhere under the same license" (Sec. 2143, 1910 City Code of Atlanta).

12. From pp. 1–2 of an unpublished report in the Atlanta Bahá'í Archives entitled "Atlanta Bahá'í History 1909–1944: A Narrative of the Early Days of the Bahá'í Faith
in Atlanta, Georgia," no date, written by Olga Finke. Finke was an early Atlanta
believer who served on the first Local Spiritual Assembly of Atlanta and was responsible for much of the early archival records. Further references to Finke's report will
be given parenthetically within the text.

13. This is consistent with Stockman's (1985) research showing that many of the early
American Bahá'ís were involved in a variety of spiritual and philosophical movements of the late nineteenth and early twentieth centuries, and often retained membership in multiple religious organizations.

14. The Rosicrucians are a fraternal order that trace their roots to the early seventeenth-
century German Christian Rosae Cross order. Their doctrine combines Egyptian occult knowledge, Christian gnosticism, Jewish mysticism, alchemy and magic, and
freemasonry (see King 1971).

15. In a study of the Canadian Bahá'í community, Van den Hoonaard said that Oakshette
claimed to have become a Bahá'í on May 21, 1897, at the same time as Lua Getsinger,
a distinguished early American believer. However, there is no record of him on Bahá'í
membership lists of that time (Van den Hoonaard 1996, 32).

16. (1) *The Bahá'í World A Biennial International Record: Volume II April 1926–April 1928*
(New York: Bahá'í Publishing Committee, 1928), 186. (2) *The Bahá'í World: Volume III April 1928–April 1930* (New York: Bahá'í Publishing Committee, 1930), 221.
(3) *The Bahá'í World: Volume IV April 1930–1932* (New York: Bahá'í Publishing Committee, 1933), 278. (4) *The Bahá'í World: Volume VI April 1934–1936* (New York:
Bahá'í Publishing Committee, 1937), 518. (5) *The Bahá'í World: Volume VII April
1936–1938* (New York: Bahá'í Publishing Committee, 1939), 568. There is no reference to Oakshette in Volume V of *The Bahá'í World*.

17. The Liberal Catholic Church (LCC) grew out of the Old Catholic Church of Holland, and came into existence as the result of a reorganization in 1916 of the Old
Catholic Church of Great Britain. The *Statement of Principles* says in part that the
LCC, although independent from Roman Catholicism or Protestantism, believes "that
there is a body of doctrine and mystical experience common to all the great religions of the world and which cannot be claimed as the exclusive possession of
any . . . it holds that the other great religions of the world are divinely inspired and
that all proceed from a common source, though different religions stress different aspects of this teaching and some aspects may even temporarily drop out of recognition" (Liberal Catholic Church 1927, 6). See *The Liberal Catholic Church: Statement
of Principles, Summary of Doctrine, and Table of Apostolic Succession*.

18. During an interview with Estelle Lindsey (14 May 1994), she said that Oakshette,
whom she described as a "deeply spiritual man," distributed a weekly bulletin that
would sometimes contain quotes from the *Hidden Words of Bahá'u'lláh*. She also said
that her husband Raymond met Oakshette through the Rosicrucians in Atlanta. My

thanks to John Haynes of the Atlanta Bahá'í Archives Committee for his assistance with this interview.

19. Also quoted in Morrison 1982, 108–109.

20. The invitation from the Atlanta Chamber of Commerce to 'Abdu'l-Bahá to visit Atlanta during his trip through North America was confirmed by Estelle Lindsey (interview, 14 May 1994).

21. Oakshette was buried in Westview Cemetery in Atlanta, receiving a Liberal Catholic funeral service. That Oakshette was actively involved in the Liberal Catholic Church and Bahá'í teaching efforts for nearly thirty years in Atlanta is confirmed in van den Hoonaard (1996, 41).

22. Report from Olga Finke to Georgie Brown Wiles, Secretary of the Regional Teaching Committee, 13 March 1938, Folder 37, Atlanta Bahá'í Archives.

23. Interview with Estelle Lindsey, 14 May 1994.

24. Doris Ebbert to Ralph McGill, editor of the *Atlanta Constitution*, 1 November 1945, Scrapbook #1, Atlanta Bahá'í Archives.

25. Olga Finke to Louis Gregory, 15 April 1951, Louis Gregory Papers, Box 1, Folder 32, National Bahá'í Archives, Wilmette, Illinois.

26. From note on Bahá'í Membership Records, Atlanta, Georgia, 21 April 1939 to 21 April 1940, Atlanta Bahá'í Archives.

27. Quoted in a letter from Olga Finke to Edward Struven, 30 August 1937, Folder 37, Atlanta Bahá'í Archives. The "recent communications from the Guardian" probably refers to a 22 March 1937 letter from Shoghi Effendi, appearing in *Bahá'í News* #108, June 1937.

28. Interview with Estelle Lindsey, 14 May 1994.

29. Estelle Lindsey said that in their neighborhood, whites lived in larger houses which faced the street, while blacks often lived behind them in small "shot-gun" houses in the alleys (interview, 14 May 1994). Raymond became friends with the black family who lived behind them.

30. Estelle Lindsey (interview, 14 May 1994) maintains that it was not racism within the Bahá'í community per se that was causing the divisions. Rather, it was differences in how the teaching work should proceed. Some felt that teaching should be done on a segregated basis—whites teaching whites, blacks teaching blacks—because of the very real dangers associated with "mixed-race" meetings in the South. Others felt that whites should actively teach blacks or whoever was receptive, and not target any population.

31. Bahá'í Membership Records, Atlanta, Georgia, 1909–1975, Atlanta Bahá'í Archives.

32. In an interview with David and Margaret Ruhe (14 December 1993), former Atlanta community members in the 1940s, and he a former UHJ member, Mr. Ruhe said that throughout their tenure in Atlanta, from 1942 to 1949, the Bahá'ís of Atlanta also united with the "liberal forces" in the city to work on three fronts: (1) to desegregate the Atlanta City Auditorium, the rear of which had a cord running down the middle segregating blacks and whites; (2) to desegregate the drinking fountains in City Hall and have the "whites only" and "colored only" signs taken down; and (3) to help lobby for the desegregation of the Atlanta Police Department.

33. From an official report to the National Spiritual Assembly entitled "Occurrence at Bahá'í Meeting, April 28, 1947" by David S. Ruhe, Chairman, and Doris Ebbert, Correspondence Secretary, Atlanta Bahá'í Archives.

34. Official Report to National Spiritual Assembly, "Occurrence at Bahá'í Meeting, April 28, 1947." Atlanta Bahá'í Archives.

35. From a letter dated 5 February 1947, written on behalf of Shoghi Effendi to the Local Spiritual Assembly of Atlanta, Georgia, quoted in *Bahá'í News* 210 (August 1948): 2; reprinted in Universal House of Justice 1984, 26. This letter was in response to a

letter written jointly by Dorothy Baker and the Atlanta LSA during their September 1946 consultation described above.

36. Annual Report of the Recording Secretary 1948–1949 of the Atlanta Bahá'í Community, National Bahá'í Archives, Wilmette, Illinois.

37. In an interview with Margaret Burns (26 April 1994), whose father-in-law was Leroy Burns, she told me that Burns would talk about the need for a Bahá'í Center using Biblical language, quoting the verse "Foxes have holes, and birds of the air have nests; but the Son of man has nowhere to lay his head" (Matthew 8:20). Making an analogy, he said the harassed Bahá'ís had nowhere to call their own. My thanks to Ann Haynes, member of the Atlanta Bahá'í Archives Committee, for her assistance in conducting this interview.

38. David Ruhe (interview, 14 December 1993) indicated that Leroy Burns initially began construction of the Center without consultation with the assembly, but records indicate (Annual Report of the Recording Secretary 1949–1950 of the Atlanta Bahá'í Community, National Bahá'í Archives, Wilmette, Illinois) that the project eventually was given unanimous approval by the Atlanta LSA.

39. Margaret Burns, interview 26 April 1994.

40. Estelle Lindsey, interview 14 May 1994.

41. Annual Report of the Recording Secretary of the Local Spiritual Assembly of the Bahá'ís of Atlanta, Georgia, 1949–1950. National Bahá'í Archives, Wilmette, Illinois.

42. The term "pupil of the eye" comes from Bahá'í scripture, from a passage that has particular significance for African American Bahá'ís. 'Abdu'l-Bahá wrote: "Bahá'u'lláh once compared the colored people [of the world] to the black pupil of the eye surrounded by the white. In this black pupil is seen the reflection of that which is before it, and through it the light of the spirit shineth forth" (quoted in Shoghi Effendi 1963, 31).

43. A letter from the NSA to the American Bahá'í community urged Bahá'ís to participate in the 1993 March on Washington to promote the oneness of humanity and racial unity. The NSA wrote: "The goals of the March, 'Jobs, Justice and Peace,' reflect the need for all people to recognize the essential oneness of humanity and to embody that reality in their daily lives. While the National Spiritual Assembly does not necessarily support each specific provision of the March, it does support its spirit in the promotion of Dr. King's vision for racial unity. Because of the opportunities the March provides for Bahá'ís to come into contact with members of many different organizations and faiths, all those who travel to Washington are being asked to report to the National Teaching Committee so that they may be counted toward the Three Year Plan goal for travel teaching" (*The American Bahá'í* 24, no. 12:1).

44. As survey results showed, Atlanta Bahá'í participation in these events is very high (nearly three-fourths of survey respondents report attending a Bahá'í-sponsored event during King Week), and is equally supported by all ethnic groups within the Bahá'í Faith in Atlanta.

45. Several other events during King Week 1993 highlight Bahá'í participation (mentioned in *The American Bahá'í* 24, no. 3: 1, 10): nine Bahá'ís joined more than forty priests, ministers, and rabbis for an Interfaith Clergy Conference at the King Center; a Bahá'í read part of the invocation at the Interfaith Service held at Bethel AME Church; a dozen Bahá'ís took part in the annual King Holiday Commission Recognition Award luncheon, including Dr. Carole Miller, who is a Bahá'í representative on the King Federal Holiday Commission; Bahá'ís contributed a float to the Parade of Celebration held two days before the march. Bahá'í country music star Dan Seals, as well as a number of local Atlanta singers, rode aboard the float and sang Bahá'í-themed songs; Bahá'ís sponsored a "Prayers Around the World" event to celebrate World Prayer and Multicultural Day; Bahá'ís Robert C. Henderson and David Hofman, former UHJ member, attended the 25th annual Ecumenical Service; and a

reception was held at the King Center at which David Hofman presented King's widow, Coretta Scott King, with a copy of *Gleanings from the Writings of Bahá'u'lláh*.

46. Again, Bahá'ís agree to disagree, and attempt to live up to "unity in diversity" when it comes to intellectual debate, as well as social relations. It is only when an institution of the Bahá'í Faith makes an authoritative decision that debate is no longer appropriate, Bahá'ís say (although sometimes, Bahá'ís admit, there is dissatisfaction with the decision). This recognition of authority is especially true of the UHJ, when it makes policy decisions or theological interpretations.

47. Yet these sentiments are not unanimously felt. One woman believed that the insularity of some of the older Persians was due to their unwillingness to cross social class lines, since some who fled Iran before the 1978–1979 revolution were able to bring their wealth with them. Most Bahá'ís, however, felt that it was language and/or cultural differences that introduced any perceived barriers between Iranian and American believers.

48. Factor analysis was done on survey items that clustered into three basic indicators or measures of Bahá'í global orientation: (1) contribution to nonlocal Bahá'í funds (Cronbach's alpha = .737; composite of contributions to national, international, and Arc funds); (2) staying informed about the national or international levels of the Administrative Order (Cronbach's alpha = .755; composite of importance given to *The American Bahá'í*, UHJ messages, Feast letters from the NSA, and "Bahá'í Newsreels"); and (3) importance given to the issue of the oneness of humanity and racial unity (Cronbach's alpha = .425; composite of variables such as participation in Martin Luther King Jr. holiday activity, and importance given to having friends of other races/ethnicities). Regression analysis was then performed with each of the above constructed measures as dependent variables.

Chapter 9 **Conclusion**

1. The Roman Catholic equivalent would be communication from the National Council of Catholic Bishops and the pope at weekly Mass; for some Protestant denominations, it would be equivalent to hearing every Sunday from both national denominational headquarters and the World Council of Churches.

2. Such as Roman Catholicism or Mormonism. A detailed comparison is beyond the scope of this research.

3. The Mottahedeh Development Services is a nonprofit agency developed by the NSA of the United States in 1992 "to facilitate social and economic development for the positive transformation of individuals, their families, and communities. To apply Universal Spiritual Principles as a guiding force for sustainable social change" (www.atlantabahai.com/mda/profile.htm).

4. See www.atlantabahai.com/mds.fui.htm.

5. The speaker's bureau offers free speakers to civic, corporate, or educational groups on issues such as race unity, the equality of men and women, human rights, education, social development, medical care, justice and the legal system, counseling and psychology, solutions to economic problems, and violence prevention, all from a Bahá'í perspective.

Bibliography

'Abdu'l-Bahá. 1957. *The Secret of Divine Civilization*. Translated by Marzieh Gail. Wilmette, Ill.: Bahá'í Publishing Trust.

———. 1978. *Selections From the Writings of 'Abdu'l-Bahá*. Haifa: Bahá'í World Center.

———. 1981. *Some Answered Questions*. Translated by Laura Clifford Barney. Wilmette, Ill.: Bahá'í Publishing Trust.

———. 1982. *The Promulgation of Universal Peace*. Compiled by Howard MacNutt. Wilmette, Ill.: Bahá'í Publishing Trust.

———. 1990. *Will and Testament of 'Abdu'l-Bahá*. Wilmette, Ill.: Bahá'í Publishing Trust.

———. 1993. *Tablets of the Divine Plan*. Wilmette, Ill.: Bahá'í Publishing Trust.

Abizadeh, Arash. 1989. "Liberal Democracy and the Bahá'í Administrative Order: An Analysis." *Journal of Bahá'í Studies* 2, no. 3:1–14.

Allen, Ivan Jr. 1971. *Mayor: Notes on the Sixties*. New York: Simon and Schuster.

Ammerman, Nancy. 1987. *Bible Believers*. New Brunswick, N.J.: Rutgers University Press.

———. 1990. *Baptist Battles*. New Brunswick, N.J.: Rutgers University Press.

Archer, Clive. 1992. *International Organizations*. 2d ed. New York: Routledge.

Archer, Mary Elizabeth. 1977. *Global Community: Case Study of the Houston Bahá'ís*. Master's thesis, University of Houston.

Austin, H. Elsie. 1998. "Faith, Protest and Progress." *Journal of Bahá'í Studies* 8, no. 2:3–12.

Babbie, Earl. 1989. *The Practice of Social Research*. 5th ed. Belmont, Calif.: Wadsworth.

Backman, Milton V. Jr. 1983. *Christian Churches of America: Origins and Beliefs*. New York: Charles Scribner's Sons.

"The Bahá'í Faith." 1985. *Update: A Quarterly Journal on New Religious Movements* 9, no. 3(September).

The Bahá'ís: A Profile of the Bahá'í Faith and its Worldwide Community. 1994. New York: Office of Public Information, Bahá'í International Community.

Bahá'u'lláh. 1976. *Gleanings from the Writings of Bahá'u'lláh*. Translated by Shoghi Effendi. Wilmette, Ill.: Bahá'í Publishing Trust.

———. 1985. *The Hidden Words of Bahá'u'lláh*. Translated by Shoghi Effendi. Wilmette, Ill.: Bahá'í Publishing Trust.

———. 1987. *Prayers and Meditations*. Translated by Shoghi Effendi. Wilmette, Ill.: Bahá'í Publishing Trust.

———. 1988a. *Epistle to the Son of the Wolf.* Translated by Shoghi Effendi. Wilmette,
    Ill.: Bahá'í Publishing Trust.
———. 1988b. *Tablets of Bahá'u'lláh.* Translated by Habib Taherzadeh. Wilmette, Ill.:
    Bahá'í Publishing Trust.
———. 1989. *Kitab-i-Iqan.* Translated by Shoghi Effendi. Wilmette, Ill.: Bahá'í Publish-
    ing Trust.
———. 1992. *The Kitab-i-Aqdas.* Translated by Universal House of Justice. Haifa, Israel:
    Bahá'í World Center.
Bainbridge, William Sims. 1997. *The Sociology of Religious Movements.* New York:
    Routledge.
Balch, Robert W., Gwen Farnsworth, and Sue Wilkins. 1983. "When the Bombs Drop:
    Reactions to Disconfirmed Prophecy in a Millennial Sect." *Sociological Perspectives*
    26, no. 2 (April):137–158.
Banuazizi, Ali, and Myron Weiner, eds. 1986. *The State, Religion, and Ethnic Politics: Af-
    ghanistan, Iran, and Pakistan.* Syracuse, N.Y.: Syracuse University Press.
Barnes, William. 1992. "Forging More Perfect Unions." *Journal of Bahá'í Studies* 5, no.
    1:1–12.
Barrett, David B., ed. 1982. *World Christian Encyclopedia: A Comparative Study of Churches
    and Religions in the Modern World, A.D. 1900–2000.* New York: Oxford University
    Press.
Bartholomew, G. A. 1989. "Harmony of Science and Religion: A Complementary Per-
    spective." *Journal of Bahá'í Studies* 1, no. 3:1–14.
Becker, Penny Edgell, and Nancy L. Eiesland. 1997. *Contemporary American Religion: An
    Ethnographic Reader.* Walnut Creek, Calif.: Altamira.
Berger, Peter L. 1954. *From Sect to Church: A Sociological Interpretation of the Bahá'í Move-
    ment.* Unpublished Ph.D. dissertation, New School for Social Research, New York.
———. 1969. *The Sacred Canopy: Elements of a Sociological Theory of Religion.* New York:
    Doubleday Anchor.
Berger, Peter L., and Thomas Luckmann. 1966. *The Social Construction of Reality: A Trea-
    tise in the Sociology of Knowledge.* New York: Doubleday.
Bergesen, Albert, ed. 1980. *Studies of the Modern World-System.* New York: Academic Press.
Beyer, Peter. 1994. *Religion and Globalization.* Thousand Oaks, Calif.: Sage Publications.
Bhabha, Jacqueline. 1998. "Get Back to Where You Once Belonged: Identity, Citizen-
    ship, and Exclusion in Europe." *Human Rights Quarterly* 20, no. 3 (August):592–627.
Bibby, Reginald W. 1978. "Why Conservative Churches Really Are Growing: Kelley Re-
    visited." *Journal for the Scientific Study of Religion* (June):129–138.
Bibby, Reginald W., and Merlin B. Brinkerhoff. 1973. "The Circulation of Saints: A Study
    of People Who Join Conservative Churches." *Journal for the Scientific Study of Reli-
    gion* (September):273–283.
Bradley, Martin B., Norman M. Green Jr., Dale E. Jones, Mac Lynn, and Lou McNeil.
    1992. *Churches and Church Membership in the United States 1990.* Atlanta: Glenmary
    Research Center.
Britannica Book of the Year. 1992. Chicago: Encyclopaedia Britannica.
Buck, Christopher. 1991. "Bahá'u'lláh as World Reformer." *Journal of Bahá'í Studies* 3,
    no. 4:23–70.
———. 1996. Review of *Rituals in Bábism and Bahá'ism,* Pembroke Persian Papers, vol.
    2. *International Journal of Middle East Studies* 28, no. 3:418–422.
Butler, David, Howard R. Penniman, and Austin Ranney. 1981. *Democracy at the Polls:
    A Comparative Study of Competitive National Elections.* Washington, D.C.: American
    Enterprise Institute for Public Policy.
Cain, Bruce E., John Ferejohn, and Morris Fiorina. 1986. *The Personal Vote: Constitu-
    ency Service and Electoral Independence.* Cambridge: Harvard University Press.
Calkins, Peter, and Benoit Girard. 1998. "The Bahá'í Village Granary: Spiritual Under-

pinnings and Applications to North America." *Journal of Bahá'í Studies* 8, no. 3:1–17.

Cantrell, Randolph L., James F. Krile, and George A. Donohue. 1983. "Parish Autonomy: Measuring Denominational Differences." *Journal for the Scientific Study of Religion* 22, no. 3:276–287.

Caton, Peggy, ed. 1987. *Equal Circles: Women and Men in the Bahá'í Community.* Los Angeles: Kalimat Press.

Chew, Phyllis Ghim Lian. 1991. "The Great Tao." *Journal of Bahá'í Studies* 4, no. 2:11–39.

Cole, Juan R. I. 1993. "'I Am All the Prophets': The Poetics of Pluralism in Bahá'í Texts." *Poetics Today* 14, no. 3:447–476.

———. 1998. "The Bahá'í Faith in America as Panopticon." *Journal for the Scientific Study of Religion* 37, no. 2 (June):234–248.

———. 1983. "Rashid Rida on the Bahá'í Faith: A Utilitarian Theory of the Spread of Religion." *Arab Studies Quarterly* 5, no. 3:276–291.

Cooper, Roger. 1982. *The Bahá'ís of Iran.* London: The Minority Rights Group.

Cooper, William J. Jr., and Thomas E. Terrill. 1991. *The American South: A History.* New York: Alfred A. Knopf.

Coser, Lewis A. 1956. *The Functions of Social Conflict.* New York: Free Press.

Curtis, James E., Edward G. Grabb, and Douglas E. Baer. 1992. "Voluntary Association Membership in 15 Countries: A Comparative Analysis." *American Sociological Review* 57 (April):139–152.

Dahl, Gregory C. 1984. "A Bahá'í Perspective on Economic and Social Development." In *Circle of Unity: Bahá'í Approaches to Current Social Issues,* ed. Anthony A. Lee. Los Angeles: Kalimat Press.

———. 1991. "Evolving Toward a Bahá'í Economic System." *Journal of Bahá'í Studies* 4, no. 3:1–16.

Dahl, Roger M. 1993. "Three Teaching Methods Used During North America's First Seven Year Plan." *Journal of Bahá'í Studies* 5, no. 3:1–15.

D'Antonio, William, James Davidson, Dean Hoge, and Ruth Wallace. 1989. *American Catholic Laity in a Changing Church.* Kansas City, Mo.: Sheed and Ward.

Davidman, Lynn. 1990. "Women's Search for Family and Roots: A Jewish Religious Solution to a Modern Dilemma." In *In Gods We Trust: New Patterns of Religious Pluralism in America,* ed. Thomas Robbins and Dick Anthony. New Brunswick, N.J.: Transaction Publishers.

Dawson, Lorne L. 1998. *Comprehending Cults: The Sociology of New Religious Movements.* Toronto: Oxford University Press.

Dawson, Paul A. 1987. *American Government: Institutions, Policies, and Politics.* Glenview, Ill.: Scott, Foresman and Company.

Dowty, Alan. 1989. "The Satanic Vendetta: Iran's Unholy War on the Bahá'ís." *Church and State* 42 (April):7B10.

Drewek, Paula A. 1992. "Feminine Forms of the Divine in Bahá'í Scripture." *Journal of Bahá'í Studies* 5, no. 1:13–23.

Durkheim, Emile. 1965. *The Elementary Forms of the Religious Life.* New York: Free Press.

———. 1973. *On Morality and Society: Selected Writings.* Edited by Robert N. Bellah. Chicago: University of Chicago Press.

———. 1984. *The Division of Labor in Society.* New York: The Free Press.

Ebaugh, Helen Rose Fuchs. 1993. *Women in the Vanishing Cloister: Organizational Decline in Catholic Religious Orders in the United States.* New Brunswick, N.J.: Rutgers University Press.

Ebaugh, Helen Rose Fuchs, Kathy Richman, and Janet Saltzman Chafetz. 1984. "Life Crises among the Religiously Committed: Do Sectarian Differences Matter?" *Journal for the Scientific Study of Religion* 23, no. 1:19–31.

Ebaugh, Helen Rose Fuchs, and Sharron Lee Vaughn. 1984. "Ideology and Recruitment in Religious Groups." *Review of Religious Research* 26, no. 2 (December):148–157.

The Economist. 1997. "Workers of the World." November 1.

Edge, Clara. 1964. *Táhiríh.* Grand Rapids, Mich.: Edgeway.

Effendi, Shoghi. 1938. *The World Order of Bahá'u'lláh.* Wilmette, Ill.: Bahá'í Publishing Trust.

———. 1963. *The Advent of Divine Justice.* Wilmette, Ill.: Bahá'í Publishing Trust.

———. 1965. *Citadel of Faith: Messages to America, 1947–1957.* Wilmette, Ill.: Bahá'í Publishing Trust.

———. 1974. *Bahá'í Administration: Selected Messages 1922–1932.* Wilmette, Ill.: Bahá'í Publishing Trust.

———. 1980. *The Promised Day Is Come.* Wilmette, Ill.: Bahá'í Publishing Trust.

———. 1995. *God Passes By.* Wilmette, Ill.: Bahá'í Publishing Committee.

———, trans. 1932. *The Dawn Breakers: Nabil's Narrative of the Early Days of the Bahá'í Revelation.* New York: Bahá'í Publishing Committee.

Esslemont, J. E. 1970. *Bahá'u'lláh and the New Era.* Wilmette, Ill.: Bahá'í Publishing Trust.

Etzioni, Amitai. 1961. *A Comparative Analysis of Complex Organizations: On Power, Involvement, and Their Correlates.* New York: The Free Press.

Fananapazir, Khazeh. 1997. "The Day of God (Yawmu'lláh) and the Days of God (Ayyámu'lláh)." In *Scripture and Revelation,* ed. Moojan Momen. Oxford: George Ronald.

Fazel, Seena. 1994. "Is the Bahá'í Faith a World Religion?" *Journal of Bahá'í Studies* 6, no. 1:1–16.

———. 1997. "Understanding Exclusivist Texts." In *Scripture and Revelation,* ed. Moojan Momen. Oxford: George Ronald.

Fazel, Seena, and Khazeh Fananapazir. 1993. "A Bahá'í Approach to the Claim of Finality in Islam." *Journal of Bahá'í Studies* 5, no. 3:17–40.

———. 1997. "A Bahá'í Approach to the Claim of Exclusivity and Uniqueness in Christianity." In *Scripture and Revelation,* ed. Moojan Momen. Oxford: George Ronald.

Featherstone, Mike. 1991. "Consumer Culture, Postmodernism, and Global Disorder." In *Religion and Global Order,* ed. Roland Robertson and William R. Garrett. New York: Paragon House Publishers.

Fenno, Richard F. 1978. *Home Style: House Members in their Districts.* Boston: Little, Brown.

Festinger, Leon. 1957. *A Theory of Cognitive Dissonance.* Stanford, Calif.: Stanford University Press.

Finke, Olga. n.d. *Atlanta Bahá'í History 1909–1944.* Unpublished manuscript, Atlanta Bahá'í Archives.

Finke, Roger, and Rodney Stark. 1992. *The Churching of America, 1776–1990: Winners and Losers in Our Religious Economy.* New Brunswick, N.J.: Rutgers University Press.

Fish, Mary. 1997. "Economic Prosperity: A Global Imperative." *Journal of Bahá'í Studies* 7, no. 3:1–16.

Fowler, Floyd J. Jr. 1988. *Research Methods.* Newbury Park, Calif.: Sage Publications.

Fukuyama, Francis. 1992. *The End of History and the Last Man.* New York: Free Press

Fukuyama, Yoshio. 1961. "The Major Dimensions of Church Membership." *Review of Religious Research* 2:154–161.

Garlington, W. 1977. "The Bahá'í Faith in Malwa." In *Religion in South Asia,* ed. G. A. Oddie. London: Curzon Press.

Garrett, William R. 1991. "The Reformation, Individualism, and the Quest for Global Order." In *Religion and Global Order,* ed. Roland Robertson and William R. Garrett. New York: Paragon House Publishers.

Geertz, Clifford. 1973. *The Interpretation of Cultures: Selected Essays.* New York: Basic Books.

Giddens, Anthony. 1991. *Modernity and Self-Identity: Self and Society in the Late Modern Age*. Palo Alto, Calif.: Stanford University Press.

Gilstrap, Dorothy Freeman. 1990. "From Copper to Gold: Finding Form." *Journal of Bahá'í Studies* 3, no. 2:25–33.

Glen, Norval D. 1984. "A Note on Estimating the Strength of Influences for Religious Endogamy." *Journal of Marriage and Family* 46:725–727.

Goffman, Erving. 1986. *Stigma: Notes on the Management of Spoiled Identity*. New York: Simon and Schuster.

Gonzales, Steven. 1995. "Affirmative Action and the Jurisprudence of Equitable Inclusion: Towards a New Consensus on Gender and Race Relations." *Journal of Bahá'í Studies* 7, no. 2:29–46.

Goode, Erich. 1966. "Social Class and Church Participation." *American Journal of Sociology* 72:102–111.

Greathouse, Elizabeth. 1998. "Justices See Joint Issues with the European Union." *Washington Post*, 9 July, A24.

Hadaway, C. Kirk, Penny Long Marler, and Mark Chaves. 1993. "What the Polls Don't Show: A Closer Look at U.S. Church Attendance." *American Sociological Review* 58, no. 6 (December):741–752.

Hall, Stuart. 1991a. "The Local and the Global: Globalization and Ethnicity." In *Culture, Globalization and the World System: Contemporary Conditions for the Representation of Identity*, ed. Anthony D. King. Binghamton, N.Y.: SUNY Press.

———. 1991b. "Old and New Identities, Old and New Ethnicities." In *Culture, Globalization and the World System: Contemporary Conditions for the Representation of Identity*, ed. Anthony D. King. Binghamton, N.Y.: SUNY Press.

Hammond, Phillip. 1985. *The Sacred in a Secular Age*. Berkeley: University of California Press.

Hammond, Phillip E., Luis Salinas, and Douglas Stone. 1978. "Types of Clergy Authority: Their Measurement, Location, and Effects." *Journal for the Scientific Study of Religion* 17, no. 3:241–253.

Hands of the Cause of God Residing in the Holy Land. 1992. *The Ministry of the Custodians, 1957–1963*. Haifa: Bahá'í World Center.

Hannerz, Ulf. 1991. "Scenarios for Peripheral Cultures." In *Culture, Globalization and the World System: Contemporary Conditions for the Representation of Identity*, ed. Anthony D. King. Binghamton, N.Y.: SUNY Press.

Hassall, Graham. 1991. "'Outpost of a World Religion': The Bahá'í Faith in Australia 1920–1947." *The Journal of Religious History* 16, no. 3 (June):315–338.

———. 1995. "Bahá'í History in the Formative Age: The World Crusade 1953–1963." *Journal of Bahá'í Studies* 6, no. 4:1–22.

Hatcher, John S. 1989. "The Equality of Women: The Bahá'í Principle of Complementarity." *Journal of Bahá'í Studies* 2, no. 3:55–66.

———. 1990. "Racial Identity and the Patterns of Consolation in the Poetry of Robert Hayden." *Journal of Bahá'í Studies* 3, no. 2:35–46.

Hatcher, William S. 1979. "Science and the Bahá'í Faith." *Zygon* 14, no. 3 (September):229–253.

Hatcher, William S., and David Martin. 1985. *The Bahá'í World Faith: An Emerging World Religion*. Wilmette, Ill.: Bahá'í Publishing Trust.

Hayes, Terrill G., Richard A. Hill, Anne Marie Scheffer, Anne G. Atkinson, and Betty J. Fischer, compilers. 1986. *Peace: More Than an End to War: Selections from the Writings of Bahá'u'lláh, the Báb, 'Abdu'l-Bahá, Shoghi Effendi, and the Universal House of Justice*. Wilmette, Ill.: Bahá'í Publishing Trust.

Heilman, Samuel C. 1976. *Synagogue Life: A Study in Symbolic Interaction*. Chicago: University of Chicago Press.

Heller, Wendy M., and Hoda Mahmoudi. 1992. "Altruism and Extensivity in the Bahá'í Religion." *Journal of Bahá'í Studies* 4, no. 4:17–34.

Hirschman, Albert O. 1970. *Exit, Voice and Loyalty: Responses to Decline in Firms, Organizations, and States.* Cambridge: Harvard University Press.

Hofman, David. 1982. *A Commentary on the Will and Testament of 'Abdu'l-Bahá.* Oxford: George Ronald.

Hoge, Dean R., and Jackson Carroll. 1978. "Determinants of Commitment and Participation in Suburban Protestant Churches." *Journal for the Scientific Study of Religion* 17, no. 2:107–127.

Hoge, Dean R., and David A. Roozen. 1979. *Understanding Church Growth and Decline, 1950–1978.* New York: Pilgrim Press.

Hornby, Helen, compiler. 1983. *Lights of Guidance: A Bahá'í Reference Guide.* New Delhi: Bahá'í Publishing Trust.

Hostetler, John A. 1993. *Amish Society.* 4th ed. Baltimore: Johns Hopkins University Press.

Hougland, James G. Jr., and James R. Wood. 1979. "Determinants of Organizational Control in Local Churches." *Journal for the Scientific Study of Religion* 18, no. 2:132–145.

Hunter, James Davidson. 1983. *American Evangelicalism.* New Brunswick, N.J.: Rutgers University Press.

———. 1987. *Evangelicalism: The Coming Generation.* Chicago: University of Chicago Press.

Huntington, Samuel P. 1993. "If Not Civilizations, What?" *Foreign Affairs* (November/December):186–194.

Iannaccone, Laurence R. 1990. "Religious Practice: A Human Capital Approach." *Journal for the Scientific Study of Religion* 29:297–314.

———. 1992. "Sacrifice and Stigma: Reducing Free Riding in Cults, Communes, and Other Collectives." *Journal of Political Economy* (April).

———. 1994. "Why Strict Churches Are Strong." *American Journal of Sociology* 99:1180–1211.

Jacobson, Gary C. 1992. *The Politics of Congressional Elections.* New York: HarperCollins.

Johnstone, Ronald L. 1992. *Religion in Society: A Sociology of Religion.* 4th ed. Englewood Cliffs, N.J.: Prentice Hall.

Kanter, Rosabeth Moss. 1972. *Commitment and Community.* Cambridge: Harvard University Press.

Kelley, Dean M. 1972. *Why Conservative Churches Are Growing.* New York: Harper and Row.

Khan, Janet A., and Peter J. Khan. 1998. *Advancement of Women: A Bahá'í Perspective.* Wilmette, Ill.: Bahá'í Publishing Trust.

King, Anthony D., ed. 1991. *Culture, Globalization and the World System: Contemporary Conditions for the Representation of Identity.* Binghamton, N.Y.: SUNY Press.

King, Francis. 1971. *The Rites of Modern Occult Magic.* New York: Macmillan.

King, Martin Luther Sr., and Clayton Riley. 1980. *Daddy King: An Autobiography.* New York: Morrow.

Kraybill, Donald B. 1989. *The Riddle of Amish Culture.* Baltimore: Johns Hopkins University Press.

Kraybill, Donald B., and Marc A. Olshan. 1994. *The Amish Struggle with Modernity.* Hanover, N.H.: University Press of New England.

Kurtz, Lester. 1995. *Gods in the Global Village: The World's Religions in Sociological Perspective.* Thousand Oaks, Calif.: Pine Forge Press.

Lalonde, Roxanne. 1994. "Unity in Diversity: A Conceptual Framework for a Global Ethic of Environmental Sustainability." *Journal of Bahá'í Studies* 6, no. 3:39–73.

Lambden, Stephen. 1997. "Prophesy in the Johannine Farewell Discourse: The Advents of the Paraclete, Ahmad and the Comforter (Mu'azzí)." In *Scripture and Revelation,* ed. Moojan Momen. Oxford: George Ronald.

Laszlo, Ervin. 1989. "Humankind's Path to Peace in Global Society." *Journal of Bahá'í Studies* 2, no. 2:19–30.

Latham, David A. 1998. "Globalization is Not New, Just Expanding." *New York Law Journal*, 30 November, 11.

Latourette, Kenneth Scott. 1953. *A History of Christianity*. New York: Harper and Brothers.

Lazerwitz, Bernard. 1961. "Some Factors Associated with Variations in Church Attendance." *Social Forces* 39:301–309.

Lechner, Frank J. 1985. "Modernity and Its Discontents." In *Neofunctionalism*, ed. Jeffrey C. Alexander and Jonathan Turner. Beverly Hills, Calif.: Sage Publications.

———. 1990. "Fundamentalism Revisited." In *In Gods We Trust*, ed. Thomas Robbins and Dick Anthony. New Brunswick, N.J.: Transaction Books.

———. 1991. "Religion, Law, and Global Order." In *Religion and Global Order*, ed. Roland Robertson and William R. Garrett. New York: Paragon House Publishers.

Lee, Anthony A., ed. 1984. *Circle of Unity: Bahá'í Approaches to Current Social Issues*. Los Angeles: Kalimat Press.

Lee, Kathy. 1989. *Prelude to the Lesser Peace*. New Delhi: Bahá'í Publishing Trust.

Lerche, Charles O. 1994. "Us and Them: Alienation and World Order." *Journal of Bahá'í Studies* 5, no. 4:17–31.

The Liberal Catholic Church: Statement of Principles, Summary of Doctrine, and Table of Apostolic Succession. 1927. Los Angeles: St. Alban Press.

Lincoln, C. Eric, and Lawrence H. Mamiya. 1990. *The Black Church in the African American Experience*. Durham, N.C.: Duke University Press.

Loeffler, Reinhold. 1988. *Islam in Practice: Religious Beliefs in a Persian Village*. Albany, N.Y.: SUNY Press.

Lofland, John, and Lyn H. Lofland. 1984. *Analyzing Social Settings: A Guide to Qualitative Observation and Analysis*. Davis, Calif.: University of California Press.

Lofland, John, and Norman Skonovd. 1981. "Conversion Motifs." *Journal for the Scientific Study of Religion* 20, no. 4:373–385.

Lofland, John, and Rodney Stark. 1965. "Becoming a World-Saver: A Theory of Conversion to a Deviant Perspective." *American Sociological Review* 30:862–875.

Lopez-Claros, Augusto. 1996. "Implications of European Economic Integration." *World Order* 27, no. 2 (winter):35–48.

Ma'ani, Baharieh Bouhani. 1997. "The Effect of Philosophical and Linguistic Gender Biases on the Degradation of Women's Status in Religion." *Journal of Bahá'í Studies* 8, no. 1:45–68.

MacEoin, Denis. 1986. "Bahá'í Fundamentalism and the Academic Study of the Bábi Movement." *Religion* 16:57–84.

Mahmoudi, Hoda. 1989. "From Oppression to Equality: The Emergence of the Feminist Perspective." *Journal of Bahá'í Studies* 1, no. 3:25–37.

———. 1995. "The Role of Men in Establishing the Equality of Women." *World Order* 26, no. 3:27B41.

Mahmoudi, Hoda, and Richard Dabell. 1992. "Rights and Responsibilities in the Bahá'í Family System." *Journal of Bahá'í Studies* 5, no. 2:1–12.

Maneck, Susan Stiles. 1989. "Táhirih: A Religious Paradigm of Womanhood." *Journal of Bahá'í Studies* 2, no. 2:39–54.

Marsden, George M. 1980. *Fundamentalism and American Culture: The Shaping of 20th Century Evangelicalism 1870–1925*. New York: Oxford University Press.

Martin, J. Douglas. 1979. "The Bahá'í Faith and its Relation to Other Religions." In *Comparative Religion*, ed. Amarjit Singh Sethi and Reinhard Pummer. New Delhi: Vikas Publishing House.

Marty, Martin E. 1959. *A Short History of Christianity*. New York: Meridian Books.

Marty, Martin E., and R. Scott Appleby. 1991. *Fundamentalisms Observed*, vol. 1. Chicago: University of Chicago Press.

————. 1992. *The Glory and the Power: The Fundamentalist Challenge to the Modern World.* Boston: Beacon Press.

McCutcheon, Alan L. 1988. "Denominations and Religious Intermarriage: Trends Among White Americans in the 20th Century." *Review of Religious Research* 29, no. 3:213–227.

McGuire, Meredith. 1997. *Religion: The Social Context.* Belmont, Calif.: Wadsworth.

McLean, J. A. 1992. "Prolegomena to a Bahá'í Theology." *Journal of Bahá'í Studies* 5, no. 1:25–67.

McMullen, Mike. 1995. "The Atlanta Bahá'í Community and Race Unity: 1909–1950." *World Order* 26, no. 4 (summer):27–43.

McPherson, James Alan. 1972. "A Solo Song: For Doc." In *New Black Voices: An Anthology of Contemporary Afro-American Literature,* ed. Abraham Chapman. New York: New American Library.

Meyer, John W. 1980. "The World Polity and the Authority of the Nation-State." In *Studies of the Modern World-System,* ed. Albert Bergesen. New York: Academic Press.

Meyer, John W., John Boli, George M. Thomas, and Francisco O. Ramirez. 1997. "World Society and the Nation-State." *American Journal of Sociology* 103, no. 1 (July):144–181.

Meyer, John W., and Brian Rowan. 1977. "Institutionalized Organizations: Formal Structure as Myth and Ceremony." *American Journal of Sociology* 83:55–77.

Miller, Bradford W. 1998. "Seneca Falls First Women's Rights Convention of 1848: The Sacred Rites of the Nation." *Journal of Bahá'í Studies* 8, no. 3:39–52.

Miner, John B. 1988. *Organizational Behavior: Performance and Productivity.* New York: Random House.

Moberg, David O. 1962. *The Church as a Social Institution: The Sociology of American Religion.* New York: Prentice-Hall.

Momen, Moojan. 1985. *An Introduction to Shi'i Islam: The History and Doctrines of Twelver Shi'ism.* New Haven, Conn.: Yale University Press.

————. 1988. "Relativism: A Basis for Bahá'í Metaphysics." In *Studies in Bábi and Bahá'í History,* vol. 5, ed. Moojan Momen. Los Angeles: Kalimat Press.

Morrison, Gayle. 1982. *To Move the World: Louis G. Gregory and the Advancement of Racial Unity.* Wilmette, Ill.: Bahá'í Publishing Trust.

Mottahedeh, Roy. 1985. *The Mantle of the Prophet: Religion and Politics in Iran.* New York: Pantheon Books.

Munje, H. M. 1970. "A Bahá'í Viewpoint." In *The World Religions Speak on The Relevance of Religion in the Modern World,* ed. Finley P. Dunne Jr.. The Hague: W. Junk N. V. Publishers.

National Spiritual Assembly of the Bahá'ís of Canada. 1983. *Bahá'í Marriage and Family Life: Selections from the Writings of the Bahá'í Faith.* Thornhill, Ontario: Bahá'í Canada Publications.

————. 1986a. *Women: Extracts from the Writings of Bahá'u'lláh, 'Abdu'l-Bahá, Shoghi Effendi, and the Universal House of Justice.* Thornhill, Ontario: Bahá'í Canada Publications.

————. 1986b. *Ḥuqúqu'lláh: Extracts from the Writings of Bahá'u'lláh, 'Abdu'l-Bahá, Shoghi Effendi, and the Universal House of Justice.* Thornhill, Ontario: Bahá'í Canada Publications.

National Spiritual Assembly of the Bahá'ís of the United States. 1975. *Declaration of Trust and By-Laws of the NSA of the United States; By-Laws of a Local Spiritual Assembly.* Wilmette, Ill.: Bahá'í Publishing Trust.

————. 1985. *Bahá'í Prayers.* Wilmette, Ill.: Bahá'í Publishing Trust.

————. 1991. *The Vision of Race Unity: America's Most Challenging Issue.* Wilmette, Ill.: Bahá'í Publishing Trust.

Nash, Geoffrey. 1982. *Iran's Secret Pogrom: The Conspiracy to Wipe Out the Bahá'ís.* Suffolk: Neville Spearman.

Neitz, Mary Jo. 1987. *Charisma and Community*. New Brunswick, N.J.: Transaction Books.

Newport, Frank. 1979. "The Religious Switcher in the United States." *American Sociological Review* (August):528–552.

Niebuhr, H. Richard. 1957. *The Social Sources of Denominationalism*. New York: Meridian Books.

Parrinder, Geoffrey, ed. 1971. *World Religions: From Ancient History to the Present*. New York: Facts on File Publications.

Perrin, Robin D., and Armand L. Mauss. 1991. "Saints and Seekers: Sources of Recruitment to the Vineyard Christian Fellowship." *Review of Religious Research* (December): 97–111.

Perry, Mark Lloyd. 1986. *The Chicago Bahá'í Community, 1921–1939*. Ph.D. thesis, University of Chicago.

Petterson, Arild J. 1989. "The Bahá'í Faith and Universal Language." In *Language in Religion*, ed. Humphrey Tonkin and Allison Armstrong Keef. Lanham, Md.: University Press of America.

Piff, David, and Margit Warburg. 1998. "Enemies of the Faith: Rumours and Anecdotes as Self-Definition and Social Control in the Bahá'í Religion." In *New Religions and New Religiosity*, ed. Eileen Barker and Margit Warburg. Aarhus: Aarhus University Press.

Pokorny, Brad. 1996. "Population and Development." *World Order* 27, no. 3 (spring):7–18.

Poloma, Margaret M. 1989. *The Assemblies of God at the Crossroads: Charisma and Institutional Dilemmas*. Knoxville: University of Tennessee Press.

Popkin, Samuel L. 1991. *The Reasoning Voter: Communication and Persuasion in Presidential Campaigns*. Chicago: University of Chicago Press.

Powell, Walter W., and Paul J. DiMaggio, eds. 1991. *The New Institutionalism in Organizational Analysis*. Chicago: University of Chicago Press.

Putnam, Robert D. 1995. "Bowling Alone: America's Declining Social Capital." *Journal of Democracy* 6, no. 1 (January):65–78.

Ramer, Linda. 1976. "Education Based on the Religious Definition of Man." In *The Religious Dimension*, ed. John. C. Hinchcliff. Auckland: University of Auckland Press.

Ray, Marilyn J. 1995. "Women and Men: Toward Achieving Complementarity." *World Order* 27, no. 1:9–18.

Richardson, James T., ed. 1978. *Conversion Careers: In and Out of the New Religions*. Beverly Hills, Calif.: Sage Publications.

Rippin, Andrew. 1990. *Muslims: Their Religious Beliefs and Practices, Volume 1: The Formative Period*. New York: Routledge.

Robbins, Thomas, and Dick Anthony. 1991. *In Gods We Trust: New Patterns of Religious Pluralism in America*. New Brunswick, N.J.: Transaction Books.

Robbins, Thomas, and Roland Robertson. 1987. *Church-State Relations: Tensions and Transitions*. New Brunswick, N.J.: Transaction Books.

Roberts, Keith A. 1995. *Religion in Sociological Perspective*. 3d ed. Belmont, Calif.: Wadsworth.

Robertson, Roland. 1987. "Globalization and Societal Modernization: A Note on Japan and Japanese Religion." *Sociological Analysis* 47:35–42.

———. 1991. "Social Theory, Cultural Relativity and the Problem of Globality." In *Culture, Globalization and the World System: Contemporary Conditions for the Representation of Identity*, ed. Anthony D. King. Binghamton, N.Y.: SUNY Press.

———. 1992. *Globalization: Social Theory and Global Culture*. London: Sage.

Robertson, Roland, and J. Chirico. 1985. "Humanity, Globalization and Worldwide Religious Resurgence: A Theoretical Exploration," *Sociological Analysis* 46, no. 3:219–242.

Robertson, Roland, and William R. Garrett, eds. 1991. *Religion and Global Order*. New York: Paragon House Publishers.

Robertson, Roland, and Frank J. Lechner. 1985. "Modernization, Globalization, and the Problem of Culture in World-Systems Theory." *Theory Culture and Society* 2, no. 3:103–117.

Robiati, Guiseppe. 1991. *Faith and World Economy: A Joint Venture, Bahá'í Perspective.* Milan: Gruppo Editoriale Insieme.

Roof, Wade Clark. 1976. "Traditional Religion in Contemporary Society: A Theory of Local-Cosmopolitan Plausibility." *American Sociological Review* 41:195–208.

———. 1993. *A Generation of Seekers: The Spiritual Journeys of the Baby Boom Generation.* New York: HarperCollins.

———, ed. 1991. *World Order and Religion.* Albany, N.Y.: SUNY Press.

Roof, Wade Clark, and William McKinney. 1987. *American Mainline Religion: Its Changing Shape and Future.* New Brunswick, N.J.: Rutgers University Press, 1987.

Root, Martha. 1981. *Táhirih the Pure.* Los Angeles: Kalimát Press.

Rosenfeld, Robert B., and Michael H. Winger-Bearskin. 1990. "Principles of Consultation Applied to the Process of Innovation in a Corporate Environment." *Journal of Bahá'í Studies* 3, no. 1:31–48.

Roth, Guenther, and Wolfgang Schluchter. 1979. *Max Weber's Vision of History: Ethics and Methods.* Berkeley: University of California Press.

Ruff, Ivan. 1974. "Bahá'í—The Invisible Community." *New Society* (September):665–668.

Rutstein, Nathan. 1993. *Healing Racism in America: A Prescription for the Disease.* Springfield, Mass.: Whitcomb Publishing.

Sancton, Thomas. 1998. "France Today." *Time*, 15 June, 86.

Sahliyeh, Emile, ed. 1990. *Religious Resurgence and Politics in the Contemporary World.* Albany, N.Y.: SUNY Press.

Schluchter, Wolfgang. 1989. *Rationalism, Religion, and Domination: A Weberian Perspective.* Translated by Neil Soloman. Berkeley: University of California Press.

Schoonmaker, Ann. 1984. "Revisioning the Women's Movement." In *Circle of Unity: Bahá'í Approaches to Current Social Issues*, ed. Anthony A. Lee. Los Angeles: Kalimat Press.

Schweitz, Martha L. 1994. "The Kitáb-i-Aqdas: Bahá'í Law, Legitimacy, and World Order." *Journal of Bahá'í Studies* 6, no. 1:35–59.

———. 1995. "Of Webs and Ladders: Gender Equality in Bahá'í Law." *World Order* 27, no. 1 (fall):21–39.

Simmel, Georg. 1955. *Conflict and the Web of Group Affiliations.* New York: The Free Press.

———. 1971. *Georg Simmel: On Individuality and Social Forms.* Edited by Donald N. Levine. Chicago: University of Chicago Press.

Simpson, John H. 1991. "Globalization and Religion: Themes and Prospects." In *Religion and Global Order*, ed. Roland Robertson and William R. Garrett. New York: Paragon House Publishers.

Smith, Huston. 1991. *The World's Religions.* New York: HarperCollins.

Smith, Peter. 1978. "Motif Research: Peter Berger and the Bahá'í Faith." *Religion* 8:210–234.

———. 1982. "Millennialism in the Bábi and Bahá'í Religions." In *Millennialism and Charisma*, ed. Roy Wallis. Belfast: The Queen's University Press.

———. 1987. *The Bábi and Bahá'í Religions: From Messianic Shi'ism to a World Religion.* Cambridge: Cambridge University Press.

Smith, Peter, and Moojan Momen. 1989. "The Bahá'í Faith 1957–1988: A Survey of Contemporary Developments." *Religion.* 19:63–91.

Snow, David A., and Cynthia L. Phillips. 1980. "The Lofland-Stark Conversion Model: A Critical Reassessment." *Social Problems* 27, no. 4:430–447.

Sours, Michael. 1990. *Preparing for a Bahá'í/Christian Dialog, Volume I: Understanding Biblical Evidence.* Oxford, U.K.: Oneworld Publications.

Spradley, James P. 1980. *Participant Observation*. New York: Holt, Rinehart and Winston.

Stark, Rodney. 1989. *Sociology*. 3d ed. Belmont, Calif.: Wadsworth.

Stark, Rodney, and William Sims Bainbridge. 1980. "Networks of Faith: Interpersonal Bonds and Recruitment to Cults and Sects." *American Journal of Sociology* 85, no. 6:1376–1395.

———. 1985. *The Future of Religion: Secularization, Revival, and Cult Formation*. Berkeley: University of California Press.

Stark, Rodney, William Sims Bainbridge, and Lori Kent. 1981. "Cult Membership in the Roaring Twenties: Assessing Local Receptivity." *Sociological Analysis* 42, no. 2:137–162.

Stockman, Robert H. 1985. *The Bahá'í Faith in America, Vol. 1: Origins 1892–1900*. Wilmette, Ill.: Bahá'í Publishing Trust.

———. 1995. *The Bahá'í Faith in America, Vol. 2: Early Expansion, 1900–1912*. Wilmette, Ill.: Bahá'í Publishing Trust.

———. 1996. "Millennialism in the Bahá'í Faith: Progressive and Catastrophic Themes." Paper presented at the annual meeting of the American Academy of Religion in New Orleans, November 25.

Stoddart, Susan Clay. 1988. "Education and Moral Development in Children." *Journal of Bahá'í Studies* 1, no. 1:59–75.

Taherzadeh, Adib. 1974. *The Revelation of Bahá'u'lláh*. 4 vols. Oxford: George Ronald.

———. 1992. *The Covenant of Bahá'u'lláh*. Oxford: George Ronald.

Takayama, K. Peter, and Diane G. Sachs. 1976. "Polity and Decision Premises: The Church and the Private School." *Journal for the Scientific Study of Religion* 15, no. 3:269–278.

Taylor, Bonnie J., compiler. 1995. *The Pupil of the Eye: African Americans in the World Order of Bahá'u'lláh*. Riviera Beach, Fla.: Palabra Publications.

Thomas, George, John Meyer, F. Ramirez, and John Boli. eds. 1987. *Institutional Structure: Constituting State, Society and the Individual*. Newbury Park, Calif.: Sage Publications.

Thomas, June Manning. 1984. "Poverty and Wealth in America: A Bahá'í Perspective." In *Circle of Unity: Bahá'í Approaches to Current Social Issues*, ed. Anthony A. Lee. Los Angeles: Kalimat Press.

———. 1995. "Race Unity: Implications for the Metropolis." *Journal of Bahá'í Studies* 6, no. 4:23–42.

Thomas, Richard W. 1993. *Racial Unity: An Imperative for Social Progress*. Ottawa: Bahá'í Studies Publications.

Tindall, George Brown. 1967. *The Emergence of the New South 1913–1945*. Baton Rouge: Louisiana State University Press.

Tocqueville, Alexis de. 1863. *Democracy in America, Vol. 2*. 3d ed. Cambridge: Sever and Francis.

Turner, Bryan S. 1991. "Politics and Culture in Islamic Globalism." In *Religion and Global Order*, ed. Roland Robertson and William R. Garrett. New York: Paragon House Publishers.

———, ed. 1990. *Theories of Modernity and Postmodernity*. London: Sage.

Tyson, J. 1986. *World Peace and World Government: From Vision to Reality*. Oxford: George Ronald.

U.S. Bureau of the Census. 1990. *City and County Data*. CD-ROM.

Universal House of Justice. 1972. *The Constitution of the Universal House of Justice*. Haifa: Bahá'í World Centre.

———. 1977. *The Individual and Teaching: Raising the Divine Call*. Compilation. Wilmette, Ill.: Bahá'í Publishing Trust.

———. 1983. *The Importance of Deepening Our Knowledge and Understanding of the Faith*. Thornhill, Ontario: The National Spiritual Assembly of Canada.

————. 1984. *Living the Life: A Compilation*. London: Bahá'í Publishing Trust.

————. 1985. *The Promise of World Peace*. Haifa: Universal House of Justice.

————. 1989. *Individual Rights and Freedoms in the World Order of Bahá'u'lláh*. Wilmette, Ill.: Bahá'í Publishing Trust.

————. 1991. *Bahá'u'lláh*. Sydney: Bahá'í Publications Australia.

Van den Hoonaard, Will C. 1996. *The Origins of the Bahá'í Community of Canada, 1898–1948*. Waterloo, Ont.: Wilfrid Laurier University Press.

Van Es, Rose. 1995. "Some Thoughts on the Teachings of Bahá'u'lláh and the Rise of Globalism." *Journal of Bahá'í Studies* 7, no. 1:57–68.

Wade, Wyn Craig. 1987. *The Fiery Cross: The Ku Klux Klan in America*. New York: Simon and Schuster.

Walbridge, John. 1996. *Sacred Acts, Sacred Space, Sacred Time*. Oxford: George Ronald.

Wallerstein, Immanuel. 1974. *The Modern World System*. New York: Academic Press.

————. 1979. *The Capitalist World Economy: Essays*. New York: Cambridge University Press.

————. 1984. *The Politics of the World Economy: The States, the Movements, and the Civilizations: Essays*. New York: Cambridge University Press.

Warburg, Margit. 1986. "Conversion: Consideration Before a Field-work in a Bahá'í Village in Kerala." In *South Asian Religion and Society*, ed. Asko Parpola and Bent Smidt Hansen. London: Curzon Press.

————. 1991. "The Circle, the Brotherhood, and the Ecclesiastical Body: Bahá'í in Denmark, 1925–1987." In *Religion, Tradition, and Renewal*, ed. Armin W. Geertz and Jeppe Sinding Jensen. Aarhus: Aarhus University Press.

————. 1992. "Citizens of the World: Power, Administration and Values in the Bahá'í Religion." Paper presented at annual meeting of the Society for the Scientific Study of Religion, November 6–8, Washington, D.C.

————. 1993. "Economic Rituals: The Structure and Meaning of Donations in the Bahá'í Religion." *Social Compass* 40, no. 1:25–31.

Warner, R. Stephen. 1988. *New Wine in Old Wine Skins*. Berkeley: University of California Press.

————. 1993. "Work in Progress Toward a New Paradigm for the Sociological Study of Religion in the United States." *American Journal of Sociology* 98 (March):1044–1093.

Waters, Malcolm. 1995. *Globalization*. New York: Routledge.

Weber, Max. 1922. *The Sociology of Religion*. Boston: Beacon Press.

————. 1946. *From Max Weber*. New York: Oxford University Press.

————. 1978. *Economy and Society*. Edited by Guenther Roth and Claus Wittich. Berkeley: University of California Press.

————. 1996. *The Protestant Ethic and the Spirit of Capitalism*. Los Angeles: Roxbury Publishing Company.

White, Robert A. 1989. "Spiritual Foundations for an Ecologically Sustainable Society." *Journal of Bahá'í Studies* 2, no. 1:33–57.

Wilson, Bryan R. 1982. *Religion in Sociological Perspective*. Oxford: Oxford University Press.

Wilson, James Q., and John J. DiIulio Jr. 1995. *American Government: Institutions and Policies*. Lexington, Mass.: D. C. Heath and Company.

Wood, James R. 1970. "Authority and Controversial Policy: The Churches and Civil Rights." *American Sociological Review* 35:1057–1069.

————. 1981. *Leadership in Voluntary Organizations: The Controversy over Social Action in Protestant Churches*. New Brunswick, N.J.: Rutgers University Press.

Woodman, Ross. 1995. "The Role of the Feminine in the Bahá'í Faith." *Journal of Bahá'í Studies* 7, no. 2:75–97.

Worsfold, Adrian. 1989. "Peace, Liberalism and Otherwise in the Bábi-Bahá'í Faiths." *Faith and Freedom* 42 (September):40–44.

Wuthnow, Robert. 1987. *Meaning and Moral Order: Explorations in Cultural Analysis.* Berkeley: University of California Press.

———. 1988. *The Restructuring of American Religion: Society and Faith Since World War II.* Princeton, N.J.: Princeton University Press.

Wyman, June R. 1985. *Becoming a Bahá'í: Discourse and Social Networks in an American Religious Movement.* Ph.D. dissertation, Catholic University of America.

Index

About the Author

Michael McMullen is assistant professor of sociology at the University of Houston-Clear Lake in Houston, Texas. His areas of research include the sociology of religion, organizational development and change, and conflict resolution and mediation. He continues to do research in the American Bahá'í community as well as various conflict resolution programs in the corporate and nonprofit sectors.